P9-AFQ-701

TIME'S MONSTER

TIME'S MONSTER

HOW HISTORY MAKES HISTORY

PRIYA SATIA

The Belknap Press of Harvard University Press

Cambridge, Massachusetts 2020

First printing

Published in the United Kingdom as *Time's Monster: History, Conscience and Britain's Empire* by Allen Lane, an imprint of Penguin Books Ltd., a Penguin Random House Company.

Library of Congress Cataloging-in-Publication Data

Names: Satia, Priya, author.
Title: Time's monster : how history makes history / Priya Satia.
Description: Cambridge, Massachusetts : The Belknap Press of Harvard
University Press, 2020. | Simultaneously published in the United Kingdom
as Time's Monster: History, Conscience and Britain's Empire by Allen
Lane, an imprint of Penguin Books Ltd., a Penguin Random
House Company. | Includes bibliographical references and index.
Identifiers: LCCN 2020011106 | ISBN 9780674248373 (hardcover)
Subjects: LCSH: Historiography. | Imperialism—Historiography. |
Great Britain—Colonies—Historiography.
Classification: LCC D13 .S3625 2020 | DDC 907.2—dc23
LC record available at https://lccn.loc.gov/2020011106

To Amann and Kabir

, , ,

For Mummy Sujaya

CONTENTS

NOTE ON TRANSLITERATION AND TRANSLATION

In Chapters 2, 5, and 6, I have transliterated Urdu and Punjabi poetry according to convention rather than adopting more precise formal transliterations—with apologies to specialists in the field. Unless otherwise stated, translations are my own and aim to provide literal meaning rather than preserve rhyme or meter. In Chapter 4, I have likewise opted for common English spellings of Arabic names, eschewing diacritical marks for the sake of readability, again with apologies to specialists.

TIME'S MONSTER

⸌⸌ *Introduction*

⸌⸌ *Historians are storytellers,* custodians of
the past, repositories of collective memory, poetic interpreters of what it is
to be human. Whether explaining our present or understanding the past
on its own terms, their work critically shapes how the past infuses our present. Apart from this somewhat numinous role, their work also has the
power to shape our future by informing debates on subjects like the war on
terror, gun control, race, women in science, immigration, and so on. Despite this policy relevance, however, their work so often casts a critical light
on the current political order that policymakers often willfully ignore it.
While we might continue to strain after a world of policymakers well informed by history, the historian's more potent role in public debate is perhaps in speaking to the public, so that people may exert pressure on their
elected representatives.

This has not always been the case, however. For much of the modern
period, historians have not been critics but abettors of those in power; history (rather than, say, economics) was considered the ideal course of study
for a young man with political ambition. This was the culture depicted,
critically, in Alan Bennett's award-winning play set in the 1980s, *The History
Boys* (2004).[1] It was a time when history was understood to be about great
men, and its study the ideal preparation for young boys aspiring to be great
men. "History is the school of statesmanship," in the aphoristic words of the
influential Victorian historian of the empire J. R. Seeley.[2]

This culture was, especially, but not exclusively, a British culture—as
captured by Bennett's play. Historians were prominent among the architects of British power from the eighteenth century until very recently, as both
policymakers and advisors to other policymakers; the rule of historians

coincided with the era of British imperialism. The most well-known and captivating historian-policymaker was, of course, Winston Churchill, the prime minister who led his people in their darkest hour and who inspires endless biographical fascination year after year. This was no accident, but an artifact of the sway of a particular historical imagination in the unfolding of empire. During the Enlightenment, history emerged as an ethical idiom for the modern period, endowing historians with outsized policymaking influence, from John Stuart Mill to Churchill. The narrative of the British Empire is, thus, also a narrative of the rise and fall of a particular historical sensibility.

After World War II, during the era of decolonization, the historical discipline was increasingly claimed as a site for protest *against* the powers that be. By the time Bennett's play premiered in 2004, the rule of historians had yielded to this new culture, in which history was an instrument of redemption for the victims of modern history. The discipline changed methodologically; stories of people long marginalized by excessive focus on "great men" began to circulate instead. When the academy was the exclusive playground of white men, it had produced the theories of history and civilization that underwrote imperialism abroad and inequality at home. Certainly, contrary perspectives took root, too. But the inclusion of women and people of color proved critical to the production of new knowledge breaking down those long-dominant narratives. Still, the old ethos maintained its influence in popular forms of history, while the cultural hold of the newer, critical brand of academic history has been compromised by a broader "crisis of the humanities" (amid charges of "overspecialization" against historians themselves).[3] And yet, historians' voices are emerging from the margins as debates about apologies, restitution, and reparations relating to the colonial past proliferate around the world.

In this book, I recount the twinned story of the history of empire and the history of history. Britain's imperial career from the era of slavery to the current Brexit crisis depended on the sway of a particular historical sensibility that deferred ethical judgment to an unspecified future time. Meanwhile, anticolonial thinkers from William Blake to Mahatma Gandhi to E. P. Thompson began to articulate alternative, "antihistorical" ethical visions that insisted on ethical accountability in the present—ultimately altering the very purpose and outlook of history itself. In braiding these two strands of intellectual history with the narrative of empire, my hope is to guide us to a more constructive vision of historians' possible public roles today, as we navigate the detritus of empire in the form of climate crisis, global inequalities, racism, diasporas, demands for reparations, and so on.

The nub of the matter is that this wreckage was, famously, unintended. Modern imperialism promised progress. It was grounded in a vision of history understood as necessarily progress-oriented. That was its justification. For the most part, empire was not the work of villains, but of people who believed they acted conscientiously. Certainly, many Europeans were in it for entirely cynical reasons—loot and adventure—but millions persuaded themselves that it was, truly, a "civilizing mission," that European conquest of the world was about upliftment, that it was fundamentally liberatory, however impossibly far (or illusory) the horizon of freedom. The British Empire, especially, embodied the apparent ideological contradiction of "liberal imperialism." But this was in fact an approach to conquest that preemptively insured against ethical doubt: the empire was an exploitative and repressive political formation built by men who often sincerely believed they were in the business of spreading liberty.[4]

Of course, it is a simple reality of the human condition that people of conscience often commit unconscionable acts—unwittingly or willfully, in a moment of fury or haplessly swept up in the tumult of their time, tragically and at times farcically. Even the Enlightenment apostle of reason Immanuel Kant recognized: "Out of the crooked timber of humanity, no straight thing was ever made."[5] It is not as though evil did not exist before the modern period, before empire and the nation, before we began to think historically. But the modern era is notably littered with examples of *well-intentioned* plans going awry, of schemes to improve the human condition ending in disaster.[6] The planetary crossroads at which we now find ourselves emerges from a particular human folly. Fueling much of human activity and invention since the Enlightenment, the conviction that history is necessarily a story of progress has conveyed us to the brink of disaster. We know about historicism's complicity in the rise of modern imperialism, how it defined progress through the rhetorical exclusion of "others" from that narrative, so that, as Dipesh Chakrabarty told us two decades ago, "historicism enabled European domination of the world in the nineteenth century."[7] What we haven't understood, however, is *how* historicism did this, not only on the level of an idea of progress or the civilizing mission but, practically speaking, in the realm of imperial decision-making—the ethical implications of this epistemic outlook, why protestations of good intentions have had such force.[8] To be sure, the sway of this ethical idiom has never been complete. The adage "The road to hell is paved with good intentions" was coined in this very time, an implicit critique of the idea that ethical judgment depends on future results. Britons used it to express their lingering awareness that good intentions do *not* excuse one from responsibility for the ill results of one's actions.

Nevertheless, belief in well-meaning liberal empire remains powerfully exculpatory; that old historical imaginary continues to collude in the afterlife of empire. Today there is neither agreement that the empire produced hell nor agreement that protestations of good intentions are an inadequate excuse. Countless anticolonial thinkers and historians have proven the British Empire's morally bankrupt foundation in racism, violence, extraction, expropriation, and exploitation. India's anticolonial leader Mohandas Gandhi adopted a nonviolent protest strategy as the empire's *opposite:* "Let it be remembered," he wrote in 1921, "that violence is the keystone of the Government edifice."[9] But the hold of this much-documented ugly reality remains slippery. According to a 2016 study, 43 percent of Britons believe the empire was a good thing, and 44 percent consider Britain's colonial past a source of pride. A 2020 study showed that Britons are more likely than people in France, Germany, Japan, and other former colonial powers to say they would like their country to still have an empire.[10] As Britain prepares for a new role in the international order after Brexit, a report on "Renewing UK Intervention Policy" commissioned by the Ministry of Defence explicitly invokes a nostalgic view of the empire to revive the case for intervention: "Because of its imperial past, Britain retains a tradition of global responsibility and the capability of projecting military power overseas."[11] Britons celebrate the virtuous heroism of the abolition movement that ended British participation in the slave trade in 1807, but often at the expense of remembering Britain's central role in the slave trade until that point and the many forms of bonded labor it exploited thereafter. The record of British humanitarianism submerges the record of British inhumanity. In public memory, redemptive myths about colonial upliftment persistently mask the empire's abysmal history of looting and pillage, policy-driven famines, brutal crushing of rebellion, torture, concentration camps, aerial policing, and everyday racism and humiliation. Balance sheets attempt to show that the "pros"—trains, dams, the rule of law—outweighed the "cons"—occasional violent excesses, racism—despite the ambiguous impact of many alleged "pros" and the deeply flawed premise that we can judge an inherently illegitimate and immoral system by anything other than that illegitimacy and immorality. The end of empire, especially, is extolled as a peaceful, voluntary, and gentlemanly transfer of power. The former Labour prime minister Clement Atlee proclaimed in 1960, "There is only one empire where, without external pressure or weariness at the burden of ruling, the ruling people has voluntarily surrendered its hegemony over subject peoples and has given them their freedom."[12] In fact, decolonization of India, Kenya, Malaysia, Cyprus, Egypt, Palestine, and many other colonies entailed horrendous violence—none of which has been formally memorialized or regretted, unlike other modern crimes against humanity, such as the Holocaust and Hiroshima.[13]

We have not arrived at this forgetting and the easy postimperial conscience it enables by accident. Public memory about the British Empire is hostage to myth partly because historians have not been able to explain how to hold well-meaning Britons involved in its construction accountable. But how can we rightfully gainsay the protests of earnest people confident in their moral soundness and in their incapacity for unjust behavior? "Hypocrisy" helps describe but does not help *explain* such human folly. No one thinks they are a hypocrite. And historical analysis framed as the unmasking of hypocrisy acquires a prosecutorial tone that vitiates understanding. Not all rationalizations are cynical and transparent. We have to take the ethical claims of historical actors seriously to understand how ordinary people acting in particular institutional and cultural frameworks can, despite good intentions, author appalling chapters of human history. The mystery here is genuine: How did Britons understand and manage the ethical dilemmas posed by imperialism? To be sure, there is a story about the "banality of evil" to be told—about the automatic, conformist ways in which ordinary people become complicit in inhumanity. But in the case of the British Empire, the bigger story is perhaps that of inhumanity perpetrated by individuals deeply concerned with their consciences, indeed actively interrogating their consciences. How did such avowedly "good" people live with doing bad things? If we can answer this question, we will be able to solve much of the mystery about the lack of bad conscience about empire among Britons today.

The quip most frequently invoked to depict the empire in charmingly forgiving terms is the Victorian historian J. R. Seeley's line that the British acquired it in "a fit of absence of mind," that they were reluctant imperialists saddled, providentially, with the burden of global rule. But it was not through absence of *mind* so much as absence, or management, of *conscience* that Britain acquired and held its empire. What we call "good intentions" were often instances of conscience management—a kind of denial—necessary to the expansion of imperialism and industrial capitalism in the modern age. The focus on intentions presumes active, unmediated conscience. We might instead ask how conscience was *managed,* what enabled individuals engaged in such crimes to believe and claim that they were enacting good intentions. Britons did this in a manner that has made historical reckoning with imperialism more complicated than reckoning with, say, the obviously monstrous aims of Nazism. This is ironic given a long-standing diplomatic discourse about "Perfidious Albion"—the idea that the British are natively dishonorable, prone to betray promises (i.e. good intentions). But it was partly the burden of this stereotype that provoked loud protestations of good intentions, which many now credit more than the evidence of their destructive impact. The claim of "good intentions" that *enabled* the violent effects of empire cannot be invoked to redeem them. It would be akin to arguing that greater discretion about their murderous intentions would have somewhat redeemed the Nazis. Nazi objectives were openly murderous—the "cleansing" of Europe—but the ideology of liberal empire required respectable cover, and lasted longer because of it. The real value of claims of good intentions lies in what they reveal about how Britons managed their own conscience about the iniquities of empire.

Historians will continue to expose the hypocrisies of imperialism, but here I want to show how certain intellectual resources, especially a certain kind of historical sensibility, allowed and continue to allow many people to avoid perceiving their ethically inconsistent actions—their hypocrisy—in the modern period. Culture, in the form of particular imaginaries of time and change, shaped the practical unfolding of empire.[14] This is a book about how the historical discipline helped make empire—by making it ethically thinkable—and how empire made and remade the historical discipline. We are looking at how the culture around narrating history shaped the way people participated in the making of history—that area of rich overlap created by the two meanings of "history": what happened, and the narrative of what happened. Essentializing representations of other places and peoples laid the cultural foundation of empire, but historical thinking empowered Britons to *act* on them.[15] The cultural hold of a certain understanding of history and historical agency was not innocent but designedly complicit in the making of empire.

I offer this narrative, not as an attack on the historical discipline (whose tools are what allow me to write this book), but to recall how it has figured in the making of our world and how the world it made changed it over time, and to defend its relevance to making new history in the present. Many scholars have tussled over the positive and negative impacts of Enlightenment values and the provincial and universal origins of those values. I want to look under the hood and see how certain notions of history nurtured during the Enlightenment "worked" in the real world and how successive generations have adapted those notions to the moral demands of their time.

In key moments in the history of the British Empire covered in this book, Britons involved in the empire appeased and warded off guilty conscience by recourse to certain notions of history, especially those that spotlighted great men helpless before the will of "Providence." This was not some amoral notion about the ends justifying the means. Machiavellianism is about political gain as its own end, without scruple. My protagonists were deeply concerned with ethical judgment but believed it was impossible without sufficient passage of time. Their understanding of conscience was grounded in different ways in notions of historical change. In the modern era, competing ideas about how such change happens shaped understandings of human agency and thus personal responsibility—the capacity, and thus complicity, of humans in shaping their world.

Much of the "modernity" of the modern period lies in a new self-consciousness about conscience. I don't mean to imply a secularization of thinking about conscience; in some instances, the historical sensibility informed, supplemented, complemented, or was grafted on to religiously based notions of conscience. (Nor is this a book about dissent or state protection of conscience.) The point is that people were thinking about and managing conscience by reference to proliferating discourses about human history—about how and why history evolves.

For instance, liberal theories of history envisioned "progress" brought about by the will, usually, of great men (chosen and guided by Providence). Marxist theories instead attributed heroic agency to the proletariat (and, to be fair, the bourgeoisie). Both were imbued with certain presumptions about race and economic progress. Such theories of history, carried around in a nineteenth-century Briton's mind, were motivating—galvanizing the exercise of agency—and exonerating insofar as they invoked higher ultimate ends or "context"—the way circumstances or the *needs* of history constrained agency and thus personal responsibility. My interest is in the cultural force of such notions; the neurological and philosophical understanding of intention and agency comprise a vast terrain of knowledge beyond this scope.

Of course, people also adapt their sense of history to the needs of conscience: an eighteenth-century plantation owner in Barbados might self-servingly celebrate his personal, entrepreneurial agency in transforming his land into an economic powerhouse, giving short shrift to the government policies and inherited wealth that in fact enabled his success. Fast-forward to 1836, after the end of slavery, and we might find his son equally self-servingly downplaying his personal capacity to ensure his continued prosperity without governmental reparations for his loss of property in slaves. The notion that change depended only on individual entrepreneurial prowess was now inconvenient. The vice of historical change in which he was caught did not stem his greed but did broaden his historical imagination so that he could perceive the role of circumstances more than his father could.

I began to perceive the link between conscience management and the historical imagination with a sudden epiphany about the protagonist of my previous book, *Empire of Guns: The Violent Making of the Industrial Revolution* (2018). The most important eighteenth-century British gunmaker was Samuel Galton. He was a Quaker, perhaps the group most associated with questions of conscience in modern Britain. As I recounted in that book, he defended his business to his fellow Quakers in 1796 by arguing that there was nothing he could do in his time and place that would not in some way be related to war—that was the nature of the British economy at the time. I used this insight to assemble a new narrative of the industrial revolution: Galton was telling us that war drove industrial activity in the West Midlands in his time. But was it true that he actually could do nothing else? On later reflection, I realized that his thinking revealed the power of historical arguments in assuaging his conscience. He *believed* that he could do nothing else, given "the situation in which Providence" had placed him.[16] A historically determined reality, in his mind, constrained his desire to fulfill his promises as a Quaker. As it turns out, his logic echoed emerging Enlightenment understandings of history as a system of ethical thought; Galton's obligations as a Quaker forced him to reveal the workings of cultural notions that were increasingly pervasive. Indeed, they likely underwrote the Quaker sect's own quiet acceptance of his family's business for nearly a century until that point. So began my thinking about this book.

I discerned then that most of my work has been about people preoccupied with history. My first book, *Spies in Arabia: The Great War and the Cultural Foundations of Britain's Covert Empire in the Middle East* (2008), was about a group of scholar-spies in the Middle East, who thought with and through history. I have written also about the alternative historical outlooks of twentieth-century South Asian poets coping with the Partition of British India in 1947 and their influence on the making of British social history, all the while engaging in a recurring effort to articulate the role of historians in public debate today.[17] From my earliest engagement with the discipline, I have grappled inarticulately with the feeling that it was somehow deeply implicated in the colonial history that had shaped me and that I sought to understand—that particular ideas of history, conscience, and agency are intertwined in our habit of understanding the formerly colonized world with balance sheets of empire. Through my work *as* a historian over the last twenty-odd years, I have finally been able to articulate that discomfort in this book.

In my previous books, I serendipitously homed in on two critical moments in which new ideas about history shaped British understandings of their agency as empire-builders. The material in Chapters 1 and 4 of this book approaches those episodes from a new and wider vantage point, towards the new end of tracing the way evolving ideas about history shaped the unfolding of the British Empire. The quietly shared preoccupation of my previous work has become clear to me over time, and this book distills a synthesis of what I have been trying to say all along. I have long perceived that "conscience" was at the heart of my work as a historian, all my efforts to understand the violence of empire. But only recently have I discerned the common way in which historical thinking shaped ethical decision-making in the distinct and critical moments I have studied.

My geographical coverage in the story that follows is uneven; so, too, is my coverage of particular thinkers. This is by no means an exhaustive account of the discipline, the empire, or the discipline's role in the empire. The episodes recounted here were not the only or the most important moments of scandal or uneasy imperial conscience; management of conscience was endemic to an enterprise based on a permanent dynamic of oppression and resistance. These stories do, however, represent pivotal moments in the history of empire—expansion, consolidation, containment, reinvention, and decolonization. They represent tortured moments in which the management of conscience became very difficult, scandals that momentarily exposed the dark reality of empire to the glare of public scrutiny and forced an explicit reckoning with conscience. They are culturally, emotionally, temporally, geographically, and topically distinct, but connected by the thread of liberal empire. Together they allow us to explore how importunate rhetoric about good historical intentions persistently stifled awareness of the destructive nature of modern imperialism. Stringing these disparate events into a single story of conscience and history wrings new kinds of truth from them about how the modern historical imagination shaped the unfolding of empire.

The debate about how and whether intentions matter in the biggest crimes against humanity typically pits crimes of the Right—the Nazis—against crimes of the Left—the Soviet Union.[18] In fact, the crimes of the Right and the Left, which were both imperious and imperial in nature, were rooted in a common ethical vision grounded in historical thinking. We know crimes were committed in the name of nationalism and imperialism in the modern period. But nations and empires exercised such persuasive power because they were the objects of a deeply influential mode of ethical thought: historicism.

To be sure, historians were crucial to proving the case against empire, especially (but not only) after the turn of the twentieth century. But even then they did not dispense altogether with the discipline's old narratives and categories. History was remade in the crucible of twentieth-century anticolonialism, but the discipline has yet to come to terms with its role as time's monster. Backlash against its remaking, such as the recent nostalgic conference on "Applied History" at Stanford's Hoover Institution, exemplifies our continued cultural attachment to the historical imagination that drove the making of empire.[19] Of course, we want policymakers and politicians today to think more historically, to be mindful of the past, but that reengagement requires first understanding the damaging ways in which policymakers have drawn on historical thinking in the past and the significance, and limitations, of their subsequent estrangement from the discipline.[20]

Because the historical sensibility that enabled imperialism is still intact, despite the seeming end of empire, we have been unable to sustain a consensus around the moral case against empire. Understanding how historical thinking conspired in imperialism offers a way out of this impasse. By uncovering how ideas of history influenced the actual unfolding of imperial history, we might dispel the perceived ambiguity around the moral case against empire *and* feel our way towards new modes of historical thinking less likely to blind us to the crimes of empire.

How we remember the British Empire matters. It shapes how we assess the seeming "failures" of postcolonial countries to "move on" from their colonial past, how we make sense of Britain's efforts to reinvent its place in the world in the current Brexit crisis, and how we think about imperial activity today.[21] The stakes for clearing up the moral fog that clings to imperialism are especially high in the formerly colonized world, where the moral case against empire encounters stubborn ambivalence despite the history of anticolonial struggle. The post-independence Indian government never really questioned the moral and intellectual underpinnings of the colonial project from which it emerged. This is as evident in its developmentalist commitments and imperial subjugation of borderlands as in its meek attitude towards securing amends for the historical wrongs of colonialism. Such ambivalence is, of course, the very mark of that state's "postcolonial" nature, the seemingly incurable hangover of colonialism. In Indian laments about the country's embarrassing failure to "catch up" after seventy years of independence lurks the fear that British assessments of their independent potential were true.

Through a series of stories about empire, we will grasp how understandings of conscience, derived from a historical sensibility, mattered in the unfolding of modern history.[22] The major forces of that history—imperialism, industrial capitalism, nationalism—were justified by notions of progress and thus liable to rationalizations about noble ends justifying ignoble means. Even those who embraced such utilitarian calculations depended on new intellectual and cultural resources that emerged to manage the conscience. Key among them was the evolving discipline of history. Instead of taking conscience and its exercise as essentially human qualities and therefore timeless, we are probing their historically contingent nature. Attending to the little voice, to conscience, has depended not only on conscientiousness but also on context. In situations of unequal power and amid legacies of imperial paternalism, love itself has led to ethical travesties.

CHAPTER ONE

`⸌⸍` *The Progress of War*

> "History has its eyes on you."
> —George Washington to Alexander Hamilton,
> in Lin-Manuel Miranda, *Hamilton* (2015)

`⸌⸍` *Let us take* "ethics" to mean the moral principles, the concepts of right and wrong, that guide a person's behavior, including a person's sense of the capacity to act, what we call "free will." Conscience is a cognitive process of rational and emotional responses to an act or situation based on that value system. Science can tell us much about its genetic and cultural foundations, but the latter requires historical explanation, too. We are occupied here with that cultural quotient. Before the modern era and the introduction of historical systems of ethical accountability, we had access to many others, which remain with us. Most were religious, and most religious traditions assume their value system to be inherent in all humans, that is, not culturally or historically specific. Many religious systems of ethical accountability took narrative form, as history does. Humans are hardwired for narrative: We tell stories to make sense of existence, and among the stories we tell are those that encompass ourselves as worldly actors, that explain how and why our own lives unfold the way they do, that tell us what stirs the cauldron of change.

Take, for instance, cosmic theories of agency, like astrology, which tell us that the positions and movements of heavenly bodies determine our nature and future. Human agency is tightly constrained in such theories;

we are pawns in a cosmic game. A believer in astrology, armed with his birth chart, would behave differently, and have a different sense of his agency, from someone ignorant of his position in that cosmic tapestry. There are several possibilities: He may be more passive, waiting for the stars to shape his destiny as predicted. Or he may use the chart as a guide on how best to cocreate with the cosmic energies at work in his life and in the world. Or, if he has kept the chart in a drawer and forgotten it, it may belatedly help him cope when his independently motivated exercise of his agency meets with defeat: the consolation that he has not failed but that it was simply not in the stars. He is aware that he is in a story whose action cannot exceed the frame made by the positions of the planets and stars at his birth; the chart shapes the script he imagines his actions to fulfill. It both shapes his sense of agency and provides ex post rationalizations of his actions and their outcomes.

Beyond the stars, for many, God is shaping how and why change happens, how life unfolds. Divine intervention—the act of God—is the ultimate force before which human agency is nothing, is annihilated. It has enormous powers to clear the conscience, the clearest basis on which to claim "It wasn't me." A belief in reincarnation might, on the other hand, mold our actions by challenging us to imagine how they might catch up with us: If we act without empathy towards someone today, will we pay karmically in the next life? Is my destiny inextricably linked to the fate of others?[1] Other religious traditions promise ethical accountability in an otherworldly afterlife—heaven or hell. The sway of original sin and the capacity for free will and redeeming grace preyed on the conscience of major Christian philosophers, most notably Saint Augustine. In the eschatological worldview of many sects within the Abrahamic tradition, the final account, Judgment Day, will come at the end of times, the last day of history. The testaments that tell us all this are related *as* histories—chronicles of human events in which the divine is an active participant.

In Hindu thought, guidance on human agency emerges from a mythical prelude to the era of human history. Our current era, the Kali Yuga, roughly coinciding with the timescale of the historical discipline, is part of a cycle of four yugas, or epochs. It is an age of darkness and destruction and relatively short human life that will be followed by a return of the Satya Yuga, an age of truth and perfection, and the cycle will continue. This yuga began in the fourth century BCE upon the end of the war recounted in the cyclical mythology of the epic poem known as the *Mahabharata*. This story of the previous yuga includes a battlefield conversation between the warrior Arjuna and Lord Krishna, in the role of charioteer. The chapters that make up this conversation comprise the *Gita*, a guide to the virtuous exercise of agency. Arjuna is unsettled at the idea that the war demands that he kill members of his own family. He cannot bear the idea of being responsible for the deaths of those he loves. Krishna persuades him that he must fulfill his duty as a warrior and engage the enemy, regardless. He must act out of duty without regard to consequence. Here is a path to absolution of conscience, an escape from bad karma, passed from a previous yuga to ours as a cultural inheritance, swept from myth into mortal, historical time, where countless people have drawn on it in decisions about when and how to act.

Along with such religious, mythical, and astrological understandings of agency, we have inherited the idea that the worldly narrative of history can guide the exercise of agency. It emerged in the eighteenth century from the Enlightenment search for a universal system of ethical evaluation based on reason that might exist apart from both organized religious belief and the internal impulses that signal the workings of conscience—a more worldly, if not secular, ethics.[2] History became central to the Enlightenment episteme of ethics, or "moral philosophy," the branch of philosophy focused on systematizing concepts of right and wrong conduct. In his *Letters on the Study and Use of History* (written in 1735 and published in 1752), the Tory politician and man of letters Lord Bolingbroke explained history's uses as moral philosophy: "These are certain general principles, and rules of life and conduct, which always must be true, because they are conformable to the invariable nature of things. He who studies history as he would study philosophy, will soon distinguish and collect them, and by doing so will soon form to himself a general system of ethics and politics on the surest foundations, on the trial of these principles and rules in all ages, and on the confirmation of them by universal experience."[3] The evolution of the work of the Scottish moral philosopher Adam Smith offers a useful example of the eighteenth-century gravitation towards history as a system of moral judgment. His first attempt at explaining moral sentiments with the 1759 version of *The Theory of Moral Sentiments* was almost entirely unhistorical. Smith expressed the experience of moral judgment primarily by recourse to visual metaphors about the internal eye, seeing inside. However, over the thirty years that Smith spent revising it, the text became profoundly historical. By 1790, it was as much about observing outside events: "It asserted a sequence over time in moral judg-ment, in which individuals start by judging other people, and then judge themselves," explains the historian Emma Rothschild. Smith piled in more and more "illustrations" from history showing the experience of moral judgment, explicitly noting history's uses in moral reflection, the way we absorb ethical values by imaginative connection with lives in the past. For him, writes Rothschild, moral sentiments were "an experiment in historical observation, and historical imagination." Observation of one's own so-ciety, in one's own time and place, might yield only a parochial rather than universal morality; history insured against this risk by offering illustrations from the lives of the great.[4]

Smith's turn to history as a mode of moral reflection was the product of the philosophical universe in which he moved. His closest associates, like his fellow Scotsman David Hume, were producing works of history. The German philosopher Immanuel Kant was most likely familiar with Smith's work.[5] In 1784, he, too, described history's potential as a guide to moral action in his "Idea for a Universal History with a Cosmopolitan Point of View." He explicitly intended this philosophy of history to help history reach the cosmopolitan end it theorized. It would proleptically guide his-tory's unfolding along the very lines it described: Among Kant's avowed motives in attempting his philosophical history was that it might "direct the ambitions of sovereigns and their agents" towards contributing to the goal of world citizenship as "the only means by which their fame can be spread to later ages." In short, rulers might better serve history with an eye towards history's judgment of them.[6] Like Smith, he anticipated that their own encounter with historical accounts of earlier governments' contribu-tions towards the goal would nurture their awareness of history's prospec-tive judgment of themselves. And his very narrating of this "idea" would help it come true. It did not perhaps even matter whether the story ever came true, whether humankind achieved its cosmopolitan purpose; Kant offered it partly to prompt ethical action now by goading political figures to act as if history had its eyes on them (as his contemporary George Washington is imagined to remind Alexander Hamilton in the epigraph to this chapter). Moral sentiments now depended on observing oneself inter-nally, observing others in the past, *and* being aware of future observation of oneself. As one scholar summarizes, "Philosophical history thus functions like the lives of the saints in the Catholic church."[7] This was history's new power as a system of ethical accountability.

Up to this point, "history" had connoted a story or narrative, such as an account of a battle or journey. The idea of history as "something that equally comprises past and future as states of a continuous subject, so that we may speak of *the* history, of history as such," emerged in the second half of the eighteenth century.[8] Like religious systems of ethical thought, history in this new incarnation had its idols: As Kant's preoccupation with sovereigns suggests, it was, expressly, an ethical system whose sacred object was the nation. In the eighteenth century, the meaning of "nation" changed "from a fact of nature to a product of political will"[9]—something that could be made by historically minded men like Washington. Hume, author of the monumentally successful six-volume *History of England* (1754–1762), confided to his publisher in 1770, "I believe this is the historical Age and this the historical Nation."[10] The imagined community of the nation possessed a worldly past narratable in secular time.[11] How did history come to acquire this power in this moment? A full account of the history of history is beyond the scope of this book; the following sketch is telescopic but necessary to understanding how the eighteenth-century embrace of history as a system of ethical thought came to fit alongside other, inherited modes of ethical accountability.

Like most Enlightenment thinkers who saw themselves as continuing the work of inquiry and illumination of the classical era, historians traced their intellectual lineage to the ancient Greek authors Thucydides and Herodotus. The latter was a fifth-century BCE historian of the Greco-Persian wars of that century. He conceived of divine and human agency as interrelated, and his history was laced with fable and ethnographic material.[12] In this sense, the worldly discipline of history emerged from the ancient swirl of poetic myth, texts like the *Mahabharata* and the *Odyssey* that defy easy categorization as fact or fiction, theological texts or humanistic artifacts. Thucydides followed in the same century; but in his account of the Peloponnesian War between Sparta and Athens, this Athenian general explicitly set out to dispense with myth and divine agency. He is taken as the father of the modern idea of history as a series of causes and effects that might be explained without invocation of divine or supernatural intervention in order to reveal timeless truth about human affairs.

Thucydides saw the contest between Sparta and Athens as a universal history—the contest between barbarism and civilization played out within the Greek world. He asks whether justice has power in the world. Athens is unapologetically imperialistic. The Athenians' assumption is that no divine powers enforce justice by rewarding the just and punishing the un-just; there is no moral accountability for the exercise of agency. Self-interest alone must guide action. Sparta, seemingly altruistically, takes on the cause of liberating Greek cities from Athenian tyranny. In fact, Thucydides says, the Spartans fought out of fear of Athens's growing power. They, too, vio-late sacred oaths in pursuit of this self-interest; they hypocritically main-tain their own hidden slave empire at home. Between Sparta and Athens, it is unclear which power behaves with greater inhumanity. Sparta, confi-dent of the morality of its cause, presumes all opponents to be unjust, swiftly condemning them. The Athenians, without this presumption of justness, instead perceive all as acting out of necessity in pursuit of their own in-terest and do not therefore morally condemn those who oppose them. But this amoral posture does not serve them nearly as well as even disingen-uous moral commitments serve the Spartans in the contest; human nature simply proves too unreasonable. Thucydides's account ends abruptly, twenty years into the twenty-six-year war, with the Athenians considerably di-minished but still hopeful.[13] Yet, ultimately, Sparta prevailed. The Athe-nians surrender to arrogance, rage, vengeance, and suspicion in ways that do not further their interests. In their certainty that they *deserved* impe-rial success by virtue of their superiority, they, too, implicitly believed in justice. They are not, then, as amoral or realist as they imagine them-selves to be.

This timeless truth is, paradoxically, revealed only thanks to the pas-sage of time. In this seemingly secular account focused on questions of ethical judgment, the judge of virtue is not God but time. In most systems of ethical accountability, the morally virtuous choice is evident in the mo-ment itself, even if justice—punishment or reward—may arrive later, in the afterlife. But Thucydides gives us the notion that "history," or time it-self, *vindicates* virtuous actions whose virtue may not be apparent in the moment itself. It is not obvious, prima facie, whether the ethical orienta-tion of the Athenians or that of the Spartans is superior; only with the passage of time and the ultimate Spartan victory does it become clear that the Spartan outlook was the right one. History thus becomes, in this text, a system of ethical accountability in itself; the end of a historical narrative framed around a contest was a kind of secular Judgment Day that re-vealed the ethical merit of the sides involved. It *turned out* in the end that Athens was wrong. Time showed this, eventually. There may be no neces-sary relationship between goodness and victory, but the triumph of good fulfills a certain *narrative* necessity common to many systems of ethical accountability.

Different conceptions of history followed. The Stoics embraced a cyclical view of history more akin to Hindu conceptions. Christian theology gave rise to theodicies that attempted to reconcile the existence of evil in the world with the existence of God. In that context, philosophers like Saint Augustine found compelling the idea that history was ultimately progressive, leading to an eschatological end—apocalypse and Judgment Day. Medieval chronicles, on the other hand, were an exercise in fairly pragmatic historical record-keeping in western Europe. No doctrinal structure was imposed on them; they did not look for meaning in the passage of time. The idea that this was a time of "the Crusades," a Christian response to Muslim incursion on Christian lands, was a later, modern invention.[14] So, too, were narratives that cast Iberian explorers in the New World as latter-day crusaders continuing the struggle to take the peninsula back from the "Moors." In fact, they were desperately searching for new commercial outlets (profiting from a technological edge in navigation cultivated *in* Moorish Spain) after the 1453 fall of Christian Constantinople shut Western Christendom out of old trade routes.

It was the Reformation that launched a retrospective search for meaning in past events. Protestant theologian-historians looked for and found God's hand in history.[15] The very rupture of Reformation fueled the notion that they were at an epochal turning point. Martin Luther's perception that the Church had departed over time from its scriptural foundations was an argument about history framed within biblical time. Viewing the rupture as providential also helped justify it. Sixteenth-century Protestant chroniclers did not apply this prophetic view of history only to the Church but also to events beyond the reach of the Christian world in time and space. Theologians like Philip Melanchthon supplied retrospective meaning to medieval chronicles by attaching forewords to new editions, in which they affirmed that history shows how God rewards and punishes earthly kingdoms. Periodization—the search for turning points in a meaningful structure headed towards the final moment, the eschaton—emerged as a Protestant passion. Catholic thinkers did not embrace a dramatic historical narrative of decline and recovery but the continual march of the true Church. Sixteenth-century accounts of explorer-missionary-conquistadors did, however, bequeath the modern age early templates for great-man history.

The tumultuous religio-political struggles of seventeenth-century England informed and were informed by the millenarian Protestant outlook, the expectation of the imminent eruption of God's power in the world.[16] To Puritans, the Reformation had not gone far enough, forcing the revolution and civil wars of the 1640s. These ideas encouraged a willingness to entertain change to political arrangements. As the historian David Como's work shows, English thinkers who wrote about the "common liberties" that we take as the essence of secular democracy did so while articulating apocalyptic notions about their time. Their capacity to dream up novel political and social arrangements depended on their faith that Christ's kingdom was about to come, that human governance might be perfected in line with the perfection of God's will.

This early modern ferment of religio-historical thought left a deep imprint on Enlightenment ideas of history. Cyclical notions of history did not disappear entirely, but history came to be understood as linear and irreversible and, especially, progressive. Classical works of history recovered during the Renaissance, thanks to Muslim preservation of those works, were appropriated into this new understanding. The works of Thucydides and Herodotus were claimed as the foundational texts for a discipline that was now all about telling the stories of nations, especially through the lives of their political makers. These narratives conferred legitimacy on national leaders and national claims to sovereignty, going well beyond earlier narratives tracing the genealogical and divine descent of individual sovereigns to substantiate their claims to rule.[17] In Britain, legitimizing the national project doubled with legitimizing the imperial one, beginning as it did with incorporation of the "four nations" of the British Isles (the Scots, Welsh, Irish, and English) into a new British "nation." Though both Thucydides and Herodotus framed their works as narratives of the contest between barbarism and civilization, the geographical assignment of barbarism to the Persian East and civilization to more westerly Greece in Herodotus's account would become foundational to British historicism; it began with and depended on the dichotomy of East and West. Indeed, as we shall see throughout this book, European philosophers' ideas about moral action were crucially shaped by orientalist engagement with alternative understandings of agency encountered abroad.

Thus, even as eighteenth-century historians adopted Thucydides's view of history as an arena of human action, they did not dispense altogether with God.[18] Instead they theorized new understandings of God's Providence. In 1710, the German philosopher Gottfried Leibniz fused a belief in the contingent nature of history with his belief in the idea that "God nevertheless exercises providential care."[19] God chooses among contingencies created by man or nature. Those contingent events are thus both accidental and chosen at once. God does not cause events but chooses among randomly occurring variations. As the literary scholar Catherine Gallagher explains, this twist on providential history created room for imagining the effects were God to choose alternative contingencies. There might be other "possible worlds." The accidents of history thus illuminated the process of divine planning. God's consciousness included countless unrealized contingencies. By speculating about (necessarily inferior) other possible worlds, we gain a clearer view of Providence's hand in our world.[20]

Leibniz's meditation on history was part of a work titled *Theodicy,* a term he coined to refer to the effort to understand why a good God permits evil in the world. In this book, we are trying to understand why good people do bad things, but he, like Augustine and other philosophers, asked why a good God tolerates bad things. His theodicy rested on the notion that our world may be imperfect but was at least guaranteed by Providence to be the best among all possible worlds. No better world must be possible according to His lights. God may be omnipotent and omniscient, but his human creations are limited; they will act erringly. The evil in the world is the necessary consequence of this metaphysical imperfection, existing so that humans might seek redemption and perceive true good. In short, the methods of modern historical thought emerged as part of an effort to make ethical sense of a world still understood to be divinely enchanted. But it was enchanted in a different way than the ancient world: The gods of antiquity acted directly in the world; the modern Christian cosmos relegated God to a supernatural realm distinct from rather than entwined with a "natural" realm governed by its own laws.[21]

And yet those laws were also divinely ordained—at first. In his 1784 essay, Kant theorized history as deterministic, destined to end in a federation of republican states at peace. His philosophy was chiliastic, he owned, "but not Utopian" since (as we have seen) it counted on itself to help the millennium come to pass.[22] Providence unfolds in human history itself, not only in sacred history (as it does for Augustine).[23] For Kant, natural laws must be guiding human evolution, precisely because of the flawed nature— or "crooked timber"—of humanity: No philosopher could find conscious individual purpose behind the malice and folly that guided men in their "great drama"; he perforce must conclude that some "natural purpose" drove "this idiotic course of things human." The need for meaning thus arises out of Christian belief in the fallen nature of man, but, as the philosopher Rüdiger Bittner explains, "Kant does not re-sell Christian thought under a philosophical wrapping. He erects a philosophy that is to allay worries induced by Christianity."[24] He is pessimistic about the rationality of individuals, but optimistic about reason's efficacy in humankind's long-run evolution.[25] For him, "reason cannot develop fully within the lifetime of any individual, but only gradually in the species as a whole," one scholar explains.[26] Human perfection might be the end of history rather than a supernatural end; the species might be perfectible in the long run, if not the individual.[27] All men are headed towards this end, unbeknownst even to themselves. They exercise free will—agency—and yet, unwittingly, act "as if following some guiding thread," furthering progress towards that end of history "even if they would set little store by it if they did know it."[28] The guiding thread of universal reason is the work of "Nature—or, better, . . . Providence." Man's unsocial, or evil, propensities generate antagonism in society, driving each to achieve status within it; man's "selfish pretensions" fuel his creativity.[29] Evil thus produces good, dialectically. Human history simply *must* fulfill some such immanent narrative structure; it cannot be without meaning. Without faith in such redeeming purpose, Kant explained, so much of human history would seem such an "unceasing reproach" to the "majesty and wisdom of Creation" that we would turn from it in disgust and hope for meaning only in another world. Kant's philosophy of history was in this sense an "expression of rational hope," writes the philosopher Manfred Kuehn. The Last Judgment was supposed to reveal right and wrong, but Kant asks us not to look for meaning in another world and rather to rely on history to reveal that truth. The modern effort to sweep religion into its own sphere thus created a space for a secular ethics that depended critically on a historical imagination.

In Birmingham, England, the Dissenting clergyman and Enlightenment philosopher Joseph Priestley shared these views. Early on, his 1788 *Lectures on History* reproduces Bolingbroke's description of history's usefulness in forming a system of ethics. Priestley was certain that proper study of history would always vindicate virtue and prove the folly of vice: "So consistent is the order of Divine Providence, that, if the scheme be fairly and completely represented, we may depend upon it that nothing will be exhibited from which it may be justly concluded, that vice is eligible upon the whole." Thus, history "*must* have an effect that is favourable to virtue." Priestley's work was also a theodicy: He affirms that by imagining the other possible worlds that might have been, we will come to recognize the rightness of God's decisions in shaping the world as it was. If there seemed to be evil in the world, such historical imagining showed that "all evils lead to, and terminate in, a greater good."[30] As Catherine Gallagher puts it, Priestley saw history as a "large-scale mechanism of incremental betterment, which makes use of the very ills it ultimately overcomes."[31] His theory of history was a halfway house between Leibniz's theory of divinely controlled contingency and the nineteenth-century German philosopher G. W. F. Hegel's secular dialectical philosophy of history. To him, God's goodness was evident in the general rule of human development *over time,* not in the everyday particulars of human life. Thus, he concludes, the study of history will compel us to look upon all events positively, which in itself will cultivate our virtue: "The more we study history . . . the more thoroughly shall we be satisfied with our situation and connexions, the more will our gratitude to the wise and kind author of the universe be inflamed, and the more desirous shall we be to promote, by our conduct, and by methods of operation, of which we are able to judge, that end, which we perceive the Divine Being is pursuing, though by methods of operation of which we are not always competent judges, and which, therefore, we ought not to attempt to imitate." He calls on readers to practice ordinary virtue and to defer judgment on seemingly vicious happenings: "Let the plain duties of morality be our rule of life. We see and experience their happy effects. But let us acquiesce in the Divine conduct, when we see him producing the same good and glorious ends, by means which are apt at first to alarm our narrow apprehensions, on account of their seeming to have a contrary tendency." He does not see this as a moral double standard but simply a temporalizing of ethical judgment, an acknowledgment of an ethical quotient that only history can reveal. For great progressive events were often "brought about contrary to the intention of the persons who were the chief instruments of them, and by the very means which were intended to produce a contrary effect." This is an early version of what Hegel would call the "cunning of reason," styled here as the cunning of God. Priestley thus advises the historian explicitly to "attend to every instance of improvement, and a better state of things being brought about, by the events which are presented to him in history, and let him ascribe those events to an *intention* in the Divine Being to bring about that better state of things by means of those events; and if he cannot see the same benevolent tendency in all other appearances, *let him remain in suspense with regard to them.*"[32]

Eighteenth-century thinkers rationalized trade, driven by self-interest, productive of luxury and fraud, as a "necessary evil" for the sake of the nation's progress.[33] But by mid-century, war, so central to the making of the British nation, became *the* testing ground for ethics for Enlightenment thinkers invested in the idea that reason, rather than violence and emotion, lit the path of progress. Of course, war has in many times and places been understood as the proving ground of ethical merit. In medieval European chronicles, it was understood as a contest of good and evil. Its outcome revealed which side was just and virtuous, favored by God.[34] This idea remained influential in the modern period: The British interpreted their defeat by the American colonies in 1783 as a sign of providential disfavor, proof of their compromised virtue. A similar moral vocabulary continues to frame discussions of the world wars, Cold War conflicts like Vietnam, and the war on terror today. In the battlefield context of the *Gita,* however, it is not clear that a particular "side" in the conflict is destined to win because of superior virtue. Rather, war is the testing ground of the ethical exercise of agency. The battlefield functions as the moral testing ground for the individual warrior—the account is mytho-history but also an allegory for any situation of moral confusion. Similarly, though the parties in the Peloponnesian War laid competitive claim to the favor of the gods, Thucydides expressly denied the obvious or automatic moral superiority of either side or the practical superiority of a morally infused outlook at all. "Higher standards" were a luxury of peacetime, he wrote. War nurtured savage instincts: people "do things the wrong way round," thinking only after acting.[35] In the age of Enlightenment, however, the question was different—not whether war would reveal the relative justness of the combating parties or whether soldiers would act ethically in war, but the ethical status of war itself: Was it something that could or even should be resisted? This was a question of pressing practical consequence in Britain, a polity almost continually at war in the eighteenth century. On the one hand, the liberal moral philosopher Adam Smith stipulated peace as the condition of progress, but many thinkers considered war a historical necessity towards that end of peace and progress, the working of some natural law that well-meaning humans might only futilely attempt to resist. Indeed, even Smith's work indulged this idea, as we shall see.

Priestley discerned the challenge that the seemingly perpetual "state of *war*" posed to the perception of divine beneficence. He offered the assuring counterfactual that those who died in war might have died from disease anyway; at least, "provided posterity be in any respect better for the war, the lives lost in it were very well lost." Class snobbery offered further solace: Considering the sort of people who made up "our armies," Priestley was confident that "in no other way could they have done their country so much service." His judgments stemmed here from the presumption that "their country"—the nation—was the obvious object of history's progress. In this light, war, far from a regrettable evil and the cause of needless suffering, was a powerful mechanism of historical change. Most especially, it was a primary engine of scientific discovery: The "salutary alarms of war . . . roused the activity, and excited the ingenuity, of men." They made things that found peaceful application after war, too. Without this motivation mankind would sink into a state of "such gross bestiality" as to risk the species' survival. The dynamic of technological progress that war unleashed and the culture of intellectual pleasure that it fostered would eventually reach such a level as to make war unnecessary for further advancement. They would arrive at a Christian millennium of equality and peace. Thus, seemingly disastrous events could efficaciously bring about "the most happy and desirable state of things."[36] Priestley's arguments about war echoed Kant's assurance that despite its immediately devastating effects, war was ultimately useful to history; competitive mobilization of forces produced cultural advances.

Priestley's ideas about history were perhaps influenced by his observations of the war-driven industrial change in and around Birmingham in this time.[37] He may also have been influenced by personal attachments to arms makers: His sister was married to the prominent cannon contractor John Wilkinson, and his great friend and champion was Samuel Galton, proprietor of the single most important gun-manufacturing business in the country. Priestley had been Galton's teacher at the prominent school for religious Dissenters, Warrington Academy. The lectures on which he based his 1788 work were given there in the 1760s, when Galton was his student. He and Galton were both members of Birmingham's celebrated club of Enlightenment thinkers, the Lunar Society. Galton helped fund Priestley's discovery of oxygen and gave him shelter when his advocacy of equal rights for Dissenters provoked massive riots in Birmingham in 1791. In 1796, in defending his business to his Quaker community, who considered it in violation of their belief in the unchristian nature of war, Galton drew on arguments similar to Priestley's. His defense shows us how eighteenth-century people came to see the war-driven economic realities of their time as irrevocable, as historically inevitable in a manner that deprived them, as individuals, of the capacity for agency.

In printing and circulating his written defense, Galton exhibited a strong sense of his own agency, but when it came to the idea of closing the gun business, his sense of agency virtually evaporated. He protested that he could do nothing to remedy the situation. His astonishment at his censure in 1795, after his family had pursued the gun business for nearly a century, suggests that his conscience had genuinely been clear up till then. As much as he may have influenced Priestley's thought, Priestley's thought may likewise have influenced him and his sense of straitjacketed agency in a providentially ordained historical process. Arguing that everyone, including his fellow Quakers, participated in war, ineluctably, he invoked the hand of "Providence" to make a point about the particular *historical* moment in which they found themselves. He lamented to his judges, "the *Practice* of your principles, is not compatible with the situation in which Providence has placed us."[38] To him, the "situation" was that of a military-industrial society progressing by leaps and bounds thanks to the spur of war. Even his supposed redeemers were complicit in it: Sampson Lloyd, one of the Friends charged with his disownment process, was the scion of a family that had long supplied iron for his gun manufactory. From where Galton sat, the industrial transformation unfolding around him was a war-driven phenomenon beyond the power of any single industrialist to change. It is not that he failed to imagine an alternate universe in which the state expended funds on peaceable "development"; historical progress, to him and many eighteenth-century men, *depended* on war. War might be unchristian, but it was the incontrovertible historical reality of their time. A generation earlier, Galton's relative the Quaker banker Joseph Freame had explained his tolerance of war-driven profits by pleading a lack of room for maneuver: "What can't be cured must be endured."[39] Galton's arguments endowed this adage designed to clear the conscience with the philosophical authority of the emerging historical discipline. Relying on providential notions of history as an ethical guide allowed Galton and other participants in the new economy to make peace with violation of purely religiously derived moral commitments; it enabled abstraction of a "distinctive space ... of economic relationships"[40]—a realm of morally neutral transaction over interchangeable "commodities"—from inherited notions of "moral economy." By thinking with history, Galton could abstract his economic acts from his commitments as a Quaker. Despite the debate's religious stakes, he did not invoke spiritual constraints or God's will to explain his actions. He explained them as the result of his place in (providentially guided) human time, not his place in God's world: He was an heir to a certain kind of business in a time in which war was providentially willed. A century later, the German social theorist Max Weber would pin the history of capitalism on the Protestant concept of the "calling," which by spinning worldly affairs as religious duty maintained the modern entrepreneur in clear conscience. But the sources of Galton's clear conscience were historically rather than religiously grounded (however providential his sense of history itself).

To the extent that Galton was familiar with Priestley's ideas, they would have bolstered his confidence in his own. No one, at least, could claim that *only* a person so obviously invested in the war economy would make such an argument: It had independent intellectual legitimacy and cultural purchase. Many Quakers apart from Galton were resigned to war as a "necessary evil," as the banker Samuel Hoare put it.[41] Quakers, too, were invested in the national destiny of Britain, and war was its central and defining fact in the eighteenth century. Beyond the world of philosophers and Quakers, many had faith in war's productive economic role.[42] The idea of "necessary evil" proved highly portable as a historically grounded concept for justifying activities manifestly offensive in other systems of ethical thought.

In a bustling town that lacked formal legal status and governing institutions until the 1830s, Galton was among the influential social elite charged with local governance on a volunteer basis, accountable to no one but themselves; de facto governing power was layered over social status. That privilege of impunity seems to have extended to his reputation within the Quaker fold, despite his acknowledged violation of Quaker principles. He insisted on his accountability to no one but his private conscience, while his consuming philanthropic engagements offered further proof (to himself as much as others) of his essential goodness. In an era in which gentlemanly capitalists invoked the esoterica of finance to absolve themselves of responsibility for crises that wiped out the fortunes of ordinary people,[43] this industrialist similarly pointed to larger forces out of his control that made it impossible for him to avoid participating in war, whatever his principles. Indeed, he, too, turned banker in 1804, as his gun fortunes sky-rocketed during the Napoleonic Wars. His son Samuel Tertius Galton was a banker and gun contractor from 1804 to 1815, when the gun business was wound up, with the collapse of state demand at the end of the wars. Tertius had by then left the Quaker fold by marrying Violetta Darwin, daughter of the Enlightenment philosopher, physician, and abolitionist Erasmus Darwin, in 1807. (We will hear about their son the eugenicist Francis Galton in Chapter 3.)

Galton's arguments are enormously helpful in illuminating the difficulty of living a life disconnected from war in late-eighteenth-century Birmingham. But they are also unreliable. Was he, in fact, as powerless to effect change as he thought? Certainly, individual responsibility was difficult to negotiate in a world of interdependent economic actors and networks, but his particular importance among the state's gun contractors suggests that he might have had a significant impact on its ability to fight wars had he decided, in the midst of war, to prioritize his promises as a Quaker and abstain from arms manufacture. This would have entailed enormous personal risk—although he might have had the support of Quaker Friends. His sense of limited agency emerged from his understanding of his historical destiny as an industrial capitalist in his time. Insofar as it was the cultural belief that informed Galton's and other contractors' passive tolerance of war, this historical imagination powerfully shaped the unfolding of history itself. The availability of modes of historical-economic thought that might even assuage the conscience of a Quaker gunmaker was critical to Britain's emergence as an industrial and global superpower. The wars against France ended in 1815 with Britain master of the Mediterranean, the Indian Ocean, and the Pacific. Twenty-six percent of the world's population was under British rule.

We take history to be an essentially worldly, secular, materialist, empirical discipline. We presume that the factors, human acts, dynamic forces that we invoke to explain why the world is as it is are of this earth and objectively discernible. And yet the discipline emerged from a search for meaning that adopted the eschatological structure of religious belief. It was built to endow morally questionable events with purpose and meaning revealed in the narrative end of history. As the anthropologist Talal Asad explains, the secular is "neither continuous with the religious that supposedly preceded it . . . nor a simple break from it," but "overlaps with 'the religious.'"[44] Most essentially for its moralizing purposes, Enlightenment historical thought embraced a particular conception of time as something that moves irresistibly forward, adopting an eschatological structure and millenarian outlook from the Judeo-Christian tradition. Hence its obsession with "progress," variously defined. The assumption about the steady and irreversible unfolding of universal time is what allows history to exercise that power of moral judgment that Thucydides detected. It is what makes "getting ahead" modernity's most overpowering impulse. History will reveal what has become obsolete and those whom Providence has seen fit to cast as "backward." Obsolescence is thus "modernity's equivalent of perdition and hellfire," writes the novelist and anthropologist Amitav Ghosh. Its most potent words of damnation, "passed down . . . from Hegel and Marx to President Obama, is the malediction of being 'on the wrong side of history.'"[45]

Enlightenment faith in the progressive nature of war helped normalize the violence of imperial conquest and industrial capitalism. Smith's pacifist vision of economic prosperity has its own legacy, but even its historical vision allowed for necessary evil in a manner that forwarded pro-war arguments like Priestley's. Thus, in his *Enquiry into the Nature and Causes of the Wealth of Nations* (1776), a "notoriously historical work," he argued that the invention of firearms, though it "at first sight appears to be so pernicious" by giving an advantage to an "opulent and civilized over a poor and barbarous nation," favored both "the permanency and . . . extension of civilization."[46] He took a Leibnizian view of guns—accommodating the existence of something that seemed evil prima facie whose actual benevolent purpose would be revealed with the passage of time. Priestley echoed this view in his argument that firearms had made war less bloody and more quickly decisive, that their effect was civilizing.[47] Galton made the same argument in his defense.

We will return to Smith and the wider context in which eighteenth-century historical thought took shape. But I want to pause here to recognize the legacy of these ideas about the place of war and industrialism in history. Like Galton, we accept industrialism as an unshakeable collective inheritance, however exceptional it is in the longer narrative of human history. We, too, readily acknowledge its unfortunate but necessary indebtedness to war- (now styled "defense-") related activity.[48] But we no longer see war as Galton did, as a contingent fact of history constraining his choices in a particular moment. In an era of a seemingly timeless global war on terror, war and other forms of mass violence have become events almost *outside* history, a permanent context with its own cyclical logic, beyond earthly control, like the weather. Technical euphemisms like "security" obscure the political and historical character of conflicts in the Middle East, Afghanistan, and elsewhere, allowing them to go on as if inevitable, without accountability; their continual damage to human lives in those places is like the routine and unavoidable damage of terrible storms.

This analogy itself is starting to break down as we learn that the weather we live with—including terrible storms—is also not as natural as we supposed. The industrial revolution that enabled mass violence on a new scale simultaneously began to change the climate. In a time in which natural disasters have ceased to be "natural," in the era we now denote as the "Anthropocene," when human activity became a dominant influence on climate and the environment, a new analogy might hold, requiring us to call for accountability for storms as well as war. We may find that we might have more room for maneuver than we have been taught to imagine since the birth of industrial capitalism.

By the late nineteenth century, the quickening historical sensibility had labeled that economic transformation a "revolution," suppressing guilty conscience about the losers in that change and claiming it for the narrative of progress. Twentieth-century labor movements made the coal miner an icon that helped awaken that conscience. Today, around the world, his image is being manipulated to *suppress* conscience about climate change. In truth, both are victims of the exploitation of environmental resources and human labor launched with the industrial revolution.

Galton's recourse to historical arguments in his defense rested on notions of selfhood particular to his time. He defended himself rather than capitulate to the sect's sudden objections out of his confidence in his capacity for private moral assessment of his actions. His point was that military contracting was so pervasive that each could only be accountable to his own conscience. The Society of Friends (the Quakers) would have to disown everyone—absurd—or simply respect "THE RIGHT AND DUTY OF PRIVATE JUDGMENT."[49] The very subjection of private motives to public scrutiny made them suspicious. Erasing the distinction between personal and public life could not but reduce his actions to mere appearances, he perceived. Certainly, he might have acknowledged the difference in *degree* of complicity between being a supplier of raw materials and a manufacturer of finished arms. But his point was that if *principle* was at stake, degree did not matter. Only individual conscience mattered—a subjective rather than objective assessment of guilt, the only kind possible in the moment, without knowledge of what the future would be. Seeing himself as a Quaker and industrialist constrained by a particular historical moment, he was accountable not to the sect's diktat but to his *individual* conscience.

The concept of a private, internal conscience distinct from, even at odds with, an institutionally supported notion of "Conscience" was integral to the Reformation and the tradition of English Dissent (including Quakers).[50] The struggle for toleration involving thinkers like John Locke was founded on that notion. Shakespeare's *Hamlet*, written at the turn of the seventeenth century, dramatized the lonely torments that highly personalized conscience could wreak. By the late eighteenth century, a time in which churches no longer gave commandments and the "shrine of morality" was understood to move within the self, the vaunting of individual conscience was part of a wider cultural focus on private moral judgment.[51] Eighteenth-century people were highly self-conscious about their moral sentiments and interested in their own consciences. Enlightenment philosophers' explorations of moral sentiments epitomized and nurtured this culture.

Partly through engagement with classical thought, the Enlightenment helped the word "moral" migrate from the world of religious belief to the domain of the political, conceived as a proving ground for individual morality, an "interior journey guided by the conscience."[52] The philosopher Charles Taylor explains that the background conditions of religious belief in the West transformed, producing an "immanent frame" that sharply demarcated the purposes of human flourishing from any supernatural order. The "self" of this immanent frame was "buffered" from forces outside the mind and was characterized by commitment to reason and linear time.[53] The novel emerged as the exemplary genre for showcasing an individual's journey of self-discovery, a form for "charting the career of the conscience," in Ghosh's words. It and other "humanitarian narratives" were essential to cultivating modern sentiments of empathy on the scale of the individual.[54] Victorian biographical writing (a historical genre), especially, perfected the art of writing about the self as though it was and could be consistent.[55] Through such forms, writes the historian Charly Coleman, the Enlightenment strove to "resacralize the self as an object of a totalizing force—situated either in the mystic divine or in a purely immanent, materialist conception of nature."[56] Rather than dispensing with the divine, philosophers effectively closed the chasm between the divine and terrestrial spheres, identifying one with the other. They valued human agency in the art of divining the world, but humans themselves became "newly alien to themselves . . . in a manner that recalled the radical distance of the divine." Historical literature helped shape this new understanding of the human. Historians were numerous among the new "public moralists," as one scholar has christened them—intellectuals who took on the burden of reminding their contemporaries of their collective moral values.[57]

In short, history's emergence as a guide to ethical action depended on, and fueled, new notions of selfhood. The evolution of Adam Smith's *Theory of Moral Sentiments* allows us to trace this change, too, in real time. In the 1759–1761 version of the text, Smith described conscience as the ability to survey one's own sentiments "with the eyes of other people"; it depended on an almost literal division of the self into the judge and the self being judged. One self restrains the other. This split self was modern relative to earlier, God-driven Protestant understandings of conscience. But the final, 1790 version of the text went further. In it, the conscience is not a distinct internal character but a more metaphorical allusion. It is a self that has transcended the internal split, that *has been civilized*. This late-eighteenth-century notion of highly individualized selfhood, possessing psychological depth and interiority, replaced more fluid and corporate understandings of identity.[58] The idea was that it took time to develop the capacity to impartially examine our own conduct; possession of it was itself the proof of modern selfhood. And historical study was key to inculcating it, as Bolingbroke, Smith, Priestley, and other philosophers urged. The idea of an inner voice may be ancient, but new understandings of selfhood explicitly concerned with individuality and individualism embedded that notion in a new frame.

This civilized self was essential to Smith's political economic thought. Liberalism is "constitutively guilty in conscience," as one scholar diagnoses, hence its prescriptions for governing sentiment.[59] Smith posited internally regulated sentiment as a constraint on the excesses of the market and on our sense of obligation to right all the wrongs it bred. Granting permission—even insisting on the need—to refuse the vision of the "miseries that we never saw," *The Theory of Moral Sentiments* preemptively offered a rejoinder to conscience's objections to the operations of the invisible hand that would govern *The Wealth of Nations* (1776).[60] The global capitalist relations being forged in the late eighteenth century depended on cultivation of a parochial moral vision. Smith prescribed for capital's agents well-regulated sympathy with a limited set of others, and for its subjects stoicism in the face of their own suffering. He called for an internal economy of sentiment, distribution of the passions within the bounds of propriety—a civilized self. In a sense, Galton's argument that everyone was ineluctably involved in war-driven industrialism attempted to puncture the illusion of wider innocence created by liberalism's parochial moral vision. But, as Marx might put it, "to call on them to give up their illusions about their condition is to call on them to give up a condition that requires illusions."[61] Marx was talking about religion, but the observation applies well to the justifying narrative of progress embraced in this time too. Even Galton did not counsel giving up their condition.

Intention was the arbiter of eighteenth-century conscience and became even more important with the rise of this modern self. Without intention, there could be no moral responsibility. In the middle of the century, the historian-philosopher David Hume explained that where actions "proceed not from some *cause* in the character and disposition of the person who performed them, they can neither redound to his honour, if good; nor infamy, if evil."[62] Criminal sentencing reflected this distinction, distinguishing more forgivable "manslaughter" committed in a moment of passion or fury from premeditatedly malicious "willful murder." But the plea of temporary fury lost purchase by the end of the century.[63] Temporary fury implied a kind of crack in the self, and by the end of the century, the British self was supposed to be more controlled and controllable, more coherent and internally consistent, less given to temporary fracture—as epitomized by middle-class British masculinity.

The growing expectation of internal consistency, of following through on stated intentions, fueled the culture of promise-keeping that gave the last quarter of the century the name "Age of Contract." The law supported this culture institutionally with provisions that made promisors generally liable for whatever expectations their promises created. Late-eighteenth-century people thus cultivated a greater sense of moral and legal liability, a greater sense of accountability to conscience. It is evident in the radical thinker Thomas Paine's public lambasting of his father's Quaker sect in 1776 for harboring "pretended scruples" as its members profanely pursued wealth by any means.[64] We see it, too, in the sect's 1779 recirculation of a minute of 1732 calling on Friends to be "exact in performing promises."[65]

Expectations of imperial accountability were part of this culture, as we shall see. Tensions with France intensified this pressure to fulfill commitments. In 1792, British Home Office spies investigated the loyalty of Birmingham gunmakers.[66] Quite apart from its specifically revolutionary context, even the Reign of Terror in France (in which Paine was jailed) was partly symptomatic of a broader culture of rooting out hypocrisy and duplicity. In England in 1795, passage of the Two Acts against sedition weaponized the promise-keeping culture against British radicals.

That was also the year in which Quakers held Galton accountable for his promises, and his defense rested significantly on denial of ill intent, the protest that he was merely a cog in an enormous, inescapable industrial machine. If pleas of temporary fury had lost conviction, late-eighteenth-century promise breakers *could* take refuge in history as a realm understood to be driven by forces beyond even a heroic individual's control, and that was Galton's tack. If "intention" was the arbiter of conscience, historical arguments—the idea that Providence constrained one's actions—were crucial to proving the absence of ill intention. The opposite of an intended act is an accident, and the consummate accident, the ultimate alibi, is the accident of history, in a time when history's unfolding was understood to be providentially designed in such a manner that even the most heroically ambitious of individuals must become resigned to being its instrument.

The new highly individuated sense of self existed in theory more than in practice, as we shall see throughout this book. But insofar as it did exist in some illusory way, it was made. The American Revolutionary War, a civil war that forced the English to question all categories of identity, was an important turning point, transforming older, unstable, malleable notions of selfhood into a more fixed concept of identity.[67] Novels and other literary forms, including history, helped too. But so, too, did the very technologies that spurred increasing faith in history as an ethical guide. In the eighteenth century, a technology was "civilizing" if it enabled greater emotional continence: self-restraint. Thus, forks facilitated self-control at the table. Likewise, firearms allowed an impersonal threat of violence between strangers, from a distance.[68] Operating outside the domain of the passions, they helped produce the late-eighteenth-century masculine ideal of the bounded self possessing bounded property. Private property was an aberration in a long history of communal landholding in England and all around the world.[69] The process of "enclosure" that drove people from the land into towns where they took up industrial labor or to colonies of settlement abroad depended on guns.[70] An advertisement from a Bristol gunmaker, shown here, helps illustrate how guns were understood to make the modern self. A generic "native" has put down his bow and arrow and taken up a musket that puts him on par with the property-owning Briton. The ship behind him symbolizes the spread of civilization, and it is a civilization based on property, embodied by the Englishman with his hound, manor, and fowling piece on the left. The armed native is not a frightening figure—though he will become one by the next century. Rather, his posture suggests liberation, a man able to stand on his own, now that he has a gun in hand. This supposed "civilizing" function—the idea that guns forwarded historical progress—routinely trumped awareness of guns' violent effects and qualms about arming potential British enemies.[71]

Why did guns imply self-control in this way? Crucially, their violence was understood as fundamentally unintentional—the result of an impersonal and highly unpredictable mechanical process that simply could not impinge on the user's conscience in the way that a purposeful, emotionally motivated act of violence with a sword, club, or hands might. The mechanical and unpredictable nature of the eighteenth-century gun made it an adjunct to the controlled, crack-free self. Smith explained in words echoing Hume's above: "He who shoots a bird, and he who shoots a man, both of them perform the same external movement: each of them draws the trigger of a gun. The consequences which actually, and in fact, happen to proceed from any action, are, if possible, still more indifferent either to praise or blame, than even the external movement of the body. As they depend, not upon the agent, but upon fortune, they cannot be the proper foundation for any sentiment, of which his character and conduct are the subjects. The only consequences for which he can be answerable . . . are those which are someway or other intended."[72] The gun was a machine that freed the conscience—absolving the shooter from "praise or blame." The consequences of its use were not grounds for judgment about the user's moral character; a man might only be judged by the *intended* consequences of his actions. The eighteenth-century gun's unpredictability allowed it to serve as a stern deterrent to property infractions without taxing the user's conscience. The presumed ease of perpetrating this mechanical, dispassionate violence *without* incurring cost to the conscience was theoretically what made waving

William Heard, Trade Card, c. 1780s–1790s. (Reproduction © Bristol Reference Library)

a gun effective in inhibiting property violations in eighteenth-century England. It supported and was supported by the legal terror of the "Bloody Code" that secured property with the threat of capital punishment.[73]

At the turn of the century, the utilitarian thinker Jeremy Bentham dreamt of a panopticon that would perfect the internalization of discipline among prison inmates: A watchman could watch them without any of them knowing in any moment which of them was watched, forcing all to act as though they were constantly watched and thus to regulate themselves as desired. This was the eighteenth-century liberal vision of selfhood that guns in the hands of property owners helped produce. British national character came to be grounded in the practice of emotional restraint symbolized and enforced by the gun-wielding property owner. The gun was a crucial accessory in the making of the modern conscience that took history as its guide: a self aware of being watched, that knew history's eyes were on it. Gentlemanliness was embodied in the authority and restraint implied by the gun. Only such a controlled self could suppress emotional impulses enough to fulfill the needs of the historical script unfolding in real time. Doing right by history required discipline.

Guns acquired new meanings and uses later in the modern period. Mass manufacture helped normalize them as ubiquitous commodities capable of forcing change—history—in any narrative, such as the epochal shift "triggered" by the assassination of Archduke Franz Ferdinand in 1914. Their presence in the colonies accordingly became a subject of increasing concern to the British. The mechanization of killing went beyond producing a controlled self, anesthetizing human sensibilities altogether. To survive the modern era, to protect the human psyche from the trauma of perpetual shock, explained the twentieth-century philosopher Walter Benjamin, we learned to insulate ourselves, to cheat ourselves of sensory response.[74] But a sense of the historical necessity of violence also eased the conscience. Galton felt no burden of guilt about manufacturing an object that itself enabled more civilized exercise of conscience, whose occasional violence was not motivated by a desire for violence but its opposite.

To be sure, a more critical view of guns was emerging in the 1790s, hence the controversy around Galton at that point. The movement to abolish the slave trade, especially, cast them in dark light, educating the public on their nefarious role in the trade and plantation violence. With increased exposure to guns in the long wars against France that began in 1793, guns began to be used in new kinds of homicides unrelated to property that also prompted reconsideration of their civilizing effect.[75] The slave trade, guns, and much else began to appear newly scandalous near the end of the century. If new ideas of selfhood underwrote the turn towards history as an ethical idiom, the British defeat by the American colonies in 1783 was what forced collective reckoning with the morality of British actions abroad in a manner that consolidated the ethical value of historical thinking in the imperial enterprise. This was the wider, political backdrop of the Age of Contract.

Up to the middle of the century, high public pride in the empire and confidence in the productive nature of war helped quiet intimations of exploitative or aggressive actions abroad. Excessive scrupulousness in the pursuit of wealth appeared as "unsophisticated carping against the public good."[76] There was little pretense that the empire was about anything other than the acquisition of wealth, little need for the justificatory narrative of the civilizing mission and plenty of opportunity for reckless fortune hunters like Robert Clive, who joined the East India Company, the monopoly charter company trading in the Indian Ocean region since the seventeenth century, and enabled it to secure its first major territorial foothold, in Bengal, with the Battle of Plassey of 1757.[77] Such companies were the primary instruments of Britain's mercantile engagement with the world. Mercantilist political economic thinking assumed a zero-sum world in which one nation's gain was the other's loss. The idea that wars of conquest supported the British public good was common, and the fate of those the British vanquished in the process was not their moral burden to bear. Invoking systemic or "market" failure, the financial elites controlling these joint-stock companies could also defraud the public of millions with impunity so long as they did not harm one another (though Britons understood bankruptcy—*individual* financial failure—through the lens of moral failure).[78]

After the Seven Years' War (1756–1763), Britons began to attack this system of "Old Corruption" for allowing the socially powerful to exploit relationships with government offices for personal gain. The middle of the century saw the most consistently negative literary depictions of merchants and capitalists up to that time.[79] Charges of corruption and malpractice against East India Company servants, including Clive, added further grist to the mill. In 1772–1773, when the company's reckless activities came to threaten both its own and the nation's finances, the government bailed it out in exchange for greater regulatory power. The sniffing out of despotism—both in England and in the American colonies—began to open up new arenas of public life to moral judgment, laying the foundation for the post-1783 reckoning with the scandal of empire.

Thomas Paine's fury about British activities in India fueled his explosive anger at British treatment of the American colonies. *Common Sense* (1776), his incendiary pamphlet released as the American colonies revolted, affirmed, "Thousands are already ruined by British barbarity."[80] That this passage gestured at India is suggested by his essay the year before on Clive's suicide. Clive had returned to England a baron, raising hackles as much for his misdeeds abroad as for this brash presumption. Paine pronounced Clive's death just desserts for the murder, rapine, and famine his greed and lust for power had caused in India.[81] (Many, including Samuel Johnson, presumed bad conscience drove him to it.[82]) In October 1775, as British and colonial clashes intensified, Paine still hoped "the Almighty" would curtail Britain's power in view of "the horrid cruelties . . . exercised in the East-Indies" and the ravaging of "the hapless shores of Africa."[83] In 1778, as the war went on, he again promised that Britain's "cruelties in the East-Indies, will *never, never* be forgotten," remarking the poetic manner in which Indian tea had kindled a war in America "to punish the destroyer. The chain is continued . . . with . . . a mysterious uniformity, both in the crime and the punishment."[84] This was a karmic vision of history.

Adam Smith's *The Wealth of Nations* (1776) also strove to puncture the attitude of insouciance towards oligarchy, reserving its sharpest attack for the East India Company then rampaging across South Asia to argue that colonialism cost the British public more than it benefited them. For all its vaunting of individual economic agency, however, Smith's vision of history gave individuals little room for maneuver in acknowledging the play of forces beyond their control. Even with respect to the East India Company, he acknowledged the "system of government" constraining its agents: Those who would criticize them would "not have acted better themselves" in that situation, he judged empathetically. Likewise, he could not see the British government backing down in the clash with the American colonies, for there was no historical script for that: "No nation ever voluntarily gave up the dominion of any province, how troublesome soever it might be to govern it." Such a sacrifice would simply be "mortifying to the pride" of the nation and "contrary to the private interest of the governing part of it."[85] Only war, he anticipated, would resolve the clash.

In this tolerance for war as a historical force, his vision of history anticipated Kant's and Priestley's in the 1780s, similarly maintaining that hidden laws ensured the ultimately productive effect of humankind's narrowly self-interested activities. If European discovery of America and passage to India via the Cape of Good Hope had caused "dreadful misfortunes" in the "East and West Indies," they had arisen "from accident."[86] Those discoveries were made when Europeans "happened to" have such superiority of force "that they were enabled to commit with impunity every sort of injustice." He writes as though the very possession of force, as a historical accident, frees Europeans from accountability for using it; the use of passive tense is notable. Crucially, he foresees everything set right *in time*: Europeans would grow weaker, or the people of the Indies stronger, and all the world "may arrive at that equality of courage and force which, by inspiring mutual fear, can alone overawe the injustice of independent nations into some sort of respect for the rights of one another." The only way to get to that point, however, was through continued commerce; progress would flow from European contact. He thus enrolled the colonial interaction, which, he knew, was devastating much of the world, as a step along the way to a happy end. Even in the end, the seemingly unhappy condition of "mutual fear" is what will guarantee collective happiness. As with fire-arms, Smith trusted in larger forces ensuring that even seemingly "perni-cious" things led to a progressive end. Smith and his circle established an influential critique of imperialism, but within a historical vision that could tolerate iniquities with a view to future improvement if not vindication. They did not object to imperialism *on principle.*

In general, Smithian thought, with its circumscribed moral vision, ap-preciation for systemic constraints, and faith in progress, did not offer a recipe for revolutionary change. Romantics, socialists, and evangelicals would insist on individual responsibility even in the context of complex processes in the next century. But they always had to contend with increas-ingly pervasive popular understandings of Smith's "invisible hand," which inhibited perception of a need for radical individual action. In the liberal view, the system is always already in optimal equilibrium, rewarding and punishing those as they merit, dovetailing with the distribution of divine grace. Markets, over time, are the judges of individual morality.

Smith could also find a reassuring historical vision in the work of Ed-ward Gibbon, probably the period's most illustrious historian, whom Smith deeply admired. Gibbon's epic six-volume account *The History of the Decline and Fall of the Roman Empire* also began to appear in 1776 (the final volumes appearing in 1789).[87] In a time of revolution in the American colonies and France, Gibbon's account of the fall of an ancient empire ex-pressed misgivings, certainly. But though its title might suggest an attempt at recovering the cyclical view of history, it in fact strove to moralize for the present through an account of the past. The world in which Rome could fall was, Gibbon hoped, safely in the past, now that the Age of Reason had finally subverted the stifling power of the Church. Certain as he was of human folly, he like many Enlightenment thinkers was equally certain that history might now be a story of progress—especially with the benefit of historical perspective. For the record of the Roman past offered a salu-tary warning of the dangers of decadence and of the corruption that came from contact abroad at the margins of the empire. Britons read the work as a guide to avoiding such pitfalls in their own imperial story. The British Empire might succeed where Rome failed.

But the British lost in 1783, and defeat against the colonies irreparably dented such self-assuredness, prompting urgent moral questioning about the nation and its empire. Attacks on Old Corruption grew insistently louder, encompassing the rogue East India Company. Not least among its irritants were the "nabobs" (a corruption of the Indian word *nawab,* or "prince") who returned with their loot to Britain, bringing the vulgar stain of nouveaux riches to an aristocratic class proud of its hereditary wealth.[88] A year after the war ended, an India Act again strove to bring the company under greater government control. Lord Cornwallis, who had notoriously surrendered at Yorktown in 1781, was rewarded with the position of governor-general in Bengal in 1786. When Cornwallis's predecessor, Warren Hastings, returned to England, he became the subject of an impeachment trial on corruption charges that lasted from 1788 to 1795. This was a part of the new moment of reflection on imperial practices as a legitimate area of public inquiry, an attempt to air the anxious conscience of empire. It echoed the public outcry against military contractors as warmongers reaping profits despite the country's humiliating defeat. The member of Parliament and liberal political theorist Edmund Burke led the prosecution (Gibbon was in the audience). In his four-day-long opening speech in February 1788, he argued, "These Gentlemen have formed a plan of Geographical morality, by which the duties of men . . . are not to be governed by their relations to the Great Governor of the Universe, or by their relations to men, but by climates, degrees of longitude . . . , parallels not of life but of latitudes. As if, when you have crossed the equinoctial line all the virtues die . . . , as if there were a kind of baptism, like that practised by seamen, by which they unbaptize themselves of all that they learned in Europe, and commence a new order and system of things."[89] Burke called for accountability to British ethical norms, indeed, for the universal applicability of those norms. He insisted that "the laws of morality are the same everywhere." The danger, to him, lay in that "baptism" abroad that altered accountability to conscience, that allowed the British conscience to contemplate actions that it would forswear and even abhor at home. (He did not contemplate the dangers of temporal morality.)

Burke had supported the colonies in the American revolution, like Paine, who, we have seen, was also disgusted by British activities in India. They were on the same page in 1788 in their apprehension of Britain's depleted moral status in the world. The French Revolution in 1789, however, revealed a chasm between their views of how history should inform ethics. Burke was repulsed by the revolution and penned a scathing critique of revolutionary change on principle, *Reflections on the Revolution in France* (1790). As in the case of India, he urged gradual change within inherited institutions and traditions. In this, he espoused a historical sensibility different from what thinkers like Priestley advocated, one that could *not* excuse immoral action on the grounds of future moral vindication but insisted on accountability to existing values in the present, however "prejudiced." It made conscience accountable to history not by asking what it made for the future but by asking how it honored the past. He could support the American revolution because a "spirit of religion" confined the "spirit of freedom," but he did not find such a sober sense of well-ordered reality animating the revolution in France.[90] The "spirit of liberty" was not a moral value in itself; *its* judgment depended on vindication in time, based on its compatibility with governance, civilization, culture, civility, order. He counseled, "We ought to suspend our judgment until the first effervescence is a little subsided, till the liquor is cleared."[91]

Paine was among the Enlightenment thinkers incensed by this argument and swiftly produced a rejoinder, *Rights of Man* (1791).[92] The past need not constrain the future, was his view; every generation had the right to remake institutions anew. They ought not to be constrained by inheritance, and they had the agency to make their own history. The spirit of liberty did, to him, possess moral value. (Such notions informed his own adventurous shuttling between scenes of radicalism in London, Paris, and the colonies.) This was a revolutionary historical vision.

Indeed, the word "revolution" was revolutionized in this very period. Etymologically, it refers to something cyclical, a return to the start of a circle, referring, for instance, to the astronomical movements that many early modernists took to be shepherding the evolution of human history. In early modern usage, however, it did not always imply a return to an original state but referred to the general vicissitudes of fortune, to the disorder and instabilities that were the natural state of human affairs, to change that *happened* but was not *made.* The naming of the political changes of 1689 as the "Glorious Revolution" thus strove to establish, rhetorically, that a great shift had occurred, providentially, and was over.[93] Before 1789, "there were revolutions but no revolutionaries," writes the historian Keith Baker. Enlightenment thinkers, with their vision of human existence framed by a social order itself created by humans, ideally according to rational principles, gave the word new meaning. To understand society as a product of human activity, of *history,* requires a different temporal logic from that implied by ongoing vicissitudes and flux. "Revolution" thus came to mean a mechanism of change for the indefinite transformation of society—understood as progress (even if critics saw it as social collapse). It became the name for "a collective political act ushering in the birth of a new world," an act rather than a fact.[94] It fit with Enlightenment historical thought, the notion that time itself was headed in a particular, linear direction—and those conscious of it must act with the knowledge that history had its eyes on them, like the revolutionaries Washington and Hamilton. A radical sense of human agency was at play in this new sense of "revolution," the idea that men can make society anew. I do mean "men" here: Though women were obviously equal participants in the history of the period, ideas about who should think with history, who might act out of a sense of historical exigency, were critical to modern gender notions. Priestley's pedagogical object in his *Lectures* was "young men of ability formed to virtue."[95] Making history was about enacting the masculine and its "other," the feminine.

The increasing currency of heroic notions of revolutionary agency were part of the reason that concern about imperialism took the form of a trial of a particular individual. The trial depended on the idea that all that was wrong in the East India Company enterprise in India *could* be the work of a single man. And redemption from it could be, too: shortly before his death, Burke instructed an associate charged with writing a history of the impeachment, "Let my endeavours to save the nation from that Shame and guilt, be my monument."[96] Arguably a positive sense of great-man destiny was also what drove ambitious men to go to India in search of loot and glory in the first place. Clive molded himself on a heroic type emerging from narratives of (what we now call) the Age of Exploration, exemplified by Hernán Cortés, the conquistador who brought treasure from abroad.[97] An understanding of history as the work of great men shaped the actions of many such figures; the conquest of India depended on men who set about very consciously trying to *make* history, based on their own understanding of the hero's role in making history. Philip Francis, Hastings's nemesis in India, acted out of a sense that he was "sent to save and govern" "this glorious empire."[98] To his endless irritation, Hastings very consciously tried to adopt a different ethical vision, borrowed from the *Gita*, namely the idea of detachment from the results of one's actions (though without destabilizing his conviction that Britain ruled India by the right of the sword).[99] Such predilections were partly why he became the fall guy of empire. The idea of heroic destiny thrived instead—most immediately in the shape of Arthur Wellesley, a latter-day Clive who conquered vast swaths of India before becoming Napoleon's nemesis in Europe under the sobriquet of the Duke of Wellington.

Though Burke and Paine were both critical of British activities in India, their competing views of the past—one seeing inherited circumstance as insuperable, the other seeing it as negligible—would serve the spread of liberal empire in different ways. The latter was the major key that licensed liberal imperialists to heroically remake other places in the world in service to historical progress (and as penance for the sins of the eighteenth-century empire). But the sense that they were doing so as unwitting instruments of Providence or esoteric natural laws meant that when such remaking inevitably wreaked havoc, they could shift to the minor key and plead powerlessness before historical forces that were beyond human control but, they assured, ultimately progressive.[100]

In the end, Hastings's trial, which ended in acquittal in 1795, helped secure the ascendancy of a historical mode of ethically assessing imperialism over Burke's plea for a more transcendent ethical idiom. Acquittal allowed the trial to function, culturally, as a ritual "cleansing and regeneration of the imperial mission."[101] "If Burke's rhetoric were followed to its logical conclusion, the trial would have had to end not with the impeachment of Hastings alone, but with the overturning of the Company's rule in India," writes the historian Thomas Metcalf. "This neither Burke nor Hastings, nor the British public . . . was prepared to contemplate."[102] Indeed, while the trial unfolded, the 1784 India Act that brought the company under closer government supervision simultaneously endowed the new governor-general, Cornwallis, with far greater powers than Hastings ever had. The trial became a theater for the spectacular enactment of penance, and an opportunity to assemble new justifications for imperial activity abroad, as we shall see in Chapter 2. By venting concerns about Hastings's particular misconduct, the trial redeemed the broader imperial project as something ultimately progressive. (Indeed, Hastings fell partly because his Indophilia irked the councilors who served alongside him [led by Francis].) Burke had complained that the Indian empire furthered the interests of only a greedy few; going forward, the trial assured, it would be about the nation's interest.[103] Scapegoating Hastings, Britons emerged confident that there was nothing wrong in empire per se. The personalized scandal around Hastings deflected focus from "the scandal of empire" itself.[104] Moreover, the trial established the *theory* that the Britons charged with ruling India would not act with impunity, that they were morally accountable—if time ever revealed a true crime. The trial thus worked to contain the guilt of empire and offered the assurance of future vindication. Imperial historians would thenceforth periodically revisit this pivotal moment to fortify the ethical foundations of empire, as we shall see.

Further historical absolution came in the form of the abolition movement, similarly fueled by national soul-searching in the aftermath of defeat in 1783. Many alighted on the slave trade as the moral liability that had caused Providence to forsake Britain in the war and allow the Americans to seize the status of freedom's torchbearers. The abolition movement offered a means of denigrating the colonial rebels as hypocrites (while American abolitionists also sought to undermine the British pose of innocence).[105] In Britain, the movement was initially led by members of the Quaker sect. (This high profile raised the stakes for ethical consistency within the sect, contributing to concern about Galton.) The French Revolution goaded the British further into making a *historical* effort to reclaim the moral higher ground as the true defenders of liberty—by abolishing the slave trade, even though it was an inheritance. Of course, skeptics saw more cynical motives at work: Rival powers dismissed British "humanitarianism" as cover for Machiavellian statecraft; radicals like William Cobbett saw it as a strategic ploy to distract attention from the plight of exploited workers at home. But the movement succeeded in 1807, and Britons understood that as the result not of mundane causes but of the "hand of divine providence."[106]

Most of those who took the lead in Quaker abolitionism were influenced in some way by Enlightenment traditions of thought. Abolitionists wanted to save Britain's soul but were also invested in cultivating a certain kind of ethical selfhood. Many aspired to save black souls by propagating the gospel among them. But many were even more exercised by the desire to produce ethical British selves: Genuine as their horror at slavery was, evangelicals hoped the campaign to abolish it might afford lessons in righteous living for Britons. It was part of a wider campaign against "nominal Christianity" that they fought on several fronts at once in the hope of making religion figure more prominently in public life. This, too, was part of the culture of promise-keeping. Quaker abolitionists likewise hoped to revive their sect's seeming reduction to "lifeless fidelity to stale customs."[107] The emerging historical sensibility bore the imprint of this reaction against nominal Christianity. Indeed, Priestley was a leader of the abolition movement. The movement was, in short, not only about freeing slaves but about shaping modern selves imbued with a particular sense of their historic agency. As the historian Chris Brown writes, "To condemn slavery in principle and colonial institutions in practice had become by the 1780s the mark of an enlightened, humane Christian."[108] Sympathy for the African exemplified moral virtue; abolitionism proved one's moral worth. Active interest in the ethics of empire endowed one with "moral capital." The British drew on that capital thereafter to sustain the paradoxical effort to be imperialist agents of liberty.

To be sure, many opposed the movement on practical grounds, arguing in a manner reminiscent of Galton's pleas of helplessness before economic realities that the "intricate web of mutual dependencies" between buyers and sellers posed an insuperable obstacle to change.[109] As the historian David Brion Davis puts it, "The knowledge that our economic acts are related in some way to most of the world's crime and oppression can blunt any sense of complicity."[110] But many who were willing to tolerate war as a necessary evil did not look upon slavery with such indulgence. Priestley deemed it an evil that Britons *must* act to eradicate.[111] Awareness of collective complicity in this context produced a sense of collective moral responsibility. A perception that slavery was the result of "human choice" underwrote abolitionists' conviction that its enablers had a moral duty to act to change it. Emancipation schemes also suggested the possibility of alternatives.[112] The sugar boycott launched in 1791 emerged from an awareness of the remote effects of individual market decisions, sensitizing Britons to their responsibility for slavery and giving them a sense of agency in effecting change.[113] Galton's arguments about arms-making went in the opposite direction, contending that when complicity was so general, individual acts of abstinence were futile. He supported his daughters' participation in the sugar boycott but was more ambivalent about abolition himself.[114] For Priestley, the difference was clear: The collective advantages resulting from war—the boost to progress and innovation—justified its continuance, but cheap sugar could not justify slavery, whose violence he judged "peculiarly shocking to humanity." Slavery violated man's capacity for "liberty and self command."[115] Modern war, by means of firearms, enhanced self-command and thus civilization, but slavery did the opposite. His seemingly antithetical views about agency in these two cases were consistent in prioritizing production of a certain kind of civilized self—the kind that might use history as the foundation of ethics. Both were also grounded in a belief in Britain's providential role in the world. Awareness of the way markets spread complicity could either blunt or enhance one's sense of responsibility and capacity to take remedial action. The distinction lay in whether the evil in question might bear sweeter fruit in the future. The distinction, in other words, lay in how history might judge it.

That slavery remained central to global production systems well after 1807 is perhaps the result of the fact that abolitionists did *not* perceive its relationship to the "war capitalism" of their time.[116] Had they attacked war—and the conquest it enabled—they might have instigated truly revolutionary change. But this was never their ambition. They sought to remove a stain from British national culture, not to transform it entirely. The movement emerged from a providential view of British history, a view that Britain's progress in a competitive global arena was blessed by Providence and that the sudden loss of that blessing was a sign of divine disfavor. It was Providence's expression of historical judgment, calling for redemptive history-making action. Through an act of redemption, like abolition, the nation might regain Providence's favor.

Something is a "scandal" because it offends collective conscience; it violates collectively held moral commitments. The preoccupation with scandal at the end of the century was the mark of bad conscience about Britain's actions, especially abroad. The campaign to end slavery launched a series of reform campaigns that analogized a range of vulnerable and exploited groups (women, animals, factory workers) to slaves. This surge in humanitarian sentiment—indeed reformism itself—depended on a strong sense of man's ability to remake his world in time, a strong sense of human agency. These various reformist causes shared a common concern with despotism and arbitrary justice; they depended on collective investment in the idea that Britons were making history, that they were guiding the world into a time of freedom. The disruptive events of the late eighteenth century—the American, French, and Haitian Revolutions—with their claims to have broken dramatically with the past, consolidated this historical consciousness, a sense of sharp contrast between past and present. In Britain, the rapidly unfolding changes associated with industrialism reinforced a sense of permanent evolution in a new direction, later acquiring the vocabulary of "revolution" too. In this period of truly dramatic historical change, ideas about history provided an additional moral compass with which to judge human activity. War, empire, slavery—all were subject to moral scrutiny, and the first two earned a pass based on faith in their usefulness in moving history towards its end of a world of civilized selves.

Notably, this Age of Revolutions, witnessing the birth of democracies drawing from the well of Enlightenment, helped popularize great-man ideas about history.[117] While ideas of human equality circulated, so, too, did the notion of genius, of especially worthy and talented men. We will hear more about the Romantics in Chapter 2. Here, I want only to recall that these critics of Enlightenment rationalism were deeply invested in notions of genius that were also indebted to Enlightenment thought—to the effort to find a source of ultimate meaning and virtue compatible with subtler conceptions of divine intervention in the world. Genius was understood to animate the most transformative historical actors. The explosion of print culture, operating in and fueling a time of dramatic political transformations, fomented a culture of celebrity. Such figures were part of an understanding of the historical process that led to the birth of a nation. If George Washington acted with an eye to the judgment of history, his contemporaries saw him as the metaphorical progenitor of his nation, a man who, the historian David Bell writes, "actually brought the nation into being by his heroic efforts," creating something that had not previously existed.[118] Books about these figures, by interpreting history in this manner, gave their leadership legitimacy in a revolutionary context (breaking with a past of hereditary continuity) where such legitimacy had to be *made*. Certainly, many warned of the risk of despotism that came with charismatic leadership. Napoleon was inspired by Washington and inspired future men with heroic pretensions in turn. He encapsulated the danger of godless pursuit of power, the risk of gaining the world at the cost of one's soul, as Galton put it to his children.[119] The ideal of heroism *with* soul was perhaps Thomas Clarkson, the leading campaigner against slavery who, as the first historian of that campaign, consolidated for a century the perception that it was the story of a few heroic men fulfilling a providential outcome. His *History of the Rise, Progress and Accomplishment of the Abolition of the Slave-Trade* (1808) explicitly invoked the motivating power of his desire to prove his genius. According to the historian Chris Brown, it was this "romantic sense of self" that set Clarkson apart from earlier critics of slavery; his awareness of how opposition to slavery reflected on himself, his sense of his providential genius and great-man historical agency, were critical to the movement's take-off.[120] Quakers provided its infrastructure, but Clarkson's and his colleague William Wilberforce's heightened aspirations gave it the grandeur it needed to become effectual. Clarkson's 1808 account of the power of individual agency and his invention of a British "tradition" of antislavery built on and furthered a providential and heroic understanding of history in his time.[121]

Theories of history—adapting different understandings of historical agency—proliferated after the eighteenth century, encompassing the unfolding of the modern forces of imperialism and nationalism. Before we watch the formation and impact of these theories in the remainder of this book, I want to think through how ideas of historical agency shape, and have shaped, how we act and how we *feel* about how we act—history and conscience. Such ideas, like astrology, shape our assumptions about what "script"—what narrative—we are cast in.

For instance, lineage was a basic organizing vector of historical understanding in the eighteenth century. Indeed, in defending his passive intransigence, Galton first cited lineage, making much of the fact that his forefathers had pursued the same business for nearly a century without inciting any criticism from the Society of Friends. His business was an inheritance that could not easily be converted to other purpose. In short, he concluded, "My Engagements in the Business were not a matter of *choice.*" A sense of the historical origins of the business, of his place in family history limited his sense of responsibility for what it was. He felt very little sense of individual agency in being a gunmaker. Structuring an explanatory narrative about one's actions through family history can radically shape one's conscience: If what I am and what I do have been determined by my lineage, my inheritance, then I am not culpable for it. Who can shake off an inheritance? In the nineteenth century, the idea of lineage determining character and behavior would merge into racial theories and more rigid and politicized understandings of colonial social categories like caste.[122] Internalized, such notions could justify and even legitimize a range of sins. I do what I do because I am from such-and-such caste. I charge extortionate interest rates on loans because as a moneylender I must. I murder on highways because I belong to a Thug caste. The very idea of such "Criminal Tribes" in British India, that there were entire groups whose social identity was based on criminal behavior, shaped not only the way the British and other Indians viewed them but their own actions.

From the nineteenth century, a Marxist historical sensibility—also eschatological in its structure—could also shape a person's sense of historical responsibility and moral accountability. Would a worker familiar with

Marxist notions of the proletariat's fated role in history behave differently from a worker ignorant of such theory?[123] A good (Marxist) materialist would say that they would behave the same, since their behavior is determined by their place in the mode of production, whether they realize it or not. But Karl Marx himself recognized the cultural power of an awareness of history in shaping how historical actors act. He recognized the objective historical constraints on human agency: "Men make their own history, but they do not make it as they please; they do not make it under self-selected circumstances, but under circumstances existing already, given and transmitted from the past."[124] But beyond "circumstances," agency also depended on a sense of history itself: "The tradition of all dead generations weighs like a nightmare on the brains of the living. And just as they seem to be occupied with revolutionizing themselves and things, creating something that did not exist before, precisely in such epochs of revolutionary crisis they anxiously conjure up the spirits of the past to their service, borrowing from them names, battle slogans, and costumes in order to present this new scene in world history in time-honored disguise and borrowed language." The "spirits of the past" evokes the occult-like power of culture and memory, of *history* to shape new history. This is why major modern historical "upsets" occurred in years commemorating earlier dramatic historic events: Stories of the past inspired the exercise of agency in the later moment. The "spirit" of the Glorious Revolution of 1689 in England animated the French revolution that erupted on its centenary in 1789; the ghost of the Battle of Plassey in 1757, when the British first established formal rule in Bengal, haunted the massive Indian rebellion exactly a hundred years later in 1857. Each successive French revolution—1830, 1848, 1871—was in turn stalked by the memory of 1789. Russian revolutionaries in 1917 consciously referenced the script of 1789. Intellectuals acting out of a sense of their own historical "chosenness" set about "converting" workers to the socialist narrative, and those workers went on to act out of a radically altered sense of their agency.[125]

The investments in universalism that characterized Enlightenment historical thought ensured this mimicry—the idea that a revolution in one place had world-historical significance, that revolutions drove a single, universal narrative of human progress, "wheels in the machine of the universe," as Voltaire styled them.[126] These historical genuflections were new. Participants in the Glorious Revolution, in a time before "revolution" was understood as a collective political act or a practice or goal of history, did not gesture to past scripts for authority. The modern historical imagination endowed its enactors with a sense that in their local crisis, they were in fact "carrying out a universal historical mission." Revolution, Baker summarizes, became a "set of moves and roles to be re-enacted, re-imagined, rewritten, elaborated and improvised upon."[127]

Some modes of historical thought accommodated more improvisation than others. Astrology can be deterministic, constraining our sense of human agency and resigning us to fatalistic acceptance. The Marxist historical imagination is deterministic in its own way, presuming a universal set of transitions between phases—feudal, bourgeois, and proletarian for the West, with the added exotic option of oriental despotism for the Rest.

Marx's very intention as a philosopher of history was to assemble a theory of history that would itself produce historical change—like Kant in 1784. He was deeply indebted to the work of Hegel, whose complex theodicy imagined history as dialectical. Following Kant, Hegel saw history as the Last Judgment, expressing this notion with a line borrowed from the Romantic poet and historian Friedrich Schiller: "*Die Weltgeschichte ist das Weltgericht*" ("The history of the world is Judgment Day"). For Hegel, the historian might only hope to interpret history after it has transpired. The reason human affairs seem so "idiotic," as Kant put it, is because of the cunning of reason: Heroes might drive history forward, but not in a manner that seems obviously reasonable. The ulterior rationality of history depends, dialectically, on the presence of irrational elements—the typically self-regarding, consuming passions that drive the great man. Intention, therefore, is no guide to history, and, by consequence, no one can be held personally accountable for the sly unfolding of history, which necessarily resembles a "slaughter-bench."[128] Philosophical understanding was inevitably belated, arriving on the scene too late to give instruction as to what the world should be: "The owl of Minerva begins its flight only with the falling of dusk."[129] Marx challenged this view of fugitive interpretation as philosophy's goal, insisting in 1845 that "philosophers have only *interpreted* the world . . . ; the point, however, is to *change* it."[130] On the now seemingly "secular" ground of modernity, humans appear as the "self-conscious makers of History" unfolding in calendrical time, making them accountable for it in a new way.[131] Marx elevated material circumstances over the spirit that animated Hegel's vision of history, but in assigning material factors historical force, Marx did not dislodge the providential eschaton that structured Hegel's vision: History was still, inescapably, heading to a liberatory end. His particular script could not accommodate a revolution in Russia, which had not gone through the requisite stage of industrialization under a bourgeoisie. So V. I. Lenin wrote a new script for that, introducing the notion of the "vanguard," which can lead even an underdeveloped proletariat into revolution.[132] The Bolsheviks accordingly rolled in by train from Switzerland to install themselves as the head of the revolution that unfolded in 1917. Much of the history of modernity was shaped by such efforts to *enact* this and other historical theories and mythologies. The British tried to create a new Rome (though there is not space to fully explore this script here).[133] History itself, like myths, gods, and stars, shaped the unfolding of the recent past. The historical imagination became essential to the modernity of the modern period.

In this sense the historical sensibility poses something of the same dilemma as divine agency for historians. A group of scholars known as the Subaltern Studies collective decades ago determined to write Indian history from the perspective of common people rather than of British or Indian elites—part of the movement for "history from below." Dipesh Chakrabarty identified the challenge posed by divine agency in this effort, invoking the historical incident at the heart of Ranajit Guha's early indictment of history-writing as "the prose of counter-insurgency." Guha's essay focused on a mid-nineteenth-century Santal rebel against British rule who attributed his rebel agency not to himself but to the god Thakur. Chakrabarty proposed that rather than simply historicize the Santal, we might see him "as a figure illuminating a life possibility for the present."[134] Can we write that divine agency into our historical narrative—as a way of acknowledging what Chakrabarty calls "the plural ways of being that make up our own present"? Or must we allow the Santal's subaltern voice to falter under the enormous condescension of posterity, since "we" after all know that his invocation of divine agency is deluded, that it was "really" the result of his class consciousness, even if in fact his actions were deeply shaped by the way he *believed* Thakur directed him? History, as a secular discipline, may not be able to do full justice to the history the Santal rebel recounts. But we at least can use the dilemma he poses to begin to understand how a particular historical imagination—in this case involving an otherworldly cast—can shape human action.

An important part of what makes modern historical activity "modern" is that modern historical actors consciously seek change that they understand as "historical." Whatever we think of the Santal's invocation of divine direction, we must concede his modernity, for his rebellion was aimed at ending British rule and replacing it with something else. Early-modern rebels rioted to restore customary rights, to restore the "moral economy" of community, when paternalistic social relations were eclipsed by more purely commercial ones.[135] Rather than move history forward or create something new, they aimed at stopping or reversing change. The eighteenth-century crowd likewise protested change—changes brought by the industrial revolution—but also demanded change itself: political changes that would empower it to address its sufferings. (To be sure, political manipulation of the "mob" endured, evident, for instance, in the anti-Catholic Gordon Riots in London in 1780, which were perhaps less about bigotry than suspicion of the government and the church hierarchy. Provincial political contests also exploited popular resentment of the wealthy to fuel the attack on religious Dissenters in the Priestley Riots of 1791 in Birmingham.[136]) By the early nineteenth century, the crowd became conscious of itself as a working class, attempting to shape its own historical destiny against the whims of more powerful social groups.[137] This awareness of its historical role is supposed to have shaped how the class acted from that point. It is hard to say which came first—the theory of history or the pattern of historical activity. Marx assembled his theory of history partly while witnessing the making of the English working class as it became conscious of itself.

Marxist historicism shaped economic understanding, too, imagining the domain of the "economy" as a distinctive space of economic relationships encompassing the production and distribution of wealth. It conceives that space historically, as dynamically evolving with the dialectic of class conflict. This historicized understanding of the "economy" built on earlier, liberal political-economic notions similarly posited along a vector of time, albeit presuming a secular trend of "progress"—glossed today as "development." When I talk about the modern historical sensibility, then, I am also talking about this intrinsically historicist modern economic imagination.

In Marxist theory, history is fundamentally materialist—a prophetic unfolding of events within an eschatological structure, but one determined by material factors: the conflict between classes with different relationships to the mode of production. But, in fact, the actions of people in these material structures are shaped by their imaginative connection to history—to myths and scripts from the past. In short, even this most materialist of historical sensibilities entails metaphysical processes. If our actions are shaped by our sense of our place in an unfolding narrative—a playing out of a familiar revolutionary script or of a long-studied astrological birth chart—we are back at the problem Chakrabarty posed about historical actors who invoke otherworldly agency. To be sure, many people join radical movements out of a sense of being wronged—an essentially emotional experience—without purporting to fulfill any grand historical purpose. John Steinbeck immortalized the image of "the grapes of wrath . . . filling and growing heavy . . . for the vintage" in the souls of the people.[138] More generally, people do what they do because that is what is done, that is the way of being where and when they live. But what of those historical actors who consciously cast themselves in a materialist, Marxist narrative—"I am joining this revolutionary movement because I am aware of my role as a member of the proletariat"? Are we bound to tell their story in a materialist manner, without any role for planets, stars, gods and goddesses? By the same token, if our historical actors cast themselves in an astrological or mystical narrative, if *they* explain their actions through divine intervention, can *we* enroll them in a materialist account? Do we whisper to our readers behind a curtain of intellectual condescension that these actors are victims of false consciousness? If we take self-conscious proletarians at their word—that they acted out of their awareness of their role in the Marxist script of history—are we not equally obligated to take historical actors citing scripts incorporating mystical, otherworldly, or other incorporeal forces at their word?

The point is that when our historical sensibility informs our understanding of how and when we can exercise agency, when we are responsible to act and when we are entitled to remain passive, it does so not very differently from the way astrological or religious guides to moral action might inform us. A theory of history comes with what Adam Smith called a "theory of moral sentiment," a guide in the exercise of empathy and conscience. For Smith, we have seen, well-governed sentiment, including a self-preservationist capacity to limit our empathy to immediate, local, and visible objects, was essential to progress; global knowledge of capitalism's troubling effects would jeopardize that progress. The consequentialist ethical vision of utilitarianism—maximizing happy ends—was a cruder sequel to this. A social Darwinist view of history quieted qualms about the annihilation of a particular people in the name of evolutionary progress. A working man's consciousness of his destined historical role, his historical *obligation,* as a member of the proletariat might free his conscience as he commits violent acts in the name of revolution. Historical thinking is like the god whispering in the Santal's ear; it is the ghost in *Hamlet,* at once goading and absolving morally dubious action.

Morality is especially adaptable in extreme circumstances, as Primo Levi has shown us. In Auschwitz, the effort to preserve life and personhood caused notions of good, evil, just, and unjust to blur. Levi perceived that we cope in the face of overwhelming grief and pain by avoiding its totality, which would be unbearable. Instead of adding up "as a whole in our consciousness," grief and pain "hide, the lesser behind the greater, according to a definite law of perspective." Because of our "ever-insufficient knowledge of the complex nature of the state of unhappiness," he writes, "the single name of the major cause is given to all its causes, which are composite and set out in an order of urgency. And if the most immediate cause of stress comes to an end, you are grievously amazed to see that another one lies behind; and in reality a whole series of others."[139] For Levi this is "human nature," "providential." He is talking about survival. But this capacity was instrumentalized by historical thinking's call to manage sentiment when coping with pain inflicted on others. Life would be unbearable if we felt all the world's pain, certainly. But the historical imagination understood "life" as the capacity for conscious exercise of agency in the name of progress. The historical imagination unleashed in the eighteenth century had tremendous power to influence the management of conscience, licensing types of action that might have seemed objectionable according to other systems of ethical accountability.

At the same time, when historical actors "fail" to fulfill their theoretical functions, historians themselves provide a kind of absolution. We explain the working man who fails to fulfill his destined proletarian role as a victim of false consciousness, duped by a charismatic leader or by mythologies of nation and manhood and so on. Duped by a system, he cannot be held accountable for his failure to do right by his and his class's interests. "Consciousness" takes us into a metaphysical realm, about being, which again asks us to perceive our existence as part of some other reality; it asks us to conceive of our selves as ensconced in a story, however material or illusory. Echoing Kant's understanding of history, the early-nineteenth-century father of modern military history Carl von Clausewitz recognized that understanding the causes of events required going beyond the perspective of historical actors themselves. The historian's role is emphatically creative. The truth of history emerged only with the help of critical analysis, making it partly the invention of the historian: "Critical analysis is not just an evaluation of the means actually employed, but *all possible means*—which first have to be formulated, that is, invented."[140] The historian has something of a God-like ability to perceive other possible worlds.

In short, the discipline of history, for all its claims to materialism, is also supposed to possess transcendental power. Kant alluded to this. Hegel spelled it out: that the point of the historical discipline is to discover the underlying rational principle behind the empirical record. History has a dual nature, a split self: at once social-scientific and humanistic, materialist and metaphysical. As a narrative form, it insists on an empirical foundation but then willfully weaves imaginative truth from it—morphing into myth when fecklessly unmoored.[141] In explaining why change happens when it does, historians invoke metaphors mimicking astrological alignment and other seemingly fatalist modes of thought—x, y, z factors created a "perfect storm," a "constellation of factors" led to the change at hand. We talk about "tipping points," "context," and "contingency," an alchemical mix of circumstances and agency. The task and purpose of history is to discover a meaningful narrative structure—that rational principle—behind events that seem (and are) chaotic and contingent; this storytelling is its own act of sorcery, creative and imaginative, however rigorously empiricist—like astrology itself. Where the latter prioritizes rigorous attention to the movement of celestial bodies, history highlights economic and social "factors." The truth is that we don't have a theory of historical agency that accounts for people acting in a manner *shaped by their own theories of historical agency,* whether materialist, astrological, mythological, or something else. Does it matter whether astrological forces themselves or the *belief* in such forces shape history? (If the former, there would be little for historians to do.) Would a historian's worldly account be convincing or even useful to those who believe the stars shape our fates?

After all, history itself is a form of mythologizing. Great-man history especially, but not exclusively, creates mythic figures, mortals embodying the heroic qualities of the gods. At times their lineage is mobilized as explanation of that heroism—just as the very heroic actions they undertake may be inspired by a sense of that family history; think of Winston Churchill and his consciousness of being a direct descendant of the Duke of Marlborough. Our cultural memory of the iconic great man, Alexander the Great, merges imperceptibly into the pantheon of Greek gods. The Romantic notion of "genius" infected the Enlightenment-derived discipline of history with a penchant for mythologizing great men. Early histories of musical lineage in particular transcended the worldly realm to connect genius to its original fount, Apollo.[142] It was not only in South Asia that myth shaped and seeped into history, quite apart from the mythologizing effects of history-writing itself. Such mythologizing presumed great men were accountable to a morality larger than life, beyond the ken and reach of ordinary mortals. We hold Churchill to a different moral standard than we do ordinary people; and *he did, too,* given his consciousness of his lineage (he was a historian himself): "I was lucky enough to start with a name very well known in England, and . . . a name counts a great deal with us," he told an American interviewer in 1902.[143] That sense of family history shaped his management of conscience as he led Britain to heroic feats during its "finest hour" *and* presided over famine in Bengal and the firebombing of Germany. The divine right of kings is the most obvious instance of a man (and occasional woman) explicitly being held to a moral standard different from that of mere mortals. The king, in this conception of monarchy, is not a mortal insofar as his power derives from God. As much as the history of the modern period was about moving beyond such a conception of rule towards the more egalitarian notion that "all men are created equal," modern history-writing itself at times perpetuated the idol worship of kings, conquerors, and other heroes, including great engineers and inventors.

It is perhaps helpful to think of ideas about history shaping the unfolding of history in a manner analogous to the way any infrastructure does. If firearms mediated conscience in the eighteenth century, liberalism's nineteenth-century urban infrastructure—lighting, sewage, roads, and so on—disciplined behavior in new ways.[144] The mutual surveillance enabled by gaslit urban streets was supposed to elevate morals, as caricatured in the accompanying image. Human agency is contingent and contextual; what we do and how we feel about doing it are shaped by the tools available to us and the systems in which we are enframed. Our very awareness of such constraints has gone—and can go—a long way in mediating conscience. Most obviously, long-distance killing, by machine gun, airplane, or drone, lowers the threshold for personal emotional investment in the act of killing, making it thinkable and doable for masses of humans. Technology shapes

A Peep at the Gaslights in Pall-Mall, 1809. Engraved by Thomas Rowlandson, after a drawing by George Woodward. (© The Trustees of the British Museum)

our agency through culture. Our understanding of city lights enables them to alter our agency: We know they will illuminate behaviors that would call into question our civility and morality, and so we behave civilly and morally. Likewise, the military symbolism of an AR15-style gun emboldens its youthful owner to exert his masculine power through impersonally lethal violence. Culture mediates the way "things" shape the exercise of human agency; this is another way of saying *belief* mediates the exercise of human agency—the story that we tell about "things," what we think the gun is, what we believe city lights are for.

What then of the planets and stars? As objects and parts of our environment, might they, too, possess the cultural power to impact our historical evolution? If culture and belief are the ultimate arbiters of how things shape human agency, planets may work, for some, not very differently from city lights: The impacts of both depend at least partly on our belief in what they are making us do or not do. Even beyond the realm of things, belief shapes our sense of agency: what a Marxist believes about the class structure, what a liberal believes is the proof of progress, what a racist believes is true of his and other races. In short, our sense of our agency as historical actors is highly subjective, and thus mutable, contingent, shifting, even capricious. As much as we like to think that historical thinking offered a secular narrative of change over time, it kept the world enchanted for us in new ways. The Romantics insisted it do so. "There's music in all things, if men had ears," affirmed the poet-hero Lord Byron. "Their earth is but an echo of the Spheres." The harsh reality of conquest, slavery, and industrialism was accompanied, indeed significantly driven by, the search for imaginative relief from the dehumanization they caused: the addictive magic of tobacco, opium, coffee, cocoa, sugar, and tea. In addition to the jinn, angels, goddesses, and shape-shifting creatures that remain with us culturally, binding us to earlier eras, the modern era produced new chimera: mythical concepts like nation, progress, and race. The longing for the sacred and magical did not disappear during the Enlightenment; even when philosophers' search for sources of ultimate meaning led away from the divine, it sacralized other objects: nature, the nation, and so on.[145] History was part of this re-enchantment, allowing us to live with and among the dead.[146] *This* mythology, as Amitav Ghosh notes, is even harder to disavow than other kinds of myth "because it comes disguised as a truthful description of the world; as fact, not fantasy."[147] Enlightenment thinkers understood the historian as a creative intermediary illuminating Providence for humanity and in that sense an angel himself. The historian was himself a great man, interpreter of muses. Kant affirmed that just as "Nature" had produced great scientists like Newton and Kepler to discern the laws of science for the rest of man, so she would produce a man capable of discovering and narrating the natural laws governing human progress. With this great-man view of the historian, Kant anticipated Marx's hopes for the historian's history-making powers: The progress of history might be continual, he explains, "when the soothsayer himself causes and contrives the events that he proclaims in advance."[148]

It is no coincidence that many of the principal architects of empire that we will meet in the next chapters claimed the expert status of the historian and drew on historical visions to justify their own actions. Since my goal is to understand and help resolve the persistent moral ambivalence around empire, they are much (though not all) of my focus. I hope this will be a beginning for a rethinking of how historical thought has shaped modern history and that future scholars might examine more closely how workers or rebels or colonial subjects drew on theories of history in the conscientious exercise of their historical agency too.

To be sure, the discipline of history—its commitments to progress, great men, and judgment, among other things—underwent many transformations in the aftermath of the calamitous twentieth century. We will get to those. Today, when we try to understand the management of conscience in the modern era, we do so with the ethical lens of a transformed historical idiom. *Today* we agree that slavery is immoral, and so we strive to understand how people in the past justified it—they appear exotic. We feel the past is another country. *Today* we recognize the horror of the Holocaust and struggle to make sense of how Germans and others could perpetrate such a horror. We feel secure that we would have known better. At the same time, it is in our very effort to explain Nazism that we make clear the ethical moorings of our own time. In the redemption of history's losers, we seek our own.

As minuscule as human history is on the scale of Time, human consciousness *feels* timeless, struggling to encompass in the time that it lives concepts as vast as Time and the Universe, accommodating an immeasurable, palimpsestic inheritance of myth and time-before-time as well as the empirical minutiae of everyday reality. Shahrazad, the great storyteller of the *Arabian Nights,* told tales without message, without end, to ward off death. Historians tell stories of the past, *with* a message, to dispel knowledge of universal sin, of the inherently flawed human self—the routine failure of conscience. In doing so, they engage in a political act that *makes* new history itself; I will have more to say about this at the end.

CHAPTER TWO

⟋ ⟋ *Progress as Penance*

> "I am going to British India,
> but I shall not be Governor General. It is
> you that will be Governor General."
> —Lord William Bentinck to the historian James Mill

⟋ ⟋ *After the end of* the Napoleonic Wars in 1815, demobilization, the postwar industrial downturn, and high food prices began to trigger radical movements among Britons. The British government took steps to disarm its people. Eventually, it created formal policing bodies, and guns in the hands of property owners disappeared, too, as did highwaymen. Gun controls remained tight in Britain, but, in the empire, increasingly fast and accurate firearms enabled new kinds of mass violence. Arms sales abroad also continued to periodically test those committed to principled governance. In a 1982 episode of the popular British political satire show *Yes Minister,* the permanent secretary and the minister discuss arms sales to terrorists. The bureaucrat's conscience is clear because he has cordoned off moral considerations from his public duties altogether. He explains, "Government isn't about morality. [It's about] Stability. Keeping things going." The minister, however, is uneasy. "What for?" he asks, "What is the ultimate purpose of government if it isn't for doing good?" The bureaucrat responds, "Minister, government isn't about good and evil. It's only about order or chaos."[1]

From the Age of Revolution, British political theorists were vexed by precisely this question: Just what is government for? In the first half of the century, covered in this chapter, they plumped for "good." Thomas Paine considered government the very guarantee of moral existence, the "badge of lost innocence." "For," he explained, "were the impulses of conscience clear . . . man would need no other law-giver."[2] We have government because virtue is not enough to guarantee our goodness. Later liberal political philosophers offered a more pragmatic view. Utilitarians like Jeremy Bentham and James Mill claimed government's objective was the greatest happiness of the greatest number. John Stuart Mill said the end of government was to guarantee liberty, a moral value in and of itself. And history was the record of liberty's progress. In the second half of the century, the answer shifted to "order," as Chapter 3 will show. But with respect to imperial governance, both—doing good and keeping order—fit within a single progress-oriented historical imagination. Indeed, the distinction became overly schematic as order itself came to possess a moral quality by the end of the century.

For the first half of the century, the burden of the empire's sordid origins, so scandalously exposed in the trial of Hastings, infused historical understandings of the empire with redemptive moral purpose: The empire must make good on its ignoble beginnings in the era of Clive, Hastings, corruption, and slavery. This was the governing historical narrative of those charged with shaping the empire. The historian Stefan Collini captures this shift: "A certain worldly tolerance of the imperfections inherent in rubbing along was perhaps lost, a more exigent notion of individual strenuousness and social harmony certainly became more prominent." This was the making of the "priggishness" typically connoted by Victorianism. The Romantics pivotally made empire's new moral stakes clear, elevating the redemptive potential of the exercise of individual agency. Their ideas of heroism fueled Victorian notions of self-help, popularized in works like Samuel Smiles's *Self-Help* (1859), whose approbation of self-assertion as a measure of "character" was empowering in a society of pervasive class-based condescension.[3] But exotic lands abroad emerged as the ideal imaginative settings in which the moral character of Victorians could be (heroically) tested and proven.

To be sure, many Romantics were skeptical of the notion that progress was an unalloyed benediction, especially if it depended on submissive acceptance of a military-industrial way of life. While Galton made his arguments from history, Romantic thinkers loudly questioned whether the changes unfolding around them were as desirable as industrial enthusiasts and Enlightenment philosophers claimed. Not that they disavowed historical change altogether: Many were abolitionists and had been fervent supporters of the American rebel cause. Although some later dialed back revolutionary sentiments and rallied to the nation in the shadow of the French Revolution, they remained sensitive to the loss, both human and cultural, that seemed to accompany "progress." They resisted especially the presumed separation of nature and culture, criticizing the dehumanized intellectual universe of "political economy" and the dehumanizing effects of industrialism. They decried the slave trade *and* their country's armed ambition, even after the catharsis of the Hastings trial.

In his apocalyptic poem *Ode on the Departing Year,* Samuel Coleridge reflected on the passing of 1796 (the year of Galton's reckoning), lamenting the direction of history: the "dark inwoven Harmonies" of the "wild Harp of Time." The line "For ever shall the bloody Island scowl?" referenced a footnote mourning "the unnumbered victims of a detestable Slave-trade— . . . the desolated plains of Indostan . . . —the four quarters of the globe groan beneath the intolerable iniquity of this nation!" In the end, the narrator resorts to withdrawal and return to a life of farming:

> Away, my soul, away!
> . . . .
> I unpartaking of the evil thing,
> With daily prayer, and daily toil
> Soliciting my scant and blameless soil,
> Have wail'd my country with a loud lament.
> Now I recenter my immortal mind
> In the long Sabbath of high self-content;
> Cleans'd from the fleshly passions that bedim
> God's Image, Sister of the Seraphim.[4]

For a poet disillusioned by the trajectory of the French Revolution as much as by his own country, withdrawal perhaps seemed the only escape from the burden of "deep guilt." Two years later saw the appearance of his ballad of bad conscience "The Rime of the Ancient Mariner." A mariner shoots the albatross that has just led his ship out of an ice jam. Wrathful spirits pursue the ship into uncharted waters, and the crew forces the mariner to wear the dead albatross around his neck. Though they die, the mariner lives on among their corpses, experiencing the absence of life, until he spies water snakes in the darkness. He responds with an outpouring of love as he glimpses, briefly, the unity and beauty of creation. The albatross falls from his neck. To complete his penance, he wanders the earth recounting his sin to all he meets:

> He prayeth best, who loveth best
> All things both great and small;
> For the dear God who loveth us,
> He made and loveth all.[5]

The mariner sinned against life and the communion of life. Although he finds atonement, he is prey to the whims of spirits and the ocean, with little scope for heroic redemption.

The supernatural elements of this tale were exotic for a time of reason that had relegated such beliefs to a premodern past. Coleridge deliberately sought to revive them, albeit as avowedly fictional. He explained later that he had endeavored to infuse his fantastic tale with sufficient "human interest and a semblance of truth" that the reader might engage in "that willing suspension of disbelief for the moment, which constitutes poetic faith."[6] This gift of imaginative literature was critical to consolidating the idea of the modern era as otherwise disenchanted, a worldly epoch in which myth, magic, and the sacred have been stripped away, *except* in books.[7] There is the real world, and there is the imaginative world—this is the duality at the heart of the modern idea of secularism. At the same time that it is exiled from the real world, myth acquired immense cultural power for its supposed capacity to reveal transcendental meaning and truth. Hence the mythic idiom adopted by many Romantic poets and the tactics they used to access transcendental knowledge: Dreams and opium— available through Britain's expanding imperial reach—supplemented ordinary perception. For modern readers, the temporary "suspension of belief" worked like a vaccination: a deliberate injection of fantasy for reasons of amusement that strengthened their immunity to its power. The supernatural was smuggled this way into the age of reason and would infect both the seemingly nonfictional realm of history-writing and the search for redemption from historical thinking later on.

In 1798, the year of "The Rime of the Ancient Mariner," another Lunar Society member, the abolitionist and industrialist Josiah Wedgwood, offered Coleridge an annuity, which Coleridge used to visit Germany with his fellow poet William Wordsworth. There Johann Wolfgang von Goethe was composing, in fits and starts, his dramatization of the crisis of conscience posed by modernity, the two-part play *Faustus* (1808, 1832) on the folly of the pursuit of infinite knowledge, represented as a pact with the devil.[8] In the final act, the old and powerful Faust is engaged in remaking the world around him in classic Enlightenment (and colonial) fashion. He uses dikes and dams to push back the sea and builds a castle on the reclaimed land. But a hut belonging to an old peasant couple and a chapel stand in his way. The devil, Mephisto, obligingly kills the couple. Faust's consequent guilt and his redemptive ethos of continual striving in the end secure him a place in heaven. A pact with the devil compromised his soul, but not in an irrecoverable way.

While Coleridge struggled with the commission to translate *Faustus,* another Romantic poet, Percy Shelley, translated parts of it.[9] But even before that, his young wife Mary Shelley's *Frankenstein* (1818), with its setting of polar exploration and explicit invocation of "The Rime of the Ancient Mariner," also captured the incalculable costs to the soul of determined pursuit of knowledge and the consoling power of imagination—"as imposing and interesting as truth."[10] The novel's subtitle, *The Modern Prometheus,* referred to the Greek myth of the Titan who creates man from clay, showering benevolence on him by stealing fire from the gods to further civilization, for which the gods punish Prometheus with eternal torment. Shelley wanted her novel to convey the inevitable fruit of the vain and presumptuous pursuit of knowledge, of human mockery of the Creator. As she explained in the introduction to a later edition, she knew "his success would terrify the artist; he would rush away from his odious handiwork, horror-stricken." It would haunt him.[11] Goethe was deeply influenced by Shakespeare's *Hamlet,* the play that can be said to have announced the modern dilemma of moral and providential agency. Both *Faustus* and *Frankenstein* also gesture at Christian notions of original sin in the pursuit of knowledge. They captured the constitutively guilty conscience of the narrative of progress, its *knowing* ignorance, and tolerance, of the miseries it caused.[12] Considering the project of improving the world in a fictional realm stripped of narratives of historical justification, these Romantic authors unveiled the moral compromise it entailed.

In *Frankenstein,* the monster and his creator are two halves of a single being—evident in the long-standing elision of "Frankenstein" as the name of the monster and his creator. The monster's vengeance against his creator is moreover the result of a frustrated desire for a companion that might make his existence whole. The shadow or double of the self is a common trope in Romantic literature. But perhaps no Romantic poet was more sensitive to the duality of nature than William Blake. Rather than the co-herent, civilized self posited by those convinced by the power of reason, Blake both experienced and felt a more agonistic form of selfhood, a self that was aware of its own duplicitous guilt even in its striving after virtue. In London, he penned his own historical myth about the revolutions unfolding abroad in his time, casting the spirit of rebellion as Orc (see accompanying image), who represents the imagination.[13] But in its apocalyptic contest with the restricting powers of reason, Orc degenerates into anarchy—another Promethean figure. Blake understood hypocrisy as an ineradicable feature of mortal life: Invoking Paine's and other Enlightenment philosophers' re-fusal to address "good and evil" in their pursuit of "Paradise and Liberty," he explained, "The Whole Creation Groans to be deliverd there will always be as many Hypocrites born as Honest Men & they will always have supe-rior Power in Mortal Things You cannot have Liberty in this World without what you call Moral Virtue & you cannot have Moral Virtue without the Slavery of that half of the Human Race who hate what you call Moral Virtue."[14] There is no need for theodicy once we accept the dual nature of the self and the divine. Orc is part of the divine energy in man, but man's internal life is cyclical, or perhaps dialectical; it is split, dual rather than sin-gular and coherent. God himself has a dual essence capable of both good and evil. Blake, who saw visions from a young age, subverted the notion of a unitary, self-conscious subject. Coleridge, familiar with opium-induced trances, thought him a "genius." Notably, Blake also illustrated those British cultural touchstones John Milton's *Paradise Lost* (1667), an epic poem about the Fall of Man, and John Bunyan's *Pilgrim's Progress* (1678), a novel about the Christian search for deliverance from sin, in 1808 and 1824, respectively.

Some Romantics' sensitivity to this internal agon produced a particu-larly British mode of guilty heroic agency as part of a narrative of histor-ical redemption. Coleridge, Wordsworth, Robert Southey, and other Ro-mantics apostasized from the radical causes they had embraced in the 1790s, becoming political conservatives by the early nineteenth century, but not all turned a blind eye to their nation's continued mortgaging of its soul in the name of progress. Lord Byron mocked and condemned the likes of Southey, to whom he ironically dedicated *Don Juan* (1819–1824), and turned himself into an icon of anti-imperialist heroism.[15] Galton and his like pleaded pragmatism and could not conceive of heroic exercise of the will; conservative Romantics like Coleridge could contemplate withdrawal

Orc, plate 12 of William Blake, *America: A Prophecy*, 1793. (The Morgan Library & Museum / Art Resource, NY) at best; but another Romantic tradition came to insist on the capacity of heroic, especially redemptive, agency, albeit usually tragic (and in a context of melancholic withdrawal and exile). Byron withdrew from Britain into exile, departing in 1816 after a scandalous divorce, rumors of an incestuous affair, and mounting debts. He was a neighbor of the Shelleys in Switzerland that summer, and it was his playful suggestion that they pass the hours of that unseasonably wet weather by writing ghost stories that prompted Mary Shelley to pen her classic. Later, in Italy, he became involved in the struggle to free Greece from Ottoman rule, dying in the midst of battle in 1824. Though his death was probably due to sepsis, he was celebrated as a hero in both Greece and Britain. With his actions, he strove to live out the life of a heroic type that he invented in his Romantic poetic works: an idealized, passionate, conscience-stricken, often exiled and self-destructive hero, who shunned convention and privilege and died tragically.[16]

Byron's works, like *The Siege of Corinth* (1816), and his actions, exemplified a Romantic emphasis on the will to power and the power of the individual to shape history, for good or ill.[17] It was an imaginary vision of human agency, wishful of heroism, which some Romantics actually tried to enact. Indeed, he was hugely influential in the development of revolutionary liberal and nationalist movements in Europe, beginning with Germany, Italy, and Poland (and would later influence colonial nationalist movements, too).[18] For Byron, Britain's imperial sins had not ceased with abolition of the slave trade. His efforts in Greece were his attempt to atone for Britain's sins in abetting Turkish rule there and for pursuing its own imperial goals in the region: During the Napoleonic Wars, Lord Elgin had taken the Parthenon marbles from Greece; Malta had become British (Coleridge briefly served in the new British administration there). Byron's gesture, his aspiration to heroic agency in the name of freeing a people in bondage, would ironically infuse the further spread of Britain's empire, as adventurers inspired by Byron ventured to free peoples from the curse of oriental despotism. Despite its ethos of gradualism, liberalism depended on such notions of revolutionary action undertaken by visionary, enlightened elites. Despite Romanticism's warnings about the danger of mankind's arrogation of creative powers to itself with the stories of Faust and Frankenstein, Romantics' very claim to a special ability to artistically capture that danger, their own claim to genius, tended to bolster the notion that men must dare to make their own history. *Even if the effort was inevitably tragic.*

Before Greece, Byron had looked to the new United States as a Romantic ideal and escape from "the closed circuit of empire and colony."[19] Indeed, in some sense, he updated Thomas Paine's efforts to free other peoples from bondage, first in the American colonies and then in France. Paine had been aware of the historical narratives of nationhood at stake in each case but in acting transnationally himself fulfilled an increasingly British historical prerogative. "My country is the world," he had explained.[20] He proved to be the first in a line of transnational revolutionaries who set out to fight despotism wherever they found it. Thomas Clarkson and other abolitionists also sought to heroically free people abroad from bondage. But it was Byron who came to exemplify that model of the Briton abroad, as a mode of *imperial* action that proved Britain's true purpose in encounters abroad. This was another, Romantic historical script that informed and guided exercise of imperial agency afterwards, infusing the narrative of civilizing mission with irresistible pathos. The idea of selflessly liberating people in bondage became the cover story of empire.[21]

South America was an important stepping-stone in consolidating the idea that British power was a vehicle of historical progress. While Byron was braving Ottoman forces in Greece, Lord Cochrane, a naval hero of the Napoleonic Wars, threw himself into the effort to free South America from Spain and Portugal. He, too, went in search of redemption, having been dismissed from the navy in disgrace in 1814 after conviction for stock fraud (he insisted on his innocence). He left England to lead the Chilean rebel navy against Spain, playing a key role in the Peruvian independence struggle, too. After helping Brazil become free from Portugal, he abruptly departed because of a dispute over prize money. Byron had died; now Cochrane headed to Greece to participate in that struggle. Soon after his return to Britain, he was pardoned and reinstated to the navy.

Cochrane and Byron were poles apart, temperamentally. Where Byron funneled his own fortune into the Greek effort, Cochrane's outlook was mercenary. He remained bitter about the absence of "more substantial reward" from Chile and Peru beyond warm expressions of gratitude.[22] Still, both exercised what they understood, romantically, as British aristocratic prerogative—somewhat different from Paine's cosmopolitan radicalism. Cochrane explained to Chile's Spanish viceroy that "a British nobleman was a free man, and therefore had a right to adopt any country which was endeavouring to re-establish the rights of aggrieved humanity."[23] These "Byronic" gestures offered a script for future adventurers abroad, who could interpret their actions as liberating even when they furthered the expansion of empire. The spread of British power was understood as the spread of liberty itself—though Chile's liberation strengthened settler colonialism there. Cochrane's liberatory heroics did not extend to Chile's indigenous people whom he condemned to an oppressed existence, scorning the "stealthy cowardice" of "Indian warfare." He did regret that the Peruvian republic swiftly fell under "despotic" rule, discovering that the "pretended liberator" of Lima's inhabitants was "in reality their conqueror."[24] But he, and many later Britons, did not hold up a mirror to their own pretended liberations.

The Romantic search for redemption in liberation abroad would infuse the history of liberal imperialism from then on. That Greece was the site of Byron's sacrifice and Cochrane's later adventures was profoundly important. Eighteenth-century philosophers had readily traced Western heritage to Indic civilization, but by the time Byron died for Greek liberation, British Orientalists were modifying this unembarrassed acknowledgment of cultural intimacy. The forging of Scots, Welsh, English, and Irish into "Britons" during the Napoleonic Wars grounded British national identity more strongly in race and the common project of empire abroad.[25] If Byron was the tragic hero, the voice of guilty imperial conscience, there was also the unapologetic Duke of Wellington, an out-and-out British military hero, who built his career as conqueror of India in those years. Missionaries gained access to India in 1813, as we shall see below, and painted Indian religion in a new negative light. These changes, followed by Greece's liberation a decade later, coincided with an effort to recast relations with "the Orient," broadly construed, and claim more selective heritage. With the Greeks now free of Turkish rule, styled as "oriental despotism," Europeans established their claims to a narrowly Greek (rather than Egyptian, Persian, or Arab) heritage. The contest between barbarism and civilization in Herodotus's history of the conflict between Persia and Greece acquired deeper resonance in a world divided into a backward East and a progressive West, becoming essential to modern historicism.

Romantic works like *Frankenstein* and the poetry of Percy Shelley both depended on and reinforced notions of racial and cultural difference.[26] The work of scholars like the jurist and philologist in India Sir William Jones fueled a view of "the East" as a realm of imaginative relief from the unsettling dynamism of Europe in a manner that deeply influenced Romantic culture. Goethe modeled the prologue of *Faustus* on Kalidasa's *Sakuntala,* based on a story also found in the *Mahabharata,* about the relationship of a woman immersed in, and symbolizing, nature with her warrior-king lover / husband.[27] This fourth- or fifth-century Sanskrit play was introduced to European audiences through Jones's 1789 translation (a German retranslation appeared in 1791).[28] Ironically, though he sought to atone for British imperialism, Byron's poetry and life helped consolidate orientalist representations of a sensual, timeless "East" that invited the spread of British power in the name of freeing the benighted subjects of oriental despotism. These hardening notions of difference were fueled, paradoxically, by greater contact abroad, in Asia, the New World, and the South Pacific. Enlightenment efforts to classify knowledge extended to new cartographic, botanical, and ethnographic knowledge arising from such contact. Hegel's posthumously published *Philosophy of History* (1837) summarized the idea that "the History of the World travels from East to West, for Europe is absolutely the end of History."[29] Notably, he wrote the lectures on which it was based while writing critically about the *Gita,* pushing back against Romantic fascination with it.[30] European notions of historical agency were formed through orientalist engagement with other ideas about agency.

In the early nineteenth century, Europeans traced the differences between East and West to culture, climate, environment, and race. Historians mapped out the progressive development of societies along discrete stages of civilization. Our concept of the "modern" was imbued with notions of racial and cultural difference from the start. Nineteenth-century ideas of liberty came to depend on an "orientalist" view of Asia and Africa, in which "the East" was the natural setting of despotism, and the West, of freedom.[31] Where the West was dynamic, the place of progress and *history,* the East was passive, timeless and unchanging, immune to history.

The abolition movement had emerged from a sense of moral obligation to emancipate oppressed humanity abroad, to bring history to those who could not make it themselves. Abolition was, of course, a very good thing, but its goodness rubbed off too liberally, tinting all British activities abroad in rose. Enlightenment thought was simply too imbued with notions of racial and cultural difference for such broad-stroke ethical judgment. It encompassed a quasi-scientific view of a racial ladder of development with white northern Europeans on top as most possessed of reason and the capacity for progress. In some geographies, freeing people would not be enough; their liberation would also require their remaking. There was the condescension of British help for the Greeks and Italians, but "other" enslaved peoples stirred condescension of another order, belief in the paternalistic spread of British power as the key to freedom. Abolitionists who went on to found the Aborigines Protection Society saw empire as a means of protecting indigenous peoples, whom it viewed as fundamentally inferior. The group's advocacy, however well meant, often abetted processes that led to greater control, marginalization, and expropriation of such peoples, including those reeling from exterminatory encounters with earlier generations of Britons. The presumption of racial difference permanently undercut the claim that the British were putting other peoples on the *same, universal* path of historical evolution that they were on.

Liberal imperialism was premised on the notion that benighted peoples around the world, lacking conscience and virtue, required a paternalistic imperial government that might at once compensate for the original British sin of conquest. It depended on a historical narrative that British rule would, as a kind of penance, civilize places and minds, that doing so would produce that internally coherent form of highly individualized conscience and selfhood that was the bedrock of the Enlightenment outlook. The racist and culturalist prejudices bundled in the notion of the "benighted," presumed as part of the flawed selfhood and conscience of others, are part of the historical discipline's colonial baggage.

Pressure from merchants, coupled with the ideas of thinkers like Adam Smith, succeeded in ending the East India Company's monopoly on trade with India with the Charter Act of 1813 (though the company retained monopoly rights to tea and trade with China). The act also opened India up to missionaries. Evangelical abolitionists like William Wilberforce and Charles Grant saw this as the next step in Britain's moral redemption—an opportunity to make amends for earlier imperial sins. Charles Grant, an East India Company man and politician, explained in his 1797 plea for missionary access that "a great deal was due from us to the people in compensation of the evils which the establishment of our power had introduced among them." He understood his exercise of imperial agency as justified by the historical necessity of making good on a shameful past; just as with slavery, historical progress was imagined as a narrative of redemptive acts. At the same time, he knew expiation was impossible, for, he argued, "we cannot now renounce them [Indians] without guilt, though we may also contract great guilt in the government of them."[32] British conscience was to be martyred for the "moral improvement" of Indians.

But views of India were shifting, as we have seen. After the moral recuperation of the Hastings trial, the taint of scandal associated with colonialism shifted from Britons to colonialism's "others." Theories of environmental determinism encouraged a habit of deflecting blame for British corruption onto India itself, with the moral dissipation of "nabobs" exemplifying the baleful taint of the Orient. Evangelical and liberal reformers led efforts to address the moral affront of Indian customs like *sati,* or widow burning. Such "civilizing" efforts invariably backfired and stifled indigenous reform movements, while exoticizing the image of India even more in Europe.[33] The scandal was no longer empire but India itself, not British corruption in India but corrupt Indian culture and customs, which justified the British presence, casting it in a humane and moral light.[34] Hastings's successor as governor-general, Lord Cornwallis, pronounced, "Every native of Hindustan . . . is corrupt."[35] As nineteenth-century British thinkers and missionaries disseminated ideas of Indian strangeness, Burke's dreaded "Geographical morality" took even stronger hold, drawing strength from the temporal morality authorized by historical thinking.

During the Napoleonic Wars, James Mill began to write his *History of British India,* which appeared in 1817, the year Coleridge defended the relevance of the imagination. Mill never set foot on the subcontinent, but this was the first serious historical account of the East India Company's rise to power there.[36] Mill was a political radical and devotee of Jeremy Bentham's utilitarian philosophy. To him, reform was a systemic matter. India's history was something to be overcome by working from theoretical principles—the ultimate aim being to use it as a testing ground for utilitarian reform of Britain itself.[37] Unlike Galton or Burke, he saw little need for resignation to the world as it was, placing tremendous faith in man's ability to shape the world through reason. As his son explained, he had little patience with those who tolerated "open contradiction" between the notion of a benevolent God and a world full of evil, preferring the Manichean view of a world in which Good and Evil compete for control.[38]

In typical liberal vein, following Adam Smith, Mill criticized the East India Company and those involved in its initial conquests, including Robert Clive. With respect to Hastings's trial, he aligned himself wholly with Burke. But Mill reserved his greatest contempt for Indians and Indian culture, which he described as backward, ignorant, savage, treacherous, morally degenerate, and so on. In doing so, he strove to distinguish his work from admiring appraisals of Indian history and civilization by earlier Orientalist scholars like William Jones. His would instead be a "critical history," in other words, "a *judging* history." Rather than be deceived like earlier scholars by a few marks of cultural advancement, he would sift the available evidence, like a judge, and compare India with past and present societies at different stages of social progress to accurately gauge India's position on a "scale of civilization." That he had not been there mattered not: "Whatever is worth seeing or hearing in India, can be expressed in writing." And a man with access to all this written material might "in one year, in his closet in England," obtain more knowledge of India than he might obtain in a lifetime there.[39] Purporting to puncture myths circulated by earlier Orientalists, Mill classified India among "rude" or "barbarous" societies.

But this appraisal was not an end in itself; Mill meant it to guide the design of British imperial rule there. India was not in a permanently barbarous condition. He posited a unidirectional historical path: Any civilization that had not progressed had simply stagnated in the culturally barbaric state in which all civilizations begin, typically as a result of despotism. To encounter Indians today was akin to encountering the Chaldeans and Babylonians, ancient Persians and Egyptians. But such a society could yet be transformed through good government. Thus had Britain arrived to free India from barbarity.[40] Challenging any notion of Indian historical exceptionalism affirmed by earlier Orientalists, he presumed a universal historical path available to Indians as much as to any other people. The book's premise was that "every society may progress if it chooses, or can be shown how to do so, but it will then follow the same road which more advanced societies have taken before it and acquire the same features which everywhere distinguish barbarism from civilization."[41] Britain's civilizing mission in the region was, accordingly, all to the good. Mill's historical outlook licensed British intervention in India in the name of progress—but also as an opportunity for Britain's moral redemption. The future-oriented vision of his history, its attempt to imagine a reformist British role unmoored from Britons' corrupt and criminal first steps in the region, "rendered the foundations of empire *ethical* in a specific sense," writes the political theorist Karuna Mantena. It implicitly disavowed conquest and force as legitimate sources of imperial authority. British reform of India would be Britain's atonement, its reparation for past sins, fulfilling a moral duty towards India and itself at once.[42] Grant's hopes for missionary access resonated with this broader historical vision of the British presence in India.

The notion of a single path to and form of modernity, originating in the Enlightenment and shaping nineteenth-century British rule in India, remains with us in the guise of "development" today. At the time, Mill's history became the single most influential book among British officials in India, eventually becoming a textbook for candidates for the Indian Civil Service and for the East India Company's college at Haileybury.[43] Its success secured him an appointment at the company's London headquarters, East India House, where he rose in the ranks to head of the department of the examiner of Indian correspondence in 1830. While reform of governance at home went on, Mill's work simultaneously triggered a new approach to governance in British India, grounded in liberal universalist notions—the idea that all races, different as they were, could ultimately be made British in civilization. He may have advocated a light touch—"light taxes and good laws"—but the creation of individual property rights and newly codified laws entailed violent revolution in Indian society.[44] Moreover, on the ground, ideas like "improvement" and "reform" were less influential than the immediate purpose of holding on to power in a region in which it remained fragmented and vulnerable.[45]

The fear of corrupting taint, of the culture of "nabobery," drove an effort to maintain the separation of races in British colonies. This meant a sharp decline in intermarriage with Indian women, which had been common in the more footloose eighteenth century, as well as de-Indianizing the governing bureaucracy, where Indians were eliminated from all but the lowest ranks of the administration of the crushing tax regime. Massive salaries and training in an ethos emphasizing character aimed to immunize British officials against the corrupting influences of their setting—ensuring the exercise of conscience. "A liberal imperialism, committed to westernization and 'manly' empowerment, [became] the instrument for removing Indians from responsible positions in self-government and degrading them to the status of an inferior breed," as one scholar summarizes the impact of James Mill's understanding of India and history.[46]

Earlier, the British had tried to mask their presence as a continuation of aristocratic Mughal rule, but as liberalism gained influence, their aims became more openly transformatory. Protecting Indian women from feckless Indian men in particular became a validating purpose of empire; much of the reform legislation of this period was gendered, often backfiring as in the case of *sati*.[47] Nomadic populations were settled forcibly. Criminal tribes legislation attempted to domesticate aboriginal groups presumed to be criminal by their heredity. Complex and communal forms of property ownership were simplified along British lines. English was adopted as the official language of India in 1837, and the spread of Western education became a priority. Indians began to study English rather than Persian as a means of self-empowerment. In his 1835 Minute on Indian Education, the liberal member of Parliament and historian Thomas Macaulay pronounced "a single shelf of a good European library . . . worth the whole native literature of India and Arabia."[48] The goal of British rule was "to form a class . . . of persons, Indian in blood and colour, but English in taste, in opinions, in morals, and in intellect." The idea was that, given sufficient training, anyone—of whatever race—was capable of this transformation presuming British cultural supremacy. Macaulay, a huge admirer of Thucydides, hoped that Britain's empire might eclipse Rome's; rather than rise and fall, it might embrace a goal of constant improvement, regardless of geographical limit.[49] This is the consummate "whiggish" understanding of history, the view, named for the Whig party most associated with liberal thinking, that assumes that history follows a path of inevitable progression and improvement and that judges the past in light of the present. Macaulay headed the commission established on Mill's recommendation to frame a body of codified law for all of British India. Mill recommended Macaulay for the post.[50] Macaulay and his fellow law commissioners completed a Code of Penal Law in 1837, but the chasm between pretension and reality in the British Indian empire was such that it remained unread and unenforced for decades.[51]

It is no coincidence that Mill and Macaulay were both Scotsmen who embraced metropolitan Englishness as they adopted Anglicization as the historical aim of colonial rule. Liberals generally conceived human nature as universal and capable of total transformation if conditioned by the law, education, and the operation of the free market. They debated methods and the urgency of reform, but for all of them, the goal was to free individuals from bondage to religious, political, and other kinds of despotism so that they could become rational, coherent, autonomous selves. If "Providence" explained and excused British rule abroad to Galton's generation, nineteenth-century liberals like Macaulay saw British rule as Providence itself—it brought the blessing of progress to degraded civilizations. Liberalism built on Christian universalism. Macaulay was the son of Zachary

Macaulay, an evangelical who became a devoted abolitionist after managing a sugar plantation in Jamaica. Zachary's search for imperial redemption earned him a posting as governor of Sierra Leone, a British colony for freed slaves. Evangelicalism gave him moral certainty in facing down those invested in perpetuation of the slave trade. To him, Christianity was the root of Britain's destined imperial role in the world, but to his son, Britain's right to govern was not so much God-given as grounded in civilizational capacities and its approach to rule itself. Britain's very capacity to rule evidenced its right to rule. Here was a new kind of moral certainty, no longer underpinned by Christian belief and soul-searching but by the confidence of imperial power itself. Indeed, Thomas Macaulay preferred not to think about slavery at all, despite or because of his father's lifelong devotion to its eradication. He was part of the government that abolished slavery in the empire in 1833; he could gauge, even from the enormous compensation package to slave owners, how much it had sustained England, but he deliberately avoided and forgot the topic. England had done its duty in eradicating slavery.[52] And that past need not detain him in his certainty of Britain's moral superiority as a civilization destined to rule over others. Still, his presumption that he had a critical role to play in ensuring Britain fulfilled its destiny seems to have been partly shaped by his consciousness of picking up the baton of liberty where his father had left off.

Instead of dwelling on his nation's sins, Macaulay determined to celebrate its progress. While in India, he decided to write a great epic of British history. His *History of England,* selling in massive numbers from mid-century, was a monumental project that occupied him for years—like Gibbon's consuming undertaking of the history of Rome before. Its story of liberal progress enfolded Romantic faith in the possibility of heroic (manly, English) individual agency in changing the world.[53] Macaulay's essays on early adventurers in India, Hastings and Clive, were likewise in a Romantic vein, engaging in some mental and logical contortions to portray Clive's greedy conquest of Bengal as an effort undertaken in the cause of justice. The deadly famine following Clive's reorganization of Bengal's government was the result of high taxation and the East India Company's monopoly of critical commodities like rice coinciding with drought, but Macaulay put it down entirely to nature. While touting unshakeable "English veracity," he paradoxically explained that dealing with "natives" "destitute of . . . honor" had, naturally, compelled Clive and Hastings to behave deceitfully.[54] Albion's perfidy was India's fault. Macaulay's redemption of Clive proved permanent; most later imperial historians continued to airbrush his vices. Burkean embarrassment about imperial conquest virtually vanished.[55] Macaulay used the genre of history as a mechanism of imperial absolution; history had vindicated the likes of Clive.

This put Macaulay in an awkward position vis-à-vis Burke, for whom, he snidely explained, "oppression in Bengal was . . . the same thing as oppression in the streets of London."[56] Rather than the mark of far-reaching empathy, this smacked of excess to Macaulay, of uneconomical management of sentiment at the expense of reason. "Burke's imagination was too vivid, his sensibility too developed in Macaulay's judgement," summarizes the historian Catherine Hall. He damned Burke with faint praise as "a great and a good man . . . led into extravagance by a sensibility which domineered over all his faculties," making him the "slave of feelings." History-writing in this key, an alchemy of fact and romance, allowed Macaulay to paper over, or rather write around, the contradictions of liberal empire. His purpose in his phenomenally popular *History of England* was didactic in the spirit of Kant's or Smith's view of history: "A people which takes no pride in the noble achievements of remote ancestors will never achieve anything worthy to be remembered with pride by remote descendants."[57] Macaulay hoped to instill pride in the nation's history specifically to inform the way his people *made* history in their time. He provided a license, or alibi, for empire. Galton had invoked lineage to minimize his agency, but Macaulay summoned ancestry—national rather than biological—to *enhance* Britons' sense of agency. He packaged the history of the seventeenth century as a story of progress, of the steady expansion of rights and inclusion in a universal civilization. Appearing in the shadow of revolutions across Europe in 1848, the work's whiggish depiction of change assured Britons that revolution was unnecessary; individual advancement would follow with the expansion of liberal empire. This kind of history-writing aimed to produce liberal subjects—law-abiding citizens who disavowed revolutionary compulsions and patiently allowed the story to unfold as it must, in a presumably progressive and morally sound direction.[58] As much as it licensed empire, it did so by inducing quietism among ordinary people, a sense of the gratuitous nature of overly zealous exercise of agency in the face of the narrative inertia of the nation and the heroism of great men. As Hall puts it, his message was that "it was the responsibility of this newly enriched elite to act <u>for</u> 'the people,' rather than allowing 'the people' to act for themselves, to lead and guide them, both at home and in the empire."[59] Macaulay mocked Burke's illiberal emotion but shared his deprecation of revolutionary sentiment; gradual evolution of existing institutions was the right path to progress, and the ideal end was limited representative government.

Historical agency was a manly quality in Macaulay's vision, as was history-writing itself.[60] His faith in great men owed something to the historical imagination of another Scotsman, the conservative thinker Thomas Carlyle. In his 1837 history of the French Revolution, Carlyle highlighted the power of individual actors in making history but acknowledged the constraints that divine Providence, or the natural laws of history, imposed on their ability to control their destinies.[61] He became most well known, however, for his 1841 celebration of heroism *On Heroes, Hero-Worship, and the Heroic in History*, which considered the Prophet Muhammad, Cromwell, Shakespeare, and Napoleon, among other great men. Here, Carlyle affirmed, "Universal History, the history of what man has accomplished in this world, is at bottom the History of the Great Men who have worked here." Or, more succinctly, "The History of the World . . . [is] the Biography of Great Men." Societies did not progress in linear fashion but thrived, then weakened, until a savior in the form of a great man appeared. He explained in the chapter on Muhammad, "The Great Man was always as lightning out of Heaven; the rest of men waited for him like fuel, and then they too would flame." This Romantic view endowed heroism with divine grace; the hero was "the light which enlightens . . . as a natural luminary shining by the gift of Heaven." Carlyle recognized the historical potential of his own writing about history, given the immense power of the "Man-of-Letters Hero" in the modern era: "What he teaches, the whole world will do and make." Books accomplished miracles, persuading men to act in certain ways. And history was the judge of rightness: "Give a thing time; if it can succeed, it is a right thing."[62] The historian, presumably, was the "Great Man" endowed with the capacity to interpret this truth. And so Carlyle did, infamously, with his "Occasional Discourse on the Negro Question" in 1849, which argued that the abolition of slavery in 1833 had been a mistake, judging by the post-abolition condition of the West Indies.[63] Rather than recognize the long shadow cast by the history of slavery, the way it continued to restrict the possibility of positive change in the West Indies (reinforced by legislation compensating former slave owners rather than slaves), he imagined that the simple alteration of one fact—the legality of slavery—might have altered an entire society overnight. His exaggerated sense of the power of history and the historian led him to scant the weight of history itself.

This essay caused a rift between Carlyle and many of his liberal friends, including John Stuart Mill, the major theorist of liberalism in this period and the son of the historian and East India Company bureaucrat James Mill. The younger Mill likewise worked out his thoughts on political economy while employed by the East India Company, which he credited for having stumbled "accidentally upon better arrangements [for India's governance] than our wisdom would ever have devised."[64] Beginning as his father's assistant, he, too, rose to the post of examiner, staying with the company until its dissolution in 1858, after a massive Indian rebellion. His sense of his own historical agency was perhaps informed by his faith, in common with Carlyle's, in genius: the idea that the exceptional individual can have an outsized influence on ordinary people, pointing the way forward.[65] He positioned himself as the custodian of British morality, with Britain, in turn, the custodian of international morality. He was the philosopher of progress whose duty it was to keep his contemporaries morally accountable, to remind them of their duty and capacity to exercise their agency. This was "character"; its opposite was apathy and passivity.[66]

The younger Mill shared his father's conviction that there was only one kind of civilization: British civilization. For societies incapable of fulfilling the necessary conditions of representative government, whose denizens evidently lacked "character," subjection to foreign and despotic government was necessary: "Despotism is a legitimate mode of government in dealing with barbarians, provided the end be their improvement, and the means justified by actually effecting that end."[67] The end—whenever it came—would justify the admittedly contrary means. Liberty was not right for all people in all times; it especially required a setting in which people have become—or been made—"capable of being improved by free and equal discussion." Liberty was for those who had evolved a certain kind of conscience—the kind of civilized conscience that could, for instance, tolerate an argument about the ends justifying the means, essentially agreeing to compromise in the present for the sake of a better future. The savage was defined by his very inability to *compromise* for a common purpose, in short, a creature without a liberal conscience. A savage "cannot bear to sacrifice, for any purpose, the satisfaction of his individual will," wrote Mill. "His social cannot even temporarily prevail over his selfish feelings, nor his impulses bend to his calculations."[68] The very failure of

India's native states to cooperatively resist English conquest was proof that their conquest was a historical necessity, for the sake of their own progress. Discipline, accordingly, was the primary attribute of civilization, and making it an unconscious habit required lengthy training and practice—perhaps centuries. The notion of "trusteeship" was key to this vision of liberal empire—the idea that Britain should rule India responsibly and paternalistically, not, as it had earlier, for profit and adventure. Leaving aside even the reality of immense British profit from India,[69] even on its face "liberal imperialism" was self-contradictory: the idea of a universalist, rule-bound, liberatory form of governance that was at once unequal, authoritarian, and exploitative. The historian's craft proved essential to smoothing over that permanent contradiction and thus enabling its survival. Historians like Macaulay and the Mills both narrated the past and made the present—in Britain and India. The younger Mill's ideas about savagery and civilization were expressed, notably, in an essay on his concerns about the state of *British* politics and culture in 1836. The denigration of India was rhetorically, as much as practically, essential to Britain's progress.

To be sure, Macaulay and the Mills are not representative of the entire world of British historical scholarship in this period. Many were occupied with other serious matters of history, both ancient and local, with little obvious connection to empire, absorbed in conversations with their Continental counterparts—as the poets Coleridge and Wordsworth were. There were also historical imaginations that allowed for anti-imperial dissent. British Positivists were influential followers of the French philosopher Auguste Comte, whose understanding of modern history led him to invent a "Religion of Humanity" grounded in a "psychology of natural affections."[70] Its spiritual outlook was historical (with echoes of Carlylean hero worship): It called for emulation of and reverence for spiritual heroes of the past through collective acts of remembrance and came with a calendar to facilitate that commemoration. Despite this preoccupation with the past, however, its transcendent belief in the essential unity of humanity made the idea of imperial intervention anathema to Comte and his followers, even in the name of furthering history. (Comte did, however, acknowledge England's and France's primary role in regenerating the world along these lines.) There were other kinds of dissent, too: We have already seen the critical views of empire offered by Romantics and, especially, Edmund Burke. These lines of dissent would remain influential; they laid critical foundations for the twentieth-century remaking of history, as we will see. But the target of romanticism, socialism, positivism, and other critical strands of thought was principally the most powerful philosophical tradition, liberalism, which arguably remains triumphant even today. It was powerful enough to infect skeptics of empire with its moral succor and co-opt historical work that was not bound up with empire. When a figure like Macaulay, stationed in India, encountered the work of the Danish-German historian of ancient Rome Bartholdt Niebuhr, it fed his faith in Britain's renewal of the Roman imperial project.[71] Adam Smith's Victorian heirs, the political-economic liberals John Bright and Richard Cobden, for all their intolerance of colonialism on grounds of cost, neither objected to empire in principle nor advocated severance from existing colonial possessions.[72]

This is partly because of the institutional authority that liberal historical thought acquired. The works of the Mills and Macaulay are my focus not merely because they were popular and influential but because they were written by historians who *also* held powerful administrative positions.[73] Departing London to serve as India's new governor-general in 1827, Lord William Bentinck assured James Mill: "I am going to British India, but I shall not be Governor General. It is *you* that will be Governor General."[74] Uday Mehta aptly describes this "offer of impersonation by power to philosophy." This coincidence, and mutual reinforcement, of historical thinking and power is our focus. These thinkers formed themselves into a canon in dialogue with one another: James Mill responding to William Jones; Macaulay putting Mill in his place; John Stuart Mill furnishing the target for James Fitzjames Stephen (Chapter 3). This conversation over time captures in itself the continual need Britons felt and the effort they made to assuage conscience, to justify empire, in new ways in new times. It is what will help us understand why the world we live in today remains in thrall to liberalism's certainties, despite mounting evidence of its folly, why it remains "the dominant framework from within which we imagine modifications on this world."[75]

Nineteenth-century novels were obsessed with moral character, and colonial locales frequently figured as the source or setting of corruption. The morally degenerate and degenerating world of the West Indies appeared, offstage, in Charlotte Brontë's romance *Jane Eyre* in 1847, just two years before Carlyle's screed. India was Brontë's other offstage colonial setting, figuring as a lethal land offering the opportunity of Christian martyrdom. It is a novel about conscience—Jane's struggle to avoid sin and Rochester's struggle to redeem his. The happy ending is brought about by the death of Rochester's mad mulatto wife, Bertha Mason, who leaps to her death as Thornfield Hall burns, in a scene recalling British depictions of sacrificial widow-burning in India. (*Frankenstein* similarly ends with the remorseful monster promising to "ascend my funeral pile . . . and exult in the agony of the torturing flames."[76]) Rochester is blinded and maimed in the incident—his atonement. He and Jane marry and live happily ever after in the English countryside.[77] This Romantic story portrayed Britons as essentially a conscientious people; taint came from naive trust of those encountered at the margins of empire. Such flattering self-portraits helped sustain confidence in Britain's moral and cultural superiority during the expansion into the South Pacific, including the Maori Wars that lasted from 1845 to 1872, the disastrous first attempt to conquer Afghanistan, the potato famine that decimated Ireland in the 1840s, and embattled expansion in India. British conquest of India was not, importantly, the result of technological or tactical superiority but of effective mobilization of resources, particularly the ability to borrow on global money markets when company revenue did not keep up with military demand.[78] Even earlier, British expansion on the subcontinent had depended on quashing and co-opting indigenous military know-how.[79] Nor was conquest final; resistance continued.

But in all this, the myth of the "Pax Britannica" helped clear the imperial conscience. So, too, did continual humanitarian engagement with imperial affairs. As two scholars summarize, "The cruelties of slave owners, . . . the perversion of justice by despotic governors, the unnecessary violence of rogue officials on the margins of empire—such allegations filled colonial correspondence . . . and peppered the headlines . . . of newspapers."[80] The "Peterloo Massacre" of 1819, when the cavalry charged into a crowd of tens of thousands of British protestors demanding political reform, killing fifteen and injuring hundreds, was recalled with such odium that it was the last time the government used such uncontrolled force against an unarmed, peaceful British crowd.[81] But violence was frequent in the colonies from the eighteenth century to the massive rebellion in India in 1857.[82] British officials reflecting on the century near its end resorted to the mind-bending logic that frequent outbursts of violence during the period of "absolute peace" that the British had brought showed what would happen if Britain were to depart.[83]

One of the most violent episodes in these decades, producing a pivotal struggle over history, was the First Anglo-Afghan War, from 1839 to 1842. The war intended to hold Russian ambitions at bay on the North West Frontier of India, but the British strategy was controversial from the start: Not all were persuaded of the Russian threat; not all agreed with the British course of displacing the Afghan emir Dost Mohammad with the former emir Shah Shuja. After initial success, the British met with shattering and humiliating defeat at Afghan hands early in 1842. That fall, a British Army of Retribution went back to Kabul on a punitive mission of revenge, departing from Afghanistan altogether after wreaking horrific violence including summary destruction of entire villages.

Key players questioned the official account of the conflict's origins from the start. But the defeat and bloody revenge raised the stakes of that debate to epic proportions, triggering a political contest over history that lasted two decades. The invasion was justified on typical grounds of imperial security. But an "Army of Retribution" was a different beast. It did not fit neatly in the liberal narrative of empire, and the struggle to accommodate it made the importance of that narrative irrevocably clear. The bloody, calamitous war punctured the confident pursuit of empire newly hallowed by the successes of the abolition movement and Macaulayite liberal idealism. It was plainly folly. By 1842, many in the public were outraged by British pursuit of an unprovoked war and saw the defeat as God's wrath upon them. The morally questionable Opium War transpiring nearby against Qing China added fuel to the fire.[84] New narratives of the Afghan war emphasized the formidable and terrible nature of the Afghan foe, transmuting Afghani resistance into treachery, thereby glorifying the heroism, however tragic, of both the initial British victory and the bloody retribution.[85] Such romantic tales could draw on the vision of heroism outlined by Carlyle just a year before the debacle.

In the end, the methods of history itself were at stake in these contrasting perceptions of the war. In 1851, Sir John William Kaye's *History of the War in Afghanistan* accused the government of deliberate forgery in presenting its case for war to the public with its infamously "Garbled Blue Books" of 1839.[86] Kaye, a military man with Indian experience, portrayed the war as evil and unnecessary, the result of poor vision and comprehension. He could challenge the official account because of his access to sources otherwise unavailable to the public, which he had received from the family of Captain Alexander Burnes, who had disputed the adopted policy from the outset and was killed in the war. As the historian Caitlyn Lundberg shows, Kaye presented himself as a man without party alliance, an objective pursuer of truth. Having discovered the unreliability of official documents, he lamented the damage to truth and the replacement of "sober history" with "florid romance."[87] Objective history depended on a wider source base and an open-ended outlook. Advertisements for his book trumpeted its source base of unpublished correspondence and diaries of men on the spot.[88] This was history as exposé. A Calcutta magazine celebrated the book's use of unpublished sources, lamenting that other histories of India presented "only the outer official side of public events," as they were written "mainly from state-papers." Historians had shown readers only "the warriors and statesmen . . . in full dress," concealing their "genuine thoughts and opinions . . . beneath the verbiage of official paragraphs."[89] Here, the discipline began to acquire another identity—as a method for using unofficial sources to ascertain the true, hidden facts of empire, an instrument for holding perfidious Albion to account. We will return to this parallel career of the discipline later in the book. For now, the point is that in stirring this alternative, mutinous understanding of the purpose of history, Kaye exposed the discipline's complicity in empire until that point. History had served the bureaucrats, and bureaucrats had served up history.

For the moment, however, even Kaye's revisionist ambitions wound up serving empire. His aim was to reveal how an evil war had spawned further evil, in Kantian fashion, according to the workings of some natural, moral law. For Kaye, the evil lay in the deliberate cover-up of a doomed policy in 1839. It has since become clear that deliberate deception was probably not a factor.[90] But Kaye's accusations kept the wound open another decade, until finally the government published a revised Blue Book in 1859. But half a century after *that,* all notion of moral failure had vanished. A historian in 1908 called it a "sorry business" resulting from "incompetence alone." Most importantly, the author of the doomed policy, Lord Auckland, "had good intentions—and we know their fate."[91] This historian, Frederick Gibbon, here summoned that classic liberal exculpatory protestation, at once acknowledging that good intentions were all but a guarantee of bad ends. Such an outlook seems to presume disastrous consequences, no matter what the intention. Disaster is thus no one's fault. How did British historians get from Kaye's moral outrage in 1851 to this indulgent view in 1908? Chapter 3 will illuminate some of that evolution.

But the seeds for it were already present in 1851. For Kaye, the primary scandal was the defeat at Afghan hands, not the activities of the Army of Retribution. The scandal of defeat may have been redeemed in 1908, but there was no need to redeem any scandal of retribution. The controversy was always about the origins of the war, not the decision to wreak vengeance after defeat.

The need for such vengeance was obvious. It was violence for the sake of violence, unapologetically enacted. It did not fit in the mythology of liberal empire, and it did not need to: Afghanistan lay beyond the pale of the empire. The violence did not, then, violate any sense of trusteeship vis-à-vis imperial subjects. Rather, the avenging violence had been undertaken for the *sake* of Britain's loyal Indian subjects; it was part of the liberal project of saving India. It was exemplary, to preempt like-minded indiscipline among them and to affirm Britain's military might and secure the paternalistic authority it claimed in the subcontinent. The British considered such exemplary, spectacular, terrorizing violence suited to an Indian mind accustomed to despotic rule, but also expiatory for a British public aggrieved and horrified at news of British defeat.[92] In this sense, the undertaking of revenge, in the name of awing and thus securing India, practically twisted violence into a moral sacrifice in the name of India's progress: The British had mortgaged their souls to safeguard the sacred project of bringing progress to India. And we encounter once again the constitutively guilty conscience of liberalism, its *knowing* partaking of sin in the name of historical progress. If defeat was God's retribution, then the Army of Retribution was Britain's audacious claim that history rather than God would be the ultimate judge of virtue. The idea of retribution, and punishment in a biblical sense more generally, was also central to the evangelical Victorian "moral cosmos," albeit in tension with the culture of improvement.[93]

As much as this violence strove to banish the thought of rebellion from all Indian minds, it was far from effectual, given the realities of colonial rule. Instead, even as the debate on the Afghan debacle dragged on, a massive uprising erupted in India in 1857, perhaps the biggest challenge till then to the idea of Pax Britannica. It emerged from long-simmering Indian frustration and discontent with the consequences of British expansion—the crushing tax regime, forced settlement, displacement of merchant communities, destruction of artisan groups, coercive cultivation of indigo and other commodities, expropriation of land and rights to land, and so on. As much as its liberal narrators imposed a sense of clear order and purpose on British actions in India, continual insurgency meant that the British often acted out of insecurity and anxiety—"irrational passions rather than calculated plans," in the words of one historian—producing chaos.[94] Indian society was astir throughout the first half of the century, but resistance reached a cataclysmic crescendo in May 1857, exactly a century after Clive's victory in the Battle of Plassey. After the company's Indian soldiers (sepoys) mutinied, diverse strands of resistance converged on a massive scale with a shared objective of ending colonial rule.[95] Rebels attacked prisons, factories, police posts, railway stations, bungalows, telegraph wires, law courts—all symbols of company authority. They destroyed official records, but also money-lenders' ledgers. Targets included merchants, bankers, and the well-off.

We are after the ethical frameworks guiding British imperial activity. But to arrive at a possible recuperation of a historically minded system of ethical accountability by the end, we must pause to explore the frameworks guiding Indian rebellion against the British narrative of progress. The revolt came as a shock to Britons accustomed to thinking of Indians as indolent, incapacitated, and effeminate—in a mind-set in which manliness defined agency. They inferred that Indian women had egged men on to be manly and revolt, to explain why otherwise loyal sepoys would mutiny,[96] smugly concluding that imperialism was successfully fostering the progress of women captive to emasculated men. But most often, Britons dismissed the alarming exercise of insurgent Indian agency as religious fanaticism, belief that was beyond reason, diabolical, and proof of a gormless inability to recognize progress for what it was. Since the Enlightenment, Burke and others cautioning against excessive revolutionary fervor had even allegorized the "fanaticism of reason" that led to the French Terror as Islam.[97]

To be sure, religious motivations mattered deeply in the rebellion—the notion of defending the Muslim or Hindu faith, on pain of damnation. Jihadis were part of the mix. Some soldiers deserted company service out of fear of going to hell for serving the kafirs. Astrological predictions guided some battle timings. But the rebellion was about much more than religion. Dynastic and patriotic allegiances mattered, too, and all these various loyalties were braided with peasants' and laborers' sense of injustice and fury against the everyday humiliation of racism. Some volunteers simply sought the opportunity for employment and service in rebel ranks. Those who traveled from far to volunteer did not just arrive at the scene and begin fighting; they felt a need to formally present themselves to the Mughal king, obtain his approval, and register in the official rolls. It was a people's rebellion, but one in which the people wanted an official endorsement and rank.[98] This may attest to patriotic loyalty or to the attraction of formal employment. As a recent editor of Indian-language sources on the rising concludes, "We need to know more about the motivations and mechanisms through which people volunteered to fight against the British."

Still, even from our existing knowledge, we can derive some conclusions about the systems of ethical accountability at work in some Indian minds. The British presumed Indians lacked a sense of history, indeed that the society itself was timeless—this was the source of its "backwardness." But in fact, a complex historical imagination, as much as religious notions, was at work in instigating insurgency. Not the least evidence of this is the rebels' consciousness of the centenary of Plassey. The idea of Doomsday—divine judgment at the end of times—fused with the sense of historical reckoning on the centenary of that epoch-making event. Moreover, the official leader of the rebellion, the Mughal emperor Bahadur Shah Zafar, then aged eighty-two, was himself actualized by a sense of being at a historic endgame; the company had made it clear on making him its pensioner that he would be the last Mughal ruler to live at the Red Fort in Delhi. He often referred to the impending end of the Mughal lineage, and his leadership in 1857 was partly his attempt at staking a claim for posterity.[99]

Maulvi Mohammed Baqar had close ties to Zafar's court and was the editor of the *Delhi Urdu Akhbar*, an important propaganda instrument during the rebellion, speaking primarily the language of defense of religion—divine will and sanction. Thus, a month into the rebellion, Baqar explained to his readers that the English were suffering under "divine wrath," and that India's people should "remain steadfast in their opposition, knowing that the English no longer have the strength to stand up to our country and our people. Since God has taken away from them their government we should all stand with one body and one mind, without hesitation or scruples, to battle with them."[100] The mutineers' agency was divine here. Still, the story of divine retribution relied on a historical sensibility. The proof that formidable rulers might be overthrown lay in the fact that "nothing is permanent" except the Primeval Deity. Muslims and Hindus alike could see "how many magnificent dynasties and kingdoms . . . in the land of Hindustan . . . all met their end. . . . Nothing can withstand divine resolution." Baqar invoked the stories of Kans and Krishna, Raja Parsuram, the Abbasid caliphs, the vanquishing of the Ghaznavids by the Ghurids, and their defeat by the Khaljis in turn, the Qajar displacement of the Safavids in Iran. He called on his listeners to emulate heroes from "history books" and "ancient Indian history—the achievements of . . . Arjun and Bhim . . . or as in Iranian history, the feats of Rustam and Saam; and in Islamic history, the victories of Saheh Qiran Amir Timur and the brave soldiers of Chengiz Khan and Halaku Khan or the memory of the Nadirshahi contingent." Quite apart from forging an imagined community through these invocations of regional history, well before the time of formal nationalism, Baqar's yoking of Hindu mythology, Puranic lore, Quranic fable, and medieval Turkish history into a "seamless whole" strove to convince readers of the "transitory and ephemeral nature of political rule," writes his translator Mahmood Farooqui.[101]

Baqar's concatenation of stories drawn from myth and history was somewhat exceptional; Farooqui speculates that it was a result of Baqar's exposure to the historical discipline at Delhi College. Macaulay's brother-in-law Charles Trevelyan was a driving force behind reorganization of an eighteenth-century Delhi madrasa into this college including English-language instruction in the 1820s. He, too, held that "only the pure fount of English literature [can make] headway against the impenetrable barrier of habit and prejudice backed by religious feeling."[102] The college remained, however, a key site of the flourishing of Urdu literary and political culture known as the Delhi Renaissance, including engagement with translated European works.[103] Christian conversion of celebrated figures in the college in the 1850s helped make it a rebel target in May 1857, but its complicated place in political culture is evidenced by its closure for three decades after the rebellion. Farooqui may be right about the source of Baqar's historical sensibility, but the fact that most rebel proclamations, despite making fewer appeals to history, did routinely cite the history of British perfidies suggests that an indigenous appreciation of historical injustice was certainly at work, too. Invocations of faith made invocations of other kinds of history redundant because they, too, were historically minded. Even Baqar's appeal to history is an effort to think through a religiously grounded notion of the transitory nature of any reality. In this, it shared an affinity with the European idea of history as a means of making sense of God's plan.

After all, Herodotus and Thucydides are not *in fact* exclusively the patrimony of the West. Herodotus himself was born a Persian subject in Halicarnassus, on the southwestern coast of present-day Turkey, and died in a Greek colony in southern Italy. Moreover, the queen of the Persian Empire was herself half Cretan and half Halicarnassian. "Ancient Greece" went well beyond Greece itself. The classical world was not "European"; it was a Mediterranean world that straddled what Europeans later ossified as "East" and "West." Palestine and Egypt were as much a part of it as Italy. Classical texts were diffused into the medieval Islamic world and were as influential in the proverbial "East." The peripatetic fourteenth-century Muslim historian Ibn Khaldun in North Africa might be seen as moving in a latter-day version of the same world. This is to say that the spark of historical imagination associated with texts like Herodotus's landed in many directions—not to mention other, entirely local foundations of historical thinking.[104] The British incursion in the eighteenth century was described in detail by Mughal historians.[105] The disruption in turn prompted invention of a new genre of moralizing histories known as *Ibrat-Nama*.[106] Scholars at the Delhi College were familiar with the joint East-West history of history. The prominent science teacher there in the 1840s, Master Ramchandra, defended his keen pursuit of translating European works into Urdu by referring to earlier Muslim translation of Greek works to the benefit of both Muslim societies and Europe.[107] (Ramchandra was one of the faculty who converted to Christianity in 1852.) In short, even the historical sensibility transmitted at the Delhi College was not entirely a Western import.

Like Macaulay, Baqar used history to sharpen his readers' sense of their heroic agency in the present moment. He pressed their direct connection to past generations for this purpose. Just as the bravery and valor of the historical figures he invoked remained on people's lips, so, too, might Indian rebels "go down in history books. . . . It will forever be recounted how and with what gallantry and daring you broke the will and arrogance of this mighty kingdom and pummelled their Pharaonic pride." They were the "progeny of the kings of old," and God had brought them to a juncture where "the descendants of these stalwarts should show the glory of their lineage and aspire to the same posts and achievements as displayed by their ancestors." He reminded readers that the British were faithless and had acquired what they had through "fraud"; they routinely violated contract, "claiming it was the translator's fault."[108] God had "sent his hidden help to defeat this hundred-year-old kingdom . . . which regarded the children of God with contempt and addressed your brothers and brethren

as 'black man' and thus insulted and humiliated them." Many "secular" issues were subsumed under the umbrella of religious offense and intolerance, ranging from unjust laws, everyday racist policies against Indians,
the rise of English, a sense of trespass, the drain of Indian wealth, and so
on.[109] Baqar wrote at length about the exclusion of Indians from top government posts and "tight fisted and stingy" use of Indian revenue, which
the British sent back to England so that "their money was of no benefit
to our Hindustan, and we derived no advantage from their savings and
profits."[110] While condemning Christian conversion, changes to religious
practices, and the introduction of English, he also expounded on British
appropriation of ancestral property that left "thousands . . . without food
or water."

The rebels must "consider God your helpers," and see the king's approval as "akin to the approval of God." Divine approval was validating (as
it was for Britons). There was allowance for magic, unlike in European appeals to history: Baqar recalled the battle of Badar in which the Prophet
aided the faithful through angels to reassure readers that momentary
British success need not lead to despair. A vengeful God would not allow
them to prevail.[111] The rebellion certainly fulfilled a religious narrative, but
one justified *by* history and designed to address a moment of historical oppression. Like liberal and Romantic historical thought, Baqar's cocktail of
history drawn from mythical and human time was ultimately a tonic to
the conscience for those having to overcome moral qualms in order to perform actions justified by their future benefit: Immediately following his
recitation of heroic past struggles, he asks, "What then may be the hesitation in, with divine help, one man taking on and killing another?"

Baqar's historical sensibility incorporated some aspects of liberal notions of history, too. While condemning British perfidy and exploitation,
he also lamented Indians' disdain for business and industry and the seeming
decline of martial ability. Comparing India to other lands, including Europe, he, too, indulged in the vision of Indian backwardness and the need
to "catch up." This vision of progress was both religious and worldly. For
Baqar, both were manifestations of divine power; India could not progress
in one while lagging in the other.[112] In this, his outlook again shared an
affinity with British historical thinking which saw the worldly position in
which "Providence" placed the nation as a measure of divine grace, too. He
saw Britain's fall in India in 1857 in the same manner that Britons themselves had interpreted military defeat by a colony in 1783. In its geograph-

ical specificity, Baqar's thought was prototypically patriotic—about the land and the people, "Hindustan"—as much as it was about anticolonial defense of religion.

Baqar often expressed disappointment in Delhi residents' lack of religious zeal, and police records from the city do not refer to religion at all, despite the emotional appeals to religion in official proclamations to soldiers.[113] This especially helps confirm that religion was as much an idiom for speaking about all manner of things, attachments to ways of life, as it offered actual, doctrinal motivations for insurgency. Religious offense was inseparable from economic suffering and the changes to ways of life that accompanied it. Under the British, "the populace was subjected to greater hardship, misery and worldly and religious loss and deprivation, and it was deprived of food and water," wrote Baqar.[114] The British plan, he discerned, was to so pollute everyone's faith as to *socially* alienate them and force them to seek refuge in the British: "They would not be allowed to eat or sit or intermingle or intermarry with their . . . communities" and would "lose their children, wives, friends and strangers and they should not have anybody to call their own in all of Hindustan except for the English." Their fate would thus be tied to the English, whose power they would have to give their lives and fortune to defend.[115] In short, the rebels were acting to prevent a kind of social atomization impending with the rise of the British. The term "saheb," used to address superiors, became associated almost exclusively with the British ruling class. It also connoted a certain "way of being," notes Farooqui. Insofar as the rebels sought to extirpate British rule, they rose up against that "way of being," perhaps that very mode of individualized liberal selfhood that the British claimed it was their goal to model and create. Baqar specifically observed that "fear and oppression" under British rule had "made a difference to the way you eat and dine, you sleep and sit." It brought the infection of a certain style of bodily discipline, personal comportment, in line with particular notions of a disciplined self, as much as "culture" writ large. Baqar saw the rebellion as the defense of a different, perhaps more complex way of being. In his writings, summarizes Farooqui, "spiritual progress, material advancement, anticolonialism and communal fraternity are conjoint, under the necessary leadership of Bahadur Shah Zafar, into a whole which would become wholly elusive after the liberal-ization of India post-1857."[116]

Apart from his participation in the Delhi Renaissance, Baqar's intimacy with the world of Urdu poets would have given him access to literary expressions of this other kind of selfhood. His close friend was the court poet Zauq. His litany of British abuses in one issue of his newspaper culminated in a line of Persian poetry that validated his mutinous posture: "The shepherd was . . . exposed and in the words of Saadi Shirazi, 'When I saw my fate, I myself became a wolf.'"[117] Poetry was also a political idiom in this period. The emperor Zafar was himself a major poet. Urdu poetry was part of courtly Mughal culture. That culture was intimately shaped by the expanding British presence from the eighteenth century. It evolved in the context of the worldly problem of colonialism and the crises of culture and identity colonialism produced. In 1835, for instance, the future poet Daagh Dehlvi's father was hanged for ordering the assassination of Sir William Fraser, Commissioner of the Delhi Territory under the increasingly subordinated emperor Zafar. Daagh's stepfather was Zafar's son, Prince Fakhru. After Fakhru's death in 1856, Daagh left Delhi, joining government service in Rampur and Hyderabad. These were "princely states"—areas of the subcontinent in which the British ruled indirectly through nominally independent local rulers in order to make their presence more discreet, especially after 1857. The vicissitudes of Mughal power shaped the work of renowned poets like Daagh, Zafar, and other court poets. They were central to the 1857 rebellion, quite apart from Zafar's role as figurehead. The Delhi poet Fazl-e-Haq Khairabadi was a key leader, imprisoned afterwards on the Andaman Islands, where he died. (Baqar, too, was executed.) Khizr Sultan, another of Zafar's sons, was a poetic disciple of the most celebrated poet of the period, Mirza Ghalib, and also took a lead role in the uprising, earning Ghalib's praise.

Poets nurtured a cult around a lost homeland as the Mughal star was eclipsed. But they also expressed another kind of selfhood that embraced incompleteness and incoherence, that was agonistic in quality. (I do not mean the "porous" premodern selfhood that Charles Taylor opposes to the modern self "buffered" from forces outside the mind.) In Shirazi's line above, the poetic subject confesses he became a wolf, but in his very recounting of this fact, we understand that he also remained himself. Where Enlightenment philosophes evolved theodicies to explain the existence of evil, here was a mode of thought, common across many South Asian philosophical traditions, in which contradiction was expected: evil and good, light and dark coexisting, the idea that the God who loves us is also our tormentor—He immiserates but is also the solace. We have seen this agon before, in strands of European Romanticism before the era of

Macaulay—and it is no coincidence, for exposure to this poetic tradition shaped the most sensitive British reflections on the nation's moral path. Blake's articulation of a divided selfhood owed something, certainly, to orientalist understandings of Indian and Middle Eastern concepts of self-hood and being. So, too, did Goethe, who, out of admiration for the Persian poet Hafez, compiled his own *West-ostlicher Divan* ("West-Eastern Diwan [Collection of Poems]") in 1819. Reading Hafez, he experienced a sense of "oscillating between two worlds, his own and that of the Muslim believer who was miles, even worlds away from European Weimar," in the words of the literary critic Edward Said.[118] The notion of a divided self was cultur-ally deep in the subcontinent, part of religiously syncretic, mystical no-tions of *birha,* the interminable longing for union with the divine, usually told through an allegory of worldly love, in both poems and popular epics (*qissas*). The subject of Urdu poetry, read throughout the north, was split, a notion captured nicely in a couplet by Blake's contemporary Mir Taqi Mir: *"Dikhaai diye yun ki bekhud kiya / humein aap se bhi juda kar chale"* ([He] was visible to me in such a way that made me intoxicated [loss of self] / [he] left me separated even from myself). Here is the nineteenth-century Delhi poet Momin: *"Tum mere paas hote ho goya / jab koi doosra nahin hota"* (You are with me thus / as when no other is there).[119] In true mystic union, the self becomes extinct. The concept of *birha* merged worldly with unworldly concerns; Urdu poets engaged political issues *through* this Sufi vein.

This form of selfhood did not go away, and it brings with it its own lib-eratory potential, as we shall see. But in the particular historical crisis under review here, it was the version of selfhood embraced by the losing side. The historian Faisal Devji helpfully describes the rebellion as a re-fusal of the modernizing uniformity the British were imposing, in defense instead of "an empire of distinctions . . . in which differences between rulers and subjects as well as among these subjects were much to be desired because they made morality possible in the form of obligation towards others." They defended the moral compact forged through *coexistence* with the alien.[120]

Before we examine the British response to the rebellion, we must finally pause to consider the Urdu word for it, *ghadar,* which also remains in the lexicon of anticolonial rebellion. Most Urdu dictionaries define *"ghadar"* as "mutiny, sedition." A *"ghadaar"* is accordingly a "traitor." This makes sense as a (British) description of the mutinous soldiers who started the rebellion (nineteenth-century British dictionaries certainly give the word this negative gloss).[121] But "*ghadar*" also means, simply, disorder—perhaps more akin to the pre-1790s understanding of "revolution" as a time of flux and thus confusion. And such a "dis-order" or undoing of order might be a nonnormative way of describing "mutiny," simply, a time of dramatic change. Farooqui defines it variously as "outburst, mayhem, rebellion, riot and disturbance, helter-skelter, turbulence." He is at pains in his work to highlight the constructive side of this complicated event—the functioning governmental structures that the rebels assembled during the time of rebellion, which were about creating the new as much as reconstructing the old. It was a radical moment in many ways, causing a "miasma of panic and suspicion" to descend on Delhi. In a fog of rumor and amid talk of impending divine and historical reckoning recalling mythic times, looting, and subversion of all kinds of authority, everyday people, from beggars to prostitutes to merchants to soldiers, and everyday acts were suspicious and politicized in a new way. Princes rediscovered their power; paupers asserted theirs; prices went awry; sahebs escaped in Indian dress; mutinous soldiers played English band songs; Indians appointed themselves collectors and generals.[122] This disorder, this temporary undoing of empire, when history remained undecided in its verdict as to whether the rebels were traitors to the righteous cause of the British or the vanguard of the righteous cause of Indians, was itself a time of incoherent selfhood, of managed contradiction, whose internal tension was a motivator of historical change, quite outside the theories of agency the discipline of history formally hands down to us as ethical guides. We will revisit this notion later.

Meanwhile, shocked as the British were by the turn of events, well outside the predictions of liberal narratives of imperial history, many did, initially, succumb to self-doubt, recognizing the rebellion as evidence of misgovernment. Karl Marx was in London then. "When the Sepoy insurrection broke out," he later recalled, "the cry of Indian reform rang through all the classes of British society." "Popular imagination was heated by the torture reports; the Government interference with the native religion was loudly denounced by Indian general officers and civilians of high standing; the rapacious annexation policy of Lord Dalhousie, the mere tool of Downing street; the fermentation recklessly created in the Asiatic mind by the piratical wars in Persia and China . . . all these accumulated grievances burst into the cry for Indian Reform—reform of the Company's Indian administration, reform of the Government's Indian policy."[123] Initially, in short, the British *got* it; British conscience was pricked. But this sympathetic view was quickly displaced as racist accounts of Indian atrocities were circulated, including mythical stories of impaled children. Telegraphed daily news reports consumed by masses recounted the heroic escapades and trials of British commanders defending their women and children. Indian motives ceased to be seen as political and were viewed as purely criminal. Formerly depicted as lazy and ineffectual, Indians now were villainized as rapacious beasts. Reform fell by the wayside as the public instead called for ruthless suppression of the revolt and reimposition of British rule. Macaulay found himself prey to bloodthirsty emotions, a vindictive hatred he had never felt before. He was "only half ashamed" at this "craving for vengeance," confessing, "I could be very cruel just now if I had power."[124] Privately, he rationalized away even his half-shame: "Is this wrong? Is not the severity which springs from a great sensibility to human suffering a better thing than the lenity which springs from indifference to human suffering?"[125] He justified his morally dubious vengefulness, shaped, certainly, by a skewed account of suffering, as a credit to his empathetic capacities—without noting the irony vis-à-vis his earlier condemnation of Burke's sensitivities or questioning why "severity" and "lenity" were the only possible responses. This was a historian's response governed not by his historical imagination of his agency but by his immediate emotions. The British wanted blood and did not need a theory of history to justify it. The rebellion was crushed with outsized violence without moral compunction. It took the British a full year to reestablish their rule. Entire cities were destroyed. Rebels were hanged, shot, or blown from cannons in thousands. Hundreds of villages were torched.[126]

The idea of retribution for retribution's sake was not new. If Indians drew on the *Mahabharata,* the British likewise responded from an ethic of Christian vengeance—"Calvinistically tinged piety" evolving from eighteenth-century Methodism whose harsh capacities had been sublimated in the gospel of improvement but which retained psychic and social charge—embodied especially in the intense evangelical ethos of military leaders in charge, such as Sir Henry Havelock.[127] This ethos elevated retribution into something nobler than coarse revenge: a visitation of righteous judgment preemptively fulfilling the work of history. The Roman playbook also offered examples of vengeful destruction, including the sack of Jerusalem after Jewish rebellion in 70 CE and the earlier sack of Carthage. They drew also, however, on the historical mythology of empire, especially the memory of the Army of Retribution that had set out to redeem the nation's honor and prestige in the face of defeat fifteen years earlier. That exercise of revenge found renewed validation in its redeployment in 1857. The British drew from the historical template of the Anglo-Afghan War to shape their practical and imaginative response to fresh imperial failure. Indeed, the Afghanistan controversy was still playing out, and many of the officers in charge in 1857, including Havelock, the heroic savior of Lucknow, had served in Afghanistan.[128] Once again, the idea that the empire's entire security was at stake in the crisis was an argument for reestablishing control through terror—collective punishment, spectacular violence—for the sake of the British reading public, the Indian public, and other colonial publics. A sense of the historical stakes assuaged moral qualms. The violence of retribution was not haphazard but deliberate and theatrical, to further its exemplary function.

I will have more to say about how racist historical theories justified and were justified by these imperial crises in Chapter 3. Here I want to address another arena of historical reckoning in which conscience *was* pricked by the brutal crushing of the rebellion: the analysis offered by Marx and Friedrich Engels as the event unfolded. This series of articles stood at an angle to, even subverted, the vision of world-historical evolution that Marx and Engels subscribed to and preached. This stubborn dissonance is a mark of the epistemological challenge the rebellion posed, which would make it a key site for unpicking and remaking history's ethical outlook in the next century.

Socialist movements, building on a range of religious and secular ideas, had multiplied in the early nineteenth century, becoming influential throughout Europe. In 1848, as revolution swept the continent, Marx and Engels had published a manifesto calling for historical change while offering a new view of history itself, months before Macaulay's *History* first appeared. Engels had already published a study based on his time in Manchester: *The Condition of the Working Class in England* (1845) documented the smoke, darkness, filth, and ubiquitous cough that marked the onset of the Anthropocene.[129] Marx and Engels's *Communist Manifesto*, laden with evocative Romantic images of veils and specters, depicted the bourgeoisie's relentless quest for profit in the mold of naively tragic heroism. Bourgeois society recalled "the sorcerer, who is no longer able to control the powers of the nether world whom he has called up by his spells"—Faust,

Sir John Tenniel, *Justice,* in *Punch,* September 12, 1857. (Pictorial Press Ltd / Alamy Stock Photo)

or Frankenstein.[130] Through its everlasting folly, from this crooked timber, each creative effort inevitably summons destruction, a dialectical evolution through continually mounting crisis. In this materialist theory, the production of goods and the organization of society into classes drive history: History consists of successive forms of exploitative production and rebellions against them, capitalism being the last such stage before a proletarian revolution that will create the liberty and equality of all.

Engels's observation of the British industrial working classes informed this vision of how history would, inescapably, unfold in the future. He and Marx drew also from the ideas of Mill and Macaulay, in addition to those of Continental thinkers like Hegel. They moved to England in 1850, and from inside the imperial metropole, the historical ideas of these imperial outsiders began to influence the unfolding of history. They, too, saw history as a universal process unfolding in a linear direction, ultimately progressive and liberatory. But there were also critical differences. In the liberal narrative, conflict between individuals or nations might productively forward progress, and progress might entail loss—of obsolete things and ways of life—but progress did not *depend* on these things. It could, conceivably, build on itself, gradually, inexorably. Whig historians of the Victorian era, especially, believed in continuity, the idea that the present ought to contain a recognizable version of the past; they strove to envision change *without* irreparable breaks, revolution.[131] The Marxist narrative, however, viewed change as necessarily disruptive and dialectical, depending on and driven by conflict, specifically class conflict. Its scientific pretensions resonated with Victorian taste, but it also drew on Romantic notions in its apocalyptic evocations, agonistic notions of "creative destruction," and tragically heroic depiction of the bourgeoisie. Marx and Engels also knew the so-called Pax Britannica in fact depended on the exercise of force to create a global economy favorable to the British bourgeoisie and elites, that they used power to open markets and keep them open.[132]

But the revolutionary *intellectual* potential of these signal differences was constrained by the narrative's faithfulness to the orientalist assumptions common to modern European historicism. Though its debts to the German philosophical tradition of "universal history" invested it in a vision of united "workers of the world," it also assumed, in Hegelian fashion, that history travels across space as much as time, that India and other colonies were Europe's past, and that Europe was the beacon of the future. To attain the proletarian utopia, every region would first have to experience despotism and emerge from the crucible of bourgeois revolution; to forge the international, each region must first incarnate the nation. The East's lack of the dynamic energy for the staging of history was integral to Marxist thought. The concept of the "Asiatic mode of production" built on older ideas of "oriental despotism," positing an economic organization dictated by geography, in which the sovereign is the sole proprietor and society is organized in autonomous villages. European dominion could be catalytic in such places, both destructive and productive. Marx wrote in 1853, "England has to fulfill a double mission in India: one destructive, the other regenerating—the annihilation of the Asiatic society, and the laying of the material foundations of Western society in Asia." To be sure, this would not be a pretty picture: "Has [the English bourgeoisie] ever effected a progress without dragging individuals and people through blood and dirt, through misery and degradation?" Indians would not reap the benefits of this process until the industrial proletariat supplanted the British ruling classes, *"or till the Hindoos themselves shall have grown strong enough to throw off the English yoke altogether."*[133] But this fleeting imagining of Indian historical agency vanishes eclipse-like in an outlook committed to tolerance of oppression—and "profound hypocrisy"—in the name of progress. England, whatever its crimes, "was the unconscious tool of history."[134] It would not be easy to stomach—the "devastating effects of English industry" in India were "confounding"—but, still, Marx counseled patience, for "the inherent organic laws of political economy" were "now at work in every civilized town." He could ultimately envision only one path for history: "The bourgeois period of history has to create the material basis of the new world," and it would do so "in the same way as geological revolutions have created the surface of the earth."

The Indian rebellion four years later gave Marx an opportunity to test these confident assumptions about the inevitable, scientifically predictable unfolding of history. From England, he and Engels reported on the conflict for the *New-York Daily Tribune,* in articles that were reprinted in a range of other publications. Their coverage, based largely on official reports, was laced with the usual orientalist motifs and stereotypes: the obstacles posed by climate, the cowardly "Bengalees," and so on—although, notably, cowardice is put down to climate and centuries of oppression rather than race or culture.[135] But they proved able to think outside the box of the liberal history of empire. However backward India and Indians were, British intentions were not, to Marx and Engels, as innocent as the British pretended. To them, the British were disrupting rather than catalyzing the formation of Indian nationhood that was essential to the region's participation in the global struggle for proletarian liberation. Rather than helping to forge this nation, the British had subjugated it by engaging in a "Roman *Divide et impera,*" using the "antagonism of the various races, tribes, castes, creeds and sovereignties" as the basis of British supremacy. Now, however, disparate groups had joined in common cause against their conqueror.[136] Marx sought to expose the great British imperial fraud, to show "that the British rulers of India are by no means such mild and spotless benefactors of the Indian people as they would have the world believe."[137] This was a challenge on historical grounds, a challenge to the dissembling narratives of progress peddled by liberal thinkers. Calling out practices like the use of torture in tax collection, Marx strove to unveil the "real history of British rule in India."

This willingness to puncture myth allowed him to arrive at a fresh ethical assessment of rebel violence itself, which he defended by asking "whether a people are not justified in attempting to expel the foreign conquerors who have so abused their subjects." "If the English could do these things in cold blood," he argued, "is it surprising that the insurgent Hindoos should be guilty, in the fury of revolt and conflict, of the crimes and cruelties alleged against them?" Indian violence mirrored British violence: "However infamous the conduct of the Sepoys, it is only the reflex, in a concentrated form, of England's own conduct in India."[138] Tearing the pages of the rebels' story from the liberal historical record in which they appeared childlike, irrational, and backward, he pasted them into another narrative, comparing them to the revolutionaries of France, thereby transforming their ethical positioning. This comparison, this evocation of a different historical script, challenged exoticized representations of Indian actions, sweeping them into a "normal," European narrative of history. (To be sure, this trope would have limited recuperative power in Britain, given popularly critical views of the French Revolution.) Marx's unmasking did not stop at calling out British brutality. He also debunked claims of imperial economic benevolence by enumerating the many ways in which Britain benefited materially from the Indian empire.[139]

By the end of the year, the British public was celebrating the capture of Delhi. But these historical commentators stood stubbornly aloof from the burgeoning British narrative of heroic success: "We will not join in the noisy chorus . . . now extolling to the skies the bravery of the troops that took Delhi by storm," wrote Engels, noting sardonically the British capacity for "self-laudation."[140] This was, again, an objection to the way the British habitually narrated history, a recognition that a particular historical outlook had become complicit in a morally dubious way of acting in the world. Reporting the plunder and outrages accompanying the reassertion of British rule, Engels's own judgment was unequivocal: "There is no army in

Europe or America with so much brutality as the British."[141] The Positivist Richard Congreve called for withdrawal from India specifically on grounds of morality, judging the Indian rebellion legitimate and the British victory a "triumph of force over right."[142] A few observers in Britain thus saw what Baqar saw. As the war ended, Marx reminded readers that the rebels had been avenging British diplomatic treachery—systematic violation of treaties with Indian rulers and confiscation of land.[143] He was certain of the judgment of history, asserting that the British would get their moral comeuppance, even if they prevailed in India, for "these treacherous and brutal modes of proceeding . . . toward the natives of India" were avenging themselves "not only in India, but in England." Indian events were intimately related to and revelatory of the progress of European history, part of a single narrative, for Marx. Perhaps he gestured here to the ongoing controversy over the First Anglo-Afghan War, or to the working-class radicalism that also strove to hold British liberalism to account.

Marx's mutinous approach towards his own historical outlook in this moment owed something to Ernest Jones, the Romantic poet-novelist who joined the working-class Chartist movement in 1846, became friendly with Marx and Engels soon after, and emerged a Chartist leader in 1848. Chartism had begun at the same time as the Anglo-Afghan War, initially arguing within the liberal historical narrative for universal manhood suffrage. Its methods were constitutional, but its ethos Romantic, infused with the work of Byron and Percy Shelley. The gentlemanly radical Jones styled himself in the Byronic mold of patriotic martyr-poet.[144] Failure of the movement's third petition in the revolutionary year of 1848, however, prompted Jones to steer it towards a socialist outlook in its declining years. The movement already had international sympathies—with Ireland, for instance, which endured famine in 1846. But in the 1850s, India became a source of inspiration. Among the works Jones produced in prison from 1848 to 1850 was the prophetic epic poem "The Revolt of Hindostan," which painted a cyclical view of history.[145] In 1853, he penned a scathing series of articles about misrule in India. More followed as the rebellion in 1857 caught his imagination. To be sure, his interest was partly instrumental, seeing in the rebellion a possible spur to militancy at home.[146] But it is nevertheless remarkable for its willingness to imagine history moving from East to West—testimony to the philosophically mutinous potential of Romanticism. Perhaps he was right in a negative sense: As the Indian rebels were extirpated in 1858, Chartism, too, was extinguished.

In the same moment, Macaulay and Marx offered different understandings of modernity. Macaulay was entirely uninterested in industrialism and what it entailed, historically. Instead, he concentrated on a Whig vision of England driven by landed and commercial interests and men of intellect like himself.[147] He saw the revolutionary energy of 1848 as a danger, although he was even more deeply affected by 1857. These were differing visions of who made history and who could rightfully make history. In one, the Indian rebels were irrational, criminal actors, like the revolutionaries of 1848; in the other, understandable and expected—like the revolutionaries of 1848. Marxism's theoretical failure to imagine Indian progress without the handmaiden of European imperialism did not trump Marx's own empathetic response to Indian rebellion against that rule, his certainty of its moral rightness (reading official sources against the grain), quite apart from whether it was "right" in terms of the progress of history. This devotee of historicism in effect allowed his judgment *in* the moment to trump history's judgment—after all, the Indians lost. This perhaps reveals something about Marx's own split subjectivity as a historicist and a Romantic; by temperament if not by philosophy, he could not but stand on the side of mutiny. The rebellion's capacity to subvert this thorough historicist's instincts almost despite himself exposed its pivotal potential, the way it had, despite its failure, punctured the logic of history and made a crack in history itself; it would thus inspire future subversions of empire and the historicism that was its alibi and furnish the primary historical terrain upon which historians would try to redeem historical thinking in the twentieth century, as we shall see in Chapter 6.

The changes upon the end of the rebellion were many. The era of company rule ended, and Crown rule began. The costs of the rebellion, roughly £50 million, were added to Indian debts to England. As Marx saw it, the prime minister, Lord Palmerston, turned the early cry for reform to "his exclusive profit."[148] Both the government and the East India Company had broken down, and Palmerston determined that "the Company was to be killed in sacrifice, and the Government to be rendered omnipotent." The company's power was "simply transferred to the dictator of the day, pretending to represent the Crown as against the Parliament, and to represent Parliament as against the Crown, thus absorbing the privileges of one and the other in his single person." Like the scandals that made Hastings the fall guy of eighteenth-century empire, now the company itself became the fall guy of empire. The problem was never empire itself, only bad imperialists.

Other historical assessments, both official and unofficial, arrived at dramatically different conclusions from Marx and Engels, testifying to a growing awareness that controlling the historical narrative was a means of controlling the unfolding of history itself. As an East India Company official, John Stuart Mill had the unenviable task of authoring the company's official defense after the rebellion to argue, somewhat futilely, for renewal of its charter. His pride in the company's achievements and faith in its disinterested benevolence fortified his view of the rebels as dupes of intrigue and fanaticism. A year later, while commenting on the Hungarian nationalist struggle against the Habsburg Empire, he wrote sympathetically that the test of a people's fitness for popular institutions was that "they, or a sufficient portion of them to prevail in the contest, are willing to brave labour and danger for their liberation."[149] This was not, however, how he saw the Indian rebels, perhaps presuming from their failure to prevail history's own judgment of their fitness. In writings soon after the rebellion, he recognized the "striving go-ahead character" of his people, but far from seeing the dangers of such overweening confidence, he proclaimed it "the foundation of the best hopes for the general improvement of mankind."[150] A decade later, however, he would condemn the brutality of British suppression of the rebellion, as we shall see; by then, history had revealed a sufficient pattern of imperial brutality that he could no longer defer judgment.

Kaye, famed historian of the First Anglo-Afghan War, immediately succeeded Mill as secretary of the Secret and Political Department of the new India Office that took over control from the East India Company in 1858. In short order, he began to produce a mammoth history of the 1857 rebellion, too, as almost a sequel to his earlier work, once again claiming a unique capacity for truth-telling based on his access to unofficial sources. If the earlier work was couched as an exposé of ill-intentioned political folly, the new one, whose first volume appeared in 1864, was framed as a recuperation of a national conscience in crisis. British "errors . . . were . . . strivings after good," he assured. "It was in the over-eager pursuit of Humanity and Civilisation" that they had been "betrayed into the excesses . . . so grievously visited upon the nation." Indeed, the rebellion was "the most signal illustration of our great national character ever yet recorded in the annals of our country." The rebellion was the fruit of over-zealous British efforts to make history, to exercise historical agency, but so, too, was its successful quelling a redemption of that presumption of the power to make history: "It was the vehement self-assertion of the Englishman that produced this conflagration; it was the same vehement self-assertion that enabled him, by God's blessing to trample it out. It was a noble egotism, mighty alike in doing and in suffering." To be English was to be a maker of history, at times tragically but ultimately in a manner vindicated by history itself. Kaye's "predominant theory" was that "because we were too English the great crisis arose; but it was only because we were English that, when it arose, it did not utterly overwhelm us." The event was made by "a few eminent men." His unapologetically great-man history gestured to Carlyle to explain that the Indian empire was the very proving ground of the agency and virtue of great men: "If it be true that the best history is that which most nearly resembles a bundle of biographies, it is especially true when said with reference to Indian history; for nowhere do the characters of individual Englishmen impress themselves with a more vital reality upon the annals of the country in which they live; nowhere are there such great opportunities of independent action; nowhere are developed such capacities for evil or for good, as in our great Anglo-Indian empire."[151]

To be sure, the text itself at times deviated from these prefatory pronouncements: Kaye acknowledged the British "reign of terror" and "wholesale confiscation" of land in Bengal, which together formed a "great war of extermination."[152] He even denounced the "heap of platitudes about Humanity and Civilisation" that sustained imperialism.[153] But the text's primary purpose remained expiatory. It styled even the worst of the retributive violence as ultimately compassionate, from an understanding that "to strike promptly and . . . vigorously would be to strike mercifully," by suppressing the conflict and thus bloodshed as quickly as possible.[154] The heroic structure of Anglo-Afghan War narratives furnished a template for histories of the "mutiny" (as the rebellion was quaintly memorialized): national glory and redemption pivoting around a central trial of temporary defeat.[155]

Historians trading in the liberal myth of empire, often doubling as bureaucrats and military personnel, as in the case of Kaye and his predecessors, were critical to making the empire resilient in the face of rebellion by its subjects and internal doubt about the violent, treacherous, and expropriatory practices it relied on. Other histories of the rebellion also betrayed ambivalent views about the British presence and response to the rebellion, echoing doubts expressed in 1842 and with the trial of Hastings.[156] We will examine the evolution of these stresses and expressions of dissent in later chapters. They were important in this moment for their expiatory function, to allow renewed investment in empire, not for undermining the imperial project. Guilty conscience had long been an integral part of the pursuit of empire. Imperial expansion in the first half of the century perhaps owed as much to a desire to atone for earlier imperial sins, including the slave trade, as it did to a belief in empire for its own sake. Even Byron, in his penitence for Britain's wrongs, fueled the spread of British power. It is not the cracks in British conscience that explain the progress of empire after 1858 but the papering over of them by recourse to historical narratives that continued to promise future redemption. Not all were unambiguously jingoistic, but enough were assuaged by the moral suturing provided by narratives like Kaye's to allow jingoism to flourish. Jingoism thrived in the ethical mud of liberalism.

Mythic accounts tracing British victory over the rebels to military prowess strengthened Victorian notions of disciplined selfhood: Samuel Smiles's 1859 guide to "self-help" included an entire chapter on the mutiny as an exemplary instance of such character.[157] But in the subcontinent, the trope of divided selfhood offered solace. Ghalib's and Zafar's brokenhearted response to Delhi's destruction fueled melancholic laments about a vanishing world and way of being. Their poetic expressions, as part of a vanquished courtly culture, were censored, limiting their capacity for ideological rebellion. In a piece of theatrical punishment, Major William Hodson shot Zafar's sons and grandson in front of a crowd, near the city gate—which acquired the name "*Khooni Darwaza*," or "Bloody Gate." Their bodies were displayed at the police station. Most other members of the family were killed, imprisoned, or exiled. Zafar was exiled to Rangoon and died there in 1862. Meanwhile, rebels who survived British retribution were scattered around the world, where they helped build global networks of anticolonial sentiment of various intellectual stripes, whose history we are only now reassembling.[158] To offer just one example, the leader of an 1865 revolt near Asyut in Egypt was a disciple of an Indian rebel who had escaped there.[159] The anticolonial ideas of the peripatetic Islamic scholar Jamal al-Din al-Afghani, which would so influence Colonel Ahmad Urabi's revolt in Egypt from 1879 to 1882, were also honed during his time in India during the rebellion.

This fallout fit neatly in the liberal narrative of empire. There was no place for the conquered in Macaulay's conception of history, notes Catherine Hall. Progress meant eradication of the weak and those meant to be subjugated. Contemporary commentators noted the way his *History of England* dispelled *doubt*.[160] The rhetorical power of the work lay in its banishment of the contradictions and conundrums of liberal empire—the pangs of conscience that might otherwise have obstructed its unfolding. Histories of the mutiny built on that foundation. That was the power of the liberal historical sensibility in underwriting imperialism.

CHAPTER THREE

ʼ ʼ Progress of Elimination

[The Englishman] is never at a loss for an effective moral attitude.

—George Bernard Shaw

ʼ ʼ *In the dominant British point of view,* the rebels of 1857 did not express legitimate political grievance against colonial oppression. Rather, they proved that Indians had still not acquired the kind of conscience necessary for participation in the world's liberal political economy and the universal narrative of progress it drove. They were perversely ungrateful and could not endure temporary discomfort for a benevolent end. The question was whether they ever could. For many, the answer was no. British revenge tried to vindicate liberal empire, but the conflict ultimately dramatically revised expectations of liberal empire. New notions of permanent difference infused imperial expansion in Asia and Africa in the second half of the century.

The effort to come to terms with the initial humiliation of the Indian rebellion immediately drew Britons into the thickets of racial explanation. This had happened before: The moment of defeat during the Anglo-Afghan War had provoked reappraisal of the opponent's merit as a warrior race.[1] Post-1842 accounts no longer dismissed Afghans as effeminate, but neither did they respect them as peers. Rather, Afghans appeared as ferocious and dishonorable; only such a foe could have prevailed against the providentially blessed British.[2] (Defeat against the Americans in 1783 had, by contrast, triggered doubts about the providential blessing.)[3] In 1857, again, belated apprehension of the fearsome nature of the adversary helped justify outsized revenge. Racial demonization of Indians likewise secured the British conscience in enacting that violence, galvanizing the support of the British public: Diabolical Indian fanatics threatened the racial purity of English women and children, as Afghans had earlier. This version of the events was expressed in newspaper accounts and historical narratives but also in novels, poetry, and art. Images of "fiendishly vengeful sepoys," like most "racialized bogeys," were "the projections, scapegoats, surrogates of some dread ultimately not external but internal," one scholar reminds us.[4] Racial stereotypes are, indeed, projections but were mobilized in this instance to enable Britons to tolerate the otherwise inexcusable violence they were committing and steel them for a new kind of imperial mission. Racist demonization suppressed enough doubt among Britons to enable renewed pursuit of empire. The terror struck into Indian hearts was also explicitly racialized: the point, Kaye explained, was to show Indians that "*it was hopeless to endeavour to resist the power of the White Man.*"[5]

The liberal assumption of universal capacity to attain British civilization was weakened as notions of permanent, insurmountable racial and cultural difference gained hold after the rebellion. Clearly, Indians were radically different as human beings if they willfully rejected the pursuit of their own best interests in the form of British tutelage. They were irrational, fanatically religious, *ineducable,* and might not ever become British. If anything, the British had naively overestimated their capacities, extravagantly showering them with benevolence only to learn they had cast pearls before swine. Sir Charles Wood, former president of the Board of Control that oversaw the East India Company, denied that the rebellion testified to hostility towards British rule. Rather, he explained in 1859 while charged with directing the new India Office, it was the result of a "mistake we fell into, under the most benevolent feelings." His exculpatory protestation of unintended error was echoed in historical accounts like Kaye's—Kaye was a secretary in the same office. Wood's conclusions about the nature of that mistake implied a radically different policy direction for the future; they had erred in "introducing a system foreign to the habits and wishes of the people." The solution, then, was to work within existing institutions and not treat Indians as if they might become Englishmen.[6] This understanding of the rebellion as the result of the failure, or rather unsuitability, of liberal reformism in India had immediate practical effect. As the Crown took direct responsibility for India, its first official act was to proclaim a policy of nonintervention in religion and custom. Post-1857 expansion took the form of indirect rule through local rulers rather than formal annexation, with the idea of keeping native society intact and avoiding further violent convulsions. Whatever the Crown did not control directly, it would control by other means, not least as its might had also been irrevocably proven.

This was a dismal, if self-serving, verdict on the ideology that had driven imperial expansion and consolidation up to this point, but it nurtured the development of new justifications for empire that were equally indebted to the historical imagination. It was not that moral justifications of empire mattered less as pragmatic notions of stability and order came to anchor policy debates.[7] Rather, ethical arguments and moral justifications changed key. Thus far, liberal imperialism had depended on a notion of original sin—the scandal of eighteenth-century conquest—that might be redeemed by a reformist style of imperialism. Its moral appeal lay in the promise of redemption. Now, new notions of permanent cultural difference made fulfillment of the promise of redemption less likely but also less *necessary* insofar as they vanquished guilt by persuading Britons of the abject nature of Indian culture; the eighteenth-century intrusion accordingly stank less. At the same time, the new sense of permanent cultural difference emphasized the potential menace of an India set loose from the imperial order—such a backward society would certainly collapse into anarchy and wreak havoc in the world. The moral appeal of empire now lay in the notion of historical burden—the idea that Britain had taken on this burden of providing security to India (and other colonies) selflessly, not as penance, but as a service to the world. In framing British rule as the "lesser evil" compared to abandoning the world to anarchic collapse, late-Victorian imperial thinkers still justified it in moral terms. Karuna Mantena distinguishes the new emphasis on stability, the idea that "native society" simply required empire, as an "alibi" as opposed to the earlier concern with "justification" for empire.[8] But this distinction may be too fine, given the continuity of the historical imagination at work. An alibi excuses one from criminal suspicion by proving that one was elsewhere: *It wasn't me because I wasn't there.* But in the case of late-Victorian empire, the argument was *I was there, for naively benevolent reasons, and thank goodness I was, and still am, lest an even worse crime occur.*

The thought and work of the jurist and legal historian Henry Maine was pivotal to the culturalist rejection of liberal universalism after the rebellion— another historian wielding enormous institutional imperial power. As Law

Member of India's governing council from 1862 to 1869, Maine oversaw passage of over two hundred acts. He was determined to understand the causes of the 1857 rebellion—the roots of Indians' fanatical behavior—as a matter of burning practical importance in guiding imperial rule going forward.[9] He nurtured a sense of moral authority in doing so, "the authority of one who unflinchingly faces up to the demands of complexity, however unpalatable"—in the historian Stefan Collini's felicitous phrasing.[10] As contemporaries noted, he imputed "an unreal influence to writers" in creating change, believing human nature "left to itself" was not intrinsically disposed to pursue it.[11] It was axiomatic that the "cause" of the rebellion could not have been the empire itself; there was no room for rebellion in its historical narrative of progress (though there was in Marx's). The coercive nature of political, economic, and social transformation under British rule could not be the cause; rather it must be the colonized society's cultural or racial intransigence in the face of the opportunity to become civilized. The British failure lay only in miscalculating the power of this intransigence.

In keeping with liberal thought, Maine was emphatic about the "unintentional" nature of British errors. He protested that he had come to India in 1862 determined to put an end to the liberal strategy of anglicizing customs and institutions there but encountered a state of affairs that left him no alternative than to "abide by actual arrangements, whether founded or not on an original misconstruction of native usage. I say, *let us stand even by our mistakes. It is better than perpetual meddling.*"[12] This was an argument in favor of continuity couched as pragmatism. But it had the effect of extending the influence of liberal practices and ideas well beyond their expiry date. Take codification of Indian law. His liberal predecessors had urged codification out of an ideological faith in the universal superiority of enlightened codification and of English common law. Maine, however, insisted on codification because the disintegration of any native alternative made rationally informed legal codes a better option than continuing to haphazardly introduce common law through judicial legislation.[13]

Maine's historical sensibility shaped his sense of extremely constrained scope for action. Like liberals, he understood history in universal terms, seeing India as Europe's past; India offered access to customs and social forms long since faded from Europe. He set about looking for those vestiges and discerned that the village-community was the primary organizing structure of Indian society, as it must have been elsewhere earlier, and that Indian society was essentially corporate, customary, and apolitical in nature, stabilized by bonds of custom and kinship.[14] This was a departure from earlier visions of Indian society as captive to timeless and politically dysfunctional structures of oriental despotism from which it had to be rescued and put on the correct, universal path of progress. Maine posited a different universal historical process, one by which in every place communal forms of property ownership evolved, inevitably, and on their own, into modern forms of private property.[15] Britain had already completed this process, but before India had had its chance, Britain had unwittingly intervened.

This intervention was itself an inescapable outcome of a universal, progressive history. Maine did not question the liberal notion that the "strong moral and political conviction of a free people" was a key influence on India. But, he argued, it competed with India's "dense and dark vegetation of primitive opinion . . . rooted in the debris of the past." This put the British in a kind of historical bind: They were "bound to make their watches keep true time in two longitudes at once." They must accept the "paradoxical position" that "if they are too slow, there will be no improvement! If they are too fast, there will be no security."[16] Maine did not give up on the idea of improvement. His commitments to universal history did not permit that; India would evolve, with or without the British guiding hand. Nor did he abandon the idea that Britain's presence in India was the result of moral conviction. Earlier liberals had reconciled themselves to the paradox of imperial rule in the name of furthering the capacities of freedom—embracing the "Geographical morality" that Burke had denounced. Maine criticized their idealism but recognized it as historically determined. He now reconciled himself to the paradox of simultaneously reforming and preserving India. This was another kind of "Geographical morality"—keeping time in two longitudes at once. History was unfolding in two keys—there was the universal master narrative of evolution from communal to private property and rights, and then there was the history of British liberal tampering with that process. The former had to be made to accommodate the latter. The British could not abandon the enterprise now; they had become entangled in India's transition from traditional to modern society. In their well-meaning debates about land revenue policy, liberal political economy (and not any "high-handed repression") had caused them to misunderstand land usage customs and contribute to crisis in the village system.[17] They had not acted immorally; there was no need for penance. They had merely accelerated the natural processes of disintegration immanent in the village-community form.[18] But they did need to finish the job, else they would abandon a native society in crisis—and that would certainly be immoral. Maine's amnesia about the history of loot and the fiscal-military priorities that governed land revenue policy did not matter in this view of history: the point was, *whatever the origins,* they had inherited a certain, paradoxical situation. Like Galton, he claimed the innocence of an heir to a situation, bound to make the best that he could of it. What can't be cured must be endured. Noting the growing "fancy" among some Indian administrators to reconstruct lost native society in the aftermath of 1857, despite their better "moral judgement," he warned that fulfilling that dream was simply "not practicable" because of the nature of British power: "It is by its indirect and for the most part unintended influence that the British power metamorphoses and dissolves the ideas and social forms underneath it; nor is there any expedient by which it can escape the duty of rebuilding upon its own principles that which it unwillingly destroys."[19] The empire was a helpless historical force of its own whose abstruse influence was impossible to resist as it did what it was destined to do. The words "unintended" and "unwillingly" signaled that it was constitutively apologetic rather than guilty as it acted as history's handmaiden. The very creation of the administrative machinery of the imperial state had altered the context of "native society." India had been swept into the storm of historical change, heading towards the evolution of individual rights. The British would protectively shepherd it through this storm; to Maine, the empire was both "cause and cure for the crisis of native society," writes Mantena.[20] Disavowing any British interest in the outcome, Maine portrayed their unintentionally destructive impact as essentially apolitical. Once again, the historical imagination, the idea that post-1857 officials were trapped by the historical moment in which they found themselves, coupled with the belief that it was a difficult moment that would nevertheless lead to a progressive end, eased British officialdom's agitated conscience.

It is a matter for debate whether the British were as powerless to effect change as Maine thought: What might have happened if those fanciful administrators had tried to undo some of the damage of the previous decades? Could the British have departed altogether, as they did after visiting their wrath on Kabul in 1842? Could they have overcome vested interests as they had in the abolition movement? We may never know, but the point here is these options were not sanctioned by the historical imaginations of those in charge. Nor was Maine's rationalization simply a "cover" for the "real interests" at stake in continued British rule of India. Those interests mattered deeply, but they were enabled by a historical imagination in which investment in India, personal and financial, was part of the discharge of a moral duty to others. That thinking had not changed but had become entrenched in new ways after the rebellion. Indeed, the rebellion had raised the stakes for its entrenchment, given the risks British violence otherwise posed to British conscience.

Maine criticized earlier proponents of liberal universalism for their overconfident exercise of agency but also excused that enthusiasm as the result of Britain's own blessed historical progress. Moreover, he remained committed to notions of universal history and morally justified empire. In all this, he, too, was invested in liberal empire. Liberalism hardly vanished with the end of the rebellion: Mill himself published his major theorizations and defenses of liberalism, including liberal empire, only after 1858: *On Liberty* (1859) and *Considerations on Representative Government* (1861). The publication of these works may have been something of a rearguard action, but they were also effective in prolonging the influence of the ideas that sustained liberal imperialism.

Maine's comparative historical work did sharpen the sense of a dichotomy of "modern" and "traditional" societies. He, Mill, and others examined Irish agrarian and social customs in parallel with those in India as the century wore on. Notions of Irish and Indian similarities were strong, not least their common resistance to the expectations of liberal reformism. Neither seemed to have advanced on the path to becoming British, and in both, agrarian strife seemed to fuel rebellious energy. Evidence from these different settings was marshaled to prove Maine's "thesis of original communism."[21] Such trends fueled skepticism about liberalism but universalized crises in colonized societies as those of "traditional" (rather than "colonized") societies.

A rebellion in Jamaica strengthened belief in a dichotomy between countries that were and were not amenable to real advance. Since 1833, many, including Thomas Carlyle, had been assessing the colonies in the West Indies for evidence of the historical wisdom of abolishing the slave trade—while indentured labor from India poured in to perform backbreaking plantation labor. The rising in Jamaica in 1865, just years after the Indian insurgency, produced a fresh crisis in imperial conscience that radically divided British opinion, revealing the fault lines in British faith in liberal empire.

Two years of drought had strained conditions for freed slaves who had become peasant cultivators in Morant Bay on the southeastern coast of Jamaica. They were also distressed at increased taxation, lack of political representation, and a legal system in thrall to planters' interests. The black deacon of the Baptist church, Paul Bogle, led a group of farmers to meet with the governor, but they were denied an audience. Confidence in the government declined, and support for Bogle increased as matters escalated. A trial that convicted a black man for trespassing on an abandoned plantation lit the match that led to the conflagration. Bogle and his supporters protested, and a conflict with the police in the market square ensued. Warrants for the arrest of Bogle and others were issued, but the police again encountered resistance. Finally, Bogle led hundreds armed with sticks and machetes on a protest march to the courthouse. A volunteer militia fired on them when they threw stones. The protestors set fire to the courthouse. The court's chief magistrate and seventeen others were killed. Participants in the uprising swelled to between 1,500 to 2,000. The rebels acted out of a sense of social, political, and economic grievance; peasant cultivation and ownership of land were central to post-slavery Jamaican ideas of freedom.[22] Historical scripts may also have shaped how they felt obliged to act in the face of such difficulty; planters accused George William Gordon, the mulatto colonial assemblyman involved in the rebellion and a vocal critic of the governor's policies, of invoking the 1791 Haitian Revolution.[23]

The man in charge was Governor Edward Eyre. Eyre's career had begun in Australia, where he was a sheep grazer and explorer. After serving as lieutenant governor in New Zealand, he had arrived in the Caribbean, from where he watched news of the Indian rebellion unfold. He, like imperial officials around the world, was wary of similar revolt in his colony.[24] He saw the beginning of just such an island-wide trouncing in Bogle's march and determined to suppress it ruthlessly. Later, he, too, drew comparisons to Haiti and the "Indian mutiny."[25] He imposed martial law and launched reprisals that killed more than four hundred black peasants. Hundreds more were flogged and arrested and a thousand houses burned. The soldiers who did all this included veterans of 1857 and 1842. They replicated the tactics of 1857, too.[26] Eyre ordered Gordon's execution for treason. Bogle was also tried under martial law and executed. Here again the object was terror designed to preempt wider rebellion.

Eyre was paranoid; there was not in fact a risk of a total rebellion. But the political stakes of the rebellion were nevertheless high; Gordon had repeatedly shown his willingness to challenge Eyre's authority and legitimacy and had been heard to cite the Haitian revolt as a model in public. In court, Eyre called him an "evil-doer."[27] Racial fear was in play from the start in press coverage of the events; the London papers saw the rebels as part of an international post-emancipation black conspiracy, even though the depressed sugar economy and the government's refusal to intervene in it had been openly debated for months.[28]

But Eyre's actions stirred British conscience, prompting a public outcry. He headed a regime of "white terror" that had "done things which should make every Englishman blush with shame and indignation," avowed a liberal Birmingham daily.[29] In January 1866, a royal commission was appointed to investigate the events; it interviewed hundreds of witnesses for months and produced a report 1,200 pages long. While it criticized the government's "excessive" violence, it did not condemn the use of martial law in principle, effectively vindicating Eyre. Still, in July, the government dismissed Eyre from his governorship.

Liberals especially could not stomach Eyre's harsh handling of the situation. John Stuart Mill was now a Liberal member of Parliament for Westminster. He had not commented on British violence in India. But he denounced Eyre for abandoning the "rule of law" to exercise arbitrary power. He was horrified by his fellow Britons' lack of sufficient horror at the events in Jamaica, the praise expressed for Eyre's quick nipping of the crisis in the bud. Mill spoke for the liberal tradition, the belief that empire was about—and only justified by—the spread of civilization, especially the rule of law. That was the commitment that secured the legitimacy of the entire enterprise. He had dismissed the violence of 1858 as an anomaly, but now it was becoming a norm. His vision of the empire's progressive historical role could not accommodate the violence against Jamaican protestors, which evoked other, un-British historical scripts. To him, Eyre recalled Robespierre, villain of the French Terror.[30] The integrity of British justice was at stake. If Eyre were not prosecuted, he feared, "every rascally colonial official would be given a free hand" to do wrong, endangering the liberties of Englishmen, too.[31] Corrupted abroad, they might bring that contagion home, as nabobs had done in the previous century. Only after this crisis would he comment critically on British violence in India in the previous decade. John Bright, Charles Darwin, Herbert Spencer, James Fitzjames Stephen, and other liberals supported his position. He took leadership of the Jamaica Committee, which sought to examine the atrocities closely and secure Eyre's prosecution for murder.

Eyre was working from a different script than Mill: the history of humiliating defeat. He insisted that in a country reliant on a mere handful of troops amid a large and hostile peasantry, only prompt and decisive action could preserve order. This was an argument explicitly in favor of terror: Only the dread of immediate and severe retribution prevented the spread of rebellion. Echoing Kaye's defense of British violence in 1857, which had just appeared in 1864, he argued that it was humane because the spread of rebellion would have vastly increased suffering and misery. In an address in Jamaica on the eve of his departure, he confessed his "regret" at the "excesses" but affirmed that such excesses were inevitable under martial law, "especially when Black Troops" were employed. He explicitly recalled 1857 to justify his actions but also to illustrate the unjust nature of his removal. Why, he asked, had there been no commission then?[32]

British public opinion was mostly sympathetic to Eyre's view, especially after workers calling for enfranchisement rioted in Hyde Park that very July, stoking fears of anarchy and armed revolution in Britain itself. Carlyle, who had long distrusted the liberal project of improving the lives of former slaves at the expense of British interests and had expressed his disillusion with the results of abolition in the clash with Mill in 1849, argued that blacks had repaid trust with hostility; the rebellion confirmed that reform was both pointless and dangerous.[33] Non-whites were fundamentally different from Europeans, beyond redemption. They deserved Eyre's rough treatment, and Eyre was an imperial hero. The poet laureate Alfred Tennyson invoked the Indian rebellion as proof of the need for vigorous and swift action. The novelist Charles Dickens and the artist and art critic John Ruskin supported the pro-Eyre side of the dispute. News of atrocities against Englishwomen during the Indian rebellion had left Dickens frothing at the mouth, fantasizing about the chance to "exterminate the [oriental] Race upon whom the stain of the late cruelties rested."[34] One scholar reads his subsequent novel, A Tale of Two Cities (1859), as an effort to exorcise that demon, expressing "revulsion from the holocaust of revenge" inflicted by the British.[35] And yet, Dickens supported Eyre. To counter

Mill's committee, Carlyle set up his own: The Governor Eyre Defence and Aid Committee.

The Eyre controversy was long, public, and divisive, probably contributing to the fall of the Liberal government that year. The new Conservative government saw no need to engage further as Eyre had evidently committed no *intentional* wrongdoing, whatever his errors of judgment. Legally, too, he was free of further accountability by the declaration of martial law. Twice Eyre was charged with murder, but the cases never proceeded. He lived in Market Drayton, the birthplace of Robert Clive, beyond the jurisdiction of the Central Criminal Court, so the first indictment failed on that count. James Fitzjames Stephen, a barrister, traveled there but could not convince the justices to endorse his case. The Jamaica Committee asked the attorney general to certify the criminal information against Eyre but was rebuffed. When Eyre moved to London to bring matters to a head and offer himself up to justice, the Bow Street Police Court magistrate refused to arrest him. The next attempt, through the Queen's Bench, also failed when the bench's grand jury declined to find a true bill of indictment. The committee proceeded through the civil courts, charging Eyre with assault and false imprisonment. That case came to court as *Phillips v. Eyre* (1870), and he was again exonerated.[36] The government covered Eyre's legal costs in 1872; two years later, he was granted his pension as a retired governor.

The uprising had attacked colonial rule itself, questioning the legitimacy of a government unconcerned with poverty, heedlessly imposing high tax rates, and inadequately representing the populace. But the Jamaica Committee was narrowly concerned with the abusive use of martial law.[37] As with his earlier pronouncements on savagery, Mill's real concern was Britain's path. As the historian Jon Connolly observes, neither his committee nor the government commission explored the issues of poverty and governance that provoked the uprising. They recall the Quaker concern with arms-making rather than collective complicity in war in the case of Galton. As in the Hastings case, too, the scandal was a bad imperialist—Eyre—not empire itself. And once again *more* imperial intervention became the means of absolution for earlier imperial sins: stronger and more centralized, rather than more representative, government, to ensure that colonial laws could not supersede British law, as Jamaican martial law had exceeded the scope of British martial law. The self-pitying liberal view of empire was "damned if you do, damned if you don't," but in the long run, at least better for "others" if you do.

So, in Jamaica, as in India, rebellion produced tighter imperial rule. The white-dominated Jamaican assembly was dissolved, and the island reverted to Crown Colony status. The Colonial Office acquired greater control over the island's affairs. Before its dissolution, the House of Assembly passed legislation sanctioning the recent use of martial law and an act of indemnity covering all acts done in good faith to suppress the rebellion after martial law had been proclaimed. The metropole could now more easily protect the planter elite from the majority black population. The new governor, Sir John Peter Grant, had been lieutenant governor of Bengal immediately after rebellion there; the assumption was that this experience would serve him well in post-rebellion Jamaica. He was succeeded by yet another former lieutenant governor of Bengal.[38]

This story testifies to the resilience of the liberal defense of empire, how much it was willing to tolerate, how much it could compromise with its avowed love of liberty in the name of future payoff, allegedly for others. At the same time, the episode illuminates the growing strength of an increasingly dichotomous view of the scope for advance in British colonies, layering a racial distinction on the distinction of "modern" and "traditional" emerging from Maine's historical sociology. By mid-century, while these crises unfolded, majority-white colonies like Canada, Australia, and New Zealand had been put on a path to "responsible government," dominion status allowing internal self-rule, the British government counting on the majority population to preserve the British tie. But in Jamaica, the white minority retreated from the path of self-government, uncertain of its ability to maintain its position without direct British rule. The distinction between the constitutional position of colonies that were mainly nonwhite versus those that had become mainly white through genocidal engagement with indigenous peoples was sharpened. This was the distinction that anticolonial movements in these colonies would later question. Shortly after the Eyre controversy, British workingmen were enfranchised for the first time, on the argument that they had proven their trustworthiness and respectability.[39] British lower classes were now no longer equivalent to colonized subjects abroad; subjecthood was clearly based on race (and gender). Race became central to national identity in a new way. Indeed, for John Ruskin, the very affront of those who censured Eyre lay in their implied support for Jamaican progress before the progress of British workers. During the debate in 1865, he described himself as a "'Conservative' . . . in the deepest sense—a Re-former, not a De-former." He supported "the emancipation of any kind or number of blacks *in due place and time*," insisting that "white emancipation not only ought to precede, but must by law of all fate precede black emancipation."[40] History must evolve in a manner that did justice to racial difference.

To be sure, the imperial enterprise had been infused with racism from the outset. Racism was embedded in the slave system and in the systems of indentured labor that emerged in the 1830s to replace it. It was embedded in city planning around the empire. We can take the racism of empire for granted, but it and its role nevertheless evolved over time. Eighteenth-century ideas about race were different from nineteenth-century ideas and mattered differently. Liberalism's universalism made it race-blind in theory, though, as we have seen, in practice it was not. Colonial subjects were thoroughly racialized, even by those sympathetic to their resistance. The very idea of "civilization" depended on the racist notion of barbarism. Liberal ideas of colonial tutelage, the very structuring of the so-called "rule of law," were founded on race, which Amitav Ghosh helpfully denotes "the silenced term" in liberalism.[41] For liberals like Mill who remained invested in the idea of tutelage even after the mid-century crises, race was "the unstated term through which the gradualism of liberalism reconciled itself to the permanence of empire." Meanwhile, for others, race became more unapologetically embedded in practice *and* discourse.

But before we trace the evolution of that overtly racial historical imagination, it is important to acknowledge the palpable moral strain caused by the temporalizing ethics of liberal empire by the middle of the century. This, I think, was an important source of the appeal of William Gladstone, probably the defining politician of this time. Gladstone, leader of the Liberal Party, was known and trusted to make his politics conform to his earnestly Anglican religious beliefs and spoke a crusading language that appealed to evangelicals and radicals alike. His political style in the age of mass politics created by the expansion of suffrage was to unite his followers around a single idea of high moral voltage. He appealed because he seemed to possess moral integrity, to be willing to stand up for what was right, *regardless of circumstances*. The British public's attraction to such a figure is revealing, bespeaking a hunger for a simpler code of right and wrong.

And it had impact in the colonial realm. In the late 1860s, Gladstone applied a fresh moral lens to rebellion in Ireland, shifting from the pattern of response seen in Afghanistan, India, and Jamaica. Ernest Jones was far from the only denizen of the British Isles to seek inspiration from the Indian rebellion of 1857. Irish nationalists welcomed it with enthusiasm.[42] While the rebellion was crushed in 1858, Irish rebels began organizing as the Irish Republican Brotherhood, or "Fenians," launching a rising to free Ireland from British rule in 1867. It was against this backdrop that Mill privately condemned the "monstrous excesses committed & the brutal language used during & after the repression of the Indian mutiny."[43] In Parliament, too, while supporting leniency towards Fenian prisoners, he recalled disparagingly the "inhuman and indiscriminate massacre" in India, "the seizing of persons in all parts of the country and putting them to death without trial, and then boasting of it in a manner almost disgraceful to humanity."[44] At the end of 1867, Irish Republicans tried, in vain, to free an imprisoned Fenian from London's Clerkenwell Prison by blowing a hole in a wall. This "outrage" caused a panic, alienating even British radicals and stoking support for the Conservative government and its repressive measures against Fenians. But Gladstone, the Liberal leader in opposition at that time, responded differently. He saw the explosion as a measure of Irish grievance and became convinced that the British had a duty to address that grievance and pacify Ireland. When he was returned as prime minister in 1868, he immediately disestablished the Anglican Church in Ireland, passed legislation to improve the position of Catholic tenants vis-à-vis their Protestant landlords, and determined to put Ireland on the path to Home Rule, or dominion status. Gladstone was semiretired in the 1870s but swept back into power in 1880, again riding the rocket of a moral crusade, this time against the government's realpolitik support of the Ottoman Empire while it repressed Bulgarian Christians—the ghost of Byron was present here. He also challenged Conservatives' outright, unapologetic mode of imperial expansion in the failed adventures against the Zulus and a second failed war in Afghanistan.

And yet, Gladstone proved unable to resist the historical logic of liberal empire. It tested his moral integrity. He had always had a pragmatic streak: He had launched on the political scene as a Tory in the 1830s, and one of his earliest parliamentary speeches was a defense of the rights of West Indian slave owners—including his father, who owned vast plantations in Jamaica and Demerara. The incident reveals signs of both an active conscience and a powerful ability to manage conscience, a capacity for moral plasticity in different contexts. The extravagant compensation to slave owners for their loss in property after slavery was abolished in the empire in 1833 included the right to six years of bound labor from their former slaves. When this apprenticeship clause was up for repeal in 1838, Gladstone rose to defend it with arguments based on history: the need to honor past contracts and to ensure the future security of the value of the estates in question. He was self-aware enough, however, to sense the way this idiom overrode more transcendent moral values. That night after his speech, he confided to his diary his hope that his prayer for success in the debate was not "a blasphemous prayer, for support in pleading the cause of injustice."[45] It was this genuine concern with morality, coupled with a capacity for accommodation, even at the risk of a tortured inner life, that made him the politician for his time. After all, his goal of Home Rule for Ireland was also about finding the best way to preserve the union with that colony. And even while his government enhanced Irish freedoms in 1868, it annexed Basutoland and, soon after, Griqualand West to "ensure the safety of our South African Possessions."[46]

Thus, even Gladstone, despite his image of heedless moral courage, proved to be a dyed-in-the-wool liberal imperialist, willing to countenance conquest so long as it could claim to be morally inspired, a civilizing force. Under his ministry from 1880 to 1885, Britain expanded dramatically, especially in Africa. Egyptian pushback against informal British and French control in 1879 prompted growing British fears about the safety of investments in Egypt and of the Suez Canal, a vital imperial conduit since 1869. In 1882, with Colonel Urabi leading a massive Egyptian revolt, Britain bombarded Alexandria and shipped the Indian Army up the Red Sea, decisively defeating Egyptian forces and taking formal control of Egypt. Again, the cure for rebellion against empire was more empire. Some liberals were outraged; John Bright resigned from the Cabinet (though he did not call for withdrawal).[47] Gladstone did not pretend that material interests like canal and bonds were not the reason for his intervention; rather they were the very infrastructure of "civilization" that he had sought to protect. This was the classic liberal justification of empire. And this is what triggered the "scramble" for Africa.

Its extended lease on life was guaranteed by the work of leading late-Victorian historians, who, Stefan Collini writes, "remained convinced of the national, and particularly political, significance of their subject and of the education it could provide to the governors and administrators of the next generation."[48] Perhaps most influential was J. R. Seeley. Like many other important historians of the period, he based his books on lectures: Speaking as a professor, with the status of the teacher and academic, had grown in importance as a source of intellectual authority. Seeley delivered the lectures that formed the basis of his classic, *The Expansion of England* (1883), in 1881 and 1882, as the events in Egypt unfolded. The book was an instant bestseller, a favorite of prominent politicians like Joseph Chamberlain and Lord Rosebery, who as prime minister knighted Seeley. Seeley's goal in the book was to correct the island focus of most histories of eighteenth-century England, to write empire back into the story of England. Revisiting the Hastings trial, he perceived its cleansing effect: "For the stain of immorality *did* pass away as by magic." He nevertheless worked to scrub it out even more. He rehearsed eighteenth-century conquerors' protestations of accidental and incidental venality and aggression but went even further in arguing that England had not conquered India at all. British guilt had been for naught. For, not having had any sense of nationality in the eighteenth century, India could not have had a sense of what was "foreign," especially since the alleged "conquerors" were Indian mercenaries employed by the East India Company. India was tending towards anarchy as the Mughal Empire disintegrated and rival Indian rulers intrigued with competing European powers. It "lay there waiting to be picked up by somebody." (The Victorian version of "She was asking for it.") What happened was not a "foreign conquest" but an "internal revolution." Thus, Britain had nothing to atone for. He acknowledged mistakes but, like Maine, saw no way to undo them: "There are some deeds which, though they had been better not done, cannot be undone." They owed it to India to remain because India would be lost without the guiding British hand.[49]

The moral ground on which Seeley based empire was different from that of earlier liberals—it was not atonement for the sin of conquest but selfless performance of duty, putting India's interests before England's and providing stability for India's own ethical failure in tending towards anarchy rather than nationhood (a strange finding of fault, given that he knew he was speaking of "a population as large as that of Europe"). He repeatedly protested that leaving India would make little difference to Britain—even taking into account the vast trade and money invested there: "A Secretaryship of State would disappear; the work of Parliament would be lightened. Our foreign policy would be relieved of a great burden of anxiety. Otherwise little would immediately be changed." But, for India, England's departure would prove catastrophic. They *could* leave India, in this account, but actively chose to remain, in a heroic exercise of historical agency. The empire's purpose was not to turn Indians into Englishmen but to act as a bulwark against the anarchy towards which India otherwise would naturally tend, given its still incompetent sense of nationhood. Like Mill, Seeley saw imperial rule as a lesser evil, albeit arriving at that conclusion from a different route. His much-debated bon mot, that England had "conquered half the world in a fit of absence of mind" expressed his conviction that British rule in India was an act of magnanimity, that it was entirely in India's interests and, far from benefiting Britain, involved considerable British sacrifice.[50] The line captured, and fed, the British self-image as an eccentric—special—but essentially *good* people. "Absence of mind" implies lack of intention of any sort. It was the ultimate exculpatory phrase when it came to reckoning morally with the empire, given the centrality of intention to Victorian judgments of conscience.

Seeley's recalibrated historical explanation of liberal empire, rewriting its origins, justified it in a manner that diminished further need to justify it. It at once extended the life of the liberal justification of empire while making it redundant and allowing other sources of imperial enthusiasm to flourish. During his campaign, Gladstone had accused the Conservative prime minister, Benjamin Disraeli, of a lack of principle. But there were other "principles"—other historical imaginations shaping morality— at work in that Conservative jingoism, which ensured the Conservatives' victory after Gladstone misread the nature of imperial sentiment in 1885. Control of Egypt had included control of the Sudan, prompting rebellion there. Defying orders to evacuate, General Charles Gordon, the governor-general in charge, and his men were besieged by Sudanese forces at Khartoum. Gladstone reacted unhurriedly to Gordon's predicament, and Gordon's consequent death at the start of 1885 made Gordon a massively popular hero-martyr of the empire to the British public. Gladstone's subsequent attempt to push a bill through for Home Rule in Ireland in 1886 finally caused a catastrophic split in the Liberal Party. The last part of the nineteenth century is often described as the period of "High Imperialism," when all fig leaves were cast aside and Britons engaged in unapologetic pursuit and celebration of empire. How did they get from the need to examine conscience, so evident in 1858 and 1865, to this blithe state? Was it, in fact, as blithe as it seems? New ideas about history shifted modes of ethical accountability, shifted the needs of conscience, in this period. Liberal justifications of empire were certainly long in leaving, going by Gladstone's popularity. Beyond liberalism's appeal, too, consciences remained active, but they were accountable to an alternative, evolutionary view of history and historical agency and obligation.

This new historical outlook drew its lifeblood from the Darwinian revolution. Science became an increasingly important basis of knowledge in the Victorian era, albeit the domain of amateurs until professionalization in the last quarter of the century. The development of scientific authority was entangled with the imperial enterprise. Darwin himself emerged from the milieu of amateur explorers collecting plant and animal specimens around the empire and the world and exhibiting them in zoos and botanical gardens. As Britain brought Christian vengeance to bear against Indian rebels in 1858, he and Alfred Russel Wallace announced their theory of evolution by natural selection at the Linnean Society of London. The theory was that only species best suited to their environments would survive. Random variations in a constantly changing environment would determine a species' ability to evolve or perish. Darwin published *On the Origin of Species* the following year, aware of the potential controversy it would incite vis-à-vis Christian belief. But his work did not obviously resonate in debates about race. During the Morant Bay controversy in 1866, Darwin himself was solidly on the side of the liberals seeking to hold Eyre accountable.

The stage was set for applying Darwin's theories to the social world after publication in 1871 of *The Descent of Man*, which extended the theory of natural selection to the evolution of the human race. Darwin emphasized the purposelessness of the evolutionary process, unlike his forerunners (his grandfather Erasmus Darwin and the French naturalist Jean-Baptiste Lamarck). But later interpreters of his work hijacked it back into a progressive framework. Another member of the Jamaica Committee, Herbert Spencer, was simultaneously fascinated by evolution towards greater complexity as a process governing the development of the physical world, biological organisms, the cosmos, human culture, and more—as a universal law. This was a time in which various intellectual domains that we only recently thought of as markedly distinct—biology, history, economy, psychology, sociology, anthropology—were still intertwined (as they are again becoming today).[51] Eighteenth-century epistemes like moral philosophy and natural history retained purchase among intellectuals still enchanted with the notion of "universal" laws—thinkers like Kant and Priestley had thought of history in terms of species evolution in their own way. Spencer is, nevertheless, most associated with the idea of social Darwinism, the idea that the principles of evolution, including natural selection, apply to human societies, classes, and individuals in historical time as much as to biological species in geological time. Insofar as it was an endorsement of belief in the market as the mechanism that enabled such evolution, this idea fit squarely within the realm of liberal political-economic thought. But the idea that society would progress through the "survival of the fittest," a term Spencer coined, fueled the notion of competitive struggle not only between individuals but between nations and races.[52] Liberals had thought in terms of equal rights even if they did not believe all humans had equal potential and talent (evident in their faith in heroism and great men). Social Darwinism now assumed the inherent, biological inequality of humans—differing degrees of "fitness." Spencer himself opposed the idea of violent struggle between peoples, seeing such conflict as an atavism in an advanced age in which struggle ought to take the form of nonviolent economic competition, but popular conceptions of social Darwinism were not so discriminating.[53]

Darwin was a grandson of the abolitionist Erasmus Darwin. His first cousin was Francis Galton, son of the gunmaker and banker Samuel Tertius Galton. Francis Galton, partly as a result of his fascination with the great lineage that had culminated in his genetically determined brilliance, transformed these evolutionary ideas into a guide for action to shape the making of history.[54] He used the leisurely scholarly existence afforded by his family's gun fortune to hatch the idea of "eugenics," arguing that the human population would evolve best through controlled breeding designed to increase incidence of desirable hereditary traits. Later adopted by the Nazis, the idea was to perfect racial development by encouraging reproduction of healthy stock, promoting social hygiene, and preventing "multiplication of the unfit." Eugenics informed the furiously competitive European conquest of Africa near the end of the century, feeding the post-1857 view of racial difference and the limits of liberal universalism.

The idea of evolutionary struggle offered a new set of ethical justifications for empire, as historically minded as the earlier, liberal model. The new scientific ideologies of evolution and race were "broadly *historical* in their thrust," writes one scholar.[55] W. D. Hay, a fellow of the Royal Geographical

Society and author of the futuristic novel *Three Hundred Years Hence* (1881), provided a stark vision of how the "survival of the fittest" would, and must, play out, and how the new historical sensibility would underwrite the unfolding of history:

> Throughout the Century of Peace ... men's minds had become opened to the truth, had become sensible of the diversity of species, had become conscious of Nature's law of development. ... The stern logic of facts proclaimed the Negro and Chinaman below the level of the Caucasian, and incapacitated from advance towards his intellectual standard. To the development of the White Man, the Black Man and the Yellow must ever remain inferior, and as the former raised itself higher and yet higher, so did these latter seem to sink out of humanity and appear nearer and nearer to the brutes. ... It was now incontrovertible that the faculty of Reason was not possessed by them in the same degree as the White Man, nor could it be developed by them beyond a very low point. This was the essential difference that proved the worthlessness of the Inferior Races ... and that therefore placed them outside the pale of Humanity and its brotherhood.[56]

British rule could now be envisioned as permanent because full reform was no longer understood as possible. This was a radical shift in historical thinking that enabled Britons to imagine "progress" in the form of permanent domination by certain, exceptionally "fit" peoples. Such a vision of "progress" could even accommodate the elimination of some "unfit" peoples; however much it might pain the sensitive soul, such elimination must be tolerated, again, in the name of future benefit. The turn to racism did not entail abandonment of the historical understandings of ethical accountability in a time of imperial pursuit. The historical ethical idiom remained influential precisely by drawing new strength from racist ideas of the second half of the nineteenth century. The Indian, Jamaican, Irish, and Egyptian rebels of 1857, 1865, 1867, and 1879 may not have succeeded in shaking off British control, but they did compel the remaking of an ethical vision that had anchored imperialism for a century. It was supplanted by something darker and more ominous, and later rebels would in turn force further reconsideration.

The idea of racial improvement (or deterioration) also infused surviving liberal notions of gradual change. The progress narrative was imagined to play out over a much longer timescale. This had practical effects, as we have seen in Maine's approach already, in that rapid, coercive improvement of other races was deemed difficult for the present. In the short term, imperial officials must remain dutifully in loco parentis. Evolutionary theory gave the gloss of scientific validation to the retreat from liberal universalism after 1857. The dream of turning Indians into Englishmen was too deeply embedded in imperial thought and practice for abrupt disgorgement or total disavowal. But added to the justification of empire as civilizing mission was the notion of an imperial dam against anarchy. The historian Thomas Metcalf summarizes the situation: "As conservative imperialists could not repudiate the idea of 'progress,' so too did liberal imperialists inevitably embed notions of India's 'difference' in their thinking."[57] Seeley set India apart from colonies tied to Britain "by blood and religion," strengthening the empire's "ethnological unity."[58] A writer in the London *Times* caught the odor of the change in liberal thought while commenting on Britons' unnecessarily harsh, "arrogant and repellent" treatment of "natives" in India: Awkward as it was to "lay bare the defects of one's own countrymen," he discerned that though "we hate Slavery," now "we hate slaves too."[59]

James Fitzjames Stephen had worked hard to prosecute Eyre. He, like Macaulay, was a son of the abolition movement: His father had drawn up the 1833 Slavery Abolition Act and then served as undersecretary of state for the colonies with a view to overseeing its implementation. This bona fide liberal became Maine's successor on India's Imperial Legislative Council in 1869 where he oversaw a flood of new legislation. The shift in liberal outlook after 1858 shaped his unapologetic attitude towards British rule in India. On his return from India, he wrote *Liberty, Equality, Fraternity* (1872), in which he attacked John Stuart Mill's liberal justification of empire as a mockery of liberalism, feebly and unnecessarily striving to mask the reality that imperial governance was based on Britain's might. There was no need for pretended paternalism. In 1883, a successor on the Imperial Legislative Council, Courtney Ilbert, introduced a legislative amendment in the old-fashioned liberal mold to allow Indian magistrates in rural districts to try cases involving Europeans. Ilbert's belated Macaulayism provoked a crisis in the government and an open airing of debate on the philosophical basis of British rule in India. Stephen emerged the most prominent spokesman for those opposed to the Ilbert Bill. He argued in the *Times*, "[The British empire in India] represents a belligerent civilization, and no anomaly can be more striking or so dangerous as its administration by men, who being at the head of a Government founded on conquest, implying at every point the superiority of the conquering race, of their ideas, their institutions . . . and having no justification for its existence except that superiority, shrink from the open, uncompromising assertion of it, seek to apologize for their own position, and refuse, from whatever cause, to uphold and support it."[60] While Seeley was just then attempting to expunge the very notion of conquest from the historical record, Stephen argued frank and proud acceptance of it rather than guilty conscience about it. Britain might be Thucydides's Athens rather than Sparta. Through a different route, he arrived at the same conclusion as Seeley, that there was nothing to atone for. His authoritarian liberalism strove to banish doubt as Macaulay once had. Good government need not be representative government. For British rule in India to "represent the native principles of life or of the government," it would have to represent "heathenism and barbarism." Authoritarian government need not only be tolerated as a temporary expedient. Insofar as Britain was there to improve Indians, it did so not out of atonement for prior imperial sins but because of its greater virtue and superiority. The expansion of liberties like freedom of speech and reliance on persuasion as the vehicle of moral improvement were not the measure of the spread of liberty in history; rather, moral progress was a product of moral and legal coercion over time. Liberty was not necessary for good government. Doubtful of the trend towards democracy in Britain, too, Stephen held that man was at heart selfish and unruly; he lived peaceably and morally only if constantly compelled.[61] His view of human nature elided the distinction between savage and barbarian. If he broke the shackles of bad imperial conscience, he persisted in defending empire as a means of producing a certain kind of conscientious selfhood. English virtue—virtue as such—was embodied in English law, now bestowed on India; it was "the gospel of the English," made none the worse for the fact that it was a "compulsory gospel which admits of no dissent and no disobedience." It conducted the "moral conquest" of India; its influence was "comparable to that of a new religion."[62]

This faith rested on somewhat mythical ideas about both the law and the empire. In fact, the law was the instrument of capital that had enabled the theft of the commons in Britain and colonial dominance in India, indemnifying the British against violence inflicted on laborers, employees, and other subordinates.[63] Colonial rule was never actually about the rule of law but about the tension between the rule of law and "emergency powers" justifying exception to the law.[64] In any case, since the subcontinent was a patchwork of hundreds of nominally independent principalities interspersed with regions of direct British rule, in which different communities were ruled differently, it was a space of legal cacophony and jurisdictional confusion rather than the triumph of the rule of law.

Perhaps the greatest proof that Stephen was revising the ethical ground of empire was his revisiting of that scene of original sin, the Hastings drama, in an 1885 work.[65] That event had defined the liberal agenda of imperialism in terms of atonement, disavowing conquest as a legitimate basis for imperial rule. Stephen rehabilitated conquest from its criminal connotations, arguing that Britain's very capacity for conquest in the eighteenth century was what mattered: It proved Britons' inherent superiority, and that was enough to legitimize British rule. History had judged not relative virtue but *fitness,* or might, and might was now right.[66] This revision was, explicitly, an effort to promulgate a new historical script to guide action in the present. This illiberal liberalism strove to overcome the moral narrative of empire in order to provide a new guide to moral action: that Britons must act, in the name of progress, without moral compunction, even if that meant countenancing the loss of those that history deemed obsolete or weak. That the new ethos depended on the rewriting of the eighteenth-century past is also indicated by Lord Curzon's determination on becoming viceroy in 1899 to erect a monument to the victims of the Black Hole of Calcutta, the controversial incident involving the death of East India Company men in captivity in 1756 that Clive had claimed to avenge in the Battle of Plassey in 1757.[67] (Anticolonial activists successfully lobbied for the monument's removal in 1940.) The history of 1857 was also written anew. Gone was the agonizing doubt, the guilty knowledge of British sin: Histories published in the 1880s exonerated the British entirely from any taint of ruthlessness or excessive retaliation accrued as a result of the "hysterical cries of ignorant humanitarians."[68]

These British conversations were part of a broader European fascination with heroic action in this time. Stephen's 1872 book had offered this concluding advice: "In nearly all the . . . transactions whatever which have relation to the future, we have to take a leap in the dark."[69] The German philosopher Friedrich Nietzsche would have roundly endorsed that view. To Nietzsche, modern conscience was a form of self-sabotage that inhibited such boldness.[70] He grasped history's central role in it: His 1874 essay

"On the Use and Abuse of History for Life" explained that acting in the present requires forgetting the past, not feeling shackled by it.[71] Making history requires letting go of history—to avoid the kind of helplessness Galton and Maine felt. Nietzsche contended that excessive preoccupation with history and knowledge was smothering the aptitude for vital action in his time, feeding complacency, cynicism, and a separation between theoretical beliefs and lived reality. The same year, the essay *On Compromise* by the historian and Liberal politician John Morley, future secretary of state for India and biographer of several great men, also bemoaned the "abuse" of the "Historic Method," through which men evaded absolute commitment to principle.[72] Morley later authored an admiring biography of his hero William Gladstone. But Nietzsche was fascinated by Napoleon, and his next work built on Carlyle's ideas to envision a superman who might redeem a decadent and disenchanted age. Such a figure was, explicitly, someone beyond the limits of ordinary morality. The Nazis co-opted this idea, along with the eugenics ideas of the period.

To be sure, there were influential skeptics of this Carlylean view of history. Gladstone's dilatory approach to the Gordon crisis in 1885 emerged partly from just such an influence in the form of his intimate friend the Catholic historian John Acton (later Lord Acton), who succeeded Seeley as the regius professor of modern history at Cambridge in 1895. In the context of the debate about papal infallibility, in 1887—just two years after Gordon's death—Acton took a stand against the notion that any man was above judgment, that in fact those with power ought to be subject to more intense judgment, given power's corrupting influence. "Great men are almost always bad men," he pronounced. The belief that an office might sanctify its holder led inevitably to the notion that "the end learns to justify the means." Recalling politically motivated murders ordered by Queen Elizabeth and William III, he wrote, "Here are the greatest names coupled with the greatest crimes." Rather than spare them, he would have them hanged, for reasons of justice, but even more "for the sake of historical science."[73] But this was a contrarian point of view in a time of popular exultation in imperial heroism; Gladstone had fallen and the Conservatives went whole hog on empire. Moreover, Acton himself embraced deeply racialized notions of history. The "only makers of history, the only authors of advancement," he certified, were the Persians, Greeks, Romans, and Teutons. Others, such as the Celts, supplied "the materials rather than the impulse of history." Like Stephen, he held that "subjection to a people of a higher capacity for government is of itself no misfortune"; indeed, for "most countries," it was "the condition of their political advancement."[74]

These updated ideas of liberal empire, muddied by conservatism, shaped imperial policy in the late nineteenth century. In 1866, before the full flowering of evolutionary ideas of history, there was a famine in Orissa. A million perished, and the government did nothing. Lord Salisbury, the secretary of state for India, condemned officials' "fetish" for laissez-faire political economic notions. Privately, he confessed, "I never could feel that I was free from all blame for the result."[75] This confession did moral work. Despite his confessed guilt, Salisbury appointed Lord Lytton viceroy of India in 1876, during another devastating famine, fully aware of Lytton's commitment to laissez-faire notions. Salisbury had a conscience but felt it was his duty to override it, to contain the unreasonable operation of sympathy, to manage it. Having assured himself of his humanity by noting his qualms about the million dead in Orissa, he martyred his conscience to the greater cause of history. This was an enactment of a dutiful suppression of humane instinct—keeping the proverbial British stiff upper lip—in deference to the economic forces that he felt must have sway. He had to refuse to exercise his agency, had to pretend he did not have the capacity to act, in order to allow those greater forces to play out as they were destined to, for the greater good of humanity. He was not very different from Galton.

Famine killed twelve to thirty million Indians in the last quarter of the century.[76] The famine that began in 1876 and lasted until 1878 stalked the colonized world from Africa to Asia to South America. This disaster of planetary magnitude, costing the lives of millions, was caused by the interaction of drought and imperial policies. The mass deaths were the result not of regions being left out of the modern global economy but of their forcible integration into it, the need for the labor and resources of these regions in the London-centered global economy. That integration enabled drought to have shattering global impact. Indian cultivators' relationship to the land had been revolutionized (as Maine observed) and artisanal capacities defeated as agriculture had become geared towards monocultural production oriented to imperial commercial ends (indigo, opium, cotton). This revolution was not peaceably wrought or the "natural" result of market competition but the product of war, invasion, coercion, and tariffs structured to favor British manufactures. The creation of a rudimentary international weather reporting network by the 1870s made it possible to perceive the planetary scale of drought for the first time, but, the historian

Mike Davis explains, the very same forces of integration also meant that economic shock waves in one part of the world were felt globally, too. A new vicious cycle linked weather and price perturbations through the medium of an international grain market: "The price of wheat in Liverpool and the rainfall in Madras were variables in the same vast equation of human survival."[77] The British response to famine in India in this moment was blind to this actual unfolding of history. Instead, officials in charge, already in thrall to laissez-faire notions, found further sanction for inaction in the social Darwinist approach to history, according to which the death of entire peoples was at times necessary for progress. There was little government could or should do. Instead, they must allow natural laws to operate as they would. The government's Famine Commission Report of 1880 absolved the government of responsibility for the millions killed, pointing to the natural cause of drought and the consequent failure of crops.[78] The Whig view of history, infused with racial presumption, papered over the bloody unfolding of actual history. It saw India's provision of raw materials and consumption of British manufactures as a reflection of racial and cultural capacities expressed as comparative advantage rather than the product of war-driven and slavery-supported industrial revolution in Britain and deliberate efforts to crush Indian industrialism since the eighteenth century.[79] From the late nineteenth to early twentieth centuries, the empire enabled the spread of famine, plague, and war, and British officials addressed all three types of crises with mass encampment that was intended to simultaneously fulfill the demands of security and humanity but that proved lethal and traumatic and produced a noxious legacy in the form of twentieth-century concentration camps.[80] Encampment was designed to prevent the itinerancy of the poor, which was seen as particularly threatening to post-1857 British officials in India and invariably cast in criminal terms.

The effort to eradicate gangs of robbers in India provides another useful illustration of the impact of evolutionist history in the late Victorian period. Liberals had launched a campaign against the scourge of "thuggee" in the 1830s in the name of social reform. The thieving gangs in question were typically "highly miscellaneous" groups—laborers, gypsy-like groups (*banjaras*), disbanded soldiers, itinerant poor, and so on—but British depictions focused on demonic images of Kali worshippers in keeping with the "mysterious India" theme.[81] Subduing wandering groups became even more politically urgent after the rebellion, and the specter of thuggee assumed exaggerated proportions. In keeping with the new "science" of human differences, the Criminal Tribes Act of 1871 affirmed that certain groups were genetically predisposed to crime. Liberal notions of the "rule of law" and individual accountability fell by the wayside, for a genetic predisposition to crime meant there was no need to show that an individual had committed a particular crime. A person could be convicted simply on proof that he was a member of a Thug gang. Criminality was collective, based on caste affiliation understood as a hereditary category. Certainly, notions of genetic predisposition towards criminal behavior also emerged in England—a belief in natively "dangerous classes"—but the children of a habitual offender were not automatically convictable.[82] In India, racial differences were equated with different potential for moral development.

Evolutionary history likewise advised tolerance in the face of the mass death enabled by the new machine guns, which ended the long technological parity between Europeans and others, making it possible for Europeans to conquer Africa at last.[83] Robert Routledge's popular 1876 history of science lifted Adam Smith's language defending firearms a century earlier to assure those concerned about machine guns' destructive nature that they favored "the extension and permanence of civilization." Their complexity and expense—itself testimony to European genius—ensured that they could be wielded only by "wealthy and intelligent nations." But for a notable substitution of "race" for "nation," he echoed Smith's language almost verbatim (without citation) in arguing that firearms gave a necessary advantage to "opulent and civilized communities" over "poor and barbarous races," which were today "everywhere at the mercy of the wealthy and cultivated nations."[84] Here we witness the literal co-optation of the liberal historical narrative into the grislier evolutionary one. In his time, Smith had referred to arms with very different capacities and had envisioned progress more in the sense of a transformation of manners; Routledge mobilized Smith's language about firearms' civilizing impact to defend racial contest as a means of progress defined in evolutionary terms. Eighteenth-century guns' unreliability had enabled new kinds of violence by eliminating accountability for intention. Machine guns *were* reliable, however; Britons excused their use for intentionally violent purposes by recourse to a new historical sensibility in which violent elimination of certain categories of people was evolutionary progress.

This was the period that shaped Churchill, the historian, man of action, and politician who dominated Britain's political scene in the first half of the twentieth century. He was conscious of his own historic destiny as a descendant of the Duke of Marlborough and of England's historic destiny based on its proven might. After early military adventures on the North West Frontier of India, he joined Herbert Kitchener's campaign to avenge the death of Gordon in the Sudan in 1898—as the fall of Kabul had been avenged in 1842 and the mutiny of Indians in 1857. At the Battle of Omdurman he witnessed the most gruesome demonstration of the power of machine guns. After five hours of fighting, there were forty British dead and eleven thousand Sudanese. We will hear more of Churchill in later chapters, but his expressed willingness to contemplate the elimination of mass numbers of people for the sake of human progress is testimony to the power of a late-Victorian historical sensibility grounded in evolutionism. In 1910, as home secretary, he proposed that one hundred thousand "degenerate" Britons be forcibly sterilized and others put in labor camps to save the British "race" from decline.[85] His rant in the 1930s on the subject of Palestine makes clear the influence of evolutionary historical notions on his unapologetic readiness to wage violence for empire out of a sense that "the Aryan stock is bound to triumph."[86] Accordingly, he explained, "I do not admit . . . that a great wrong has been done to the Red Indians of America or the black people of Australia. I do not admit that a wrong has been done to these people by the fact that a stronger race, a higher-grade race, a more worldly-wise race to put it that way, has come in and taken their place."[87] He oversaw the deaths of three million Bengalis in 1943 as the result of a famine created by wartime grain distribution policies. Explaining his refusal to send aid, he invoked the vision of "Indians breeding like rabbits."[88]

The influence of such thinking was never absolute. Social Darwinist theories competed with new ideas of poverty stimulated by the global economic recession that began in 1873. The overnight increase in unemployment rates in Britain made it obvious that poverty was the result of systemic causes. A new concept of "the social" mitigated older liberal notions of poverty as a reflection of individual moral failure. The job of government was increasingly understood to be that of intervening to prevent hunger.[89] Works like *Progress and Poverty* (1879) by the American Henry George, who visited India, questioned the wisdom of liberal political economy, asking why poverty persisted despite economic and technological progress. This work deeply influenced the founder of Britain's first socialist party, H. M. Hyndman. Hyndman, who popularized the works of

Marx in English, criticized the 1880 Famine Commission Report on India: "We attribute all suffering under native governments to native misrule; our own errors we father on 'Nature.'"[90] Indian critics like Dadabhai Naoroji likewise wondered why the British failed to see that they were the cause of the destruction that followed droughts: "Why blame poor Nature when the fault lies at your own door?"[91] Naoroji became a member of Parliament in London for the Liberal Party with the help of Irish nationalists. I will have more to say about his revisionist take on the history of British rule in India; I invoke him and Hyndman here for the way they sought to expose the fraud of the social Darwinist theory of British rule in India.

At the end of the century, the radical journalist William Digby was certain that historians would consider the "unnecessary deaths of millions of Indians" as the "principal and most notorious monument" of the nineteenth century.[92] The naturalist Alfred Russel Wallace considered the mass starvation not a "natural disaster," but avoidable. His 1898 audit of the century, *The Wonderful Century*, openly called out the way narratives about the spread of security, commerce, and civilization "distract attention from the starvation and wretchedness and death-dealing trades at home, and the thinly veiled slavery in many of our tropical or sub-tropical colonies." The empire's failure was obvious: "The condemnation of our system of rule . . . is to be plainly seen in plague and famine running riot in India after more than a century of British rule and nearly forty years of the supreme power of the English government. Neither plague nor famine occurs to-day in well-governed communities. That the latter . . . is almost chronic in India, a country with an industrious people and a fertile soil, is the direct result of governing in the interests of the ruling classes instead of making the interests of the governed the first and the only object." Generous as Wallace was towards Indians here, he did not think they were worse off than immiserated workers in Britain itself. He judged the condition of the latter "even more disgraceful than the . . . famines of remote India" in proportion to British wealth and their nearness to the center of government. The comparison of misery is always invidious and has been the bane of disputes about the merits of abolitionist sentiment by those unperturbed by the vigorous exploitation of factory labor in England itself. Without wading into such a debate, we might still diagnose Wallace as succumbing to the liberal habit of contained sympathy. The death of millions at British hands, however far from London, was a crime against humanity. His rhetorical equation of mass deaths with the chronic suffering of the poor spared him from acknowledging the particular illegitimacy of imperial rule abroad. Once again, the problem was bad governance, not illegitimate rule. He concluded, "Both are the result of the same system . . . and both alike are the most terrible failures of the century." This was not "progress, but retrogression." He predicted that historians would look back and see that the Victorians were "morally and socially unfit" and "that our boasted civilization was in many respects a mere surface veneer."[93] With this assessment of moral "fitness," Wallace explicitly pushed back against the legitimacy of the evolutionary narrative of historical progress. Though he was a founding proponent of natural selection theory, he opposed the eugenics view of history, judging contemporary society too corrupt to allow reasonable assessment of relative fitness.

Too many historians have yet to realize Digby's and Wallace's prophecies and fully acknowledge the grim reality of Victorian empire, even after passionate anticolonial movements fully exposed it.[94] This says something about the historical discipline. Charles Dickens's appeal to social conscience has proved more lasting, untainted even by his racism. Despite real moral shame about British imperial rule by the end of the nineteenth century, despite the exposure of the "apologies" of empire as mere apologies, the pursuit of empire went on. Digby and Wallace indicted the present by forcing their readers to adopt the viewpoint of history as judge: How will historians judge us? they asked. But they did not realize how much of the shameful present had been enabled by historians in their own time, by the likes of Mill, Maine, Seeley, and Stephen, who in their continual rewriting of the past, especially the Hastings trial, authored new ethical scripts for empire in their present. Historians continue to do this today (more on this in Chapter 6). A historian at the University of Sussex recently caricatured the dynamic implied by such exhortations to mind the future judgment of history, as though historians were not already shaping the present (see accompanying image).

Today historians like myself quote the likes of Digby and Wallace for the evidence they offer of just how atrocious British rule was—enough to offend even some Britons in that moment. But Hyndman, Wallace, and so on were not a few good men among a sea of monsters. It was their critique, the moral compass that they provided, like Burke's in the eighteenth century, that enabled the idea of empire to survive intact while its excesses came under attack. There were no monsters; liberals, as much as conservatives, believed in the legitimacy of empire. I don't mean to scant the rich

Chris Kempshall
@ChrisKempshall

People: 'Historians in the future will judge this harshly'
Historians: 'We already have thoughts.'
People: 'I wonder how the history books will explain this?'
Historians: 'Well actually–'
People: 'We'll have to wait and see...'
Historians: 'Oh for the love of God.'

3:45 PM · 12/14/18 · Twitter for iPhone

Twitter frame of an imaginary exchange, 2018. (Courtesy of Chris Kempshall)

vein of British socialist and anti-imperialist thought in this period, which bore important fruit in the next century, as we will see.[95] But, insofar as they stopped short of challenging the historical sensibility underlying so much of public ethics by this time, their critical edge was blunted. The most famous turn-of-the-century liberal critic of empire, J. A. Hobson, whose work would inspire Lenin's critique of imperialism as the highest stage of capitalism, objected to empire, but, more specifically, he objected to it being hijacked by capitalist oligarchs from its legitimate task of offering morally inspired tutelage to backward people as part of a "rational cosmic plan," as he put it in a 1897 article titled "Ethics of Empire."[96] The dynamic of apology and aggression together allowed the enterprise to endure. Critical as they were, liberals were not calling for India's freedom. Building on the abolitionist tradition, late-nineteenth-century humanitarian movements focusing on coercive labor systems, especially in other European colonies like the Belgian Congo, fortified the trusteeship justification of empire. These movements emerged less from the evangelical Christian ethics of the earlier period but were informed by similar notions of individual responsibility and altruism: Even Victorian "unbelievers" subscribed to a "rhetoric of sincerity," the moral duty of being true to oneself, to demonstrate the sovereignty of the secular self.[97] The scandal for them, too, was not empire but the miscarriage of its objective of trusteeship. They supported the establishment of the Indian National Congress in 1885 not to encourage anticolonial sentiment but for the moderating purpose of creating an outlet for it to prevent truly revolutionary colonial unrest.[98]

They and the Indian elites who joined the Congress asked for change by appealing to the English conscience, their voices growing louder from the sidelines through the turn-of-the-century scandals of the concentration camps of the South African War. But much of British society had learned that real virtue lay in overriding the impulses of the unsophisticated vestiges of premodern conscience—which had led them, for instance, to foolishly carry a burden of guilt about eighteenth-century conquest. Instead they must defer to the higher-order morality of an updated historical sensibility that saw progress in economic and biological terms. Like Salisbury, they recognized but knew better than to become susceptible to momentary moral compunctions. The historical stakes were too great. As the Irish playwright George Bernard Shaw explained in an 1897 play, the Englishman "is never at a loss for an effective moral attitude. As the great champion of freedom . . . he conquers and annexes half the world. . . . There is nothing so bad or so good that you will not find Englishmen doing it; but you will never find an Englishman in the wrong. He does everything on principle. . . . His watchword is always duty; and he never forgets that the nation which lets its duty get on the opposite side to its interest is lost."[99] Fittingly, this speech (quoted in the epigraph to this chapter) comes from the mouth of Napoleon, the epitome of impenitent pursuit of glory. Shaw finishes by calling the English cynical—aligning principle with their interest. But they did not see themselves as cynics. They were, emphatically, in earnest, hence the sanctimonious "moral attitude." Late-Victorian Britons were not so much unapologetic about empire but believed in the value of willfully overcoming the naive impulse to apologize for the sake of historical progress. They made a pact with history and strained to do so without the guilt that burdened Faust.

Their sense of high historical stakes was founded ultimately on a sense of the precariousness of Britain's global supremacy by the end of the century. History must prove that the British did have might and were innately superior, for the claimants to such fitness were multiplying as

Germany, the United States, and Japan rivaled Britain's imperial and economic power. The imperial expansion of the period was part of a panicky effort to prove that in the contest of survival of the fittest, Britain would prevail. That was not obvious, going by the state of Britain at home. In a deeply interconnected world, rivalries grew more pronounced. National myths became dearer as the world grew more international. Darwinist notions shaped understandings of the contest among nations for Great Power status. Francis Galton established his Eugenics Laboratory at University College in London in 1904; around the world, biologists and politicians contemplated the implications of eugenicist ideas. As Churchill's quote as home secretary in 1910 attests, anxiety about Britain's racial decline was rampant, stoked especially by the poor state of recruits for the turn-of-the-century war in South Africa. Empire boosters from Rudyard Kipling to Lord Curzon harbored an inner core of doubt and fear as challenges to British rule not only persisted but grew stronger and offered alternative narrative framings in which the end of history was not Indian Englishmen but the end of empire itself. While the end remained uncertain, British officials could continue to imagine themselves unaccountable to any authority but the story of imperial might and order they had authored. Colonies remained sites of exception where they could behave with relative impunity.

To be sure, scandals like the South African concentration camps erupted, recalibrating the balance between apologetic and unapologetic justifications of empire. (Those who defended the camps did so in classical liberal terms—as a technology for protection that had unintentionally become massively lethal.[100]) But in 1919, General Reginald Dyer was able to act much as Governor Eyre had in 1865, massacring Indians gathered in a garden in Amritsar, Punjab; a similar drama of divided British public response followed.[101] Churchill asserted that the event was an exception "without precedent or parallel" in the history of the empire.[102] But in fact the precedents were many, and Churchill had participated in a few himself. The "cold-blooded approval of the deed" in many British quarters "shocked" the future prime minister of India Jawaharlal Nehru into an irrevocable realization of "how brutal and immoral imperialism was, and how it had eaten into the souls of the British upper classes."[103] On his death in 1927, Dyer was given the funeral of a national hero. The evolutionist historical perspective called for deference to biological and economic forces greater than man. Though a great man might occasionally act in the furtherance of progress—like Kitchener at Omdurman or Dyer at Amritsar—in its demand that men suppress their instinctive desire to act out of compassion, this was a historical imagination that diminished Britons' sense of individual historic agency. In India, the sense of one's duty *not* to act in the face of famine, for instance, was compounded by British officials' growing awareness of being cogs in a vast administrative machine designed to allow "natural laws" to do their work. From the 1830s to the 1870s, the British empire in India functioned more bureaucratically.[104] Less a playground for adventurers to enact heroic fantasies, it was the realm of endless paperwork, the daily grind of menial tasks, in which ethical decisions about whether to act in a time of famine were reduced to signing off on routine administrative correspondence. (The insubordinate Gordon of Khartoum caught the imagination of the British public partly because it was hungry for stories of heroic men on the spot.[105]) Even a great man, as Salisbury surely saw himself, could not exercise greatness thus constrained. Officials perceived limits on their scope for individual action in an administrative hive that was itself understood as the fulfillment of a historic destiny, just as Galton could not see how to take major steps in his industrial hive.

In the early years of the twentieth century, the German social theorist Max Weber, who was much influenced by social Darwinism and evolutionary thought, looked upon this development with worry. Highly bureaucratic forms of social organization were a measure of cultural progress but also an "iron cage" that risked dehumanizing individuals into cogs in the machine.[106] Bureaucratic inertia created modern individuals incapable of principled moral action. They were part of modernity's "disenchantment of the world," explained Weber, quoting the Romantic Schiller.[107] We have seen the audacious sense of personal agency that animated empire- and nation-builders of the eighteenth century, which built on and fueled Enlightenment and Romantic ideas of history as the work of great men. Weber described such individuals as "persons of vocation" or, alternatively, "charismatic individuals."[108] He traced their empowered sense of agency to the Reformation: The history of capitalism was the result of the Protestant work ethic, though it had yielded a society offering little space to such individualism. Reflecting on the history of the nineteenth century, Weber theorized charismatic leadership as a revolutionary, highly personal form of political authority, perceived by its followers as rooted in godlike powers and unaccountable to worldly moral norms. He hoped the possibility of such leaders might mitigate against the dangers of rational-bureaucratic rule, though at the end of World War I, a war that seemed to reveal in the most tragic and irrevocable way the impossibility of individual heroism in the modern era, he was pessimistic in the extreme: "How is it *at all possible* to salvage any remnants of 'individual' freedom of movement *in any sense* given this all-powerful trend towards bureaucratisation?"[109] His pessimism about modernity extended to a pessimism about the possibility of historical progress.

The price of disenchantment was cultural as much as political and social: loss of "sublime values" and dissipated art. British cultural commentators were also prey to disillusionment about the promises of the liberal industrial order in their perception of cultural decline in the midst of historic economic and technological progress. Their assault on the presumption of historical progress took the form of imagining time standing still—a nostalgia that echoed the Romantics but abandoned any liberatory narrative vis-à-vis the colonies. The Crown-ruled colonies were celebrated as places where, through heroic—historic—sacrifice and effort, the British had created a refuge *from* history. Great men had wrested the colonies from the grip of those natural laws governing history everywhere. In India, at least, they felt, aristocratic grace and a traditional order had been preserved. The founders of the Arts and Crafts movement, William Morris and John Ruskin, known for their concern about the conditions of industrial workers, found gratification in India's stubborn attachment to artisanal traditions and immunity to industrial progress. Other socialists lamented the failure of liberal political economy, but Morris and Ruskin merely appreciated the result. They argued for the moral virtue of defying progress. Medievalism was the rage, inspiring the aesthetic of "Victorian Gothic." Modernist fascination with the primitive was also part of an incipient cultural relativism that endeavored to interpret "the cataclysmically expanding and collapsing modern world."[110]

Indeed, the hankering after times lost was partly triggered by the unraveling of the very notions of time on which faith in progress had been founded. The eschatology of Marxist and liberal historical time had been based on the template of religious, Christian time, but by the late nineteenth century, the work of evolutionary biologists and geologists had made muck of inherited notions of time. From the "cramped temporal estimates of Biblical chronology," the earth's age now oscillated between millions of years and infinity, notes the historian Stephen Kern.[111] In this limitless span, the history of mankind appeared parenthetical at most, raising doubts about the meaning of existence and the workings of the universe, and shaking the comfortable certainties underlying the liberal narrative of progress. Meanwhile, telegraphs, railways, and steamships created a new kind of time travel for information, prices, and people—at times with devastating effects, as we have seen with the famine of 1876.[112] Railways, especially, were said to "annihilate" time and space. Time also became money with hourly wages. The spread of factories displaced the "task time" of the artisanal and agricultural way of life with "disciplinary time" that clearly demarcated work and leisure and in which minute-to-minute motions of the body were choreographed and regulated for machinelike efficiency, to the tune of bells and clocks. The diffusion of homogeneous, empty time through technologies of communication such as daily newspapers and telegraphs was critical to modern nationalism, allowing people to imagine themselves as participants of such wider communities.[113] Enthusiasts nurtured utopian visions of universal time that permits unhindered flow of people, goods, and ideas and thus worldwide progress. But many were also disturbed by the new uniform time and its effects. The more time became empty, uniform, quantifiable, monetizable, the more it became narratable in terms of the secular march of progress, as history, year by uniform year, the more many Britons longed for nonempty time, an experience of the fullness of time. This was time that could not be narrated in linear fashion, that was not teleological but palimpsestic, a telescoping of past, present, future in each lived moment. Philosophers expressed doubt about the notion of time adopted by historical thinkers like Spencer. The French philosopher Henri Bergson argued that the very evanescence of time made it unamenable to the kind of measurement presumed by notions of uniform, serial time that were the backbone of historical thought. He proposed instead the notion of *durée*, time as something pervasive, ineffable, and unrepresentable, accessible only through intuition and the imagination. Man experienced time in this manner, in its fullness.

The combination of the dream of recovering this experience of time with an already deeply internalized historical sensibility could be imaginatively fruitful. In his utopian novel *News from Nowhere* (1890), Morris envisioned a historical path to his ideal society—a period of revolutionary conflict—but that society's utopian-ness lay precisely in its timelessness: The book's subtitle was *An Epoch of Rest*.[114] It is a place that has escaped the relentless churning of history, a kind of rural idyll, a romance of the pre-industrial English past. This vision was at odds with most exemplars of the genre of futuristic socialist utopias that so represented this time, a genre all about imagining future payoff for present struggle. Others included the American Edward Bellamy's *Looking Backward* (1888), which envisioned an unapologetically industrial socialist future, and W. D. Hay's *Three Hundred Years Hence,* whose social Darwinist affirmation of the idea of progress conjured an all-white socialist utopia in the future. Morris's ideas inspired Robert Blatchford, author of perhaps the best-selling socialist work of the period, *Merrie England* (1893), which likewise emphasized the value of the arts and the culture of the English countryside. As its title suggests, it offered an autarkic "Little England" ideal in place of the image of England as the workshop of the world.[115] This was a futuristic vision, but Blatchford's own sense of commitments to the past made it impossible for him to imagine a route to it. Thus he argued, "We ought never to have conquered India; very well. But we *did* conquer it, and we must govern and defend it, or give it up. And if we are to give it, to whom is it to be given, and *when,* and *how?*"[116] The dream of "Little England" would continue to offer an antidote to the reality of the imperial past, as we shall see, and the search for an experience of the fullness of time would also shape the history of twentieth-century imperialism.

But before drawing the curtain on the nineteenth century, I want to briefly describe how moral skepticism about progress shaped policy prescriptions of the post-mutiny order in India. Though Western education went on and the queen pledged to an equal system of government in 1858, hardening ideas of permanent difference informed the idea that policy must be tailored to unchanging communities. If Indians could not be made into Britons, they might be best ruled through their own, "traditional" institutions. Maine's ideas about "traditional" forms were important here. Indirect rule became the new mantra. The rebellion had shown the enduring influence of Indian princes, and so future expansion would take the form of ruling indirectly through them rather than outright annexation—colonial India's "princely states."[117] This would also, in theory, make the British presence less obtrusive. The "Victorian Gothic" celebrated the alliance of the seemingly feudal power of princes with the pomp of the British crown.[118] At the same time, the idea of evolutionary struggle gave policymakers confidence in the rightness of these policies and of their continued presumption to make policy.

Indirect rule found acceptance as the proper way to govern racial others who could not be expected to conform to any universal civilizational standard: It was exported to Malaya, Fiji, sub-Saharan Africa, and elsewhere. Supported by emerging notions of cultural relativism, the goal was to protectively maintain newly annexed territories in a museum-like manner, while their resources were exploited for wider global development: This was how the colonial administrator Frederick Lugard would summarize the "dual mandate" fulfilled by indirect rule in his influential 1922 book *The Dual Mandate in British Tropical Africa*.[119] Insofar as the protective role was understood as a patient shepherding of "natives" as they progressed through their own institutions, the approach preserved much of the ethos and appeal of liberalism, as evolutionary history in general did. (The leader of the new Labour Party, Ramsay MacDonald, who was much influenced by Hobson, supported a similar vision of the empire.[120]) It was not understood merely in terms of expediency,[121] but rather continued to present imperialism as the performance of a paternalistic moral duty to native society—and a moral duty to Britons themselves. For, they were engaged in a belated but heroic struggle to preserve the rest of the world as a patrimony for mankind's future. Second, they were, equally heroically, allowing evolutionary laws to run their course by tolerating the mass death that was endemic to the expansion that put them in the position to preserve. This was an ethics informed by a blend of the evolutionist historical imagination and the embrace of tradition as timeless.

The late-Victorian preservationist outlook required more precise knowledge of custom, and the tools and rubrics of scientific racism were mobilized to this end. Colonial officials conducted ethnographic surveys, using anthropometric techniques to identify and classify and govern different communities, understood in biological terms. This data was simultaneously understood to be historically informative for the light it could shed on the evolutionary history of Aryan civilization (of which India represented an ancient version, and Britain the apex). In India, ethnography came to be based on scientific claims, and data about caste and ethnicity were enrolled in censuses and revenue records that formed the basis for imperial administration. Though anthropology offered the primary methodology in achieving empire's new administrative ends, as opposed to the historical-textual methods favored earlier, its importance was founded, morally, on particular, evolutionary theories of history.[122] Holding a place in timeless suspension, or watching its "naturally" induced destruction, required no apology. Imperial officials had no agency in this.

The power of Victorian historical narratives cannot be underestimated. The story of empire is one in which the villains of history, if there are any, were historians themselves, partly because of their idolatrous belief in the power of the individual. Carlyle and his ilk offered historical visions that indulged the great-man pretensions of those who sought license to exceed ordinary moral bounds in their actions. The liberals screwed their eyes shut and put their fingers in their ears, muttering "progress." The social Darwinists and Marxists sympathized with the reflexive pity that violence abroad aroused but counseled stoic tolerance in the name of momentous ends. The nineteenth century pivoted around these modes of history-writing. At its start, a liberal universalist vision of history condoned expansion and violence in the name of progress; by its end, a racist historical outlook similarly condoned expansion and violence in the name of progress. The kind of progress envisioned shifted between these two main modes of thought, but the teleological format of history itself enabled tolerance of pain as merely birthing pain in the cause of some greater epochal labor.

If history was the cover story, the enabling soother of imperial conscience, other forms of expression, other moral compasses that could not be fully suppressed, gave it the lie. The sneaking suspicion that all this was rot, that the moral case for empire was rotten, bubbled below the surface, as we have seen with Gladstone's electric appeal in the 1860s. Most famously, Joseph Conrad's novella *The Heart of Darkness* (1899) unmasked the moral bankruptcy of the imperial endeavor—albeit obliquely, displacing focus onto a Belgian colony, the Belgian Congo. The rogue ivory trader Mr. Kurtz is a prodigy and poet, "an emissary of pity, and science, and progress," with the heroic ambition typical of the liberal-romantic empire-maker. He has extraordinary qualities and a powerful sense of agency: "higher intelligence, wide sympathies, a singleness of purpose." But he ultimately unmasks the darkness of the seemingly uplifting liberal imperial mission, its direct path to the evolutionist tolerance of mass elimination: At the end of his immaculate report for the quintessentially liberal International Society for the Suppression of Savage Customs, Kurtz scrawls, "Exterminate all the brutes!" Conrad recognizes the Victorian elision between upliftment and genocide as the madness that it is. On his deathbed, the rationalizations of history dissolve and Kurtz confronts the reality of another, more primordial ethical compass, whispering the final judgment, "The horror! The horror!"[123] The novel's narrator, the seaman Charles Marlowe, is wizened by the experience and returns to Europe doubtful of the "civilized" world: What was savagery and what, civilization? Like most British critics of empire in this moment, Conrad stopped short, however, of envisioning a "fully realized alternative to imperialism."[124]

The Romantics sought to capture the moral peril of the hunger for power and knowledge: Frankenstein, "horror-stricken" by his monster, goes mad and becomes one with him. Frankenstein's is an individual tragedy—the wages of his personal arrogance; Kurtz's tragedy is societal ("All Europe contributed to the making of Kurtz," writes Conrad), calling into question the human capacity for civilization. World War I amplified this question in shattering ways. And yet, in its shadow, the British reassembled the narrative of liberal empire all over again. That cultural feat is the subject of Chapter 4. But the reassembled narrative came with a twist—one augured by an encounter that transcends the divide between fiction and nonfiction. In the Congo, Conrad encountered a young Anglo-Irish civil servant, Roger Casement, son of a veteran of the 1842 war in Afghanistan. Casement went on to great fame for exposing Belgian atrocities against the Congolese (commissioned to do so by a British government recovering from controversy about its own human rights abuses in South Africa). He was knighted after his subsequent uncovering of rubber slavery committed by a British company in Peru. But knighthood did not tame the poet Casement. He turned revolutionary, joining the effort to free Ireland, liaising with Indian revolutionaries, too. During World War I, he worked to smuggle German guns into Ireland for the ill-fated Easter Rising of 1916, for which he was stripped of his knighthood and executed for treason. His story foreshadowed the dawn of new kinds of secret and doubled agency that would shape twentieth-century notions of history and historical action as empire faced new challenges.

CHAPTER FOUR

⸗ The Redemption of Progress

> Those who dream by night in the dusty recesses of their
> minds wake in the day to find that it was vanity; but the
> dreamers of the day are dangerous men, for they may
> act their dream with open eyes, to make it possible.
>
> —T. E. Lawrence

⸗ *As the British fell prey to* a sense of vulner-
ability, an arms race between the Great Powers vying for supremacy raised
more doubts about the narrative of progress. Would they produce a massive destructive war? In this moment, around 1907, a descendant of the
eighteenth-century Quaker Sampson Lloyd reflected approvingly on the
Galton affair of 1795. Considering Galton's arguments through glasses
tinted rose by the recent conquest of Africa, this younger Lloyd recalled a
childhood encounter with the missionary explorer David Livingstone, a
"peaceable man" who affirmed the usefulness of guns for an Englishman
in Africa.[1] But in this tense international moment, Lloyd also deplored the
statesmen driving an arms buildup that threatened war between "Christian nations." That seemed to him to fall outside the liberal narrative of
historical progress, which envisioned violent struggle only against uncivi-
lized "others" beyond Europe. But the Christian bond evaporated in the
heated contest of twentieth-century nationalism. Seven years later, Lloyd's
worst fear came true as the machine guns used to conquer Africa created
a bloodbath in Europe—the First World War. "Christian nations" were
coping with a range of cultural challenges, including doubt about foundational biblical chronology, as we have seen—this, too, was part of the
turn-of-the-century crisis of liberalism (in Britain, manifested also in

suffragette militancy, massive workers' strikes, and brinkmanship over Irish Home Rule). From the late nineteenth century, Britons yearning for an experience of the fullness of time turned towards new kinds of spiritualism. Aesthetic revulsion at the fruits of capitalism, epitomized by William Morris's Arts and Crafts movement, reinforced an interest in the mystical. Fascination with occultism flourished in the search for release from capitalist time. Discovery of the invisible electromagnetic forces that made wireless telegraphy possible encouraged a "will to believe" in all manner of invisible, seemingly magical telekinetic and telepathic phenomena, including the active agency of spirits and the divine in the real world.[2] Christian orthodoxy may have lost some purchase, but elites, especially, dove into the world of medieval and Renaissance Christian mysticism and other forms of spiritualism, searching for what the historian Alex Owen describes as an "immediate experience of and oneness with a variously conceived divinity."[3] According to Christian tradition, we rejoin with deceased loved ones after the resurrection on the Day of Judgment; spiritualism opened up the possibility of encountering them *now*, in the very historical time spiritualists sought to escape. In this it was "very much a product of a modern sense of secular time and of a world far removed from that of traditional religious sensibilities," explains the historian Thomas Laqueur.[4] Orientalist interests in "Eastern" mystical traditions dovetailed with this search, fueling the invention of universalist mystical philosophies like Theosophy. Henri Bergson's mystical ideas, themselves unimaginable without Europe's long engagement with "oriental" thought, were part of this intellectual swirl; many Bergsonians shared an interest in the occult. Workers in factories resisted time-discipline in a variety of ways, earning a reputation for rebellion, laziness, and lack of initiative and drive; occultism was the bourgeois resistance to uniform time and the rational economic action it enabled. Rebellion against the normalization of empty, secular time was wide, if not universal. Change was not unidirectional, however much whiggish historians hoped it would be.

The spiritualist trend introduced new ideas about agency that shaped the reinvention of empire in the twentieth century. A "medium" was central to spiritualist practice and revived ideas of split selfhood (which also found new scientific sanction in Freudian theory). Typically female, it consisted of a being in a middle position, a transmitter of the agency of occult beings. It subversively endowed women with agency by denying that this agency was their own.[5] But the notion of the gifted man was also in the air, building on Victorian ideals of heroism. It is no coincidence, given this backdrop, that British imperial expansion transpired in the ancient seat of occultism, the Middle East, in the era of World War I. Notions of the occult agencies alive in the region dramatically shaped British activity there, inspiring paranoid historical narratives among "experts" who themselves claimed preternatural understanding of the region. These narratives licensed violent imperial activity in the Middle East—much of it covert, since explicitly imperialistic actions increasingly risked condemnation at home and abroad. The remaking of notions of expertise and of experts' relationships to state institutions, meanwhile, shook the foundations of historians' institutional authority, opening the door to their displacement by social scientists in corridors of power.

The young men who greeted the announcement of war with excitement in July 1914 looked forward to the opportunity for revitalizing chivalric glory and escaping dull bourgeois existence. Stalemated trench warfare soon revised expectations. Many took comfort from the idea, dating from the Enlightenment, that seemingly evil events are necessary for progress: This most painful episode in history might in fact be the apocalyptic end to which history had been heading all along, the cataclysm preceding ultimate peace, the "war to end all wars." Nevertheless, those in the trenches confronted a frustrating loss of agency in a war of attrition. For middle-class soldiers raised on the Romantic poets, the technological nightmare of attrition left little room for fulfillment of the Byronic vision of individual heroism. Soldier-poets struggled to convey the unspeakable pain and horror caused by military paralysis and stillborn battlefield agency. Bitterness produced satire, too: Perhaps no one was better positioned to mock the dashing of heroic hopes than Lytton Strachey, descended from a long line of Indian officials, named after a viceroy, and author of a four hundred–page hagiographic dissertation on Warren Hastings. In 1918, his book *Eminent Victorians* skewered Victorian ideals of heroism, particularly the hypocritical penchant for violence in pursuit of allegedly divine aims.[6]

But the ideal of heroism survived via new notions of occult agency in the desert, particularly the story of Lawrence of Arabia. Soldiers in the Middle East, perhaps uniquely, found some expectations of war-as-romance fulfilled. The Palestine campaign, in which Britain fought Germany's Ottoman ally, was hailed as the "last crusade."[7] Moreover, in his history of the campaign, *Seven Pillars of Wisdom* (1926), T. E. Lawrence self-consciously undertook to narrate it as a heroic tale: "My proper share was a minor one, but because of a fluent pen . . . I took upon myself . . . a mock primacy."[8] Indeed, his actions were shaped by his ambition to acquire experiences worthy of an epic historical account.[9] The recovery of great-man history on a *legendary* scale was part of his search for escape from the "iron cage" of time. His account explicitly strove to transcend its historical empiricism with an antihistorical preoccupation with the power of the desert setting and his own avowedly epic intentions and creative license.

Violent agency remains a suppressed subject of the First World War. Among soldiers' incommunicable experiences was the intimate history of killing—how young men coped with the violence they meted out, how their consciences bore that burden.[10] Most historical accounts focus on soldiers' suffering and victimhood rather than that common experience of killing. Lawrence, however, publicly shared the experience of killing, depicting the setting in the Arabian deserts as a uniquely licentious moral universe where killing and narrating killing made a different kind of sense. Lawrence was an advisor to the Arab Revolt against the Ottomans, with which the British effort in the region was allied. He wrote at the start of his history of the campaign, "Blood was always on our hands: we were licensed to it. Wounding and killing seemed ephemeral pains, so very brief and sore was life with us. With the sorrow of living so great, the sorrow of punishment had to be pitiless. . . . When there was reason and desire to punish we wrote our lesson with gun or whip immediately in the sullen flesh of the sufferer, and the case was beyond appeal. The desert did not afford the refined slow penalties of courts and gaols." Later in the text, he recounts the "burden" of an execution that he was obliged to perform to preserve the peace among his men, describing the shooting in excruciating, confessional detail: Hamed stood in a narrow gully, and Lawrence "shot him through the chest. He [Hamed] fell down . . . shrieking, with the blood coming out in spurts over his clothes, and jerked about till he rolled nearly to where I was. I fired again, but was shaking so that I only broke his wrist. He went on calling out, . . . and I leant forward and shot him for the last time in the thick of his neck under the jaw. He shivered a little." After the night passed, the men loaded up to leave. "They had to lift me into the saddle." Finally there is the account of the retributional killings that Lawrence encouraged when his men witnessed the results of a massacre at Tafas by Turkish troops. "In a madness born of the horror of Tafas we killed and killed, even blowing in the heads of the fallen and of the animals; as though their death and running blood could slake our agony."[11]

Peter O'Toole as T. E. Lawrence in David Lean's *Lawrence of Arabia*, 1962. (*Lawrence of Arabia*, Horizon / Columbia, 1962)

Hundreds were shot by machine gun. But to convey the horror and moral breakdown, David Lean's 1962 film *Lawrence of Arabia* depicts the event as a reversion to an intimate, premodern form of violence—a crazed Lawrence wielding a blood-dripping dagger.

The desert setting of this narrative was everything in permitting Lawrence to describe his violent agency. As Indian village life found renewed appeal among those in search of a lost world, so, too, did the Arabian deserts. Britons in the era of World War I romanticized the Middle East more than any other region as an escape from the stultifying time of bourgeois Europe, a place where medieval, mythical, and mystical pasts could be found together and in whose deserts the sensation of timelessness could be fully realized. Lawrence's confessional prose, his guilty conscience, and much else besides, put him in a line of descent from the Romantics. His conscience suffered especially under the knowledge of British duplicity towards Britain's Arab allies against the Ottoman Empire in the war. In correspondence with Sharif Hussein, provincial ruler of the Hejaz in the Arabian peninsula, British officials promised to support creation of an independent Arab kingdom from the peninsula to Damascus. However, as Lawrence knew, Britain also signed the secret "Sykes-Picot" treaty with France and Russia to divide the spoils of the Ottoman Empire between themselves—allotting the region around Damascus to France. Farther east, the campaign in the Ottoman provinces of Basra, Baghdad, and Mosul—the Mesopotamia campaign in present-day Iraq—likewise betrayed its promises of liberation with an enormous Indian-style occupation regime. Much ink has been spilled on the validity of British promises about the postwar disposition of the Middle East.[12] The point here is that Lawrence was conscious, and felt guilty about, this double-dealing, so that during the war he "was continually and bitterly ashamed."[13] He at times presented himself as working to subvert imperial ambition in favor of the Arabs. (Notably, he later contemplated writing Casement's biography.) This divided loyalty, echoed in the figures of other British Arabists, drove the Colonial Office to endless anxiety about officials who became "more arab than the arabs."[14] It was a product of the development of a new, covert mode of great-man agency in the Middle East during a time in which the British also searched for an antidote to modernity. The expertise of the British Arabist was understood to depend on sympathetic mimicry of the Arab mind—an analogy of the occult medium—making him constitutionally unreliable to the British state. Seemingly privy to occult political forces shaping the region's history, these experts, despite their avowed sympathy with Arabs, authored a violent system of aerial policing in the postwar British-ruled Middle East.

In *Spies in Arabia*, I related this story as one of British cultural representations of the Middle East inspiring the invention of air control. But, more specifically, they were representations anchored in particular notions of history and historical agency. As in 1857 and 1865, a particular historical sensibility enabled officials to overcome ethical scruples over colonial violence, but this time it was a more sinister view of history, licensing shadowy imperial action, too. The postwar political climate was different: The obvious barbarism of the Western Front weakened faith in the narrative of imperial progress, casting doubt on European claims to superior civilization. But as anticolonial movements strove to take over the narrative of national liberation, the romantic image and relative discretion of the aerial regime gave the narrative of imperial progress a new lease on life. Experts claiming oracular insight into the region insisted that aerial control was the best midwife of the region's historical progress: In a land trapped in biblical, medieval, and mythical time, and subject to the machinations of malevolent occult forces, its modern reinvention of destruction wreaked from heaven by British knights in the sky made a unique sort of sense.

British Arabists began to articulate their view of the medieval-biblical Middle East before the war, as they searched for escape from bourgeois

England, repulsed by the effects of progress there. The growth of German ambitions and nationalist movements in the region also stoked their interest, as did anxiety about the spread of weapons around the empire, which they had hitherto tolerated and from which they had liberally profited. In the late nineteenth century, while the British congratulated themselves on their continued commitment to saving India from anarchy, political anarchism became a deeply influential political current among anticolonial networks,[15] sparking fresh concern about arms in the colonies. Political terror emerged as a new tactic on the global stage with the assassination of Tsar Alexander II in 1881. We will trace some of the ideas of this "global Left" later; here I want to focus on British efforts to contain it.[16] Arms traders continually adapted to new legislation attempting to stem the tide of arms flowing into colonial hands, resorting to shipping them in smaller and smaller lots to avoid detection. These adaptations made Muscat a major arms entrepôt on the Arabian Sea.[17] The flood of arms reaching India's North West Frontier became especially concerning. On the frontier in 1897 with the Malakand Field Force, the young Churchill was dismayed to discover "weapons of the nineteenth century, are in the hands of the savages, of the stone age."[18] The Afridis had long been paid by the British to guard the Khyber Pass at the frontier, but they revolted that very year. After suppressing the revolt, the British obtained Muscat's permission to search vessels in its waters to limit the flow of guns to the frontier. This led to massive arms seizures in the Persian Gulf in 1898 (infuriating Birmingham's gunmakers). The 1900 Exportation of Arms Act added further regulations. Criticism of arms trafficking grew more pronounced as the world war neared, as did Indian anticolonialists' turn to tactics of political terror. In 1908, J. G. Lorimer, a colonial administrator in the Persian Gulf, condemned the arms trade as "at least as great a public evil as the slave trade." It drove "anarchy and bloodshed" in Arabia and threatened "widespread and incurable disorder."[19] It was no longer merely tainted by association with the slave trade, as in Galton's time, but was morally objectionable in its own right, threatening the sacred Pax Britannica itself. (Still, the government found the need to deepen alarm about Casement's gunrunning by associating it with his rumored homosexuality.) In 1912, the Sultan of Muscat surrendered to British pressure to regulate the trade, triggering revolt by Omani tribes.[20] At the same time, British colonial authorities engaged in the trade, too, when it served their interests.

Against this backdrop of escalating tensions in the region, gathering intelligence in the Ottoman Empire acquired new urgency. Though intelligence work was generally becoming more professionalized in the aftermath of the South African War, Britain's formal alliance with the Ottoman Empire prompted a turn to informal rather than professional spies in the Middle East: diplomats, soldiers on leave, journalists, businessmen, and so on. Archaeologists, whose excursions to the region were part of a renewed effort to assert influence in the Ottoman Empire in the face of German competition, were also part of the group.[21] Such excursions proliferated with the rising interest in occultism. Britons searching for the ancient origins of occultism staked a claim to continuity with traditions rooted in "Arabia's" past in particular. The occultist G. R. S. Mead compared the "rising psychic tide" in London to that which had inundated the Alexandria of Hellenistic times, "where Egypt and Africa, Rome and Greece, Syria and Arabia met together."[22] They were after a new historical script. If the eschatological narrative of liberalism had brought Britons to a cul-de-sac of progress accompanied by spiritual and cultural emptiness, perhaps buried beneath its biblical template they might find a new historical guide to purposive existence. Works on archaeological discoveries buttressed the search for spiritual lineage: W. St. Chad Boscawen's *The First of Empires: "Babylon of the Bible"* (1904), R. Campbell-Thompson's *Semitic Magic, Its Origins and Development* (1909), Gertrude Bell's *Palace and Mosque at Ukhaidir* (1914).

This cultural project muddied the approach to intelligence-gathering in the region, as I described in *Spies in Arabia*. British agents complained of, yet relished, the difficulty of gathering intelligence in an essentially mysterious and otherworldly land ("peopled," as one put it, "by the spirits of the Arabian Nights"), expecting the company of genies, liars, and biblical characters.[23] Many spent as much time investigating the sites of biblical lore—Jonah's route, the Tower of Babel, the Garden of Eden—as they did gathering intelligence. Cartography was challenging; in the apparently featureless, horizonless, protean, and mirage-ridden desert, dreamy and distracted agents often had great difficulty simply determining where they were, finding the region "very much the same everywhere."[24]

But "Arabia," as they referred to this geographic and cultural imaginary, did seem to possess virtues lost to Britain. Many of these volunteer agents were drawn to the work as patriotic cover for their dream of escaping linear history, to "step straight from this modern age of bustle and chicanery . . . back into the pages of history to mediaeval times."[25] Gertrude Bell, the lone woman among this set, titled her 1911 record of her travels in the region *Amurath to Amurath*—an homage to Shakespeare's pithy comment on the serially unchanging imperia of the Turkish court.[26] This timeless place offered escape from "news," from history itself. There they might recover "boundless liberty,"[27] something different from the freedom that "liberalism" offered—primordial, elemental, the freedom *not* to be part of human society, freedom from bourgeois human law, from the "iron cage"—a place where one was accountable only to cosmic forces. Travelers in this generation were self-consciously heirs of the Romantics in their turn to "Arabia" as a refuge from modernity where the West's spiritual origins were preserved. Early among their numbers was Byron's granddaughter Lady Anne Blunt and her husband the poet Sir Wilfrid Blunt, whose travels turned him into an anticolonial agitator a generation before Casement.[28] As one of the few places geographers considered "Still Unknown," Arabia was off the map, a land not yet incorporated into universal time.[29] This was at once a relief and a temptation to those eager to fulfill heroic ambitions to put Arabia on the map. The agents experienced intelligence-gathering there as entry into a fictional world—at the very moment in which the genre of spy fiction was coming into its own.[30] They self-consciously followed their fictional contemporary, the eponymous hero of Rudyard Kipling's *Kim* (1901), in being both spies and spiritual disciples, deeply conscious of working in the land of the Bible and the *Odyssey,* where espionage had always been an integral part of the epic struggle for self-knowledge. Reference to these different, mytho-historical scripts shaped their actions, their sense of their capacity to act, and their ethical judgments about their actions very differently from those of their counterparts elsewhere. "Crossing the Mediterranean," explained one agent, "one entered a new realm of espionage . . . full of Eastern . . . cunning and subterfuge . . . in which the spy no longer emerged bogey-like as in the West."[31]

They evolved a distinct methodological outlook, boldly concluding that they need not follow scientific precepts in a place where facts and visual data were evidently scarce, that seemed to license recourse to other epistemological modes. Arabia's seemingly complacent, anti-intellectual endurance, this generation felt, was an antidote to the ills of "progress." The journalist Meredith Townsend's immensely influential *Asia and Europe* (1901) articulated this notion: "Imagine a clan which prefers sand to mould, poverty to labour, solitary reflection to the busy hubbub of the mart, which will not earn enough to clothe itself, never invented so much as a lucifer match, and would consider newspaper-reading a disgraceful waste of time. Is it not horrible, that such a race should be? more horrible, that it should survive all others? most horrible of all, that it should produce, among other trifles, the Psalms and the Gospels, the Koran and the epic of Antar?" For what if, Townsend asked, "Mecca survives Manchester," and "when Europe is a continent of ruins, the Arab shall still dwell in the desert, . . . living on like the Pyramids"?[32] Here was a new perspective on the idea of a contest for "survival of the fittest," in which Europeans are discovered to have got it all wrong. Such thinkers turned received wisdom about civilizational progress (equating Western civilization with Civilization as such) on its head, building on new notions of cultural relativism. The diplomat-agent and historian Mark Sykes (of later "Sykes-Picot" fame) mocked the European "civilised community" as "living in towns and in houses, suffering from infectious and contagious diseases, traveling in railway trains, able to read and write, possessing drinking shops, reading newspapers, surrounded by a hundred unnecessary luxuries, possessing rich and poor, slums and palaces, and convinced that their state is the most edifying in the world."[33] He appropriated the alleged symbols of progress—newspapers, railways, literacy, and so on—as evidence of Europe's cultural vacuity. Byron and Shelley had looked to the "Orient" to escape personal sorrow; now it offered a balm for society-wide nostalgia for faith. In his 1915 history of Turkey, Sykes explicitly instructed those who would go to Arabia, "Wipe John Stuart Mill, Omar Khayyam, Burke, Ruskin, Carlyle . . . out of your mind" and instead "learn the Book of Job by heart for philosophy, the Book of Judges for politics, the 'Arabian Nights' . . . for ethics."[34] He at once acknowledged that the works of historians like Burke, Carlyle, and Mill *had* been functioning as a moral compass, like religious texts, and that Arabia was a place where such a moral compass was no guide. They must look instead to the Bible and myth. They had to excavate an older form of knowledge from repressed cultural memory, from the biblical past that located their roots in Arabia.

The wanderers in the Middle East funneling information to the Foreign Office did not go there in search of the sensual indulgence the Orient is generally supposed to have offered Europeans but to escape what they saw as the moral decadence of their own society—the fruit of adhering to an ethical path hewed by the likes of Mill and Carlyle. Travel there was conceived as a journey into a past that was not merely further back on the secular time scale of history but on a different scale altogether, outside secular time. Moving in the desert itself allowed the mind to "wander into the past and . . . pry into the future," explained Sykes.[35] It challenged the historical sensibility that had been the mainstay of British interaction with the world since the eighteenth century. Scientists had wreaked havoc with the notion of the Bible as an *actual* historical account, so travelers conscious of moving in a biblical region located themselves in a mythological landscape, in a time and space that they knew existed somewhere in the shadow of reality.

This outlook, along with the empirical challenges they encountered, infected our informal intelligence-gatherers with a particular intellectual and ethical flexibility. Travel in Arabia numbed the senses, but it also, one wrote, allowed one to "'see, hear, feel, outside the senses.'"[36] These agents were willing, like avant-garde philosophers and artists, to experiment with new theories of perception and more "unscientific" ways of knowing. In the deserts of Arabia, where empiricism seemed impossible, they settled on faith as a reasonable alternative.[37] As a basis of knowledge, faith could at once solve their intelligence-gathering difficulties and soothe their spiritual cravings. Arabia, of all magical places, was *the* place for miraculous conviction: Sykes wrote, "The desert is of God and in the desert no man may deny Him." This was the birthplace of the three monotheistic religions, all launched by visionary prophets.[38] To this generation of Britons, Arabia was a biblical homeland to which they might *return* to find the "perfection of mental content" that Arabs "alone" seemed to possess.[39] This was an orientalist stereotype, but one spun as newly admiring.

The very act of wandering unraveled the knots of the overcivilized mind, yielding access to that mystical ethical realm beyond the senses. The archaeologist and spy David Hogarth recognized the desire to wander as "a temptation of original sin," an impulse by its nature subversive of the object of the scholar.[40] They might travel in Arabia to gather knowledge, but that travel could not but morph into a profounder quest to recover a primitive spiritual understanding. Henri Bergson's sense of time and his anti-empiricist emphasis on intuitive insight were dear to these wanderers.[41] Arab wisdom was rooted in primitive certainty, to British observers, intuitive rather than intellectual: "The European thinks, the Oriental only reflects," theorized Townsend, "and . . . the idea, turned over and over endlessly[,] . . . is part of the fibre of his mind."[42] This was a product of the place itself: Another traveler echoed, "In . . . desert countries . . . the essential facts . . . sink into you imperceptibly, until . . . they are . . . woven into the fibres of your nature."[43] To this generation, to be primitive was to know, without Cartesian proofs or theodicy, whether human existence mattered and whether there was a god. Travel in the desert restored that "savage" condition.[44] British agents accordingly prioritized intuitive knowledge acquired through lengthy immersion in the region, for, "only by Orientals—*or by those whose long sojourn in the East has formed their minds after the Oriental pattern*—can the Orient be adequately described."[45] Agents determined to "merge . . . in the Oriental as far as possible, [to] absorb his ideas, see with his eyes, and hear with his ears, to the fullest extent possible to one bred in British traditions."[46] This determination to "go native" reprised a Romantic trope. In Byron's *The Corsair* (1814), the European antihero disguises himself as an Islamic holy man; in *The Siege of Corinth* (1816), the European protagonist becomes an Islamic convert fighting for the Turks.[47]

By the time war broke out, the understanding was that what made an expert on Arabia *expert* was his ability to see, like Arabs, beyond surface deceptions, to discern the real from the unreal, the mirage, the lie. Knowing Arabia was a matter of *genius*. Book knowledge mattered little, an agent explained: "We 'sensed' the essence of a matter."[48] The gifted few claimed a kind of omniscience, so that at the outbreak of war, they exercised enormous influence over the Middle East campaigns, with a lasting effect on notions of expertise thereafter. They had ventured to desert Arabia in search of a new experience of consciousness but also to recover alternative guides to *conscience*. There, the presumed rightness of progress, whatever its costs, seemed dubious. Instead, a biblical, unworldly moral standard seemed to apply. In shaking off the historical ethical idiom, they evolved new understandings of their own agency: They nurtured ambitions of heroism but acted in occult fashion behind the scenes, assuring the military establishment that Arabia was a region in which different ethical rules applied.[49] They did not understand their agency as "greatman" agency but as the power of man as a divine vessel fulfilling cosmic destiny. It was not *God made me do it,* but *What anyone does in this divine place is beyond apprehension by a worldly narrative like history.* As the occultist Mead wrote shortly before the war, "The idea of the adept and initiate in secret knowledge, the ideal of the divine man or woman, of the god-inspired, or at any rate of the human with superhuman powers, is in the air."[50] If man was merely enacting what God desired, the question of moral accountability was moot. Everyone knew that God moved in mysterious ways. Likewise, "The ways of the Political Officer [British intelligence and administrative officer in wartime Iraq] are mysterious, his manner quiet and inscrutable, like the Arab's," wrote one officer, explaining, "The desert gets a hold of some white men, as it does upon the Arab." Thus, he described the intelligence officer Gerard Leachman's uncanny way of knowing things: "He heard, as though the wind had told him."[51]

This ethical outlook shaped the tactics of the campaigns fought in the region, informing British commanders' unique willingness to use craft in this region.[52] Both campaigns against the Ottoman Empire were highly mobile and relied on creative tactics unlike anything seen on the Western Front, incorporating deception, airpower, and irregular warfare in a manner that would deeply influence the tactics used in World War II. Most especially, British Arabists assured that the Bible and the Crusades offered a historical script for these actions. As soldiers visited biblical sites, they became convinced that the "tales of the Old Testament were based on fact."[53] In the Middle East, wrote a war correspondent, "you live the story of the Bible, and you do not wonder . . . if it is true; you know it is."[54] Officers consulted biblical battles to plan their own. In Palestine, General Edmund Allenby emulated the wars of Joshua. He learned surprise by studying the night attack of Gideon's three hundred in Judges 7.[55] Devouring histories of the Crusades, he became convinced that "in the unchanging East history would repeat itself . . . and the decisive battle . . . would be fought at . . . Megiddo."[56] And this certainty ensured that it was. Long viewing guerrilla warfare as the illegitimate recourse of backward peoples, the British now naturalized it as a modern British tactic. "The Hejaz war is one of dervishes against regular troops—and we are on the side of the dervishes," Lawrence explained.[57] This was again about reading history backwards, reviving the past in the present, abandoning the premise that what is old is obsolete: "Our text-books do not apply," he urged. Instead of Clausewitz, they must think of "Mohammed and the Crusades!"[58] This necessarily entailed revision of ethical values: Lawrence traced his taste for guerrilla attacks on trains and bridges, the "gospel of bareness in materials," to "a sort of moral bareness too."[59]

He and other commanders approached war in the region with a moral license unimaginable in France, justifying it as mimicry of Arabs. "Leave your English . . . customs . . . and fall back on Arab habits . . . to beat the Arabs at their own game," Lawrence advised. "The more unorthodox and Arab your proceedings," the better. They had to meet "cunning with cunning," confirmed another agent.[60] The British took inspiration from the way Arabs used mirages in battle, found cover in shadows and "folds in the ground," and used dust storms to create surprise. In such "ruses" could be found important "lessons," concluded British experts.[61] So it was that the British first attempted to hide an entire offensive *in a desert* in the Third Battle of Gaza in 1917 and the preparations for Megiddo in 1918—the war's only successful major deceptions, which inspired the deceptions before the invasions of Sicily and Normandy in the next war.

In the Middle East, Britons felt, they could intrigue without scruple because the place seemed to demand it. Lawrence reported admiringly on an agent in Mesopotamia who, besieged by spies, had begun to spread "wild fictions" and was "willing to do everything or anything" to spy on the spies in turn.[62] Unscrupulousness was, paradoxically, a virtue in this setting. The British had always intrigued abroad, but here they freely admitted it without recourse to euphemism, protestations of innocence, or blaming the needs of history. It was not that Arabia was culturally corrupting but that, practically speaking, it demanded ethical flexibility. The agents thus made the imaginary Arabian spy-space real. This was a conscious, purposeful adoption of "Geographical morality," normalized with the help of the new cultural-relativistic view of the world. Noting Leachman's efforts to divide and rule tribes by arranging for one to carry off the women of another, one observer conceded that British actions in the region were at times "odd in the extreme," but Leachman, as "the Romantic" of the intelligence officers, was practically an artist in his work.[63] Indeed, spies were "the pluckiest of all men."[64] The idea of the English as a plucky, eccentric people who had absentmindedly acquired an empire served them here. The British were suited to irregular warfare, Lawrence assured, given the similarity of desert tactics to naval warfare and that "nearly every young Englishman has the roots of eccentricity in him."[65]

Airpower was critical to this creative warfare. From the start, Arabist experts deemed it essential in a land they persisted in imagining as "flat as your hand," despite its varied topography.[66] A postwar cabinet paper acknowledged that airpower saw its greatest development and proved its independent capabilities not in Europe but in the "more distant theatres" in the Middle East.[67] Control of the air was essential to deception and irregular tactics; it was used to conceal movements, watch enemy movements, coordinate irregulars, and conduct mapping and reconnaissance, providing views even of the forbidden holy cities. It was also employed in irregular action itself, in train-wrecking. Aerial photography and signaling were developed in the Middle East. In the Hejaz, unlike France, experts insisted, a shot could not be fired without aerial observation.[68] The British invented the "aerial trap" when they bombed Turkish troops retreating through the canyon of Wadi Faria, spearheading the fall of Damascus. "We were butchers," admitted the commander, but he hoped this "new feature in war . . . can be made use of."[69] Official assessments of wartime air-power held up this "disaster wrought . . . by bombs" as "a classic instance of the proper application of air power."[70] Most notably, commanders praised the "political" uses of the "terror" of aerial bombardment in disciplining tribes.[71] These violent uses would be sanctioned as acceptable military practice thanks to the ethical latitude the British perceived in the Middle East.

Now, what justified much of this activity was the old-fashioned liberal historical narrative that the British had come to the region as liberators, promising independence to Arabs in the Ottoman provinces they "freed." This promise was crucial to securing Arab cooperation in the war. But British officials also considered the region crucial to the security of imperial sea and land routes *and* the new air route. Without their old ally, the Ottoman Empire, securing it for them, and with Bolshevik Russia making a fresh play for control, they grew determined to hold it themselves. The region also had oil. But the moment for might-makes-right arguments articulated by the likes of James Fitzjames Stephen had passed; security and resources were no longer legitimate grounds on which to make a bid for colonial rule, especially given the diplomatic promises they had made. Apart from the Arabs, they had assured President Woodrow Wilson and the American public that the war was not being fought for the expansion of European empire but in the name of self-determination and liberty. The world had become increasingly hostile to the idea of colonial acquisitions with the growth of anticolonial movements all over, drawing inspiration from the communist revolution in Russia in 1917. The war's violent exposure of the sham of the European "civilizing mission" made it even harder to make a case for outright annexation. The British swallowed Iraq into the empire by rehabilitating that historical script of liberal empire as a chance at redemption once again.

During the war, the mobile and tactically innovative campaigns in the Middle East offered morale-boosting narratives for Britons at home, at times the only source of positive war news while the Western Front remained in stalemate. Their accounts of plucky agency and romance helped keep the British public invested in the war, despite horrific losses in Europe. They affirmed the historical vision of evil ultimately producing good. This long-suffering public became enamored of the idea of "developing" the ancient cradle of civilization to redeem the war's losses—hopes that were steadily encouraged by government propaganda. By rescuing it from devastation at the hands of the Turks and restoring it to its ancient position as the crossroads of the globe, the British would find redemption themselves. Contemporaries judged that by "rebuild[ing] a civilization after many years of anarchy and desolation," and that, too, a civilization of "mysterious and divine" origins, they would give meaning to the sacrifices of British soldiers.[72] Those who continued to interact with their family members as ghosts were invariably dressed in uniform, itself an exhortation to make good on their unfinished work.[73] An officer prayed, "We'll fix this land up . . . and move the wheels of a new humanity. Pray God, yes—a new humanity!"[74]

The idea of reforming or uplifting colonial people had fallen somewhat out of favor in the late nineteenth century, as we have seen; the focus had been preservation of traditional society. But in Mesopotamia, the old liberal ethos found a new lease on life, for there the reformist goal was packaged *as* restorative. There, noted the British press, the bearers of technological change would be akin to the sorcerers who had made Sinbad the Sailor turn airman on the back of a great bird; motorcars would be like "snorting land monsters" rushing across the deserts—they would cause the happy return of "the age of miracles," which the local people would take in stride "as a matter of course."[75] Improvement would recover the style of ancient empires in the region—the Persians, Seleucids, Parthians— explained the historian Edwyn Bevan. As the Romantics had claimed Greece as a lost part of the West, so wartime British representations of Mesopotamia stressed its bonds to Hellenistic-Christian culture. "When European Christendom looks to-day at the desolation of these lands," Bevan wrote in 1918, "it is looking at a lost piece of itself."[76] This was another opportunity for Britain to fulfill its destiny as the new Rome.

Humbled by the war's devastating effects, Britons reached, again, for the trope of atonement to underwrite their efforts to make history in the Middle East—just as atonement had guided imperial activity after defeat and scandal in the late eighteenth century. In 1917, a naval sailor in Mesopotamia foresaw that this "new burden of Empire" would prove once again that "we Britons spend our lives in making blunders, and give our lives to retrieve them."[77] A general was certain that the struggle in Mesopotamia was "being fought for the sake of principles more lofty . . . for issues of higher service to the cause of humanity, than those that had animated the innumerable and bloody conflicts of the past."[78] Far from breaking faith in Britain's destined greatness, the war raised the stakes of proving its truth, redoubling determination to act in a manner validating Britain's providentially blessed role. The war that seemed ideologically bankrupt elsewhere could find meaning in Mesopotamia, fulfilling the millenarian hopes that had been pinned on it. They would prove empire was about not "conquest but . . . redemption," Sykes affirmed in an official note.[79] Mesopotamia would prove that the British could still civilize, even if they had lost civilization itself. An enthusiastic author admired the "power and vision which sees the British Empire as a vast army of many nations and cultures sweeping up the varied civilisations of the past in the march forward to that ideal world of brothers."[80] This historical vision neatly co-opted the evolutionary view of history into the progress narrative; a future of "brothers" posited an end to the racial struggle that many Britons thought had precipitated the war. In this moment, Britons recuperated the liberal myth of empire as a story of human fraternity *against* the rival internationalism of communism.

With this historical vision in mind, ex-soldiers sought transfer to the Middle East. James Mann, who became a political officer in Iraq, explained to his mother, "If one takes the Civil Service, or the Bar, or Literature, or Politics, or even the Labour movement, what can one do that is constructive? Here on the other hand I am constructing the whole time."[81] This was a region where a postwar British man might feel *effectual* in a historical way, rather than a cog in an aimless machine. Such men were often inspired by Lawrence, whose story was central to the idea of redemption in Arabia. The only heroic action figure to emerge from the war, he both renewed and exceeded Victorian ideals of heroic historical agency, at once expressing his generation's sense of disillusionment and betrayal by blind statesmen and stupid generals.[82] He was praised for a special perception as much as his physical exploits, qualities held to have "deepened and matured in the solitude of the Arabian desert, ever the breeding place of saint and prophet."[83] His power was not only his own but derived from some greater, more occult force. Comparisons to Christ were frequent. The military theorist Basil Liddell Hart wrote, "The young men are talking . . . of him in a Messianic strain—as the man who could, if he would, be a light to lead stumbling humanity out of its troubles. . . . He is the Spirit of Freedom come incarnate to a world in fetters."[84] This is not the freedom that John Stuart Mill devoted his life to but something more transcendent, invoking a more transcendent understanding of historical "progress" itself. Lawrence, carrying the burden of perfidious Albion, offered deliverance for a civilization reeling from discovering its feet of clay. As Arabia supplanted Greece as the most romantic backdrop for the enactment of aristocratic English heroism, Lawrence was the apotheosis of the Byronic figure in his time. He, too, had leapt into the battlefield to free another people from chains. The *Daily News* insisted, "There has . . . been no English soldier so astonishing in his character and circumstances since Byron was at Missolonghi," with whom Lawrence shared "the genius of literature and . . . adventure."[85] Lawrence's friend Robert Graves, soldier-poet of the Western Front, also compared him to Byron.[86] Lawrence produced his epic history of the Arab Revolt, *Seven Pillars of Wisdom,* in an artisanal style recalling Blake's illuminated works: each of its two hundred copies bore a unique handcrafted binding and illustrations by renowned painters of the day. Much came to be staked, culturally, on the image of redemption in and a redeemer from the Middle East.

Britons' prophetic expectations of the Middle East informed the case the British made for control of the region. In 1920, following the 1919 Paris Peace Conference, the League of Nations was founded as an institution for international governance in fulfillment of Woodrow Wilson's vision of the war's goals. It provided for a "mandate system" assigning newly "freed" countries to tutelage under a more "advanced" power. This was liberal empire 2.0, a rebooted internationalized version of the "civilizing mission," in which the "trustee" relationship was more explicit and international oversight offered at least a theoretical check on the trustee. The popular script of redemption ensured the buy-in of the British public. The British now claimed postwar control of Mesopotamia before the world as restitution for its sacrifices for the country's development. The gambit worked. Iraq, made up of the former Ottoman provinces of Mosul, Basra, and Baghdad, became a British mandate, along with Palestine (soon divided into Transjordan and Palestine). Though denoted "mandates," these territories were nevertheless administered from the "Colonial" Office—giving the lie to the cover story.

The goal of the Paris conference was a peace "settlement" that would secure the world against war going forward. As an instrument of international
governance, the League of Nations was supposed to contain conflict, to
prove that the war had ended all war—had ended history itself. But the very
terms of the settlement were profoundly unsettling. Iraqis knew that the
mandate system was colonialism by another name and challenged the recuperative script the British had embraced, erupting in rebellion that very
year. Development projects, which were designed largely to serve army
needs and were debited to the Iraqi state, were abandoned as counterinsurgency became the colonial state's priority. At the same time, the British
faced anticolonial resistance in India, Egypt, Ireland, and elsewhere as colonial subjects called in promises of postwar reforms in exchange for wartime loyalty.

As in the previous century, the British saw these rebellions as mali-
ciously anarchic, fueled by the spread of decommissioned arms at the end
of the war, which they now struggled to contain. A wartime committee
had brooded over the costs of unilateral operations to control the arms
traffic in the Gulf and the erosion of the Omani sultan's power due to his
cooperation with the British blockade. Sykes warned the committee of the
dangers they courted: Smokeless magazine rifles had spread around the
world, "enough to arm every black man who wants a rifle." Small, cheap
arms had revolutionized their capacity for history-making action. Sykes
foresaw a world in which unrest took the form of terrorism by pistol-
armed anticolonial individuals: "Any fool . . . can shoot a viceroy."[87] After
the war, the committee resolved to launch international talks. The Paris
arms convention in 1919 framed the problem as a "high moral issue."[88] The
immorality of arms trading delegitimized and depoliticized rebellion in
imperial minds (and vice versa). The convention forbade export licenses to
any country refusing to accept the "tutelage" under which it had been
placed and defined a prohibited zone including the Middle East. British,
French, Italian, and Japanese representatives agreed to carry out these
provisions even before ratification as a "moral duty of all civilized States."[89]
In the end, the convention remained a dead letter as each waited for the
others to ratify and left enough loopholes that firearms continued to flow
to the region. (International efforts to come to agreement would be renewed in Geneva in 1925, again abortively.) Anxiety about these arms
flows during the 1920 rebellion fueled British aggression and fear of imminent collapse.

Britons were attracted to the idea of redemption in Mesopotamia, but they had not signed up for war in defense of it; they wanted demobilization and attention to reconstruction at home, not expenditure on new colonies. Middle Eastern experts' taste for and belief in occult exercise of agency allowed them to maneuver in this fraught moment. Impatient with red tape, they were accustomed to acting independently, even covertly, in service to their intuitive insight, often securing official approval after the fact. During the Iraqi rebellion, Lawrence took it on himself to expose British betrayal of promises to the Arabs in the *Sunday Times,* at once burnishing his heroic image: "The people of England have been led in Mesopotamia into a trap[,] . . . tricked into it by a steady withholding of information. . . . Our administration [has been] more bloody and inefficient than the public knows. . . . How long will we permit millions of pounds, thousands of Imperial troops and tens of thousands of Arabs to be sacrificed on behalf of a form of Colonial administration which can benefit nobody but its administrators?"[90] He blew the whistle on the occupation of Iraq as imperialism without moral justification. In another article, he called British counterinsurgency tactics, including burning of villages, "immoral." He may also have been behind a London *Times* article a few days later that wisely deduced, "When our beneficial railways are cut, our engines and trucks seized, and our telegraph wires torn down, it is time for us to drop the pose of liberators."[91]

As scandal threatened to rear its head again, however, Lawrence proved critical to assembly of a new story and practice of empire in the Middle East. In March 1921, his great admirer the colonial secretary Winston Churchill called a conference of experts at Cairo. Churchill had already made his mark as a historian and empire builder, emerging a pivotal figure on the global political stage. At the conference, he and the experts decided to establish an Iraqi monarchy that would appease Iraqi rebels *and* guilty imperial conscience about the broken promises to Sharif Hussein. Hussein's son Prince Faisal had commanded the forces of the Arab Revolt and set up a government in Damascus that lasted several months before the French had booted it out to establish their mandate in Syria. (His tragic position struck a familiar chord for Britons: At the Paris Peace Conference, the writer and diplomat's wife Vita Sackville-West described him as "prey to a romantic, an almost Byronic, melancholy."[92]) Faisal now received the consolation prize of Iraq, though he had no ties to the region. The British would rule Iraq indirectly through this monarchy, as in an Indian princely state, but with a new twist: Instead of boots on the ground to enforce British will, the veiled colonial state would rely on the newly christened Royal Air Force (RAF). It would police Iraq from the air, coordinating information from agents on the ground to bomb villages and tribes.[93] This revolution in imperial governance is partly explained by air control's relative cheapness. But it also emerged from a conviction that airpower was particularly, even uniquely, suited to the region. Lawrence insisted at the time that the scheme was "*not* capable of universal application."[94] To someone searching for avenues for exercising heroic agency, in the aftermath of a war of attrition, airpower seemed promising. Lawrence frequently likened man's conquest of the air to the arrival of the stars in Coleridge's "The Rime of the Ancient Mariner," "as lords that are expected."[95] He, too, joined the ranks of the RAF in 1922 (pseudonymously, adopting the surname of another Irish troublemaker, his friend George Bernard Shaw).

The aerial regime was deadly and did not work entirely as expected. The experts imagined that an aerial point of view would allow them to overcome the mirages, haze, flatness, and other features that made the desert so difficult for them to reconnoiter. But the regime was plagued by information failures: pilot disorientation, visibility problems, inaccurate identification of tribes and villages.[96] The wrong targets were bombed. Iraqis found cover in watercourses, hillocks, and other features of the allegedly "featureless" landscape.

But air enthusiasts drew on the new historical scripts mobilized to justify British action in the region to buttress faith in the experiment. As I described in *Spies in Arabia,* casualty counts were not made, out of a sense that any data gathered in the region was necessarily unreliable. The 1920s saw the rise of a new government emphasis on not only collecting but publicly circulating statistical information as part of the postwar effort to justify colonialism on developmental grounds—an updating of the liberal-historical narrative of progress, though, the political theorist Timothy Mitchell reminds us, colonialism itself caused so much displacement and disruption that accurate statistics remained elusive.[97] Postwar Iraq, however, was an exception to this practice, being located, to British experts, beyond the pale of the empirically assessable world. A record of what happened there—a historical account of air control—need not be kept. Arabia could not be host to history. This willful ignorance of the outcome of air control let it sit more easily in the British official mind. Only in "Arabia," a place romanticized as being without linear history, where nothing could be known with precision, indeed where the objective of precise knowledge was a kind of smallness, a betrayal of the opportunity to know something deeper, did such fecklessness make sense and thus make air control acceptable. In its Iraqi cocoon, the RAF was safe from criticism, protected by the notorious fallibility of all worldly news from "Arabia."

The inaccuracy that made record-keeping impractical at once enabled aerial policing to fulfill the historical script of the civilizing mission. It did not matter what the aircraft actually did so long as they appeared to be everywhere at once, "conveying a silent warning," as Arnold Wilson, head of political intelligence in Iraq, put it.[98] Terror was the admitted principle of the scheme. It fulfilled Jeremy Bentham's dream of a disciplinary panopticon, which guns had partially fulfilled in the eighteenth century. Air control now attempted to realize it in postwar Iraq. An official memo explained that "from the ground every inhabitant of a village is under the impression that the occupant of an aeroplane is actually looking at him . . . establishing the impression that all their movements are being watched and reported."[99] If pilots could not be sure whether they were looking at "warlike" or "ordinary" tribes, Bedouin could not discriminate "between bombing and reconnaissance expeditions."[100] This use of terror was, ironically, held up as the source of the regime's humanity. In theory, airpower would bloodlessly awe tribes into submission, or interference with their daily lives through destruction of homes, villages, crops, fuel, and livestock would produce the desired result.

In keeping with this vision of automated discipline, the regime was accommodated in the revitalized liberal narrative of empire. Officials held that air control itself would now fulfill the dream of developing Iraq and redeeming the cradle of civilization. By demonstrating "the power of modern inventions . . . to conquer vast open spaces of the world," desert flight helped resurrect Victorian faith in the progressive, constructive power of technology. From the air, they would witness "adoring Asia kindle and hugely bloom," in the poetic allusion of the *Illustrated London News*.[101] Flying over Iraq showed that "a new era had dawned" and that with the help of the RAF, Iraqis would "win their independence at last," affirmed an enthusiastic official.[102] The violence was a temporary birthing pain—a rite of passage necessitated by history. A wing commander explained, "The cheaper the form of control the more money for roads and development and the sooner it will be no longer necessary to use armed forces to do with explosives what should be done by policemen and sticks."[103] Air control would thus fulfill hopes that Iraq would "safeguard humanity from famine, wars" and compensate for "sacrifices . . . made in the Great War."[104]

But these hopes apart, in that moment, the "pacification" of Iraq was proving horrifically costly in Iraqi lives—a hundred casualties were not unusual in a single operation, besides those lost to starvation and the burning of villages. Witness this 1924 report by Arthur Harris, a squadron officer in Iraq: "The Arab and Kurd . . . now know what real bombing means, in casualties and damage; they now know that within 45 minutes a full sized village . . . can be practically wiped out and a third of its inhabitants killed or injured by four or five machines which offer them no real target, no opportunity for glory as warriors, no effective means of escape."[105] Whether attacking British communications, refusing to pay taxes at crushing rates, or harboring rebels, many tribes and villages were being bombed into submission.

The liberal defense of air control was not enough to quiet criticism of this violence. The war secretary himself doubted the logic that "peaceful control of Mesopotamia depends on our intention of bombing women and children."[106] But where the liberal defense failed, defenders of the regime had recourse to more resigned defenses of colonial violence from the second half of the nineteenth century. With arguments recalling those of Kaye and Eyre, some protested the "great humanity of bombing," arising from the way "continual unending interference with . . . normal lives" forced the enemy to give up sooner, thereby lowering their casualties, too.[107] Imperial ideology encompassed wrath and benevolence in a single paternalistic vision of progress. But more than these worldly defenses of air control, what ultimately made its violence tolerable even to Britons who professed deep love for the region was the notion that Arabia was simply otherworldly, outside the time-space continuum of the historical imagination. It was a timeless place of biblical violence and chivalric contest, a mystical land beyond worldly convention, a place of perennial and objectless conflict. The usual norms could hardly be held to prevail there, especially when the war had proven them outdated in Europe itself.

In a timeless land, all that transpired was part of an endlessly unfolding epic that repeated ad nauseum. One could merely revel in the retelling of its tales within tales, like Shahrazad's regaling of Shahriyar with stories unburdened with moral or message. So the history they made in Iraq need not serve an obvious immediate moral purpose for the Arabs (it was enough that the British knew its promise of progress). The RAF intelligence officer John Glubb insisted, "Life in the desert is a continuous guerilla warfare." You had to strike hard and fast; that was the way of "Bedouin war."[108] For Bedouin, war was a "romantic excitement"; its production of "tragedies, bereavements, widows and orphans" a "normal way of life," "natural and inevitable." Their appetite for war was what made them feel "*élite* of the human race."[109] They possessed "depths of hatred, reckless bloodshed and. lust of plunder of which our lukewarm natures seem no longer capable," explained Glubb, "deeds of generosity worthy of fairy-tales and acts of treachery of extraordinary baseness."[110] Their "love of dramatic actions" outweighed "the dictates of reason"; it even, the General Staff affirmed, overcame the "inherent dislike of getting killed."[111] Arnold Wilson echoed that Iraqis were used to constant warfare, expected harsh justice, had no patience with sentimental distinctions between combatants and noncombatants, and viewed air action as "legitimate and proper."[112] Having served as chief of the Air Staff during the establishment of air control, Hugh Trenchard assured Parliament in 1930, "The natives of a lot of these tribes love fighting for fighting's sake. . . . They have no objection to being killed."[113] In this view, it would be a cultural offense *not* to bomb them. The British were certain that Bedouin retained their dignity under bombardment and did not need the condescension of pity. They possessed the "gallant humanity which thrills us in the pages of Homer," explained Glubb.[114] And in Homeric ethics, courage and skill in battle were what mattered in judging a man's value and virtue. A British commander assured, "[Iraqi sheikhs] . . . do not seem to resent . . . that women and children are accidentally killed by bombs"—a mood, Lawrence acknowledged, "too oriental . . . for us to feel very clearly."[115] Indeed, if aircraft were "knights of the air," reviving chivalry in an otherwise "vulgarised" modern warfare,[116] they even allowed the British to recuperate their own Homeric virtue. The vindication of air control depended on long-circulating ideas about Arabia as a place exempt from the this-worldliness that constrained human activity elsewhere. It was a place of heroes and villains, where, as in books, agents could escape from the pitiful reality of human suffering into an exalted sphere in which action possessed a cosmic significance. Strikes against Abdul Aziz Ibn Saud's puritanically Wahhabi avant-garde forces who raided into Iraq from neighboring Nejd particularly stoked this romantic vision. From her perch in the Iraqi government, Gertrude Bell was fiercely proud of "our power to strike back" at these Ikhwan, who, "with their horrible fanatical appeal to a medieval faith, rouse in me the blackest hatred."[117]

The book the region most recalled was the Bible, and its imprisonment in the time-space of the Bible rather than the secular time of history especially required ethical accommodation. Its moral universe was biblical, beyond the reach of ordinary mortal law. In 1932, when the inhumanity of air control was under discussion at the World Disarmament Conference in Geneva, the British high commissioner in Iraq explained that Iraqis regarded bombing "as an act of God to which there is no effective reply but immediate submission."[118] Lawrence agreed that it was seen as "impersonally fateful"—"not punishment, but a misfortune from heaven striking the community."[119] Arabia was a biblical place, and the people who lived there *knew* that, expecting periodic calamity and divine visitation. Air control played on their presumed fatalism, their faith in the incontrovertible "will of God." Such people could bear random acts of violence in a way that Europeans, coddled by secular notions of justice and human rights, could not.

The morality that applied in Arabia was the stuff of myth and romance: The transposition of real Arabia into a biblical, storybook land made bombing acceptable to those who believed they would object to it in any other context—even to Arabist agents enchanted with notions of Arabian liberty. They loved Arabia for its otherworldliness, the very quality that also made it fit to bear the unearthly destruction of bombers, as if a distinct moral world. Thus, in 1932, when Iraq joined the League of Nations as a nominally independent country, the RAF remained in control on the logic that "the term 'civilian population' has a very different meaning in Iraq from what it has in Europe."[120] Social Darwinist military science added further support for this claim: In "rude societies," Herbert Spencer had explained, "all adult males are warriors; consequently, the army is the mobilized community, and the community is the army at rest."[121]

The Air Ministry put on pageants of airpower attended by hundreds of thousands in England to sell the vision of air control as both an instrument of progress and a compliment to Arabia's timelessness to the British public. The demonstrations represented desert policing as a scene of thrilling rescues of white humanity from a "barbarian mob."[122] Recruitment tours and other kinds of propaganda reinforced this narrative. The Middle East Department at the Colonial Office eagerly proffered publicity material promoting it, too. Lectures, books and articles, exhibitions, films, and photography pressed the romance of the aerial regime in Iraq.[123] Progress, if it was possible at all in such a society, could come only in the form of violent military engagement. Its population was so compulsively martial and aimless in its martial exploits that the British, who were increasingly in thrall to notions of cultural relativism, need not scruple over principles of *ius in bello* there. The British government sold the new warfare by promoting an image of its constructive capacity in a famously romantic place where the now bankrupt laws of humanity and warfare did not apply anyway.

In a place stuck in a timeless loop of conflict, existing somewhere on an otherworldly timescale, the British felt they could exercise violent imperial agency without moral accountability. Without history as an ethical guide, the only test was emotional: A year before the Iraqi revolution of 1958 finally ended air control, Air Marshal Sir John Slessor defended the regime by citing the approval of gifted officers "so attached to their tribesmen that they sometimes almost 'went native.'"[124] Into the 1980s, Glubb insisted that "the basis of our desert control was not force but persuasion and love." In 1989, a military historian cited Glubb to vindicate the regime, because "no European was ever closer and more sympathetic to the Arabs than [he]."[125]

But these attempts at sentiment-driven moral reflection were based on counterfeit empathy. From its prewar invention as an intelligence epistemology, British sympathy with the Arab mind had signaled not recognition of common humanity but an effort to adapt the British self to what Britons thought of as a radically different physical and moral universe. Postwar agents inspired by the legends around their predecessors still sought to escape the bonds of *too much* civilization to a fictional, biblical, enchanted, and uncanny space beyond secular time. They, too, saw desert travel as an escape into the blue, a truant fulfillment of patriotic duty and exit from the customary world, the world of everyday moral judgment.[126] The RAF's tenuous links to "civilisation" through a seemingly magical wireless infrastructure, and rumors of Lawrence's presence in the ranks, fed this mystique.[127] Flight over biblical terrain was sublime but also produced "a bad effect upon one's nerves," a feeling that "the end of the world had really come," said one RAF officer. Pilots knew "that air of quiet weariness which comes to those who have been in the desert too long" and made them go mad.[128] This was not a place for empathy but for psychic breakdown, without some kind of bracing. Emulation of Arabs was intended to enable British survival in this extraterrestrial space but did not

Poster by Frank Newbould, 1922. (Crown Copyright, Royal Air Force Museum Collection [FA11012])

produce compassion for the victims of the surreal world of bombardment the British actually created by pulling the strings of fate from the sky. Iraq was for them a place beyond the reach of ordinary moral sentiments.

If Iraq was outside the space of history, it nevertheless was understood to matter deeply to the historical fulfillment of empire. If it offered the chance to resurrect the cradle of civilization, it was also, in the British imagination, a pivotal, borderless region of nomads through which unrest could spread like a contagion throughout the empire and the world. Everything was at stake in disciplining it. The British had imagined conspiracies behind specific rebellions before—as in Jamaica in 1865. But conspiracy-thinking, based on belief in the working of occult agencies in the Middle East, became a primary mode of justifying the British presence there. The stretch of land from the Mediterranean to the Indian frontier was, in Gertrude Bell's dramatic phrase, a "devil's cauldron."[129] Imagining a Pan-Islamic combination with Moscow controlling everything from Constantinople to Afghanistan "pursuing a policy specifically designed to destroy the British position in the Middle East and India," British officials saw British Iraq as a "wedge directed towards their vitals."[130] Were the British driven out, "only anarchy can supervene."[131] In 1920, Churchill ominously lectured to the City of London about a "world wide conspiracy . . . designed to deprive us of our place in the world and rob us of victory." Britain must overcome this "malevolent and subversive force."[132] In a public lecture, Valentine Chirol, the historian and diplomat who popularized the term "Middle East" from the start of the century, conjured a reawakened Orient surging with "many Old World forces . . . tending more and more to combine together against the common menace of the Occident."[133] Officials committed to the idea of a hidden reality in Arabia believed that various movements striving for autonomy in the region were part of a single "Eastern Unrest," a malicious plot to undermine the British Empire.[134]

To be sure, there were connections among anticolonial movements around the empire (as we'll see more in Chapter 5), and many did operate under cover of secrecy, but they were not all part of a single conspiracy against Britain (however much they were all bred by British rule). British faith in the value of British rule to others was too strong to contemplate the possibility of genuine, widespread political resistance to it—as in 1857 and 1865. The idea of a mean plot explained rebellion and provided the justification for British rule as a bulwark against anarchy. But the threat of this anti-British plot was particularly menacing this time because the sinister bleeding of Soviet power into the Middle East had sabotaged the East-West divide that was the foundation of the liberal historicist imagination. Conspiracies in the Middle East seemed to threaten not only the empire but history itself—only lately settled at the Paris Peace Conference. The experts feared that the new, rival claimant to the mantle of liberty would exploit the incessant mobility of nomads and pilgrims to fulfill a giant Bolshevik-Islamic conspiracy against liberal empire. Lawrence warned of "a Wahabi-like Moslem edition of Bolshevism."[135] Before he became an influential universal historian, the young Arnold Toynbee (nephew of the economic historian of the same name who had given the Anglophone world the term "industrial revolution") germinated his ideas about civilizational decline as a wartime intelligence analyst reflecting on the game-changing breakdown of the East-West divide. In a 1918 memorandum, he observed that distance, race, and history distinguished the European and oriental parts of European empires, but "two great states, Turkey and Russia . . . occupy between them the landbridge between Europe and the East, and embrace Europeans and Orientals in one political body without any clear-cut division between them. . . . Europe and the East merge into one." In the war, the despotic Russian and Ottoman Empires, which had long held the shifting sands at bay, had yielded to the forces of change, and in their new volatile incarnations had become the "political conductor between Europe and the East."[136] They threatened to subvert what he took as the premise of Western historical understanding since Herodotus. In 1923, witnessing the exchange of minority populations between Greece and the new Turkish nation-state, Toynbee warned of the possibility of "catastrophic conflict between the British Commonwealth and the Oriental world."[137]

The government assiduously shared its portentous conspiracy theories with the public as part of the effort to stoke support for air control.[138] The narrative of apocalyptic contest between Orient and Occident, and between good and evil, in the Middle East guided British action there. The notion of a clash of civilizations raised the stakes of holding on to the region and made violent counterinsurgency and policing more tolerable to an otherwise skeptical public. In a work written to persuade that public, Thomas Lyell, an officer who served in Iraq, conceded that Britain's Iraq policy might look "wantonly extravagant" in isolation but made eminent sense considered as part of the "immense problem of empire—as the key to the future of our dominions."[139] In 1923, the *Times* praised Air Secretary Samuel Hoare (descended from the eighteenth-century Quaker banker who had accepted war as a "necessary evil") for awakening the public to the "reality of the danger" and fully justifying the air control regime in Iraq "on the two grounds of economy and humanity."[140] Britain itself was at risk. The reviewer of a history of the French Revolution found the moment resonant with that crisis and called for arrest of all the Bolshevik-backed "polyglot rascals" in the country, lest they witness the "degraded spectacle of honest Englishmen murdered by the worst Chinamen and the worst niggers whom brutality can control."[141]

The perceived collapse of the foundational East-West separation consolidated the new, occult approach to history and the exercise of historical agency. Bolshevism's and Pan-Islamism's narratives of liberation challenged imperialism ideologically on the ground of historical narrative. In this contested field, the British nurtured a more fantastical sense of agency indebted to their occult fascinations with the Middle East. Reports of potentially devastating conspiracies were often proleptically dismissive, but always with a remnant of lingering danger. Informing Wilson of a terrifying Moscow-Berlin-Irish-Egyptian-Persian-Indian conspiracy, the War Office consolingly told him not to lay "too much stress" on it.[142] Such reports seemed to irrepressibly relish the frisson of hidden forces stirring a momentous time. Bell hoped she was not witnessing "the crumbling of the universe" but found it "too immensely interesting to be in such close touch with it."[143] Part of the draw of working on and in the Middle East was the opportunity to steep oneself in extraordinary, epic fictions and romantic scenarios, to face in theory if not in reality situations faced by spies of lore—like the spies in a John Buchan novel (his *Greenmantle* appeared in 1916). There was some reciprocity between fiction and real life here: Buchan, the director of Intelligence during the war, was an intimate of the community of Arabist experts and spies, on whom he modeled his heroes. He was also instrumental in the making of the Lawrence legend.[144]

A conspiracy theorist discerns a "plot," a narrative, behind otherwise random events. He searches for a *story* to knit them together. He is a fantasist. Conspiracy theories were a way to envision change in places otherwise thought of as timeless and incapable of change; they attributed agency not to Middle Easterners but to Russian or Jewish actors behind the scenes, even at times to a sort of elemental force or spirit, a kind of generic subversive energy.[145] Conspiracy thinking was symptomatic of intense psychological and cultural strain produced by the upheavals of war and ideological challenges to the old justificatory narratives of empire. It also testified to an epistemological shift in British thinking about empire in a mystical direction as Britons set out to govern a place that they thought of as essentially unknowable. British officials searched for the hidden will not of humans or God but of the region itself—a divine region after all. (The "real" force, if any, uniting the region against them was the British Empire itself; that common factor was what led Egyptians, Irish, and Indians to see themselves engaged in a single struggle.)

The notion that the Middle East was a kind of occult world licensed unorthodox, covert exercise of great-man agency accountable to the morally ambiguous spy world rather than the "straight" world of mass politics, where the British public, rewarded for war service with expanded franchise untethered at last from property qualifications, was loudly asserting its right to control foreign policy to ensure politicians did not land them in another disastrous war. Toynbee's *Study of History* began to appear in 1934 and argued that civilizations rose by responding successfully to challenges under the leadership of creative minorities composed of elite leaders.[146] The novelist and social commentator H. G. Wells, who deeply admired Lawrence, laid out a program, notably titled *The Open Conspiracy* (1928), of visionaries who would lead humankind out of crisis into a utopic cosmopolis. It was, explicitly, a work on revolutionary agency urging "human control over the destinies of life."[147] In the interwar period, spies and former spies filling the expanding intelligence and policymaking bureaucracies understood themselves as that elite. If the foundational geographical separation of historicism had collapsed, history's "natural laws" could no longer operate as they ought. The conspiracies bridging the East-West divide subverted their operation, making covert British activity an entirely appropriate response. The genius of British Middle East experts was already understood to give them special insight into hidden realities. That hidden reality, the world of cloak-and-dagger, the world of spies, was a space of moral exceptionalism, and Arabia was the quintessential land of hidden realities, a spy-space in its very essence. Justificatory ends were not necessary; actions need only forward the "game." It was in that sense celebrated as a space for real liberty among Britons weary of the spiritually crushing results of bourgeois social and cultural discipline. If liberalism was founded on the notion of the watched self—the panopticon disciplining individuals or the inner eye watching the self—a hidden reality was an unwatched space, enabling other notions of conscience and systems of ethical accountability. As the German philosopher Hannah Arendt observed, Lawrence's story was that "of a real agent . . . who actually believed he had entered . . . the stream of historical necessity and become a functionary or agent of the secret forces which rule the world."[148]

The air control regime, cloaked in secrecy, was part of this hidden world. As much as it sought to discipline Arabs by making them feel watched, it eluded the gaze of the British public, and this licensed its ethical liberties. Many were satisfied with the official justifications of the regime, as we have seen, but many remained skeptical, especially those invested in asserting the mass democracy's right to control foreign policy and receptive to the unflinching critique of the League of Nations mandate system coming from anticolonial bodies like the transnational League against Imperialism.[149] Government secrecy, including closeted reliance on experts, was the answer to this intransigency. Aspects of air control that could not be airbrushed or justified as part of a progressive narrative of history were simply hidden. Casualty figures were not collected anyway, but news from Iraq was also censored, airmen were not decorated, and travel to the region was strictly controlled.[150] The more the mass democracy asserted itself, the more the state found ways to keep foreign policy out of reach, adopting a covert modus operandi. British MPs pressed futilely for "particulars of where and why these bombardments have taken place . . . [and] whether inhabitants have been killed."[151]

Dissent was never fully stifled, however. The *Times* and the *Guardian* accused the state of having become numb to violence; its covert prosecution of small wars testified to its distance from a public that had exorcised the demon of militarism.[152] The novelist and journalist George Orwell's sharp nose for humbug did not fail him: "Defenceless villages are bombarded from the air, the inhabitants driven out into the countryside, the cattle machine-gunned, the huts set on fire with incendiary bullets: this is called *pacification*."[153] As in 1857 and 1865, news of rebellion and oppression abroad resonated in radical quarters at home, reviving the old worry about despotism. Once again, complained critics, colonial subjects and Britons suffered at the hands of a corrupt elite. Iraqis were subject to an unaccountable, authoritarian form of imperial rule, and the British public was, too; their will was ignored as the government, fulfilling the will of interested experts, unapologetically pursued its belligerent ("hunnish") and greedy ends, conspiring with oil and arms magnates.[154] Radicals compared the evasion of Parliamentary oversight of Middle East policy to the days of the Stuart kings.[155] The notion that the source of this scandalous despotism was ultimately oriental corruption also revived: The *Round Table* warned that if the RAF used bombers for everyday purposes like tax collection, "our rule will have become Oriental and its end will be near."[156] Such critics also adopted a conspiratorial understanding of history. The *Times* scoffed at "innocent imperialists" going on about the civilizing mission without an inkling that the government was fraternizing with oilmen "behind the scenes" on the assumption that the British taxpayer "inoculated with imperial enthusiasm" would be duped into paying for a permanent garrison to protect their interests.[157] As we will see in Chapter 6, in this atmosphere, new kinds of historical narratives began to appear as exposés of official mendacity, building on the work of anticolonial thinkers and earlier critics of jingoism.

Lawrence's awareness of his participation in government deception was the source of his guilt and his awareness of his moral ambiguity as a historical actor. In the twentieth century, the spy, bearing this kind of moral burden, emerged as a new archetype of British masculinity. If the novel dramatized the making of liberal conscience in the eighteenth century, the spy novel dramatized its unmaking in the twentieth century, elevating British stoicism as an ability to live with an internally fractured conscience—John Le Carré's George Smiley comes quickly to mind, as do the heroes of Buchan's novels. The late-Victorian view of empire as a burden to be selflessly borne was a stepping-stone to the formation of this new type. The burden of guilt came with the growing awareness of liberal empire as a mere cover story, cynically purveyed by a postwar government adept at propaganda. On grasping that the empire is "a despotism," "the secrecy of your revolt poisons you like a secret disease," explained Orwell in 1934 in his first novel, *Burmese Days*. "Your whole life is a life of lies." Orwell had resigned from the Indian Imperial Police in Burma in 1928 after just such a realization, but the passage refers to his protagonist, the dissolute Burma-based timber merchant John Flory, who represented a hapless version of the internally divided interwar imperial self. Flory begins to live "inwardly, secretly, in books and secret thoughts that could not be uttered"—a "corrupting" way to live. He, like Frankenstein's monster, longs in vain for a companion to share his secret life and "love Burma as he loved it and hate it as he hated it." Like the monster, Flory (who bears a disfiguring birthmark) ends his life with suicide.[158] The spy-hero offered a more resilient model for coping with postwar realities—Orwell himself had sought redemption in "undercover" life as a tramp in London and Paris, morphing from the policeman Eric Blair into the writer George Orwell. Thus, Lawrence's story was an essential historical script for many young men who went to the Middle East as travelers or to serve in the British administrations there, but even beyond them, his complicated moral graph—hero, traitor, redeemer—opened up the possibility of new kinds of agency. His public image recalled Byron, but unlike Byron, this was not a case in which one heroic death might atone for collective guilt. Rather he embodied a new kind of hero who *bore* guilt for life, a burden that made him elusive and morally slippery—a figure complicit in betrayal, who had himself been betrayed by government. Lawrence's invention of the figure of the special operative showed that the government might sinisterly use such a figure to betray the public in covert pursuit of unpopular imperial ends. The fight for "democratic control" was an assertion of the historical agency of the people over "agents" of the state, fueled by a postwar belief that state actors were conscienceless and that the story of liberal empire merely veiled Machiavellian pursuit of interest.

The continued flow of arms to the region amplified these suspicions. Radical members of Parliament asked questions about Britain knavishly subsidizing both its wartime Sharifian allies and their rival, Ibn Saud, who prevailed in the contest to control the Arabian peninsula in 1925, generating fresh fears that the Saudis would next turn British arms against the British.[159] In 1926, the Labour Party politician Hugh Dalton condemned the directors of arms firms as "the highest and completest embodiment of capitalist morality."[160] Between the world wars, arms-makers came to embody for the British public the most nefarious form of the amoral exercise of agency in their single-minded devotion to profit—the villainous "merchant of death." Echoes of the debate around Samuel Galton emerged as a movement to abolish private arms manufacture took center stage. In 1931, H. G. Wells pushed back in a manner recalling Galton by reminding the public that they were collectively invested in the arms trade; evil arms-makers profited from war, but so, too, did "thousands of persons of all ranks of life . . . as lesser shareholders" and workers in arms firms, though they were innocent of any desire to do so.[161] He was more optimistic than Galton, however, about the capacity for change, imagining that these thousands of workers would gladly endure loss of this fraction of their wealth for the greater good. In 1932, the Union for Democratic Control, an organization fighting for the public's right to control foreign policy against the monopoly of oracular experts, published an exposé about the "secret international," a complex of arms firms and government driving belligerent foreign policy. Two years later, the leftist politician and champion of Indian independence Fenner Brockway offered an unsparing indictment of the arms trade with his book *The Bloody Traffic*. Concerted public pressure forced a royal commission to investigate private arms manufacture the next year. Like Galton, however, it concluded that there was no room for exercise of remedial agency, for "the whole field of industrial activity" was complicit in arms-making; nationalizing arms manufacture would mean nationalizing all of industry.[162] In any case, the commission's report was buried before it could have any effect as German forces occupied the Rhineland. Meanwhile, air control, having spread to the North West Frontier, helped quell concerns about arms flows to India.

The British public did not shake its suspicion of secret forces guiding foreign policy. As it struggled to rein in the state's foreign policy, it remained skeptical of whether it ever could: quite apart from the evil agendas of arms-makers, through the means of an "invisible arm"—heroic secret agents like Lawrence—the state might continue to pursue unapologetically imperialistic ends. Socialists burned Lawrence in effigy in 1929 when revelation of his pseudonymous presence with the RAF on the Indian frontier prompted rumors of a secret imperial agenda, only strengthened by the clumsy secret operation to bring him home. In 1930, he was suspected of being in command in Baghdad.[163]

But the state itself mistrusted these figures, too. Lawrence was known to bridle at bureaucratic constraints on his capacity to act even during the war. Churchill felt proud of having put him into a "bridle and collar" at the Colonial Office, but the wary undersecretary of state doubted Lawrence would ever fit into the "official machine," accustomed as he was to dealing directly with ministers, "and Ministers only—and I see trouble ahead if he is allowed too free a hand."[164] Other bureaucrats chafed at Middle East experts' pretensions to heroic powers and systemic insubordination as they were ensconced in the imperial bureaucracy. Bell took "some handling"; Glubb was "unreasonable" (he defected to an Iraqi government post when the War Office recalled him from his post in 1926).[165] Others who were once treated like prophetic oracles later fell foul of the government, including H. St. John Philby, who defected to the service of Saudi Arabia and self-servingly described this pattern: "Most of the giants of

Arabian adventure . . . have displayed a tendency to fall foul of their own folk. . . . [Sir Wilfrid] Blunt . . . had a perpetual feud with the British Government in his fight for the rights of Arabs and Irishmen. . . . Lawrence himself was a declared rebel. . . . Bell was never popular, and was regarded rather as a nuisance than an asset in British official circles. . . . My own case was similar."[166] Official and popular mistrust of Middle East experts was part of the growing paranoia about the region and about British actions there. These figures had opened up a realm of covert agency, heroic but also possibly unaccountable to conscience—public or private. Lawrence was perennially suspected, by both the public and the government, of being liable to engage in "some diabolic trick for raising mutiny or revolt."[167] In 1929, just before leaving the Air Staff to become commissioner of the Metropolitan Police, Trenchard forbade him from leaving the United Kingdom and speaking to any of the "great," particularly Opposition politicians.[168] The type of the Arabia expert, drawn to the desert as the place to be authentically free, would not cease bucking against an imperial bureaucracy (the "iron cage") bent on constraining the liberty of Arabia and their liberty in Arabia. The "English Turk pro the Irish Arabian" was a recognizable type by 1922,[169] variously encompassing Casement, Lawrence, Blunt (who died that year), and others. The British state mistrusted the Lawrentian agent as constitutionally contrarian and prone to succumb to Bolshevik or Arab blandishments, so much so that the Colonial Office refused to appoint a British representative to Ibn Saud's government for a decade out of concern that "very close association with an Arab . . . regime does, in practice, make nearly all European officers very unreliable agents of their own Governments."[170] In 1923, British governors in Iraq were restyled as "Administrative Inspectors" overseeing Iraqi governors in response to Iraqi demands for greater autonomy but also to British concern that they were becoming "more native than the native himself."[171] Those who learned to "see things from the Beduin standpoint" seemed to lose "their English outlook . . . and . . . British character."[172] While the public thought Lawrence might be the instrument of imperial aggression, many state officials questioned his—and his emulators'—loyalty to empire. History was now understood as an occult world in which certain heroic types might exercise outsized agency. It was no longer the realm of natural laws or progress but of plots and machinations, a contest in subversion in the clash of civilizations.

Though the public thought the government behaved cynically, in pursuit of interest without regard for principle, government officials in thrall

to conspiracy fears remained certain of the principled nature of the empire, perceiving even public pushback as the work of malevolent forces (the
Russian hand). They saw press criticism of Middle East policy as the conspiratorial work of traitorous regional experts.[173] They excused their own
resort to covert means as merely a response to such forces. In the face of
Iraqi resistance that it understood as conspiratorial, the Air Ministry felt
discreet use of air control was appropriate: "In countries of this sort . . . the
impersonal drone of an aeroplane . . . is not so obtrusive as . . . soldiers."[174]
Air control was a mechanism of control in a time and place in which anti-
imperialism made more overt colonial rule a political impossibility, but
government officials denied that political reality by instead pointing to
malevolent conspiratorial forces to excuse their turn to covert tactics.

This view of history ensured that even decolonization might be a means
of extending imperial rule. The British presence was a provocation, creating instability. Air control, however discreet, continued to compromise
the legitimacy of the mandatory Iraqi government, which strained after
greater independence, forcing continual reframing of the mandatory ar-
rangement. Finally, Iraq was admitted to the League of Nations as an independent nation in 1932, but the British remained in charge behind the
scenes. British officialdom intended the grant of independence as window
dressing, "more apparent than real."[175] After all, the reason for holding on
to Iraq still stood: the risk of catastrophic anarchy instigated by evil plot-
ters. Over Iraqi objections, intelligence-gathering, aircraft, wireless, and
tanks remained in British hands even after 1932. The British high commissioner held a right of intervention, and British officials ensured the "independent" Iraqi government conformed to British priorities.[176] The Air
Ministry defended these continuities in Parliament by explaining that
Iraq was "an oriental country where intrigue is rife." Making it just that
themselves, they privately conceded, "we really have no defence."[177] This
fascinatingly disruptive comment is a singular instance of an official acknowledging the cynical use of historically grounded ethical arguments in
defense of empire. Its private nature suggests the author had adopted the
Lawrentian mode of living with duplicity. A Victorian would in Mill-ian
fashion have resigned in high dudgeon or proclaimed dissent some other
way. But this was an era that believed in the power of words uttered in
shadowy spaces.

Despite its failures, air control was pronounced a success. After a decade, it was exported to other areas, albeit in modified fashion. By then,

experts considered it "absurd" to think "some peculiar quality about [Iraq] . . . enabled aircraft to achieve [there] what they could not achieve anywhere else."[178] But the making of that original window of acceptability was crucial, and it depended on a powerful blend of historical narratives of imperial redemption and Arabian timelessness. The liberal defense of air control claimed it redeemed Arabia for the world, but tolerance for the violence of that project depended on the notion that Arabia existed outside history. Such legitimating notions gave air control a place to become normalized within the tolerance of postwar British conscience. Presumably, once air control had done its work, Arabia and its denizens would no longer be able to tolerate bombardment; they, too, would expect to be treated as ordinary mortals. From the British point of view, that would be a win for history but a loss for culture.

Air control extended the myth of liberal empire just enough to convince those who could be convinced, and it was cheap enough and discreet enough to dodge the check of those who were no longer buying.[179] Enough were convinced, enough consciences soothed or evaded, for the regime to last the entire interwar period. The British fully reoccupied the country in World War II. At that time, the Arabian window of acceptability opened the door to wider use of bombardment. Arthur Harris applied his experiences bombing Iraq and the Indian frontier as head of Bomber Command— he was the man behind the firestorms of Hamburg and Dresden that killed half a million people. Churchill was prime minister and, under Harris's influence, warded off pangs of conscience about bombing Germany with faith in the higher poetic justice that "those who have loosed these horrors upon mankind will now in their homes and persons feel the shattering stroke of retribution."[180] They adapted the historical script used against the Ikhwan; now Europe had become the scene of a clash between good and evil. Churchill emerged a hero from the war, and, as a historian, he knew that the power of the pen would safeguard that reputation—as he is famously misquoted: "History will be kind to me for I intend to write it."[181] That cracks have nevertheless opened in the self-righteous portrait he painted is the result of the discipline's dramatic reinvention beginning just then, as we shall see in Chapter 6.

Meanwhile, the aura of occult knowledge acquired by British Arabist experts in a time when Lawrence of Arabia was a household name colored notions of expertise more generally. The aura of the expert evolved into one of almost magical objectivity, someone whose knowledge depended on genius rather than intensive study. The British adventure in the Middle East, though rooted in humanistic curiosity, galvanized faith in the expert as someone possessing "abstract" knowledge—knowledge abstracted from context—building on James Mill's confidence that he could know India from his closet: from expert in a closet to closeted experts. Indeed, British Arabist experts did not pause in using their humanistic knowledge as a basis for the techno-scientific effort to police and "develop" the region. The techno-scientific experts who came to "fix the economy" in the Middle East did so having absorbed the aura of absolute authority from the dreamy spies who wandered there first.[182] As Timothy Mitchell tells us, the idea of "the economy" was first realized at the level of the colony, as part of the scramble to reassemble imperial authority on the eve of its collapse. Colonies were the sites through which the rule of historians yielded to the rule of economists, just when the historical discipline itself was being reframed as the province of rebels, as we shall see. The archetypal economist John Maynard Keynes followed the Mills in developing his intellectual expertise while employed at the India Office just before the war, producing a study of the Indian economy. This new domain, which claimed to abstract the material sphere of life for rational and numerical study, leaving culture, history, and other realms to humanistic contemplation, took its full form in the 1930s–1950s: The world was bifurcated into "the real and the abstract, the material and the cultural."[183] British spies in Arabia were the midwives of this partitioning. But the reign of historians did not end overnight, as Chapter 5, on decolonization, will show.

After World War I, British officials drew liberally on new understandings of history that sought to recover the possibility of individual heroic agency. Their cloak-and-dagger sensibility depended on an oriental setting where secrecy and mystery were imagined to be not only permissible modes of operation but culturally expected. This view of history enabled the British to invent and implement the world's first air control regime with mostly clear conscience and even with confidence in a consistent paternalism, a renewal of the Victorian story of liberal empire.

Soon after the Second World War, Hannah Arendt located the origins of the deadly totalitarianism of her time in European imperialism: the belief in the power of "white skin," the British administrator's belief in "his own innate capacity to rule and dominate," *and* the attraction of intelligence work for British men. These were, in fact, the dominant justificatory frameworks for empire from the mid-nineteenth to mid-twentieth

centuries; here we have re-attached them to the series of historical narratives that gave them ethical legs. Arendt saw that "the stage seemed to be
set for all possible horrors" in the British Empire, with all the elements in
place for totalitarian rule based on racism. But totalitarianism instead
emerged elsewhere, and, Arendt concluded, "the happy fact is that although British imperialist rule sank to some level of vulgarity, cruelty
played a lesser role between the two World Wars than ever before and a
minimum of human rights was always safeguarded."[184] Certainly, the interwar empire was not the same as Stalinist Russia or Nazi Germany, but it
was hardly a scene of diminished cruelty. Human rights were not safeguarded, and air control's panoptic ambitions in particular betray a substantive affinity for the totalitarian style. Arendt's free pass testifies to
the twin successes of British propaganda and secrecy about the reality of
interwar empire, such that the Amritsar Massacre of 1919 appeared an
anomalous episode. Like air control, that episode was justified as the heroic foiling of a vast "conspiracy . . . to destroy our sea power and drive us out
of Asia."[185] Meanwhile, the "cuteness of the English aeroplane," ironically,
helped anchor the myth of the "peaceable kingdom" between the wars.[186]

We are the heirs of this mythology. The British-backed Iraqi monarchy
was overthrown in the Iraqi revolution of 1958. But just two years later, the
United States began covert interventions in the country, attempting to as-
sassinate the head of the new republic. Through long cooperation during
World War II and the Cold War, the American intelligence and military
establishment absorbed the lessons of covert and aerial imperial control in
the region.[187] The conspiratorial view of history sank deep roots in the paranoid atmosphere of the Cold War, fueling conspiratorial use of covert
agency to make imperial history. Special operatives modeled on Lawrence
played an important a role in World War II and have remained a primary
mode of Western engagement with the Middle East, especially. Lawrence
remains an indispensable guide to military thinking about the region. The
ghost of empires past haunts American use of drone surveillance and warfare in the very regions the British once controlled from the air: Afghanistan, Pakistan, Somalia, Yemen, and Iraq. Secrecy remains key to evading
questions about inhumanity. Generalized terror remains the tactical objective. This violence, too, is justified by the notion that the "Arab mind" can
tolerate force in a manner that others cannot.[188] As one senior counterinsurgency advisor to the American military regime in Iraq recognized, people
in the region see drones as "neo-colonial."[189]

CHAPTER FIVE

ˊ ˊ *The Division of Progress*

> Serious nationalism is tied to internationalism.
>
> —Benedict Anderson

ˊ ˊ *The empire did end,* after a fashion, despite repeated renewals of its script. It ended in fits and starts, cracking first in 1776, and still cracking today as Scotland and Northern Ireland confront the implications of Brexit. The story of modern empire flowed, in a sense, from the opening crack in 1776: The need for a historical narrative to explain and make good on that loss drove much of British imperial activity afterwards. The empire continued to crack, and each desperately contained rebellion prompted further soul-searching about the historical necessity of the empire. The end of formal empire in Iraq in 1932 was a sham, a morphing of direct empire into indirect and even covert rule. More credible, if ephemeral, was the revolutionary end of British rule in Iraq in 1958.

In general, the reality of post–World War II decolonization was attenuated, for the British especially, by the idea of the Commonwealth. This body had been inaugurated between the wars to frame the shifting relationship between Britain and the "white dominions." As Canada, New Zealand, and Australia asserted their autonomy, the Commonwealth preserved the imperial bond in other ways. Economic ties with colonies and dominions remained important, particularly the imperial trade bloc known as the sterling area. Until the 1970s, Britain stood back from the emerging institutions of the European Union, maintaining its orientation towards the empire. British imperialism had always been flexible, granting real and nominal autonomy as needed in order to better preserve the imperial bond. Informal, indirect, and covert forms of imperial rule were part of its tool kit. Against this backdrop, there was little reason to think that granting independence to India in 1947 would substantively alter its relationship to Britain. Indeed, many could reasonably read the moment of formal decolonization as yet another strategy for keeping the moral case for empire intact while maintaining the relationship in substance. That India became a member of the Commonwealth was spun as the culmination of liberal empire, another signal transition moment in its unfolding. There was no embarrassment in it. The postwar Labour government was deeply committed to this narrative and its incorporation of the notion of "colonial development"—that the empire could produce commodities that would earn much-needed dollars. In 1960, while the former Labour prime minister Clement Atlee extolled the empire for "voluntarily" surrendering sovereignty to its colonies, the ruling prime minister, Harold Macmillan, spun the "wind of change" blowing through Africa as fulfillment of the imperial narrative.

Such narratives of continuities with the past, real or imagined, framed understandings of decolonization. The British did not simply let go of the empire after the Second World War—whatever Atlee claimed. They fought hard and long to hold on to some colonies, such as Kenya and Malaya. In others, the promise of substantive continuity allowed more graceful transition. In India, the anticolonial movement forced the British out, despite efforts to crush it with massive force. As prime minister during the war, Churchill refused to countenance loss of the "jewel" anchoring the empire.[1] Even those on the Left were not contemplating a total break between India and the empire. Like Fenner Brockway, George Orwell was born in India and concluded (from his service in the police there) that it was an "evil despotism."[2] Still, in a 1941 essay, he argued that Britain must offer India not "freedom" but "partnership," although "we must also tell the Indians that they are free to secede, if they want to." This, he said, they would never do. For what they really wanted was merely recognition of their power to secede, not actual severance of the imperial bond, which would spell "disaster for India no less than for England." He dreamt of socialist revolution offering a chance at imperial expiation: Indians and the English would work "side by side for the development of India." The English would finally pass on the training from which they had "systematically" excluded Indians.[3]

Indian anticolonialism challenged Orwell's confident assumption of Indians' joint investment in the historical narrative of ever-evolving liberal empire. That was why it was brutally repressed during the war, in a manner that weighed on Orwell's conscience, at least: He confessed in his diary in August 1942 that "the way the British government is now behaving in India upsets me more than a military defeat."[4] Mutinies and the need for American troops to secure against Japanese and anticolonial threats together made it clear that the British could not hold the subcontinent by force alone. Nothing in the 1930s negotiations with Indian anticolonialists suggested that the British would concede real independence after the war; it was a decade of formal concessions designed to maintain ties in substance—akin to the granting of Iraqi independence in 1932. That the British departed relatively quietly in 1947, compared to, say, the French in Vietnam or the British in Kenya later on, testifies to British faith that India's official new status as a dominion of the Commonwealth was a guarantee of substantive continuity.

That faith was strengthened by the fact that decolonization took the form of devolution to two rather than one new dominion: India and Pakistan. This crack in British India, known as Partition, became the biggest human migration in history, accompanied by horrific violence on a mass scale. Fifteen to eighteen million people moved; more than three million were missing or dead; hundreds of thousands of women were raped or abducted.[5] The event gave us grisly images of trains full of corpses; dismembered and burnt bodies abandoned in canals and along roads and tracks; entire villages executed; stories of women raped and mutilated or killed by themselves or their families to escape rape, the shame of rape, or conversion. This violence on an unprecedented scale was not the haphazard violence of a barbaric society suddenly let loose upon itself. It was systemic. It was committed by paramilitaries composed of former soldiers and well-trained young men, gangs with machine guns in jeeps, efficient bodies who took the shame, honor, and protection of their communities into their own hands, with the support of those communities.[6]

What was the role, or responsibility, of the departing British rulers in this violence? To many, it seemed to substantiate the narrative that the British presence was what had long held anarchy at bay—the late-Victorian justification of empire that predicted that the minute the British left, the subcontinent would erupt into barbaric violence. Britain's only sin, then, was in giving up the selfless burden of maintaining order in South Asia

after shouldering it for so long—which it had done only out of gracious-
ness, in response to insistent, if naive, local demands. Thus, the violence
need not weigh on British conscience at all. British narratives of decolonization emphasize the ceremony of the transfer of power in 1947 as the fulfillment of the paternalistic goals of the empire, while at once resignedly
viewing the violence as proof that those paternalistic goals could never be
fulfilled; clearly, only a steadying British hand could keep a lid on the native
tendency to anarchy.

South Asians are of course responsible for the violence they committed.
But the violence was also directly and intensely shaped by the colonial
context in which it erupted. Before British rule, conflict had flared at times
between different religious communities, but the violence of Partition was
something new. Religious identity had been transformed by the experience of empire. The violence of Partition was grounded in modern, colonial notions of difference, not ancient hatreds. Moreover, it was itself
transformative, laying the groundwork of a new, divided form of national
selfhood that shaped both South Asian consciousness and conscience.

Mixed populations have long existed and have gotten along in many
times and places. The Indian subcontinent is no more riven by ethnic, linguistic, social, and religious divisions than similar-sized Europe in the
same period. The assumption of some sort of permanent incompatibility
between Muslims and Hindus defies the evidence of history. To be sure,
there have been times of conquest and subjugation, but also indigenization
of Muslim conquest and coexistence alongside Hindu rulers. Hindu and
Muslim interactions varied, encompassing production of new religions
(Sikhism), combined mysticisms (Sufism), syncretic beliefs and practices
in coastal communities, and also radical hatreds in some times and places.
Hinduism and Islam are not monolithic and unchanging religions but systems of belief that evolved in the subcontinent together since the time of
the Prophet. They are no more intrinsically incompatible than Protes-
tantism and Catholicism or Judaism and Christianity or Judaism and
Islam. Political context and the quality and legitimacy of governance determine when religious groups live together peacefully. If the concept of
"partition" had been available in seventeenth-century Europe, would it
have been sensible to simply partition Protestants and Catholics given
their evident inability to get along in that time? The fact is that in most
times and places, Jews, Muslims, Christians, Hindus, Buddhists, and others
have lived together without violence, even when there has been tension

between them. The seemingly intractable hatred between Jews and Muslims in Palestine, between Muslims and Hindus in South Asia, and between Catholics and Protestants in Ireland is emphatically a modern phenomenon, shaped by the history of colonialism.

The British, however, were impervious to this reality. From the start, British narratives had justified Britain as a benevolent force come to rescue India from dereliction under "foreign" Muslim conquest. From the second half of the nineteenth century, social Darwinist thinking about race and culture ensured that the British interpreted eruptions of violence among their subjects as evidence of the primordial hatreds of irrational people without a sense of history rather than the result of bad governance or traumatic social upheaval caused by imperial capitalism.[7] Intercommunity violence was, to them, an atavism. The same dismissive language of fanaticism was used across colonial contexts from Ireland to India. The empire's very purpose, in this understanding, was to impartially and selflessly impose peace among such people.

In fact, it stoked rather than dampened such conflict. An 1888 history of British India by the career Indian official Sir John Strachey (uncle of Lytton Strachey) closed by affirming the "absolute peace" wrought by the "blessing of Pax Britannica" in India—apart from when Muslims and Hindus "sometimes for a moment . . . burst into violent conflict." The 1894 edition replaced "sometimes for a moment" with "not unfrequently." The historian Mark Doyle rightly calls attention to this subtle but important change: "'Absolute peace' except for 'not unfrequent' outbursts of 'fanaticism and intolerance'? Frequent communal violence under British rule as a sign of what would happen if Britain ceased to rule? Just what kind of 'Pax' was this?"[8] How did this make any sense? In fact, as Doyle shows, the empire helped cause much of this "not unfrequent" violence between communities. It did so by pressing different communities into vulnerable forms of mobility, forcing settlement of others, and framing policies that ossified formerly fluid communal relations so that caste, tribal, and religious identities became more rigid. I don't want to attribute too much creative force to colonial power—there are longer trajectories to many of these things—but, nevertheless, British colonialism significantly shaped South Asian religious identity from the outset, as we have seen. The British saw religion (like other identities) as a fixed, mutually exclusive badge of identity, despite its often fluid and locally determined nature. While continually dis-ordering Indian society, they endeavored to impose administrative "order" on diverse communities. Orientalist scholars codified religion in new ways; the colonial legal system enforced those new, codified identities; maps, censuses, and the revenue system built them into the administration of the government. It is worth recalling, for comparison, that Britain's own common law, while resting on the authority of antiquity and honoring precedent, remained flexible in accommodating varied interpretations, reflecting change in custom and understanding over time. But British codification rendered Hindu and Muslim legal practice immune to change out of the presumption that they were timeless, like India itself.[9] The British revolutionized Indian social structure, and caste distinctions were clearly not rigid enough to prevent them from doing so. Rather, British administrators disembodied caste from mutable social, political, and cultural processes and networks and, as nationalism took off, made it the fundamental organizing category for censuses and ethnographical surveys informing government activities, politicizing it in an entirely *new* way. Caste as we now know it "is not a residual survival of ancient India but a specifically colonial form of civil society," writes the historian Nicholas Dirks.[10] The objective of such policies was administrative efficiency—the hope of easing tax collection, for instance.

But fear of rebellion also shaped colonial social engineering. The British emerged from 1857 determined to prevent South Asians from ever combining into a bloc against their rule again. Theorizing South Asian political identity through social distinctions grounded in the new science of race, the British built them into the colonial state—even public infrastructure, as, for instance, in the "Hindu" tea stall at Gondia station pictured here. In 1905, the British partitioned the province of Bengal along religious lines expressly to stifle rising anticolonial sentiment emanating from Calcutta. The plan was masterminded by Herbert Risley, the race scientist who codified the caste system (based on nose measurements) in the 1901 census. His logic was simple: "Bengal united is a power; Bengal divided will pull in several different ways."[11] His aim was "to split up and thereby weaken a solid body of opponents to our rule." Resistance to this "divide and conquer" tactic was vociferous, exploding into the swadeshi movement, including boycott of British goods and institutions. The anticolonial Jugantar revolutionaries drew on many ethical guides, from international anarchism to the *Gita,* in their turn to political terrorism.[12] The British were forced to annul the division in 1911. They also conceded a measure of local participation in government for Indians in 1909 but, here

Tea Stall, Gondia Station, 1932. (Reproduction © Ravindra Bhalerao, Courtesy of Narrow Gauge Railway Museum, Nagpur, and South Eastern Railway, Garden Reach, Kolkata)

again, cannily based political identity on religion, creating separate electorates for Hindus and Muslims. In Britain, the move was hailed for "pulling back ... sixty-two millions of people from joining the ranks of the seditious opposition."[13] Once electorates were framed by religion, attendant forms of political association and communication—from parties to newspapers—had to be, too, hardening differences and irrevocably politicizing religious identity.

Besides fabricating it with administrative policy, the imperial crucible forged communal identity in other ways. Anticolonial movements drew intellectual and political strength from religious ideologies that strengthened communal identity, including, for instance, Wahhabism, which sought to purify Islam of external contamination and unite Muslims under a caliphate, rather than the British Empire. Queen Victoria's affirmation of the policy of noninterference in religion in 1858, coupled with political repression, also encouraged anticolonial activists to couch their protests in religious terms.[14] The very illegitimacy of the imperial state, including suspicion of state bias towards particular communities, mistrust of its motives, and alienation from its forces of law and order, also caused communal disturbances across the empire. Moreover, communal violence *worked* in pushing back against empire—albeit bringing its own harrowing costs. Though not directed at the state, such violence helped destabilize its hold by exposing its façade of omnipotence, questioning its impartiality, exposing its brutality, and targeting its policemen. The violence itself showed that communal identity was a powerful basis for political mobilization.[15]

Interwar tensions between Indian Hindus and Muslims were also part of a moment of global reckoning with minority populations in a time when, also thanks to European colonialism, the idea of a homogeneous ethno-nation-state had become a norm. Fought in the name of national self-determination, the First World War had established the norm of a world order made up of homogeneous ethnic nation-states participating in an internationalized order (the League of Nations), giving new purchase to the categories of "minority" and "majority" all over the world. This new international order could oversee the ethnic unmixing of parts of the world straining after the status of homogeneous nation-state. Following the genocidal elimination of Armenians from Turkey, the pattern was officially consolidated by the 1923 exchange under League of Nations auspices of Greek and Turkish minorities in the name of pacification. The German vision of a minority-free Europe emerged from a similar outlook. The ethnic cleansing that accompanied Partition in 1947, though exceeding others in scale, was part of a wider post–World War II phenomenon, when minority populations became refugees all over Europe and the Middle East, producing a crisis in the very nation-state system that had made their expulsion necessary.

Even with these antecedents and this context, it was by no means a foregone conclusion that South Asian religious communities would turn hellishly upon one another in 1946–1947. There was still plenty of evidence of cooperation and coexistence among groups. The Punjab province, one of the two provinces that were partitioned, was under a Unionist Party government. Members of all religions fought the British side by side in the Indian National Army raised by Subhas Chandra Bose in World War II. But a historical imagination that gave great men an outsized role in history and the requirements of the powerful historical narratives jointly sustaining understandings of imperialism and nationalism colluded explosively in creating Partition and its violence.

As colonialism set various forces in motion abetting the consolidation of communal identities in India, British control of the Middle East also began to inform the British attitude towards Indian Muslims. Paranoid fears of telepathic unity across deserts raised the stakes for interactions with Muslims in India. In this view, a "mistake" with Indian Muslims would reverberate destructively throughout the empire. This Islamophobic background mattered deeply in British willingness to entertain the idea of Pakistan. Muslim members of the Indian National Congress, who did not seek the creation of Pakistan, disturbed the British political imagination of India and were marginalized as independence approached.[16]

Even more importantly, the practice of attempting to order peoples and polities by drawing lines on a map had become an established imperial practice, as the attempted partition of Bengal in 1905 shows. The scramble for Africa had begun with a conference geared to just such an end in 1885 in Berlin, with eager European officials gathered to score the map of the continent. In 1893, the Durand Line had fixed the border between British India and Afghanistan (whose sovereignty was nevertheless constrained by British influence). The imperial prerogative to arbitrarily draw such lines is perhaps most famously captured in Churchill's apocryphal boast that he "created Jordan with a stroke of a pen one Sunday afternoon."

These earlier divisions were not lines drawn as part of an alleged "solution" to political conflict between different groups. That type of partition began with Ireland in 1920–1922, as the price of Home Rule (Northern Ireland remaining within the United Kingdom), which then became a template for applying the same "solution" to Palestine in the 1930s (as illustrated by the accompanying maps).[17] By the 1940s, "partition" was part of Britain's decolonization tool kit. The same officials transferred the idea from context to context, especially the prominent historian Reginald Coupland. Coupland was a student of Alfred Zimmern, a classicist historian who read the history of the Greek city-state system as a playbook of imperial survival, as captured in the title of his 1911 work, *The Greek Commonwealth*. He embraced the notion of federalism as a way forward for the British Empire, a means of accommodating local patriotism within an enduring imperial framework. Such ideas had found fertile soil in the nineteenth century, too, especially in Seeley's work. Their life was also extended in the work of Hugh Edward Egerton, whose 1911 historical survey *Federations and Unions within the British Empire* foresaw that the empire would

Map of the Partition of Ireland, 1921. (World History Archive / Alamy Stock Photo)

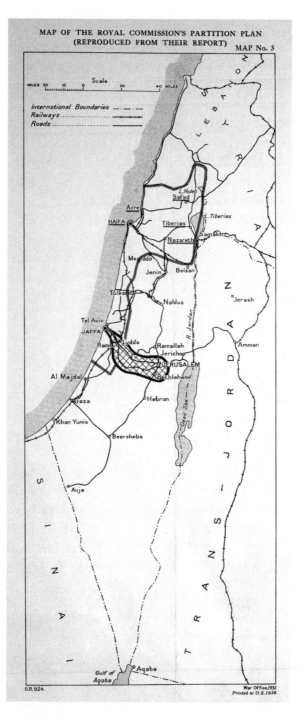

Proposed Partition of Palestine, Peel Report, 1938. (The National Archives [UK], ref. MFQ1/465[3])

"organically" evolve in a federal direction. The Commonwealth would be the culmination of this evolutionary vision. Coupland absorbed these ideas, presenting Zimmern's book and a copy of Thucydides to Churchill during the First World War in hopes of influencing him.[18] After the war, Coupland saw partition as a useful technology not so much because it could separate people at odds but because it promised to fulfill that federal dream of empire. The empire would be the umbrella structure encompassing fragments that were *temporary* incubators of federal wisdom. In a 1946 essay on Palestine in the *Times,* he explained that partition was the only way for Arabs and Jews to finally come together in a "real and durable" settlement.[19] It was, in short, a stage, a historical phase, through which they must pass. As the historian Arie Dubnov writes, "Coupland justified partition as a form of federalist eschatology: the End of Times would witness the reunification of the Jew and the Arab, who would outgrow their tribal idiosyncrasies and join the Commonwealth of Nations."[20] After all, Britain itself had gone through this very process: The people of Wales and Scotland, whose nationalism was the subject of his last book, had gotten over contemplating "a Welsh or Scottish 'Pakistan.'"[21] Britain was a federal unit and had helped form federal structures for South Africa and Canada, too.

Coupland was not only sanguine about his historical vision; he also had great faith in the power of heroic men to achieve it by sheer will. This, too, he had inherited from his liberal predecessors. As Beit Professor of Colonial History and Fellow of All Souls College at Oxford, Coupland was an influential proponent of "imperial trusteeship" as a tradition dating from the time of abolitionism.[22] In 1923, he published a popular biography of William Wilberforce. In 1933, centenary celebrations of the end of slavery in the empire, along with the interwar mandate system, helped renew this narrative of empire. Coupland went on to write hagiographic works on the founder of modern Singapore, Sir Stamford Raffles, and on Sir John Kirk, the explorer and administrator in East Africa credited with ending slavery there. He (like Toynbee) was among the set of experts at the new Royal Institute of International Affairs, known as Chatham House, which advised the government on policy—the closeted postwar decision-making that so incensed those demanding democratic control of foreign policy. Partition became another instance of great men attempting to exercise godlike authority in determining the fate of millions; indeed, Cyril Radcliffe, the man appointed to draw the border between Pakistan and India, went beyond closeted expert in being "shut up in a lonely mansion" under heavy police guard while he did his work, per the poet W. H. Auden.[23]

Intention was key in distinguishing the type of partition proposed for Ireland, Palestine, and India.[24] In purporting to solve a conflict defined as perennial and intractable, this type of partition provided a further rationale for imperial oversight and preservation of the imperial bond despite devolution. Dubnov summarizes, "Partition finds its origins in both the now-forgotten imperial federalist vision of bringing to life a Third British Empire and to [sic] the interwar discourse that considered population transfer a pragmatic, liberal, and legal mechanism for overcoming ethnonational strife."[25]

British (and other European) imperialists thus staked empire's claim as an international formation in a competitive field of internationalisms including the international communism of the Soviet Union, Pan-Islamism and other "pan" movements, and the liberal internationalism of the League of Nations. Many interwar British leaders saw a "natural evolution from the British Empire to worldwide organizations." The South African general Jan Smuts saw the empire as the "embryo League of Nations."[26] This was the vision of empire Orwell's talk of international partnership also affirmed during the war. The idea of federalizing newly "free" states in the Commonwealth appealed symbolically but also geopolitically in a world dominated by continental superpowers—the United States and the Soviet Union.

In this outlook, partition presented a means of internationalizing conflicts, of containing nationalism and extending empire as a force of international oversight of those conflicts. Arie Dubnov and Laura Robson write, "Partition . . . belonged firmly within the imperial realm; it was less a vehicle for national liberation than a novel, sophisticated *divide et impera* tactic that sought to co-opt the global tilt toward the ethnic nation-state." It was originally conceived as part of a "new type of imperial governance in the guise of internationalism" and, even after 1945, offered the promise of continued postcolonial influence.[27] The British priority for decolonization was that whatever new entity emerged must remain in the Commonwealth to ensure continuity of the imperial order. Partition was fully compatible with that vision; both Pakistan and India *were* initially dominion states of the Commonwealth. Britain had a taste for partnering with reliable local elites to federate territories and societies—it tried (unsuccessfully) to federate the Indian princely states with British India in the 1930s. Partition was "a method of intraimperial political rearrangement" that at once furthered the liberal narrative of "dominionization."[28] It emerged from a liberal historical imagination whose telos was the rationalizing of the world into a system of nations framed by the Commonwealth. Partition was an acceptable compromise for ensuring all territory wound up within the Commonwealth even if in fragments. It could be spun as the fulfillment of historical narratives that had long justified the empire, a fusing of the story of progress with the story of permanent difference. The very success of the gambit—the willingness of former colonies to be Commonwealth members—would be history's verdict on the empire, that expiatory moment towards which imperialists had strained since the trial of Hastings: proof that it had been an altruistic enterprise. These were high moral stakes for the British. That 1947 yielded two new Commonwealth members rather than one was immaterial to them.

In short, as Dubnov and Robson put it, partition was an "imperial survival tactic" that helped smooth the afterlife of empire: Britain sought to create new forms of informal authority and friendly client states in the postcolonial era, without heed for the human costs. This was why Gandhi mistrusted British mediation of the conflict between the Indian National Congress (or Congress) and the Muslim League (the party advocating for creation of Pakistan), preferring direct confrontation between them.[29] Dubnov and Robson seek to disabuse us of partition proponents' actual desire to solve conflict, but those behind it did not see their aims so cynically. The stated intentions mattered. The allegedly good intentions behind Partition were powerfully exculpatory when it came to assigning moral responsibility for the deaths and mayhem it caused, casting the British as naive but otherwise clear of fault. Figures like Coupland testify to the power of an updated evolutionary historical narrative of empire and to the renewed postwar sense of heroic imperial agency that emboldened people like him to work towards fulfilling it.

But India's partition did not in the end come about because of Coupland's confidence in that narrative. Whatever his theoretical enthusiasm for the practice, Coupland ultimately concluded that partition was not appropriate for India given the absence of natural boundaries, the presence of other minorities (like the Sikhs), and the sheer size of the population and territory in question.[30] So it was not simply the case that the colonial ordering of society by fixing religious identities led directly to the colonial division of land based on those identities. How then did Partition come to pass in India, and to what extent were the British in fact accountable? They did create the conditions for Partition and put the idea into circulation. But it wound up on the table in devolution negotiations in the end because the idea took on a life of its own through the colonially framed evolution of historical, and antihistorical, thought among South Asians.

European Orientalist ideas about South Asian religion shaped South Asians' study of their religions, too. Scholarly conventions made it difficult for anyone to understand questions about Islam or Hinduism and worldly affairs *outside* of European orientalism. Mohamed Iqbal is the poet and philosopher credited with inspiring the movement for Pakistan. He was a disciple, by correspondence, of the poet Daagh Dehlavi, mentioned in Chapter 2. Iqbal went to Europe in 1905 in the steps of another beloved teacher, Thomas Walker Arnold of Government College in Lahore. Arnold was a historian of Islam and Islamic art. He was a great friend of Sir Syed Ahmed Khan, who had helped found a new college at Aligarh in 1875 on the model of Oxbridge in order to belatedly fulfill Macaulay's dream of producing an Indian class in the British image: The failed rebellion of 1857 had confirmed for him that Muslims must acquire the skills necessary to navigate the structures of power and prosperity in an India clearly ruled by Britain. Khan was knighted for his efforts. Arnold, meanwhile, participated in the turn-of-the-century makeover of Islam that helped draw eccentric Britons to the Arabian deserts. His books punctured notions that Islam had spread through belligerence to show instead that it spread because of the appeal of its religious and moral message. In 1904, he returned to England to work for the India Office, the department that oversaw the Government of India. He had introduced Iqbal to Western oriental scholarship on Islam and now helped him further his studies abroad in Cambridge, Munich, and London. His influence on Iqbal was "both ideological and practical." Iqbal dedicated his PhD dissertation to him.[31] Researching Islamic mysticism in these settings, while reading Goethe and Nietzsche, whose own work was shaped by interest in "the Orient," Iqbal became convinced that mysticism had no real foundation in original Islam, that it was alien and even unhealthy. He became interested in "real" Islam's potential as a social and political organization. He sympathized with Syed Ahmed Khan's view, supported also by the poet and critic Maulana

Khwaja Hali, that Urdu poetry, and Muslim elite culture generally, had become decadent and required reform. In 1909, he thought of the British Empire as embodying the antinational, universalistic political ideal of Islam.[32]

And yet, while embracing the empire, he at once disavowed the historical narratives that were its justification. The empire was framed as a mechanism for unleashing the moral consciousness of nationhood around the world. But Iqbal's sensibility was not historical in this worldly sense. As the historian Faisal Devji has argued, Iqbal's was not a "properly historical inquiry" into Islam but a search for a "constitutional model for a future society freed from its grandiose past," like republican Rome in the West. He admired the French philosopher Henri Bergson, whose work was just then also shaping mystically minded British venturers to the Middle Eastern deserts.[33] If Bergson's ideas depended on long European engagement with "oriental" thought, now they resonated with Iqbal in Europe. He, too, rejected the notion of uniform, serial time that was the medium of history and rejected national history—the raison d'être of modern historicism and its accompanying notions of time.[34] Islam's origins therefore were not something consigned to a past that was past in serial time but might yet constitute a future.

After the First World War, Iqbal emerged a critic of empire. By demonstrating nationalism's destructive effects, the war redoubled his determination to think outside that box. Many anticolonial thinkers saw an alternative in communism. Iqbal's problem with communism, like territorial nationalism, was its essential worldliness, its perpetuation of the condition of alienation that made imperialism and capitalism so oppressive.[35] This was an argument against the historicism that had made these four isms the dominant narratives of his time. As Devji writes, Iqbal "argued that the 'interests' to which historians routinely attribute all actions and ideas were themselves the products of history and could not have existed before the establishment of property as the foundation of social order." That order had made "ownership of some substance" the heart of "interests," defined by general historical categories like class rather than "natural or individual reality." In modern nation-states, the material and spiritual realms were divided—the one worldly, the other otherworldly. Ethics had been split—the preceding chapters are evidence of how worldly systems of ethical accountability ushered in by the Enlightenment's historical sensibilities subverted the call of religiously grounded or more transcendent understandings of ethics. Iqbal put this in his address to the Muslim League (the party claiming to speak for Indian Muslims, founded in 1906 out of Syed Ahmad Khan's Muslim upliftment efforts) in 1930 in Allahabad, where he first uttered his dream of a "Muslim India within India": "The universal ethics of Jesus is displaced by national systems of ethics and polity. The conclusion to which Europe is consequently driven is that religion is a private affair of the individual and has nothing to do with what is called man's temporal life."[36] In societies in which property was not the sine qua non guiding an irrevocable march towards nation-statehood, as he felt was the case in India, moral ideals remained compelling interests, and he devoted himself to preserving them.

Iqbal's alternative view of human agency was that humans are meant to "partner and even compete with God," writes Devji.[37] However mistakenly Iqbal faulted Urdu poetry's Sufi idiom for politically passivity, he turned it to explicit political use in his own work, expressing this view of agency in his masterpiece "*Jawab-e-Shikwa*" (Response to the Complaint), which he recited at a political rally in Lahore in 1913.[38] In this poem, God reminds his followers to act, "*Waqt-e-fursat hai kahan kaam abhi baaqi hai*" (Where is the spare time, much still remains to be done), and to act powerfully, "*Naghma-e-mauj hai hungama-e-toofan ho ja*" (You are the song of a wave, become the tumult of a storm). As His followers, they hold their fate in their own hands: "*Tu Musalman ho to taqdir hai tadbir teri.*" The poem closes with the assurance that if they proved faithful to Muhammad, He (God) would be theirs: "*Ki Mohammad se wafa tu ne to hum tere hain.*" Not only would they inherit this world, the tablet and pen with which divine fate is written would be theirs: "*Ye jahan cheez hai kya lauh-o-qalam tere hain.*" This is a strong sense of God-given human power to shape the world, to make history, but history with an otherworldly more than worldly objective: the evolution of humankind into the divine. His 1915 poetic work in Persian, *Asrar-i-Khudi* (Secrets of the Self), reprised the theme of the divine spark animating each human self, the realization of which is the evolutionary journey of every life. Man's capacity to act in the world, an echo of the divine capacity for creation, is central to this self-realization. As he put it in a well-known couplet, "*Amal se zindagi banti hai jannat bhi jahannum bhi/ye khaki apni fitrat mein na noori hai na naari hai*" (Through deeds life becomes heaven and hell/this earthly being is by its nature neither full of light nor full of fire).[39] It is a less gloomy appraisal of human nature than Kant's notion of crooked timber; more importantly, it spells out Iqbal's sense that the "world" the human creates through his actions is a subjective one. Iqbal's sense of human capacity and duty to act is as strong or perhaps stronger than that of the most zealous great-man theorist of history, but, crucially, the aim of this action is not to change the world and times outside but to become self-conscious—an internal transformation. The one fearing a storm must remember that he is the sailor, the ocean, and the boat and the shore ("*Nakhuda tu, beher tu, kashti bhi tu, sahil bhi tu*").[40] He is the navigator through change, and the maker and object of it.

Iqbal echoed these themes in his prose work in 1930, the year of his speech. In a collection of his lectures published that year, *The Reconstruction of Religious Thought in Islam,* he openly criticized Nietzsche, who had proclaimed God dead and looked to a superman to redeem his resulting spiritual hunger. Iqbal affirmed the value of religion, arguing that prayer induced a self-awareness that allowed transcendence of petty individualism and material reality. It was an ethical necessity for the modern age—and the historical imagination of the survival of the fittest: "It is only by rising to a fresh vision of his origin and future, his whence and whither, that man will eventually triumph over a society motivated by an inhuman competition."[41] Iqbal's final book of Urdu poetry, published in 1936, also explicitly contested contemporary normative notions; it was subtitled "*Elan-e-Jung Daur-e-Hazir Ke Khilaaf*" (A Declaration of War against the Present Times). In it, he again urged that new worlds are born not from material but from spiritual change. A poem titled "*Takhleeq*" (Creation) began with the couplet, "*Jahan-e-taza ki afkar-e-taza se hai namood / ke sang-o-khisht se hote nahin jahan paida!*" (It appears from the fresh thoughts of a new world / that worlds are not born from stones and bricks!).[42] Another couplet pronounced, "*Wahi zamane ki gardish pe ghalib aata hai / jo har nafs se kare umr-e-javidan paida!*" (He conquers the vicissitudes of the age, / who with every breath creates the life of eternity!). In short, Iqbal, through his study of a combination of European, Persian, and South Asian thinkers, distilled a powerful sense of human historical agency but for the sake of making higher selves. History was not something with direction but the unending flux of life, the world through which a person must strive to redemptively transcend his humanity.

Crucially, the transcendence was not a kind of navel-gazing, but social in its call to overcome individualized selfhood. It took the form of love: "The real test of a self is whether it responds to the call of another self."[43]

Truth, or the "ultimate Reality," was the state of love. This is why the Sufi idiom of Urdu poetry was so relevant to Iqbal's thought. As Devji beautifully observes, Iqbal used traditional motifs of lovers endlessly separated, ships never reaching shore—that idiom of *birha* or *hijr* at the core of modern Urdu poetry—to demonstrate the "power of negation as a principle of movement." We have seen how the notion of split selfhood at the core of this idiom was evoked in the time of the *ghadar*. Here, again, it expressed a rejection of the historical imagination implicit in justifications of imperialism—and nationalism. Devji invokes a couplet from Iqbal's Persian poem *Javid Namah* (1932), translating it as "The traveler who knows the secrets of journeying / Fears the destination more than the highwayman." Life is a journey *without* destination, in other words, whose ethical bearings can be judged only in the moment, not belatedly by history, by the flight of the owl of Minerva when we are already in the darkness. Why should the nation be the end of history, when we in fact desire the infinite? Was there a way to make India "a country without a nation," as Devji expresses Iqbal's imaginative quest?[44] Considering the problems posed by nationalism, secularism, and the vitiated state of Islam, he dreamt of Muslim political autonomy fostering in one place a less divided and exploitative society on the basis of an Islamic moral system that would serve Muslims and non-Muslims alike. This political vision emerged from his refusal of the historical narrative behind empire—his conviction in man's entitlement and obligation to make his world towards an end of ethical rather than material or "civilizational" refinement.

T. E. Lawrence and other British Arabists sought escape from serial time into an experience of the *durée* in the Arabian desert. Their sense of that region as a place out of time emboldened them to practice violent policing techniques there that would not otherwise be justified in conventional narratives of imperial progress. Iqbal's contemporary attempt to recover the fullness of time also bore monstrous fruit. Devji homes in on Iqbal's exceedingly protective attitude towards Muhammad as the final prophet and thus the "founder of humanity as history's true actor." Islam in his vision was "a pure idea," "divested of all materiality"—geography, time, nation, race, and so on—and thus "uniquely vulnerable to disruption." It was universal and powerful but also permanently at risk, requiring "of Muslims a touchy and even aggressive defensiveness." Its doctrinal vulnerability was akin to that of communism in the same period. To Iqbal, one of the empire's sins was its nonchalance towards the integrity of Islam, its indifferent tolerance of the emergence of new sects and claimants to religious authority. This fragmenting of the "portable fatherland" of Islam consigned Muslims all over to some kind of minority status.[45] There are many paradoxes here. The point is that Iqbal's logic ended in a conservative protection of Muslim practice, despite its revolutionary and liberatory aims. His vision of a new kind of tolerant and inclusive society empowered a defensive politics based on religion; his vision of a "Muslim India within India" was swept up with the buzzing imperial concept of partition in directions he had not anticipated. The Partition that emerged in 1947 did not fulfill his vision of a non-national society but was rather co-opted into the historicist imagination of nation-statehood and imperial survival.

Iqbal's close friendship with Muhammad Asad in Lahore from 1934 offers a measure of the irresistible pressure historical thinking came to exercise on his effort to escape historicism. Asad was a figure cut from the same cloth as Lawrence, Philby, and Glubb. Born Leopold Weiss, he was an Austro-Hungarian Jew who grew up reading Nietzsche's *Thus Spake Zarathustra* and felt alienated by the "worship of material progress" that was the only faith left to the average European in his time. He, too, found a tapestry of all times in the desert: "The images of past and present intertwine, separate again and call to one another with wondrous sounds of evocation, backward through the years." His travels in the Middle East led him to convert to Islam and become an advisor to Ibn Saud in the 1920s, for whom he also engaged in secret missions. He exercised the power to reinvent himself and harbored a sense of his own agency as a power behind the scenes. However, he and Saud fell out, and Asad concluded that the Saudi kingdom had corrupted Wahhabism's striving after inner renewal of Muslim society. Moreover, the "gush of oil" had crumbled the "solitude and integrity" of Arabia.[46] Arabia had been sucked into the vortex of worldly history. He went to India in 1932 in hope of finding the Islamic practice and thought to which he was committed, immediately concluding (in a manner echoing European beliefs of the time) that a "chasm" divided Muslim and Hindu practices and beliefs.[47] Asad was a kind of historical idealist; he believed there was a right way for history to unfold. Saudi Arabia had betrayed its historic destiny. So, too, had Zionists, he felt. He was vehemently critical of Jewish settlement in Palestine even while conceiving his own travels in the Arabian deserts as a "home-coming" to the land of "my ancestors . . . that small beduin tribe of Hebrews."[48] By becoming a Muslim, he was fulfilling a historic destiny that had been disrupted by Jewish migration to Europe: Had they stayed in Arabia, he presumed, Jews would have become Muslims.

He saw the Pakistan idea as a fresh chance at renewing Islam now that the Arabian peninsula had failed in that cause. In his 1954 autobiographical account of these years, his encounter with "the great Muslim poet-philosopher and spiritual father of the Pakistan idea, Muhammad Iqbal," is momentous and pivotal. From that point, he devoted himself to the ideal of creating "a political entity of people bound together not by common descent but by their common adherence to an ideology."[49] He credited Iqbal with persuading him to stay in Lahore rather than continue his travels eastward so that he might "help elucidate the intellectual premises of the future Islamic state which was then hardly more than a dream in Iqbal's visionary mind." Now, Iqbal died in 1938, without knowing what form Pakistan would take. But he did disavow the goal of a separate "state" as early as 1934, writing to his friend the historian Edward John Thompson, "Pakistan is not my scheme. The one I suggested in my address is the creation of a Muslim Province. . . . This new province will be, according to my scheme, a part of the proposed Indian Federation."[50] Even Chaudhry Rahmat Ali, the Cambridge student who coined the name "Pakistan" in the early 1930s, envisioned a country or set of countries distributed across India in a "counter-nationalist vision."[51] But there was no room for such lost causes in Asad's account, in which the goal was always a "state"—a vision in which, he claimed, Iqbal fully concurred.[52] Nor is this merely the result of a post-1947 attempt to project the desire for a state backwards in time; Asad had thought in terms of a state earlier, as part of a historical narrative about non-normative nationhood. In an essay of May 1947—a month before all parties agreed to partition—he asserted that Pakistan was not designed to "solve the minorities problem," which was merely "an *incidental* accompaniment to the movement's intrinsic objective—the establishment of an Islamic polity in which our ideology would come to practical fruition." Muslims "are a nation unto themselves," he insisted.[53] This was a rejection of "national interests" as conceived in the West and urged followers of the Pakistan movement not to surrender to the dangerous "temptation to regard their movement as just another of the many 'national' movements so fashionable in the present day Muslim world."[54] Pakistan must have nothing to do with racial, cultural, or economic nationalism; in words anticipating those in his 1954 account, he explained that it was about "common adherence to the ideology of Islam."[55] He faulted the "majority of our intelligentsia" for forgetting this point. Asad shared some of Iqbal's motivations for thinking of an Islamic solution to the problem of the nation-state in his time but did not abandon a worldly historical outlook—partly because of his orientalist commitments: He saw the movement as evidence that Indian Muslims had "at last awakened from their political torpor." The Pakistan idea had brought a sense of history to a people long without one. Its goal was to revive Islamic history, not escape history altogether: It would prove "that it is possible to establish an ideological, Islamic polity in our times no less than it was possible thirteen hundred years ago." These essays appeared in Asad's "one-man" monthly journal *Arafat*, which he launched in 1946 specifically to aid the cause of Pakistan.[56]

It is hard to say how influential Asad's thought and writing was—he claimed it was significant.[57] Muslim opinion on Pakistan was varied and complicated, drawing on historical, anthropological, and theological political imaginaries—as Asad's frustrations with the "majority of our intelligentsia" suggest. The Jamiat Ulema-e-Hind, the senior party of Indian ulema founded in the 1920s and led by Maulana Husain Ahmad Madani, did not support the Pakistan movement. It, like the Congress, sought abolition of separate electorates. Madani called on Muslims to refer to the Prophet's example in Medina—the city to which He fled from Mecca in search of refuge (the hijrah) and which became the capital of his expanding empire where Muslims and non-Muslims lived together. To be sure, some Muslim thinkers in the United Provinces (roughly Uttar Pradesh and Uttarakhand in present-day India) thought of Pakistan itself as a new Medina, "an Islamic utopia" and "a worthy successor to the defunct Turkish Caliphate as the foremost Islamic power in the twentieth century."[58] This was another narrative about reprising Islam's interrupted post-prophetic, worldly history that emerged from more immediate events.

The Turkish Caliphate had been abolished in 1924 after the breakup of the Ottoman Empire and the establishment of the new nationalist Turkish state under Kemal Atatürk. In 1919–1922, the Congress and the Muslim League jointly launched the Khilafat movement to preserve the caliphate against the twin pressures of the postwar partitioning of the Ottoman Empire and the rise of the Turkish nationalist struggle. Although it did not achieve its aim, it was another postwar anticolonial movement that attempted to think beyond the nation. The Middle East was in rebellion at the time, as we have seen, and Iqbal's old teacher Arnold was a key advisor to the British government on handling the Khilafat movement while the government put air control in place in Iraq. The experience occasioned his book on the caliphate in 1924 in which he condescendingly explained that Indian Muslims had misunderstood the institution: The proclamation of the Turkish republic in 1922 showed that even Muslims recognized that the caliphate did not fit in the world of modern constitutional government.[59] Indians were thus futilely clinging to an ideal of a united Muslim community that had no political future, fueling their resentment of European domination with the pain of that loss. This avowed sympathizer with Muslims proved blind to the historical effectiveness of Muslim aspiration in his single-minded devotion to the idea that history unfolded teleologically towards the end of nation-statehood modeled on European nations. In the 1930s, by embracing the idea of Pakistan, South Asian Muslims defied this presumption. A different historical imagination animated those looking for a new Medina, quite apart from Iqbal's initially antihistoricist ethical objectives in dreaming of an Islamic utopia. To be sure, apart from a historical imagination, Islamic notions of jihad informed decisions to pursue the end of Pakistan. Whatever thinkers like Asad or Iqbal may have had in mind, Indians joined the Pakistan movement from a variety of motivations that varied across space and class.[60] Asad knew that the movement's leaders were not on the same page about the struggle's aspirations: "Do we all mean the same when we talk and dream of Pakistan?" he asked pointedly in May 1947.[61]

Asad was definitely influential enough among elites to secure an important role in shaping Pakistan's constitution and other government appointments until 1952, after which he traveled and lived in many other places until his death in 1992. I invoke him to highlight the colonial intellectual context in which the idea of a Muslim nation-state—quite apart from Iqbal's nebulous ideas—necessarily took shape. Rather than the bonds of blood and soil central to much of modern nationalism, Pakistan was the brainchild of those invested in Enlightenment ideas about organizing society according to first principles in a world in which minorities had become a "problem" in regions with national aspirations.[62] In this, as Devji observes, it had much in common, genealogically, with the thought behind the creation of states like Liberia, Israel, and settler colonial societies. It was also the dream of those who felt a sense of their own agency to so organize society, the idea that great men can defy the past to make a new history, even behind the scenes. Muhammad Ali Jinnah, who presided over the Muslim League in the years before Partition, deeply admired John

Morley's 1874 essay *On Compromise,* defending the idea of acting out of principle rather than becoming mired in the obfuscations of the "Historic Method." His byword was "faith" in the ability to forge one's own destiny, whatever the reality one confronted, the transcendent power of pure will.[63] Maine and Galton would have disappointed him, Paine or Carlyle perhaps not. Though there were many imaginings of what it might be and how it might be made, the ultimate decision to partition Punjab and Bengal was the product of pragmatic negotiations between elites who were ambivalent in varying degrees towards the idea of Pakistan. It was perhaps only in Pakistan's division into two wings separated by about a thousand miles of Indian territory, that the creative anticolonial effort to think outside the nation-state found practical expression. Iqbal's and others' adumbration of alternatives to racial and cultural forms of national identity in order to escape the telos of modern historicism was co-opted by an updated version of that historical imagination in which imperial federation provided an incubator for the maturing of inchoate nations.

Apart from ensuring that whatever new entity or entities emerged in South Asia would join the Commonwealth, London officials paid little attention to Indian daily life in the run-up to the transfer of power, focusing instead on the Cold War, British balance sheets, the safety of British civilians in India, Britain's international reputation, and challenges in Greece and Palestine. At every turn, they sped up events, stunning the Indian public with announcements about the accelerated calendar—which made partition, and violent partition, more and more unavoidable. The historian Yasmin Khan has shown how hasty dismantling of the imperial state not only made it harder to address the violence; it also made much of the violence possible in the first place. The British administration withdrew provincial control as eager Indian leaders seized it after provincial elections early in 1946. The imperial state shed its law-and-order capacity and sense of responsibility, offering little support to administrators trying to deal with routine local politics. The British aim was to cut losses by avoiding investing any more in India's infrastructure. Intelligence units were run down, which meant local officials had less and less information and warning to cope with threats of violence. The government stopped counting people, right when information of that type was most needed.[64] It is also important to recall that the Bengal famine in 1943, resulting, again, from British grain distribution policies, had decimated that province, killing millions. It dramatically compromised Bengal's capacity to cope with Partition and all that it entailed.

In the summer of 1947, the British Army began to depart just when India's own army was being divided and could not be relied on to control violence. In Punjab, while trouble unfolded, the British command confined troops to barracks and evacuated them as quickly as they could. Confidential instructions insisted that British army units had no operational functions except in emergency to save British lives. Instead, the British created the Punjab Boundary Force, which lasted a mere thirty-two days, from August 1 to September 1, 1947, when it was disbanded out of ineffectualness. It was too small and too thinly distributed.[65]

How did Britons reconcile themselves to the violence? Here, again, inherited notions about history that had long justified the empire shaped both the unfolding of history and British conscience about it. When Iraqis massacred the Assyrian minority in 1933, a year after the British granted Iraq nominal independence, the British saw it as proof that Iraqis needed a firm imperial hand rather than apprehending that their long cultivation of that minority to serve in the levy forces that supported the RAF had irreparably compromised Assyrians' position in the country—they looked like colonial collaborators. A similar logic prevailed when it came to Partition violence. The British felt entirely justified in adopting a passive position when it began, for it was entirely expected given their narrative of an eternally fractious subcontinent—whatever the evidence they had seen and fears they had harbored about unity in the region. Their approach to the violence was thus fatalistic. In Benares in 1946, the British district magistrate simply assumed the city would be "burnt down" and that "Hindus and Muslims will fly at each other's throats."[66] With this outlook, it made sense for him to prioritize planning his departure rather than taking measures to prevent violence. Such fatalistic thinking underwrote hasty withdrawal of resources and manpower and ensured that the British conscience nevertheless remained easy.

The actual form that Partition took, accompanied by mass violence and population exchange, was not part of the plan elites agreed to.[67] It was the result of the decisions, some taken freely and some out of desperation, of millions of ordinary people coping with this breakdown of governance and nurturing their own interpretations of Partition's historical significance—whether it was temporary or permanent, a question of national commitment or religious obligation, and so on. We can look back and say that people in the subcontinent made their own history, but, per Marx, not in circumstances of their own choosing. Colonial sociology shaped their outlook and political objectives; imperial indifference created a climate of insecurity that could not but give rise to violence. What were Indians thinking when they acted violently? What historical or other ethical frameworks shaped their actions and conscience? What happened to the commitment to nonviolence that so many had embraced as part of the independence movement? How did the same people commit the unconscionable, leaving bodies unburied and uncremated—perhaps the most obvious sign of total civilizational breakdown? If they were not merely enacting ancient hatreds, as the British presumed, was this momentary insanity? the wages of fear? desperation? amoral fulfillment of a rational political objective?

The context of world war and the transfer of power mattered deeply in shaping South Asians' sense of their agency in this moment, as Khan has shown. During the war, the British killed thousands of protestors and jailed much of the Congress for launching the massive Quit India movement demanding immediate independence.[68] As one officer wrote, the police were "given a free hand . . . to use force where necessary without the usual rigmarole of getting a magistrate's written sanction."[69] The Jamiat Ulema also did not support the British war effort. This allowed rival parties invested in religious separation, like the Muslim League, which supported the British war effort, and the right-wing Hindu Mahasabha (founded in 1915) to flourish. Jinnah's standing with the colonial government was also enhanced. The historical visions they offered, drawing on British as much as their own notions of inherently incompatible religious "nations," gained traction. Meanwhile, in Southeast Asia, the Indian National Army gained fame for fighting the British alongside the Japanese army. After the war, Congress's commitment to nonviolence was diluted as it belatedly tried to latch on to these rival popular movements, particularly the cause of the Indian National Army.

The war gave many Indians violent experiences. Recruitment was in the millions. After the war, disgruntled soldiers who had fought for Britain were recruited into military and police units and new defense groups and volunteer bodies forming across the north. Deserters joined such groups with their guns. These groups often shared an imprint of Western fascism and race pride, even acknowledging the example of Hitler and the Nazis.

Their commitments were adaptations of the social Darwinist notions that underwrote European fascism and colonialism. Such groups, holding rallies in uniforms with flags, also attracted students, youth, and opportunistic criminals. For instance, members of the Hindu Mahasabha's Ram Sena, in khaki uniforms and orange caps, pledged to sacrifice for the Hindu cause. Some started as sports or youth clubs. Some were large, well organized, and professionalized, more like private militias, such as the Rashtriya Swayamsevak Sangh, or RSS, a Hindu paramilitary volunteer organization, and its counterpart, the Muslim League National Guards.[70] Future scholars may probe other religious ethical systems that may have informed their thought and action. From the British perspective, these armed groups posed no direct challenge to British interests.

Some provincial politicians began to use such groups for policing as they shifted from being the opposition to being *the* government, eager to show their power on the eve of independence. Now that wartime British repression of the nationalist movement was over, Indian politicians could roam freely, devise laws, spread propaganda. Police and other officials who had earlier feared showing nationalist support now openly celebrated particular party leaders, losing their image of neutrality. Everyday life was shaped by committees organized or divided along Muslim League and Congress lines. In this polarized atmosphere, politicians' words were overly incendiary, close to incitement.[71]

These dynamics were clear after the Cabinet Mission negotiations of 1946 over a proposed federal structure for independent India. Though the Muslim League (and the Jamiat Ulema) agreed to the plan, Congress refused, adamant about inheriting the centralized imperial state as it was, partly out of a shrewd suspicion that a weaker center would not be able to resist post-independence British machinations, but also because it was invested in that end point of the liberal history of empire as an incubus for the nation-state—what the Congress leader and India's first prime minister, Jawaharlal Nehru, called India's "tryst with destiny." A strong central government would also more effectively fulfill the developmental vision adapted from the imperial historical script. To strengthen his hand, an infuriated Jinnah called for Direct Action Day on August 16 to show the power behind the Pakistan idea. He understood the move as a willful embrace of historic agency. In his speech before the Muslim League after the resolution was passed, he affirmed, "What we have done today is the most historic act in our history. Never have we in the whole history of the

League done anything except by . . . constitutionalism. . . . This day we bid goodbye to constitutional methods. . . . I am not prepared to discuss ethics. We have a pistol and are in a position to use it."[72] Fascinatingly, committing a "historic act" was for him synonymous with suspending ethical considerations; to act historically was to suppress ethical qualms for an end that would be deemed worthy in hindsight. It was to consciously disavow an obligation to ordinary ethical norms in a bid to orchestrate a great event as a great man—to dare to be a great man and thus someone held to another moral standard. This was James Fitzjames Stephen's "leap in the dark." The call for "direct action" was a call to abandon the diffident exercise of agency demanded by accommodation to a system of laws and procedures—to act like Lawrence rather than Maine. Jinnah, probably the most Westernized of the nationalist elite, had a fascination with *Hamlet* (at one point aspiring to a stage career), and one senses that in this moment he saw himself in that mold, at last resolving to act decisively, outside his ethical comfort zone, even if it ended tragically—for "conscience does make cowards of us all," Hamlet tells us.[73] He hoped that history would vindicate him, as was history's purpose in such ethically dubious situations. He likened the power of Muslim masses to a pistol—the easy plot fix in any story, whose blunt exercise of power from a distance had by this time anesthetized human sensibilities and was known to enable violence that more easily eluded the check of conscience.

Jinnah called for a strike, but August 16 became a day of violence throughout northern India. The violence was organized and enabled by a sense of immunity from the governing provincial party. For many reasons, the local population understood it as a situation of war, not politics or riot.[74] In a Calcutta reeling from the famine and postwar unemployment, Muslims armed with *lathis* attended a meeting where the Muslim League's chief minister gave crowds the impression that the police and military would not be called out.[75] When victims noted that the police did not come, they inferred that the murderers were acting with the League's and the government's blessing. Hindu militias were ready to retaliate. The carnage was on an unprecedented scale in a place of strong regional patriotism and coalition government. Soon after, the coalition provincial government in Punjab tried to restrict militia activity by banning the RSS and the Muslim League National Guard, but the resulting uproar forced it to lift the ban in days, showing its weakness. The evident breakdown of law and order produced paranoia and fear in everyday life. In this atmosphere, all forms of identification were subordinated to faith in a single political identity: If you aren't with us, you're against us. Whatever religious justifications may have been in play in the violence, many actions emerged from a sense of the desperate need for survival in a harrowing environment—a breakdown of all systems of ethical accountability.

At the same time, peasant insurgencies infused with communist ideas gained strength in Bengal, the Deccan, and elsewhere, frightening Congress as much as the British. The threat was credible—next door, China underwent a massive communist revolution just two years later. As Yasmin Khan recounts, this was the tense backdrop against which political elites (except the Jamiat Ulema) agreed to the Partition plan in June 1947, without anticipating what it would entail, and without offering assurance that citizenship, property, and lives would be guaranteed everywhere. Without such assurance and without information for two more months about where the line would fall, terror reigned. It was a time of extreme mental stress, nerves on edge under curfew, the sounds of drums, sirens, militias in the streets. Decisions—about which land and which infrastructure went to which side, how substantive the separation would be, whether people would move, what would happen to major cities like Calcutta and Lahore—were hasty and confused. People began to move out of fear, out of conviction, by accident, *and* because they were driven out, systematically. Bureaucracies became dysfunctional as officers thought of migrating or tried to please new masters or gave in to anxiety themselves. Officials were openly partisan or not at their posts.[76] News of the army's division was a further blow. Without functioning army or civil services, Punjab was held hostage by militias. Now fearing backlash, the government allowed ringleaders to go free.[77] In 1857, a "miasma of panic" had descended on Delhi and licensed various subversive activities, but not intercommunity violence like this, which testifies both to the relative competence of rebel governing bodies in that time and to the newness of the mutually exclusive communal identities at stake in 1947.

As every community in every place feared becoming a persecuted minority, it made a kind of sense to wage a violent battle to preserve the land from intruders or outsiders. All the ingredients for ethnic cleansing were in place: a feeble, polarized police force; absence of troops; and a petrified, well-armed population.[78] Whatever sense of agency Indians had

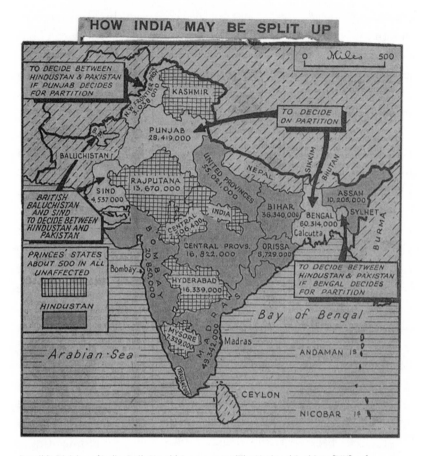

Possible Division of India, *Daily Herald,* June 4, 1947. (The National Archives [UK], ref. CAB21/2038)

access to in that time—religious, historical, astrological—was deeply conditioned by a reflexive survival instinct in a moment of cultural and institutional breakdown, when the usual compasses by which we assess our scope for action had vanished.

When Cyril Radcliffe's land award was finally announced, complaints by leaders fueled the willingness to fight. Bitterly disappointed groups on the wrong side of the line fought to cleanse their areas, reverse the line, or rob it of meaning.[79] Soldiers hearing of villages wiped out or sisters abducted deserted to join the militias. Besides guns and swords, there were bombs left over from the war. Research in a new archive of ordinary people's recollections of this time may at last provide deeper insight into the ethical imagination of those involved in the violence of 1946–1948.[80]

In short, the violence of Partition was not "caused" by religion or religious fanaticism; the exclusionary politics of that time, the scale of killing and grouping along religious lines, were new. The violence marked the crumbling of an old order and abdication of responsibility for minorities by all those with any kind of power. That abdication of responsibility was in turn underwritten by long-circulating narratives of South Asian history that on the one hand depicted religious divisions as perennial and unchanging and on the other insisted that evolution out of that trap of timelessness into a space of more rational order would require a certain amount of blood and loss.

That said, in a time of such uncertainty, it is not surprising that the narratives through which Indians interpreted events around them and their own actions were highly unstable. There was a notable lack of durable conviction in those narratives. The killing was genocidal in some places, but there were also countless acts of heroism and generosity *and* a deep desire to return home after moving. Reports of help and protection offered by strangers, neighbors, and friends suggest that even while religious identification mattered in a new way, other kinds of moral community survived.[81] Violence temporarily forged national community, but contradictory allegiances related to class, caste, language, and so on endured, complicating the task of turning South Asians into Indians and Pakistanis. Colonial social engineering had layered a 0 and 1 sense of religious identity on top of enduringly complicated selves.

This is where we must encounter, again, the complexity of the colonized mind, the way in which indigenous ways of being and modes of ethical practice were in dialectic struggle with other modes shaped by generations of colonial rule.[82] The British justified their presence in India as a catalyst for the nation-building necessary for progress to unfold. Even Marxists agreed with that notion. Many Indians did, too. However, that "nationalist" struggle had been inflected with other concerns that diverged from the colonial narrative—opposing the colonizer's "not yet" with an insistent "now," as the historian Dipesh Chakrabarty puts it. Chakrabarty nicely captures the Janus face of anticolonial thought: "It is true that nationalist elites often rehearsed to their own subaltern classes . . . the stagist theory of history on which European ideas of political modernity were based." At the same time, practically speaking, given their desire for self-government *now,* they implicitly rejected "stagist, historicist distinctions between the premodern or the nonmodern and the modern."[83] The assertion that the rural, illiterate, nonmodern, nonsecular Indian "common man" was capable of self-rule *now* was a rejection of the developmentalist excuses for empire, the idea of colonization as a "waiting room of history," in Chakrabarty's apt phrase. It was a Byronic vision in calling on Indians to exercise heroic agency in overcoming the apparent limitations of their historical moment.

Some went further, rejecting the nation-state as the end point of their efforts. Decolonization narratives have taken a colonial form by presuming the nation-state as their exclusive horizon. But all over European colonies, anticolonial thinkers imagined other collective futures. If interwar communists and liberal imperialists were committed to international visions, so, too, were many anticolonialists.[84] They tried to imagine and create *alternative* forms of community and tried to articulate other historical trajectories, distinct from what liberal empire had to offer. We have seen this in nineteenth-century India and Jamaica. The Egyptian revolt of 1882 likewise drew on locally derived (rather than European) notions of freedom and on ideas spread through the exiling of Indian rebels in the region.[85] Indian protestors before World War I similarly drew on South Asian traditions for alternatives to the colonial narrative of history. It was the vibrancy of those alternative outlooks that drew Britons craving alternatives to South Asia and the Middle East in that time. Meanwhile, nineteenth-century Caribbean writers thought in terms of the hemispheric and local, imagining autonomy and unity at different scales of social organization.[86] Indeed, perhaps the most effectual expression of such alternative visions would come from the twentieth-century Marxist anticolonial poet and thinker Aimé Césaire of the French Caribbean island Martinique, who favored Martinique's departmentalization as part of France rather than its independence, preferring reformation of the interdependent, cosmopolitan bonds created by empire over the autarky or neocolonial status that might follow their formal severance. He echoed the vision of the Senegalese poet and leader of the negritude movement Leopold Sedar Senghor, with whom he sat in the 1946 assembly to write a new constitution for France. African anticolonial thinkers also imagined various forms of Pan-Africanism and federalism, including a United States of Africa. This was the same time that the possibility of a European political and economic community was being discussed, with the one, the idea of a federal, transcontinental France, complicating the other.[87] Historians thinking in national frames risk reproducing the narratives of immature nationhood that justified empire in the first place. The British saw the varied regional, linguistic, ideological, and religious commitments fueling early-twentieth-century Bengali revolutionary sentiment as evidence of the failure of Indian nationalism. We might instead recognize the richly imaginative nature of those tangled sentiments and the alternative collective futures they hoped to produce. They certainly possessed enough strength to frighten the British, whose concerns about interwar arms trafficking included a particular anxiety about smuggling into Bengal via China and Burma.

Following that era of revolution, many Indians tried to move beyond nationhood, understandably skeptical of a form of social organization that justified imperialism—especially after the First World War's demonstration of nationalism's monstrous effects. Thus, Iqbal, we have seen, looked to Islam as a means of social and political organization. The late twenties and early thirties also saw "the mobilization of a collective identity for and by women in the public realm," writes the historian Mrinalini Sinha.[88] The Bengali poet and educational reformer Rabindranath Tagore dreamt of a world "not broken up into fragments."[89] During the First World War, he criticized the destructive tendencies of nationalism in lectures in Japan and the United States. After the war, he used his Nobel Prize money to found the Vishwa Bharati college, with a name reflecting the idea of Indian communion with the world and a curriculum departing from Western methods, which, he felt, eroded a person's natural capacities for joy, love, and creativity. He warned Indian nationalists against modeling themselves on "Garibaldis and Washingtons" and adopting self-evidently corrupted ideologies of European origin; instead they must rely on local inspiration.[90] His 1931 book *Religion of Man,* based on lectures he gave at Oxford, put forward a humanistic vision based on love, drawing inspiration especially from the Bauls, mystic minstrels of Bengal from mixed religious, caste, and class backgrounds who repudiated established social norms in devotion to spiritual and personal freedom and an ethic of love and spontaneous emotion. The word "*baul*" means "god's madcap." Their goal, according to Tagore, was "love's emancipating us from the dominance of the self."[91]

Tagore's critique of Western education emerged partly from his own abortive attempt to study in England. Mohandas Gandhi, whose activism based on noncooperation secured the Congress a mass base, had a law degree from London, but he, too, became famously critical of Western education. (His favorite song was Tagore's *"Ekla Cholo Re"* [Walk Alone].) He conceived of the "Indian" as itself an "international" category.[92] He turned Maine's fetish for the Indian village-community into a vision for a postcolonial order based on interdependent yet independent village republics. "The future of India," he said, "lies in its villages." Much ink has been spilled in assessing whether Gandhi was a "traditionalist" or "progressive" in his antimodernist idealization of the village. In fact, it was a refusal of that dichotomy grounded in historicism.

As any good Gandhi biography will recount, that refusal was founded partly on Gandhi's long engagement with thinkers like Leo Tolstoy and William Morris, whose *News from Nowhere* (1890) envisioned a utopia of English villages formed after a revolution in 1952. Its denizens recognize that the "the crude ideas of the first half of the twentieth century" had allowed fear of future ruin and tales of "past miseries" to destroy the "present pleasure of ordinary daily life." Their utopia offers no formal education, and history is no longer a reading preference, since "it is mostly in periods of turmoil and strife and confusion that people care so much about history."[93]

Gandhi similarly explained in *Hind Swaraj* (1909) that history was the record of conflict; violence was its motor—as, indeed, it was to thinkers as varied as Priestley, Carlyle, and Marx. But if this was all that actually happened, the world would have ended long ago. Its survival was due to the sustaining force of love that routinely defused would-be conflicts in a manner illegible to history. Gandhi's aim of nonviolence implied a refusal of history in favor of these sustaining quotidian practices that were not the stuff of history understood in that sense—per the Enlightenment proverb "Happy is the nation without a history." He explained, "History is really a record of every interruption of the even working of the force of love or of the soul ... [,] a record of an interruption of the course of nature. Soul-force, being natural, is not noted in history."[94] An ethical vision indebted to history constrained human action towards violence; nonviolence created new possibilities for the future precisely by allowing humans to be morally accountable exclusively in the present. Iqbal diagnosed the manner in which Gandhi and the British talked past each other: The mind of "Western man" was "chronological" in character; he "lives and moves and has his being in time." On the other hand, the "world-consciousness" of Gandhi, as an "Eastern man," was "non-historical"; things are "purely present." Hence, his effort to attain *immediate* self-rule. But for Western man, "things gradually become; they have a past, present and future."[95] British insistence on gradual political evolution blinded them to, and indeed, enabled their present status as oppressors. Gandhi thus rejected Western education out of the conviction that "the foundation that Macaulay laid of education has enslaved us." Instead, he called for religious, or ethical education.[96] Institutions like the National College in Lahore, where the Marxist Punjabi revolutionary Bhagat Singh studied, emerged out of the anticolonial boycott of British educational institutions.[97]

Gandhi effectively turned the orientalist notion of "timeless" India on its head in the interest of recovering an experience of the fullness of time. His fascination with the *Gita,* including his attempt to translate it despite weak knowledge of Sanskrit, was part of his search for alternative ethical guides to exercising human agency—he called it his "eternal mother."[98] He felt he lived the *Gita* for forty years; he did not live only in secular historical time. He insisted that the *Mahabharata,* which includes the *Gita,* "is not a history; it is a dharma-grantha." The *Gita* was a nonsectarian work of "pure ethics."[99] It instructed in action untethered from the calculus of future effect—the "instrumentality that sacrificed the present for the future," as Devji puts it.[100]

To be sure, the *Gita*'s influence in this period was itself framed by colonialism. Before the European incursion, stories from the *Mahabharata* were part of popular discourse, as were the tales of the *Panchatantra,* but the *Gita* was a text for theologians and philosophers.[101] The East India Company Orientalist Charles Wilkins translated it into English in 1785 under Hastings's patronage—Hastings wrote the preface. Friedrich Schlegel, the German Romantic poet and philosopher credited with coining the word "historicism," translated the first half into German; his brother August produced a full Latin translation in 1823, sweeping the *Gita* into the German Romantic and Orientalist tradition, so that, as we have seen, Hegel wrote on it, too, while thinking through his philosophy of history. It is allegedly he who made the *shloka* (verse) about acting without regard to the fruits of action the text's centerpiece. Gandhi first read the text in English while in London among the Theosophists. He and other anticolonial thinkers reappropriated the *Gita* as an alternative guide to ethical action. The psychologist and critic Ashis Nandy notes that Gandhi's rejection of history as "a guide to moral action" in deference to myth, put him in a line that traces back to Blake, from whom Gandhi also took his credo, "My religion is my politics and my politics is my religion."[102] His activism against British rule was on the ground of ethics rather than politics, designed to establish the Indian cause's moral superiority in the eyes of the world. Nonviolent protest was to him an end in itself, not a means to achieving a *future* political end.[103] It was in its very practice that self-rule was attained. This argument repudiated the historical idiom that justified empire: "Civilization" is not the end point of some historical process for Gandhi, but a term with a "purely ethical and moral meaning," writes Uday Mehta. It operated at the level of the individual, in the form of an ethical mode of conduct, which might be followed no matter how developed or primitive his society was; it had nothing to do with history. Hence Gandhi's confidence that India was ready for self-rule *now,* on the ground of culture. His oft-cited quip when asked his opinion of "modern civilization," that "it would be a good idea," played on these competing understandings of the term. Mehta explains that a "prevalent response to imperial historicism is almost by necessity a form of parochialism, because what has to be valorized is a set of conditions whose normative and experiential credence can be justified without reference to a future or a necessary past and prescribed path of development."[104]

The Khilafat movement was another attempt to think beyond the historicist category of the nation. Its leaders also engaged in creative efforts to think outside the historical imagination of empire—evident in their investments in educational reform. While participating in the Khilafat movement, Maulana Abul Kalam Azad, the poet Mohammad Ali Jauhar, and Maulana Madani founded the radically anticolonial university Jamia Millia Islamia (JMI). They did so out of frustration with the Aligarh college's colonial sympathies; JMI's objective became the development of new, anticolonial educational methods, for which it earned international fame. In 1923, Jauhar briefly presided over the Congress. In his presidential address, he articulated his cherished, post-national dream of "a federation, grander, nobler and infinitely more spiritual than the United States of America."[105] "Providence," in the form of "this Country of hundreds of millions of human beings" of diverse faiths and backgrounds, had given them the opportunity to create such an entity, a "new synthesis." The federalism bug scuttled hopefully through anticolonial discourse, too—informing Iqbal's thought, too, as we have seen. This was partly because of the inspiration of the new Soviet Union, which offered a vision of a federal, communist form of social organization in which nationhood was, at least in theory, subordinated. The Russian Revolution, in the midst of the bloody struggle for national supremacy that was the First World War, was a crucially important inspiration in these efforts to imagine a world that might be both postcolonial and postnational.[106] Many anticolonial thinkers drew on a Leninist historical narrative in perceiving the Indian struggle as part of a wider, global revolutionary cause. But quite apart from the goal of international communism, many were inspired simply by its defiance of known historical scripts: the idea that every society did not have to go sequentially through the phases of industrialism, capitalism, liberalism, and so on, that they might invent new scripts altogether. It was a revolution in historical thought.

A network of South Asian revolutionaries ensured that these thought experiments infected conversations far and wide. Early in the nineteenth century, Sayyid Ahmed of Rai Bareilly had brought Wahhabi influence to the North West Frontier region to fight the Sikh kingdom. The British referred to the group of followers who remained as the "Hindustani Fanatics." Following the 1857 rebellion, many revolutionaries escaped dire fates by leaving the subcontinent.[107] The Muslim concept of *hijrat,* referring to the journey of the Prophet and his followers from Mecca to Medina, was an important ethical framework informing this exercise of Indian agency. Influenced by these earlier hijrats to escape colonial rule, in 1915, during World War I, a group of anticolonial activists established the Provisional Government of India in Kabul with the support of Britain's military opponents, Turkey and Germany. The British uncovered the group's plan to create an Army of God to liberate Islamic countries under infidel rule, the so-called Silk Letter Plot. Working with the British Indian intelligence services, the Middle Eastern intelligence establishment staffed by the intuitive experts covered in Chapter 4 called these activists "Hindustani Fanatics," too, and divined a conspiracy "spread over . . . the whole mohammedan world" requiring continual watchfulness—at once tempering this fear with the confident assertion that the conspiracy had no teeth.[108] These were among the fears that inspired postwar repressive measures in India and Iraq, including air control. In the moment, however, the British deported many of the activists to Malta, where the experience of imprisonment intensified their anticolonial commitments. The student and devotee of one of these activists, Maulana Madani, was then in Mecca, and Britain's wartime ally, Sharif Hussein, obligingly ensured that he, too, was caught in the dragnet late in 1916. Madani returned from Malta to India in the midst of the Khilafat movement.[109]

I called this wartime plot "paltry" in an earlier book.[110] I was so taken by the breathtaking extent of British paranoia that I shortchanged the substantive efforts and creative notions of the revolutionaries—quite apart from the role the affair played in triggering the Third Anglo-Afghan war in 1919 and in postwar colonial repression and appeasement in India, culminating in the notorious Amritsar Massacre of 1919. Several members of the Silk Letter Plot went on to become important nodes in international networks of anticolonial activism. They met with Bolsheviks, Pan-Islamists, and other kinds of anticolonial activists in Europe, the United States, all over Asia, and beyond. Many led wildly peripatetic lives, "calling their travels hijrat or migration and building networks for emancipating the Indian people." In this tribute to the Prophet's journey they saw themselves as "revolutionary pilgrims," in the historian Yasmin Saikia's phrase.[111] It was their incessant mobility across borders that made the British so paranoid between the wars.

Such figures subvert the easy categorization of anticolonial activists as either Congress or Muslim League supporters. Raja Mahendra Pratap, president of the Provisional Government, met with Lenin and Trotsky, the German kaiser, the khedive of Egypt, and Enver Pasha (the defense minister of the Ottoman Empire). Hailing from a royal family, he had studied at Aligarh but did not complete his degree and, in a familiar pattern, had established an innovative educational institution of his own in 1909, Prem Mahavidyalaya. Though a Hindu, he embraced the concept of jihad to define his struggle for freedom.[112] Muhamed Barkatullah Bhopali was the prime minister of the Provisional Government. He had worked with the Ghadar Party in San Francisco, another node in these cosmopolitan revolutionary networks. Internationalist and ecumenical in outlook, the Ghadar Party was founded in 1913 by Punjabis, who had been venturing to California to escape British rule from the late nineteenth century. Some had ties to 1857, and the party's name was an homage to that early generation of rebels. The rebels of 1857 had bequeathed their generation a revolutionary script that could animate an anticolonial historical imagination. Many Ghadarites returned to Punjab during the war to launch an armed rebellion to free India, but thanks to the help of American intelligence agencies, the British hanged or imprisoned them in the Andaman Islands, like their predecessors in 1857. Bhopali edited the Ghadar Party journal. He died in San Francisco in 1927. Pratap also met Ghadar members after the war and before a long sojourn in Japan, where he published the journal

The World Federation, promoting the idea of an Asian federation against colonial rule. His ethical motivations defy easy categorization—he spoke in terms of jihad but also *"prem dharma"* (an ethics of love), internationalism, nationalism, and communism.

Though some of these figures reappeared in the Khilafat movement and thought in terms of hijrat, their aim was not an Islamic state. Rather, the network itself was the object—the intermixing of Muslims with non-Muslims in an echo of the ummah created by Muhammad in Medina. Their international networks were their Medina and the key to achieving the kind of freedom implied by their concept of *"azadi,"* which went beyond political freedom guaranteed by the nation-state to encompass self-awareness: in Saikia's phrase, "an existential concern of being human." The revolutionary effort to bring diverse people together to think about their own liberation "enabled human agency," she writes.[113] It attempted to recover the ethical compass of Medina that had been the secret of Muslim immunity to colonization in the past, the view that the "support and friendship of multiple partners engaged in a common effort" could once again disrupt colonial rule. Maulana Obaidullah Sindhi, the home minister of the Provisional Government, understood his struggle as jihad made accountable to *zameer,* or conscience, understood as the acceptance of the truth of all communities, as modeled by the Prophet in Medina. That was the ground from which they might create global revolution. He, too, imagined an Asian federation; a single nationalist struggle lacked ethical merit to him. For these thinkers, the antidote to the historical imagination that had given rise to imperialism and nationalism was to hold their actions accountable to another ethical standard: The ethical merit of the end they desired lay in the ethics of their means. Their goal appears historical in that they aimed to end colonial rule. But in fact the concept of *"azadi"* collapsed ends and means into one: The existential concern with being human was the condition of possibility for creating the network of partners, and the network of partners was the condition of *azadi.* It was an ethics derived from religio-historical memory but that could not be captured by historicism's linearity. This, too, was a legacy of the revolutionary script of 1857.

It is difficult to place thinkers of this time into tidy boxes with the vocabulary that the discipline of history, shaped during the era of colonialism, offers us. Hasrat Mohani was a poet and journalist who presided over the Muslim League in 1921 but also wrote devotional poems to Lord

Krishna and helped found the Indian Communist Party. Was he a Muslim? a Hindu? a nationalist? if so, for which nation? an internationalist? In the early 1920s, he like other radicals was impatient with the Indian National Congress's liberal nationalist goal of dominion status. Instead, the Hindustan Republican Association (HRA), founded in 1924, engaged in a substantive effort to actually create a United States of India. In contrast to the Congress, they adopted an ethic of revolutionary violence, inspired partly by Irish and Russian scripts. They dubbed their targeted attacks against British officials and symbols "actions." Their most iconic representative, Bhagat Singh, stressed the impersonality of this violence, aimed as it was at the "capitalist and imperialist system."[114] This activity fueled British fears about Islamic-Bolshevik conspiracy, strengthening commitment to air control on the frontier and in the Middle East. But the HRA and Congress were not entirely distinct. HRA membership intersected and interacted productively with that of Congress, radicalizing it towards adopting "*purna swaraj*" rather than dominion status as its objective by 1929.[115] Many were simultaneously sympathetic to violent revolutionary methods and Gandhian nonviolence, without a sense of contradiction.[116] As late as 1946, the Congress politician Rajendra Prasad, future president of independent India, argued in favor of allowing India to remain an "unnational" state.[117] Colonized people managed complex and contradictory identities in creative ways, attempting to think through alternative ethical and historical frameworks as they acted.

Take the example of the vice-chancellor of Jamia Millia Islamia in the 1920s, Mohammad Mujeeb, a staunch Congress supporter boasting a social circle encompassing all religions. Despite this, in Delhi markets in the years leading up to Partition, he resolved to "buy Muslim" to support his religious community. In the end, however, he surrendered to pragmatism, concluding that there were good and bad salesmen irrespective of religion and deferring to the insistence of the women of his house that they shop wherever they got the best goods and service.[118] Managing contradictions produced ironic outcomes. During World War II, the Hindu Mahasabha and the Muslim League, two groups that both embraced and peddled the idea of Hindu and Muslim incompatibility, formed successful coalition governments in three provinces. They were incompatible yet compatible. The historical narratives that framed their actions were a complex blend that we have yet to fully grasp.

Common to them is the embrace of a certain agon, a refusal to commit wholly to one narrative or another, resignation to cognitive dissonance. We have seen already the way the notion of a divided self mediated responses to colonialism. Many scholars today criticize historical accounts that focus on British oppression of Indians, arguing that they do not do justice to Indian agency and depict Indians as passive victims. However, in seeking to recognize or recover their agency, the works of such scholars often wind up showing how Indians in effect collaborated with or enabled the imperial structure.[119] Lost in this debate is the agonistic complexity, the queering, of Indian agency and Indian conceptions of agency and historical and ethical obligation, which drew on multiple cultural sources at once. Just as the British paradoxically pursued liberal empire through authoritarian means, Indians resisted empire even while working for it; they bought into the liberal myth of empire—that was the very premise of the Congress—even while challenging it. Just as Romantic poetry illuminates British notions of heroic yet tragic individual agency, poetry captured much of the agon of South Asian selfhood in the same period.

The collusion of nationalism with imperialism in the making of Partition suggests the marginalization of the alternative political imaginaries articulated by revolutionary thinkers who rejected the historical imagination of empire and nation. But the agonistic quality of their thought found extended life in South Asian subjectivity after Partition. It emerged from the older history of Indian selfhood and extended it further. The history of another kind of selfhood, founded on a sense of individual incompleteness, helped produce the violence of Partition, but it also helped mitigate Partition's impact.

The subject of northern Indian poetry had long been understood as split, we have seen. This poetic idiom had evolved to express loss and exile of many kinds. The mobility that empire encouraged and that revolutionaries increasingly embraced added new layers of meaning to the trope of *birha*. The *pardesi,* the one gone from home or the one from another land, is a name for the beloved in this idiom. In this period, the longing for erotic or spiritual union with the beloved morphed into a longing for *home,* for the *des* from which the *pardesi* is exiled. Iqbal expressed this sentiment with his well-known poem "*Tarana-e-Hindi*" which he wrote in 1904, on the eve of his departure for Europe: "*Ghurbat mein hon agar hum, rehta hai dil watan mein / Samjho wahin humein bhi dil ho jahan hamara*"

(If we are in an alien land, the heart remains in the homeland / Understand us to be there wherever our heart is).[120] Ghadar fighters imprisoned on the Andaman Islands wrote love poetry in which the motherland from which they were exiled stood in for the beloved. When Bhagat Singh and his companions launched a hunger strike in prison in 1929, five thousand supporters gathered in Amritsar to recite poems comparing their love of country to the love of Heer-Ranjha, the Punjabi *qissa* of star-crossed lovers who die before their chance at union.

The pain of Partition gave this idiom a new incandescence. The Punjabi poet Amrita Pritam left Lahore during Partition. She expressed her anguish in a poem addressed to Waris Shah, the eighteenth-century author of the most famous narration of the Heer-Ranjha *qissa*. The poem, "*Ajj Aakhaan Waris Shah Nu*," asked Waris Shah to speak from his grave and turn the page of the book of love (" . . . *kiton qabran vichon bol/te ajj kitab-e-ishq da koi agla warq phol*").[121] The poem highlights women's sufferings during Partition and the poisoning of Punjab's rivers, wind, and land. A *qissa* is a story, but Heer-Ranjha was also a legend, historico-myth, based on the ethics of divine love. Pritam called on the poet-historian Waris Shah to *speak from his grave,* to come back from history to write a new history for Punjab envisioning a path out of the hell into which it has descended, *back* into a *new* page in its *old* history of love. Pritam is not thinking in terms of linear time here.

Her sense of Waris Shah's power, and of the importance of her own poetic voice in this moment, arose from her participation in the Progressive Writers' Movement that had begun in the 1930s. This movement gave fresh impetus to the idea of poets' and poetry's relevance to politics. The writer Sajjad Zaheer had left for London after a stormy controversy around his coauthored short story collection *Angare* (1932), which had criticized the Lucknowi Muslim culture from which he emerged. The British government in the United Provinces banned the book. The polarized political atmosphere between fascism and communism following the economic crash of 1929 made the 1930s a decade of "commitment" for European intellectuals, too. Writers everywhere claimed a central role in political and social change, building on older, Romantic notions of the poet's special role in history. Writers with revolutionary commitments gathered in Paris and Madrid as the Nazis came to power in 1933. The Soviet Writers' Congress met in 1934. The first International Congress of Writers for the Defence of Culture met in Paris the next year, and Zaheer went. In 1936, British writers he knew, like Ralph Fox, went to fight in the Spanish Civil War, which was seen as an ideological contest between fascism and international communism. Orwell went, too. His and other writers' sense of their particular historical agency also led them to assertively try to remake British public opinion through the Left Book Club. Zaheer joined other Indian students in England to form the anticolonial and leftist Progressive Writers' Movement in this political and intellectual climate; the All-India Progressive Writers' Association was affiliated with the International Congress of World Writers as its Indian branch. The group held its first official meeting in Lucknow in 1936 with the support of literary giants like Josh Malihabadi and Premchand. Progressives, like some of the earlier cosmopolitan revolutionaries, sought "freedom" in a broader sense than conceived by the mainstream nationalist movement. They aimed at a full social, economic, and political transformation of India that would make India truly free. They were not working within a historical narrative that necessarily culminated in the birth of the nation. Many members were communists, including Mohani. Urdu writers took a lead in the movement at the national level. The poet Faiz Ahmad Faiz, another communist member, was also a leading labor activist in Punjab. In Amritsar, at a 1937 meeting of the Kisan Sabha, a communist peasant movement, he affirmed that middle-class writers *could* relate to peasants and workers.

Iqbal and Tagore gave the group their blessing. Nehru did, too, but though he was a literary figure in his own right, he urged the group to include writers exclusively rather than politicians like himself. But the group's entire purpose was to transcend that divide; it had adopted a new script for historical action in which the poet played a central role. One senses that for some, the memory of poets' role in 1857 was as galvanizing as that of their European and Soviet contemporaries. Some were literally heirs of 1857: the Progressive poet Jan Nisar Akhtar was a great-grandson of one of the leaders of that rebellion, Maulvi Fazl-e-Haq Khairabadi, whose grandson (Jan Nisar's father) Muztar Khairabadi had penned the despondent lines often invoked to express the anguish of the generation of 1857 (often misattributed to the poet-emperor Zafar): "*Na kissi ki aankh ka noor hoon, na kissi ke dil ka qarar hoon*" (Neither am I the light of anyone's eyes, nor the tranquility of anyone's heart). With this lineage and an enhanced sense of poets' historical agency, during World War II, many Progressives disregarded Nehru's admonishments that they prioritize the nationalist movement and heed the Congress's Quit India campaign. Those who saw the war as a struggle against fascism and *for* socialist revolution spearheaded by the Soviet Union supported the British war effort, including Faiz, who had just married the British communist and poet Alys George. By the time of Partition, the Progressive movement had grown to four thousand members and fifty branches. Their sense of the agency of poets ensured that poets became outspoken and influential commentators on the unfolding of Partition.

Urdu as a poetic language figured critically in the articulation of South Asian subjectivity in that time. Indeed, its poetic idiom seems ready-made to address the post-Partition condition of a partial, parted, or divided self.[122] Part of the psychic inheritance of the trauma of Partition has been the enhanced resonance of this split selfhood—the split consciousness of Indians and Pakistanis and the split conscience of victims who were also perpetrators.

The Muslim short story writer Saadat Hasan Manto, who left Bombay for Pakistan, dramatized the absurdity of the choice before him in his story "*Toba Tek Singh*" (1955), which ends with its deranged central character, Bishan Singh, refusing to choose between the two countries, depicted as lunatic asylums behind barbed wire borders—hardly an endorsement of the triumphant making of the nation-states of Pakistan and India.[123] Bishan Singh dies in the no-man's-land between them, bodily inhabiting the division. Tormented by loss of homeland, Manto did, too. He struggled with depression, entering a mental asylum; alcoholism killed him in 1955.

Indeed, the very movements of these poets dramatized the agon and agony at work. The poet Josh Malihabadi was Nehru's close friend and chief editor of the Indian government's Urdu periodical *Aaj Kal*. But he remained torn and indecisive, going back and forth until he finally migrated to Pakistan in 1958. Still, he pined for India. Hasrat Mohani stayed in India and joined the constituent assembly that drafted the constitution, but he became so skeptical of the process that he never signed it. He died in Lucknow in 1951. Would he have moved had he lived longer? Some, like the poet Nasir Kazmi, who initially *had* conviction about his choice and embraced the cause of Pakistan, lost that certitude and wound up with a resigned ambivalence, accompanied often by a sense of transcendental connection across the border.

Others denied the border outright. Gandhi defiantly declared, "I do not consider Pakistan and India as two different countries. If I have to go to the Punjab, I am not going to ask for a passport . . . and I shall go walking. Nobody can stop me."[124] He was not alone in insisting on continued connection that would render the border meaningless. Many imagined friendship between the new nations, the border functioning as a bridge rather than a divider. The many deferrals and reversals of the decision to move were evidence of that possibility. They represent a willful and wishful belief in the prerogative to remain locally and regionally rather than nationally embedded as long as it was practicable. Many strove to defer fulfillment of any one historical narrative, to embrace inconclusiveness and internal division.

Leftist poet-activists in particular hoped Partition was a transient event in a longer struggle for far more radical ends. Their agreement on that point across the border, their continued solidarity, was a mutual affirmation. The object of Amrita Pritam's own tragic love story was the Progressive poet Sahir Ludhianvi, who also incorporated Partition into the antihistorical Sufi idiom of eternal longing. Sahir went to Lahore from Ludhiana in 1943 and stayed there after Partition, but his communist views quickly made him a target of the new government of Pakistan. He left for India in 1949 and settled in Bombay, where he wrote lyrics for cinematic narrations of love stories based on eternal division. He openly challenged the establishment narrative of the fulfillment of the anticolonial movement in August 1947. In the 1957 film *Pyaasa* (*Thirsty*), a story of a disillusioned and exploited poet, he only slightly altered his pre-independence poem "*Chakle*" (Brothel Area) for the song "*Jinhen Naaz Hai Hind Par Wo Kahan Hain?*" (Where Are Those with Pride in Hind?).[125] As far as he was concerned, the anticolonial movement he had taken part in remained unfulfilled, whatever the change in 1947. Notably, "Hind" referenced a vaguer geographical imaginary than the national space of India. In a 1958 film, he assured, "*Woh Subah Kabhi To Aayegi*" (That Dawn Will Surely Come Some Time).

Faiz Ahmad Faiz was repeatedly persecuted in Pakistan for his revolutionary politics. In jail in 1951, he wrote "*Subh-e-Azadi* (August '47)" (The Dawn of Freedom), which closed with the line "*Chale chalo ki woh manzil abhi nahi aayi*" (Keep going, for that destination has still not come).[126] For him, too, Partition was not a stopping ground of history; it could not be allowed to become a stopping ground. The struggle for the as yet unattained end had to go on, although it was unclear what shape it might take. His literary and political commitments continued to outrun the bounds of the nation. The late 1950s found him at work on an Indo-Pak cross-border film *Jago Hua Savera* (*The Day Shall Dawn*) about Bengali fishermen.

Other poets on both sides of the border criticized the false dawn of August 1947 and looked forward to the coming of real freedom, some explicitly calling on workers to rise up and exercise their collective agency in creating that reality. The Indian poet Ali Sardar Jafri's "*Fareb*" (The Deception) asserted, "*Ab bhi zindaan-e-ghulami se nikal sakte hain/apni taqdir ko hum aap badal sakte hain*" (We can still get out of this prison of slavery/we ourselves can change our own fate). It ended prophetically: "*Phootne vali hai mazdur ke maathe se kiran/surkh parcham ufuq-e-subh pe lehrate hain*" (The sunray is about to burst from the forehead of the worker/red flags flutter on the horizon of the morning).[127] This idea of Partition's only transitory quality was different from Coupland's belief in partition as a necessary phase in a march towards imperial federation. Progressive poets harbored a future-oriented historical imagination, a dream of progress in the Marxist mold, but subverted that narrative in their prioritization of the journey over the telos. Working within the Sufi idiom, they were able to express that their goal—substantive freedom and equality—had not been fulfilled in 1947 but was also necessarily unfulfillable. It was a utopic end to be eternally strived after. After all, "utopic" implied an unrealizable ideal, something unattainable by definition; but the longing for it was nevertheless deeply agitating and motivating. This was a reworking of *birha,* something to long for interminably. The Sufi idiom of Urdu poetry thus once again allowed South Asian anticolonial and revolutionary thinkers to work outside the episteme of history. As Faiz wrote in another poem, "*Faiz thi raah sar-ba-sar manzil*" (Faiz, the path was entirely the destination).[128]

The scope for human agency in this outlook remained wide despite its elusive goal. Such agency was not ethically accountable to the judgment of time, or Marxist theory, or God; its ethical vision was secular and social, even as it worked within the Sufi idiom.[129] Connection itself was the end and judge. This was an ethics of love: the idea of mutual *co*existence, rather than individuals existing side by side, based on the assumption that an individual is not in fact complete in himself or herself but exists partly in others and finds completeness through that connection with others. It might be understood as a deeply humanistic echo of earlier cosmopolitan revolutionaries' devotion to friendship and partnership as a revival of Medina. For Faiz, the self finds meaning through connection with others;

that *was* the script for action. Though he rooted his art in worldly reality—his consciousness of human suffering—he drew on the imaginative motifs of Urdu poetry to express the irrepressible nature of human connection and aspiration. The prison poem *"Zindaan Ki Ek Shaam"* (An Evening in Prison) ends with the defiant affirmation that those who spread the poison of injustice will never prevail; they may have extinguished the lamps that light the place of union, but let's see them snuff out the moon (*"Zulm ka zahr gholne vale / kaamraan ho sakenge aaj na kal / Jalva-gaah-e-visaal ki sshamein / vo bujha bhi chuke agar to kya / chand ko gul karen to hum jaanen"*).[130] The moon, a heavenly body typically representing the glowing face of the beloved in Urdu poetry, is here the infinite if unattainable source of hope visible even from a prison cell.

To be sure, both denial and the idea of a long, joint journey ahead, despite borders, were mechanisms for coping with the trauma of Partition. But they also made a kind of sense given the events unfolding around these poets at the time—the ongoing sense of *ghadar,* or tumult, of the disordering of history: A clash was unfolding in the massive princely state of Hyderabad at the heart of India. The Nizam of Hyderabad refused to join India while also struggling to crush a massive communist peasant rebellion. He lifted the ban against the Communist Party in 1948; the Communist Party also opposed joining the union. A leader in the peasant movement, the Progressive poet Makhdoom Mohiuddin, helped inaugurate the Paritala Republic, a village republic independent of both India *and* the Nizam that survived for one year and seven days. It was unclear where history was heading; perhaps this Telangana rebellion would herald a subcontinental peasant revolt. To be sure, in September 1948, the Indian Army violently repressed it, restoring land to the *zamindars* (landlords), but the very next year saw a successful communist revolution in neighboring China. As mentioned earlier, the global system of nation-states was in severe crisis after the world war, with displaced minorities all over Eurasia. The historical narratives that had sustained the era of empire and nationalism seemed to be collapsing. Many reasonably continued to nurture hopes of moving *beyond* nationalism *and* the new border.

The Congress leader Maulana Azad was among such thinkers. His father was an influential Islamic scholar who had left for Mecca during the 1857 rebellion. The family moved to Calcutta in 1890. In a familiar pattern, Maulana Azad was a poet in his youth. During Partition, he called on Indian Muslims to make a "leap of faith" by refusing a politics based on fear and refusing the very notion of a Muslim "minority" in India.[131] He insisted on the existence of a "composite culture" shared among all and possessing secular and cosmopolitan dimensions.[132] The literary scholar Amir Mufti describes him as having found a way of living as if in exile even when at home, given his unconventional background among Congress leaders and his relationship to Muslim and nationalist politics in his time. (He had not studied in Europe but was home-schooled and an autodidact who became a master of many languages, religious scholarship, and Urdu literature.)[133]

Maulana Madani was certain that Partition served British interests, that the British had connived in it to maintain control of Muslims and India.[134] Like Azad, he counseled Muslims in India to forget notions of "minority" and the lack of power that status implied. In a 1948 address in Bombay to the Jamiat Ulema-e-Hind, he categorically disavowed as blasphemous the idea that the violence of the time could be defended as jihad; it was not worldly exercise of agency that mattered but "patience, forbearance, and high ethics . . . jihad-i-akbar ('the greater jihad')," which required not the sword but other kinds of resolve.[135] He traveled continually during Partition in the interest of promoting peace. His own actions and his prescriptive calls to adhere to a higher morality that enjoined a tempering of the will to act emerged from a remarkable historical imagination, which saw history as deeply contingent rather than a working out of ideals, natural laws, or destiny. The historian Barbara Metcalf has given us a critical interpretation of Madani's historical thought. For him, the practical reality was that Muslims were historically rooted in the geographical space of India: The Prophet had visited India; the subcontinent was home to countless tombs, mosques, and other Islamic institutions; thousands of Muslim holy men, scholars, and martyrs, and millions of ordinary Muslims, were buried in its soil. It was their ancestral home.[136] Indeed it was, he argued, the second-holiest place on earth for Muslims after Mecca because Adam, the founder of the Islamic prophetic tradition, descended on Adam's Peak in Ceylon after his expulsion from Paradise. India was thus the site of the first manifestation of the "eternal light of Muhammad," he wrote in 1941. "Among various communities residing in India . . . Muslims alone, because of Adam, can legitimately claim they are the original inhabitants of the land." This narrative challenged the right-wing Hindu claim that India was a land sacred only to Hindus, itself grounded in the colonial narrative of empire that positioned Muslims as foreigners, making the British seem less intrusive and more benign in their attempt to rescue India from "foreign" rule. Madani ingeniously pointed out that Hindus, believing in reincarnation, might be reborn anywhere, meaning that Muslims, who buried their dead, had a deeper bond to Indian land. Living Muslims visited those graves, which were sanctuaries till the Day of Judgment; the spiritual influence of the dead emanated from them.

This was a historical narrative that encompassed what might be considered otherworldly forces, but in fact Madani was making an argument about *belief* in reincarnated versus buried souls—he understood that it was belief in a particular historical vision, even visions that transcended worldly existence, that guided human action. His was a pragmatic narrative, as opposed to the historical vision of Islamist thinkers who looked to Pakistan to fulfill some Islamic ideal based on theoretical abstraction. Such a vision was futile, according to Madani: Politics could not be resolved through philosophy, he thought (in a manner recalling Burke); it could not be based on abstraction but must be based on history and existing circumstances. Pushing the British out was thinkable, perhaps because their intrusion was grounded in fulfilling an abstract theory of progress. But mass expulsion of India's Muslims was unthinkable, given the heritage at stake. He accepted the deeply interwoven nature of Hindu and Muslim life in the territorial space of India as a reality of the time—a historical reality that they could not but accept, as much as they must not accept the historical reality of British imperialism. His counsel to accept the Indian reality was not the same as Galton's plea that providential circumstances prevented him from fulfilling his ethical commitments. Madani challenged Indian Muslims to fulfill their ethical commitments in those circumstances and saw the Constitution of Medina as religio-historical proof of the real-world possibility of doing so. He approached the contemporary struggle with a historical imagination that demanded the transcendence of ethical obligations across time rather than leaving ethical judgment *to* time.

The wounded optimism of these outlooks in the immediate aftermath of Partition created the space for a post-Partition South Asian selfhood that could both encompass *and* transcend the new division, even perhaps the violence that accompanied it. This was a fragile utopian vision, a refusal of received historical narratives akin to the madness of Bishan Singh, with his stubborn attachment to the no-man's-land of *"Toba Tek Singh."* Manto's story showed that madness in a dark, Chekhovian manner, but in

Urdu poetry, madness is depicted not as the breakdown of reason but as the hopeless idealism of the poetic subject, the lover. The g*hazal* titled "15 August 1947" by Jagan Nath Azad, who reluctantly left Lahore for Delhi in September 1947, begins, "*Na puchho jab bahar aayi to deewanon pe kya guzari / zara dekho ki is mausam mein farzaanon pe kya guzari*" (Don't ask what befell the madmen when spring came / just look what befell the wise men in this season).[137] "The madmen" embraces the world of Azad's fellow poets, his friends, fellow idealists, those who were seemingly the losers in the understanding of history inherited from the imperial masters. Perhaps more importantly, the friendship among poets was one critical way in which the border *was* rendered meaningless.

Faiz's poetry, especially, expressed the condition of a self not at home with itself and yet aware that its feeling of incompleteness is the source of its movement and life, as masterfully shown by Amir Mufti. Here are two lines from the 1962 poem "*Marsia*" (Elegy): "*Dur ja kar qarib ho jitne, ham se kab tum qarib the itne / Ab na aaoge tum na jaaoge, vasl o hijran baham hue kitne*" (The extent to which you are close now that you have gone far, when were you ever so close to me / Now you will neither come nor go, how as one union and separation have become). Separation and union are collapsed into one; distance and nearness coexist. Self and other do not become one but are simultaneously near and distant, uncertain.[138] Indianness came to encompass the disavowal of Indianness, Mufti argues. Faiz worked within an idiom in which indefinite separation from the beloved was the only ground from which to contemplate union. On Jagan Nath Azad's first visit to Pakistan after his departure, he wrote, "*Main apne ghar mein aaya hoon magar andaaz to dekho / ke apne aap ko manind-e-mehman leke aaya hoon*" (I have come into my own home, but look in what manner / for I have brought myself like a guest).[139] It remained his home. Alienated as he was, he was still not a guest but guest*like*. He was split into host and guest, both at home and not at home, *desi* and *pardesi*.

After Partition, when the acclaimed Pakistani short story writer Intizar Hussain invoked Ved Vyas, divine author of the Hindu epic the *Mahabharata*, as if this was emic (insider) knowledge, he affirmed this split or indeterminate South Asian selfhood. This was a political and humanistic claim about his ethos and sensibility and what he took as "his" past. Post-Partition Urdu poetry likewise continued to invoke places across the border as part of the same space—as if Sialkot, Delhi, Karachi were equally within reach of poets on either side of the border.[140] Pakistani poets continued to rely on the non-Islamic symbolism of *but* (idols), *puja* (implying idol worship), *chitaa* (pyre), and so on, on which the ironic idiom of Urdu poetry depends. The Indo-Islamic poetic tradition presumes a world of Muslims coexisting with non-Muslims (the world of Medina) to dramatize the ironies of worldly and unworldly faith at its core; it depends on a split social body. Partition was supposed to fulfill the religious historical narrative of virtuously abandoning a heathen land—*hijrat*—but in this poetry, the abandoned home became the longed-for beloved. The religious *hijrat* yields to the mystical-poetic *hijr*—to *birha*.[141] The idea of imaginatively transcending borders was also a reworking of *birha*. This poetic idiom was all about transcending worldly reality for something more meaningful. Indeed, the Sikh ethical outlook, which sees the world as real and man's deeds in this ordinary world as a mode of experiencing God, infuses Punjabi culture in particular with this capacity. (The Gandhian ethic was also about finding spiritual liberation in immersion in, rather than retreat from, the world and the sufferings of others.) The Urdu poetic idiom remains popular because it resonates with the real experience of millions.

Intersecting stories might be told about Bengali, Hindi, Punjabi, and so on. This is no specialized intellectual history but part of the cultural mainstream, evident in films, plays, and other art forms.[142] After 1947, the Indian and Pakistani governments engaged in a "long partition" of land and peoples that worked to produce "Indians" and "Pakistanis" over time.[143] Theirs was nevertheless a condition of a self that could both encompass and transcend division. Oral histories of Partition survivors confirm the widespread enduring prevalence of this split selfhood. Even those who moved out of conviction felt a bond with the "home" they abandoned because of ongoing relationships and memories: "There is not a clear line for these people," writes the oral historian Anam Zakaria. "It is difficult to decipher what they love more, where they belong more. *This confusion is the only truth for them.*"[144] Partition did not create two new, coherent national identities (Indian and Pakistani) but a population of divided selves. The exile, the refugee, the orphaned, the converted, the abducted and reclaimed—all these survivors were in different ways split, in many cases violently split, selves. Post-Partition identity was about belonging in new nation-states but also about exile and unbelonging emerging from a refusal of the linear teleology of modern historicism. Notably, in the realm of performance, those who comfortably inhabited and exhibited this kind of limitless selfhood acquired massive cultural traction in this period: figures like the *qawwal* Nusrat Fateh Ali Khan, the actors Nargis and Amitabh Bachchan, the rock singer Freddie Mercury come to mind.

This sensibility is South Asian, but it was forged through contact with the wider world, including the colonial experience and contemporary European attempts to recover a more numinous sense of self through engagement with Eastern thought—like the self-styled eccentrics who ventured to the Arabian desert. Progressive Urdu poets subverted the mission of Victorian-era Urdu reformers like Sir Syed Ahmed Khan and Maulana Khawaja Hali to fulfill Macaulay's task of casting Indian minds in a British mold. Instead, they embraced the cracks in the Indian mind, evoking a particularly South Asian way of being idiosyncratically modern, drawing on this heritage in their immediate context in new ways.

All this helps us understand the survival of other kinds of moral community in the region despite Partition. But when it came to acknowledging guilt for complicity in it, adapted narratives of progress remained robust—the idea that Partition was the price of national progress, for instance. The centrality of displacement to Punjabi identity was reinforced by continued turmoil in the region from the 1960s onward, which sharpened the image of the Punjabi as beloved *pardesi*. (Punjabi writers and artists who found refuge in the Bombay film industry helped popularize this image and the idea that love lies in separation.) But it is distinct from, say, displacement in Jewish or Armenian identity, in that the Punjabi is aware of his *own* role in his tragic severance from his home and violent division of his homeland. His (and I do mean "his" here) is a self-imposed exile guiltily justified by one or another promise of historical narratives of modernity—personal prosperity for economic migrants, national prosperity for Partition refugees. He self-consciously martyrs the homeland for the progress of its children, secure that in dutifully pursuing his worldly ends he nevertheless maintains a timeless bond with it, a bond made more transcendental at each remove from the geopolitical reality of a place called "Punjab." When Jagan Nath Azad was leaving Pakistan after a visit, Muhammad Tufail, editor of the Pakistani Progressive literary journal *Nuqush*, bid him farewell at the station with a box of sweets, quipping, "*Tumhein to yun rukhsat karte hain jaise beti ko rukhsat kiya jaata hai*" (You we send away in the way one sends off a daughter).[145] Instead of separation from a beloved, he rendered Azad's exile from his homeland in the more clearly gendered form of the daughter leaving her parents' home to join her new family after marriage—a rite common to Hindu, Sikh, and Muslim traditions in the region. Playing on the land-as-mother trope, he rendered the departure in forward-looking terms, as a rite of passage to adulthood—progress itself. It is more final than the beloved's separation, but also less rigid, in that a woman can and does go back to her old home at times, albeit to be indulged as a guest with few substantive entitlements.

The split self is a self that can watch itself; this is the foundation of most understandings of conscience. Whether as an inner observer, inner voice, internal messenger, or simply the absence of a sense of a unitary self, across most religions and ethical systems, we understand conscience as a capacity to disrupt selfhood in some way, as a splitting of the self into observer and observed. This is what Galton, as a committed Quaker, claimed to do with his defense in 1796, but his providential sense of history disrupted the effort. The Enlightenment goal of papering over internal splits in the interest of producing internally coherent individuated selves had the effect of outsourcing judgments of conscience to time, to history. It did not do so without struggle: This is why the historically minded administrators we have examined frequently confessed doubt about their actions in diaries and private letters, confidential literary spaces where the pressures the historical ethical idiom exercised on ordinary moral compunctions are revealed, ironically, for posterity—designedly, insofar as men conscious of their great-man destiny may have been aware of the humanizing power of such sources for those who might tell their story. From the turn of the twentieth century, some Britons rebelled against the conception of unitary selves and sought instead the self's dissolution by wandering in the desert and dabbling in mysticism and occultism. Both Gandhi and Lawrence emphasized the value of absorption in craft as a means of dissolving consciousness. Their appeal was similar—Lawrence made the comparison himself. A photographer who chased him down explained, "You and Gandhi are the two people I want to take."[146] Both were known for their struggles to subject the body to the mind, through fasting, sexual abstinence, and a Morris-inspired absorption in craft—Gandhi at his spinning wheel, and Lawrence with his mechanical work at the RAF in which he sought "complete emptiness of mind."[147]

Morris had turned to artisanal crafts as a remedy for the alienation from creativity and social connectedness (i.e., humanity) produced by the

Mohandas Gandhi, 1946. (Photo by Margaret Bourke-White / Time & Life Pictures / Getty Images)

capitalist-industrial mode of production. Lawrence desired absence of mind to cope with consuming guilt and shame. Gandhi saw crafts as a cure for the unsound ethical bearings, the endless material craving of Western civilization, which left judgment to history and was thus essentially about being absent from the present time. For Gandhi, craft was a cure for *that* absence of mind, an invitation to another kind of absence of mind in which conscience and consciousness were once again the same. Faiz's contemplation of the moon through prison bars perhaps went even further in reminding us of the cosmological context of human aspiration, love, and creativity.

The very nature of rule without consent meant that the British ruled in a state of continued insecurity, verging often on paranoia. Their rule was thus characterized by outbursts of rage and a desire to fragment societies, tendencies variously accommodated in their own historical mythology of the empire. The fractured condition of so many societies today is a *postco-*

T. E. Lawrence in
Miranshah
(present-day
Pakistan), 1928.
(Chronicle / Alamy
Stock Photo)

lonial condition. Nationalism and colonialism have been forces of violent displacement, disrupting social and cultural relations by unleashing dynamics of inclusion and exclusion. Those who participated in them became houses divided unto themselves in coming to terms with complicity in their destructive dynamics. The violence of empire has not been memorialized like other instances of mass trauma—the Holocaust or Hiroshima—as I observed at the start of this book. But neither, too, has the violence of Partition, partly because of widespread *bad* conscience; those who were victims were often also perpetrators. Moreover, both India and Pakistan have been complicit in appropriating the violence done to women within an ideology of community and nation. The imminent passing of the generation of Partition survivors has unleashed a scramble to collect testimony and memorialize the event before it is too late.[148] Undertaken with sufficient sensitivity, this effort may enable a new reckoning with conscience and allow us to fully understand how Indians and Pakistanis dealt with the burden of conscience after Partition. The intimate history of killing is, indeed, difficult to write.

Indians invested in the nationalist narrative see Partition as a betrayal or failure of the nation-building project. Indian Muslims are often treated as a traitorous fifth column. Many Pakistanis saw and continue to see Partition as fulfillment of a brave and visionary nationalist vision and the ambition to create a new Medina, and yet it is a nation-state without a coherent political project, where militant Sunnism engages in continual assault on the inner life of its citizens.[149] As both countries continue to cope with the unfinished business of Partition—incorporation of minorities, ongoing crisis in Kashmir, communal violence, religion and the state—they might do better to understand it as the monster-child of imperialism and nationalism. Partition changed minds and consciousness. Going forward, its heirs might recover the alternative ethical frameworks embraced by thinkers of that revolutionary time: Medina, love, networks, regionalism, connectedness, a wider conception of *azadi* and self-rule.

Understanding it within the historical narratives that undergirded British imperialism, to the British, Partition proved that they were right about the incompatibility and barbarism of Muslims and Hindus without their staying hand. Even twenty years later, W. H. Auden described the event as the creation of a border "Between two peoples fanatically at odds / With their different diets and incompatible gods." Radcliffe never collected his fee of 40,000 rupees for drawing the boundary, allegedly out of guilt for the millions of lives lost in the nightmarish process of making it a reality. But this attitude of renunciation smacks more of the self-pity of the martyr than real conscience: Less than a decade later, he was urging partition of Cyprus.

Today, international policy "experts" continue to look to partition as a useful tool of "conflict resolution" between allegedly intractable communities, despite its evident failure to solve any of the problems it claimed to solve—in Ireland, India, Cyprus, or elsewhere.[150] As Dubnov and Robson note, it is invoked in discussions of Syria, Israel / Palestine, the Sudan, and other regions. The total absence of any evidentiary basis for claiming that partition "works" is of no moment in such discussions. They are a product of the continuing intellectual and moral grip of an imperial historical imagination that sees partition as the logical way of paternalistically bringing order to a disordered world. The violence it will inevitably entail is considered the tolerable price of "nationhood," a historical object of mythic status whose achievement licenses abandonment of ordinary ethical considerations.

With an uncanny sense of poetic justice, the vulture of partition now circles Britain itself. The Brexit movement, calling to partition Britain from Europe, is the culmination of a long struggle to accommodate the presence of immigrants of color in postwar Britain, many of whom were refugees from India's Partition. The racial sentiments deployed in the empire found amplification in nasty and violent political debates at home as they arrived. Brexit is also about imperial nostalgia—resurrecting Britain's island glory and ties with the wider world. As Britain faces a messy partition from Europe, ghosts of partitions past sit at the table. The permanent irresolution of conflict represented by the 1921 partition of Ireland haunts discussions about the practicality of Brexit. Joint membership in the European Union—that supraimperial federal structure—had helped smooth relations between the two Irelands. Now, the border between the Irish Republic, still in the European Union, and the proposed non-European United Kingdom of Great Britain and Northern Ireland, will become a security nightmare once again. Meanwhile, Scotland contemplates partition from Britain, too—making mince of Coupland's smug confidence in the immunity of Britain's constituent nations from the idea of "Scottish 'Pakistan.'" In 1977, the Scottish political theorist Tom Nairn's book *The Break-Up of Britain* predicted that the United Kingdom, as an imperialistic relic, was doomed to fall apart into its constituent units.[151] The anthropologist Benedict Anderson, perhaps the most well-known recent theorist of nationalism, wrote his classic *Imagined Communities* (1983) in conversation with Nairn's book and a body of theory on nationalism authored almost exclusively by Eastern European Jews displaced to the United Kingdom after World War II—thinkers like Ernest Gellner and Eric Hobsbawm, who, ironically, were attached to the United Kingdom for its supranational resemblance to the defunct Austro-Hungarian Empire.[152]

As in the breakup of South Asia, today's Brexit mess is a product of the feckless and ignorant nonchalance of Britain's ruling elite, setting rushed calendars for departure, oblivious to the mayhem to which it will give rise.

As Fintan O'Toole observes with delicious irony in the *Irish Times,* the chaos in Britain recalls the situation in many a colony transitioning to self-government: "Let's just say that if Theresa May were the head of a newly liberated African colony in the 1950s, British conservatives would have been pointing, half-ruefully, half-gleefully, in her direction and saying 'See? Told you so—they just weren't ready to rule themselves. Needed at least another generation of tutelage by the Mother Country.'"[153] O'Toole, an Irishman invoking Shaw's earlier parodies of British justifications of empire, perceives in the Brexit shambles an upending of the historical logic that sustained empire—and nationalism. He adds, "As every former colony knows, nationalism is a great beast for carrying you to the point of independence—and then it becomes a dead horse."

CHAPTER SIX

ʹ ʹ The Past and Future of History

> What could have been the intellectual history of any
> discipline if it had not . . . been forced into, the waste of
> time and life that . . . dominance required—lethal
> discourses of exclusion blocking access to cognition
> for both the excluder and the excluded.
>
> —Toni Morrison, 1993

ʹ ʹ *Edmund Burke's anxiety about* the "Geographical morality" of his countrymen proved accurate over the long run. Colonial atrocities continued through the period of decolonization. British counterinsurgency in Kenya in the 1950s resorted to concentration camps that killed millions.[1] In 1959, the Conservative politician Enoch Powell echoed Burke in one of the signal speeches of his controversial career, urging, "We cannot say, 'We will have African standards in Africa, Asian standards in Asia and perhaps British standards here at home.'"[2] Powell was an imperialist and a racist. He had served in military intelligence in India from 1943 to 1946, authoring the last British report on the Indian army in which he recommended increasing the proportion of white officers. In May 1946, he projected that India would require at least another half century of direct British rule.[3] In 1968, he became infamous for his "rivers of blood" speech calling for a stop to immigration from former colonies to the United Kingdom.[4] In 1959, his concern was that Britain had become too "African" in Africa. But the camps and the massacres were not "un-British," when set against the record of British imperial activity; they were only un-British set against the myths the British told about themselves. Powell was another in a long line of imperialists who deflected responsibility for the crimes of empire onto its victims.

The British Empire was acquired not in a "fit of absence of mind" but by minds committed to certain cultural notions and theories of history. A defining quality of the modern period is a self-conscious and worldly understanding of conscience, shaped by a historical sensibility. We are reflecting here on the metaphysics of historical thought, how a particular theory of history can influence our deeds by influencing our sense of agency and responsibility in shaping the world around us. Eighteenth-century sugar boycotters acted out of an awareness that their agency as consumers contributed to the slave production of sugar. British imperialism emerged from well-meaning but destructive faith in Britain's providential historical role in the world. If you believe that the proletariat makes history, you will act differently from someone who believes that the alignment of the planets and stars shapes human action. The modern era is one in which men (and I mean men) increasingly conscious of their own agency as historical actors tried to shape world events according to certain historical scripts, whether as revolutionaries or conquerors or industrialists or settlers. The notions of "progress" that drove the spread of industrial capitalism, imperialism, and nationalism depended on an ability to suppress conscience by recourse to assumptions about race, religion, and culture; dreams of utopic ends again and again justified horrific means. Modern history has been one of marginalization and uprooting on a massive scale; split selfhoods are *typical*—in South Asia, but also in Germany, the Balkans, Cyprus, Palestine / Israel, Ireland, Vietnam, Korea, the United States (including what W. E. B. Du Bois called "double consciousness"), and elsewhere—much of this traceable to colonial rule. These events, however, also crucially reshaped the historical discipline and the imagination behind it in ways that leave open possibilities for alternative ways of acting and being in time.

In the early twentieth century, Indians, Arabs, and others pushed back against the colonial historical sensibility. Some did so by appropriating it to serve anticolonial ends. British celebrations of the fiftieth anniversary of the 1857 rebellion in 1907, just when Bengal was in radical rebellion, made that event ever more pivotal to debates about and in imperial history. In 1909, the Indian historian and future leader of the Hindu Mahasabha V. D. Savarkar published a revisionist account of the 1857 rebellion as a national uprising, specifically in response to British commemoration of the fiftieth anniversary.[5] He imported a different historical script into his interpretation, writing it in London while immersed in histories of the French and American revolutions. In the face of intense British efforts to ban the book, Savarkar had it printed in the Netherlands. It became a much-read banned book in India. Its printing and circulation were part of interwar anticolonial revolutionary activity.[6]

The 1857 rebellion came to haunt the discipline's own history—Baqar's son, Mohammed Husain Azad, became Urdu's first modern historian. Sir Syed Ahmed Khan emerged as a Muslim reformer while writing the first Indian account of the conflict in 1859.[7] Kaye, too, made it an object of literary devotion for over a decade. The traces of ambivalence in many British accounts of the rebellion left an opening for more critical future revisionism. Thus, when a British World War I veteran became suspicious of received historical wisdom about the empire, he turned first to the 1857 rebellion. This was Iqbal's friend Edward John Thompson, a missionary in India who served with British forces in the invasion of Iraq as an army chaplain and became deeply disillusioned by his experience, resolving, in a letter to his mother, that if he survived, he would stand "finally & without question, with the Rebels," for Western civilization was bankrupt.[8] He re-signed from his mission after the war and began to write. He first turned poet, with a 1919 volume, *Mesopotamian Verses*. His next major literary work was the play *Atonement* (1924) about an English hero who renounces vio-lence against Indians and adopts a self-sacrificial role.[9] Then, his first major historical work—his first attempt to enact that atonement himself—was a revisionist account of the pivotal rebellion of 1857, from the Indian point of view (paternalistically undertaken out of the presumption that "Indians are not historians, and they rarely show any critical ability"[10]). He told Tagore, another of his anticolonial poet friends, that the book was an "in-dividual Englishman's act of atonement."[11] *The Other Side of the Medal* (1925) strove to displace the long-standing narrative of diabolical Indian attack on an entirely benevolent British presence by acknowledging at last the real political protest the rebels expressed and the British violence that had provoked their own. He recognized the power of British myths about this event in sustaining the empire and harsh retribution afterwards—and that the book risked his lectureship at Oxford.[12] It became part of public debate about the increasingly powerful Indian anticolonial movement. The *New Statesman* praised it for uncovering the "policy of terrorization" behind the rebellion.[13]

This book was a crucial anticolonial precursor to the trend in writing "history from below" that became popular in Britain after World War II. It was a radical intervention in the discipline of history made possible by Thompson's sense of his own duties as a historical actor. His friends already included two poet leaders of the Indian anticolonial movement, Iqbal and Tagore. In Oxford, as he wrote, his neighbor was the war veteran, poet, and classicist Robert Graves—the friend and biographer of T. E. Lawrence. Thompson came to know Lawrence himself. Unsurprisingly then, given his close acquaintance with such figures, he nurtured a fascination with the Byronic type—the poetic hero who sacrificed in the name of a beloved enslaved people, at once redeeming the sins of British imperial power. Though many young Britons found their heroic aspirations quashed by the First World War's degeneration into a war of attrition, Thompson felt he experienced it fleetingly in Iraq, where he earned a Military Cross for attending to wounded soldiers under fire. When Lawrence died in a motorcycle accident in 1935, Thompson attended his memorial service at St. Paul's.[14] In Calcutta the next year, he invoked his wartime experience in a letter to his elder son, describing "the spontaneous rushing-out of our wills into selfless action," the way certain individuals "get gripped by something that fills their lives with personal communion, & gives them a sense of destiny which makes them fearless." He spoke of heroes who periodically appeared to redeem their country's bad faith, recalling Byron's death while "encouraging the Greeks still firing at their Turkish oppressors." He wondered, "Can one man today achieve anything that matters by a gesture?"[15]

Thompson's revolutionary approach to the history of empire in India was his Byronic gesture. It was also self-assertion shaped by the proactive culture of mass democracy in the aftermath of the war, the growing sense that it was citizens' duty to exercise a check on government and ensure that its actions conformed with their wishes. While Lawrence exercised the agency of the great man in the shadows of the secret state, Thompson articulated a vision of history-writing as active public citizenship, and the historian as the archetype of the active citizen: "Now . . . the historian cannot be historian only."[16] After the First Anglo-Afghan War, Kaye had revolutionized the discipline's methodology, urging the need for unofficial sources to get at the truth. Thompson now fully unleashed the idea of history as a means of truth-telling against a government bent on covert pursuit of empire. En route to India during the decade of "commitment," he met another Mesopotamia veteran, Geoffrey Garratt, with whom he co-wrote the anti-imperial work *The Rise and Fulfillment of British Rule in India* (1934).[17] Thompson targeted his government's brutality *and* the secrecy and propaganda used to conceal it, cultivating a passionate faith in the historian's craft as the most effective means of truth-telling against the imperial state—history itself as a means of redemption.

As imperialism became more embarrassing, however, historians like C. A. Bodelsen and R. L. Schuyler mitigated the impact of indictments like Thompson's by arguing that Britons had in fact been antipathetic towards imperial expansion from about 1815 to 1880, producing a sticky myth that the Victorian era was a time of "anti-imperialism."[18] This historiography recalled the theoretical anti-annexationist arguments of free-trade critics like John Bright and Richard Cobden, without their willing tolerance of empire so long as it did not cost (not to mention their unwillingness to sever existing colonial ties). It extended the life of Seeley's "fit of absence of mind" explanation of empire and enrolled turn-of-the-century critics like Hobson in a longer liberal lineage. (Hobson himself noted in 1930 that the Seeley thesis "played into the hands of mysticism," for, in fact, "there was no absence of mind in the makers of [the empire's] several parts, or even in the gradual bringing together and extension of these parts."[19])

But the work of dismantling the historical narratives that sustained empire went on in the empire, as we have seen in Chapter 5. Moreover, the paths of interwar anticolonial thinkers from all over often crossed in London, infusing British political and intellectual culture, too.[20] In 1933, the British celebrated the centenary of the abolition of slavery. Two years later, Italy invaded Ethiopia, the only African country not under American or European control. From 1935 to 1938, riots and strikes erupted in Barbados, Jamaica, Guyana, and elsewhere. Against this backdrop, a Trinidadian in London, C. L. R. James, penned his classic 1938 history of the Haitian Revolution, *The Black Jacobins,* replete with asides denouncing British perfidy during the Napoleonic Wars.[21] A Pan-Africanist and socialist, James moved in the same circles as Fenner Brockway in London, producing plays, novels, and cricket commentary alongside his historical works. These works and his peripatetic life, lived between London, the United States, Ghana, and the West Indies, evidenced his search for an answer to colonialism that went beyond the nation. Eric Williams was a student of James's in Trinidad and would later become prime minister of Trinidad and Tobago. His 1938 dissertation was the basis of his 1944 classic history of abolition, *Capitalism and Slavery,* which sought to expose the hypocrisy of abolition *and* its celebration, grounding the story in economic interest rather than moral virtue.[22]

Thinkers who took to history as the terrain on which to make the case against empire implicitly recognized the discipline's collusion in empire. They recognized that history could not function as an autonomous foundation for ethics, as Lord Bolingbroke had imagined, because it is constructed through minutely political decisions. As the Haitian anthropologist Michel-Rolph Trouillot put it in the 1990s, "Why bother with the Holocaust or plantation slavery, Pol Pot, or the French Revolution, when we already have Little Red Riding Hood?"[23] History was never simply a universal moral philosophy. As Trouillot shows, "Either we would all share the same stories of legitimation, or the reasons why a specific story matters to a specific population are themselves historical." What is said to have happened is distinct from what happened, and deeply political decisions mediate the construction of the former from the latter. By opening up 1857, abolition, and the rest of the imperial record to fresh narrativization, anticolonial historians recognized that claims about history's ethical uses had long served to cover up its political uses. "Our writing of India's history is perhaps resented more than anything else we have done," Thompson noted in 1943.[24]

This fracturing of the discipline shaped the writing of British history, too. Thompson's children grew up in this atmosphere, with Gandhi, Nehru, and Lawrence visiting their Oxford home, and their father instructing them in Byronic heroism and the power of individual agency in political activism and narrating the past. His younger son, the poet, historian, and political activist Edward Palmer (E. P.) Thompson, later recalled cadging stamps from the Indian "poets and political agitators" who visited their home and his knowledge that these were their "most important visitors."[25] One senses that for both father and sons it was as much the life that such poets lived on the front lines of history as the poetry they wrote that made them so admirable. Thompson's elder son, Frank, was an aspiring poet, too. He spent much of World War II in intelligence in the Middle East before he was killed during a Lawrence- and Byron-inspired Special Operations Executive mission to free Bulgaria.[26] E. P. inherited his father's struggle to solve the mystery around his brother's death in the face of the "British anti-historical device known as the Official Secrets Act." He learned that "reasons of state are eternally at war with historical knowledge."[27] This experience confirmed his father's lessons in government mendacity; he had grown up "expecting governments to be mendacious and imperialist and expecting that one's stance ought to be hostile to government."[28]

Churchill had modeled the Special Operations Executive on Lawrence's activities in the previous war. But the resistance groups they helped warily eyed the "average SOE officer as a would-be Lawrence of Arabia," and thus the "perfidious arrogant champion of an Empire," in the words of one Yugo-slavian partisan.[29] Lawrence's shifting image in a time of growing anti-imperialism made it difficult for post–World War II Britons to emulate him or Byron uncritically. Even the elder Thompson suffered from specula-tions about his possible Lawrentian qualities: When he was in India in 1932 on behalf of the Rhodes Trust to explore possibilities for cooperation be-tween Indian and British writers, Tagore's circle suspected he was a gov-ernment agent. For his younger son, empire was embarrassing enough, more so his father's embodiment of that quintessentially imperial Byronic English character. He described his father harshly: "It is as if he wishes both to challenge with his pen the imperial power whose rule provokes emergencies, and yet to reassure the rulers that, at the point of emergency, he could be counted on to take up a rifle with the best."[30] After his brother's death, E. P. channeled his own Byronic ambitions domestically. His father's intimacy with and Byronic attitude towards Indian anticolonialism, in-tensified by his brother's loss while attempting to fulfill a similar destiny at the frontier of Western and Eastern imperialism, sparked E. P.'s critical stance towards the British state's imperiousness at home and his interest in exploring the history of the English working class to guide Britons out of darkness in his own time, resulting in his classic work *The Making of the English Working Class* (1963). (The title echoed that of his father's last work of history, *The Making of the Indian Princes* [1943].) He looked to the his-toric libertarian tradition of working-class people for ways to check the excesses of the "secret state" in the Cold War era that shaped his life. As Britain's "warfare state" boomed despite the loss of India, Thompson saw empire at home: "Inter-recruitment, cross-postings and exchange of both ideology and experience" meant that methods designed to pacify crowds and invigilate subversives abroad—the "world of a John Buchan novel"—were now applied to the disciplining of the unemployed, women, and crowds at home.[31] He understood his role as a historian-activist as a By-ronic gesture to liberate working people in his time. He defended the "En-glish notion of radical intellectual practice based on the widest possible interchange between intellectuals and workers." Intellectuals were located "'inside' the struggle," using their position to "articulate the experience and aspirations of the subordinate classes."[32] This was his Byronic view of his own role in British socialism (though, of the Romantic poets, he most admired Blake, identifying with him as a "witness against the Beast."[33])

Through these shifts in writing history during the era of anticolonialism emerged the popular twentieth-century understanding of the historian as critic of government. Bad conscience about empire was critical to the new, more inclusive modes of history-writing that emerged in the last century. History set out to expose the scandal of empire.[34] E. P. was wary of "progress" as a category through which to understand history, after a world war that had ended with the dropping of the atomic bombs, capping a modern period that was a record of devastation as much as progress—or perhaps progress based on devastation. Of the industrial revolution, he averred, "It is impossible to designate as 'progressive' . . . processes which brought about the degradation, for twenty or thirty years ahead, of the workers employed in the industry." Mindful of his nuclear-armed time, he admonished, "Our only criterion for judgment should not be whether or not a man's actions are justified in the light of subsequent evolution. After all, we are not at the end of social evolution ourselves." The "lost causes" of the past might even yield "insights into social evils which we have yet to cure."[35] This was an outright rejection of the notion dating to Thucydides, that history vindicates. It was not history that judged, but the historian who decides where the story ends. History was written by victors or those who choose to side with them, and victory then became the judge of ethical merit. Even in Priestley's time, Isaac D'Israeli, father of the future jingoist prime minister of Britain, mocked the conceit that history offered insight into God's plan, for the moment at which we close the account is arbitrary: History is "so ductile . . . in the hands of man" that it bent towards "the force of success."[36]

Still, as Thompson's words show, he remained committed to the idea that the study of history offered insight into the problem of "evils" in the world and that "social evolution" can reach an "end." Moreover, he remained committed to the idea of progress insofar as he imagined a "cure" sometime in the future. He wanted to rummage through lost causes as an end in itself but also for the more pragmatic purpose of recovering ideas that might further progress in his own time. He was critical of the cultural costs of "progress" but nevertheless still invested in the idea of universal history, imagining the eighteenth-century British story as a harbinger for what would evolve everywhere in due course. In a celebrated essay on time a few years later, he avowed, "Without time-discipline we could not have the insistent energies of the industrial man; and whether this discipline comes in the form of Methodism, or of Stalinism, or of nationalism, it will come to the developing world."[37]

Continental thinkers were even more ambivalent about progress in the shadow of the Holocaust. The German Jewish philosopher Walter Benjamin had already perceived how industrial life and mechanized warfare anesthetized human sensibilities. Exiled from Germany in the 1930s, he was persecuted even in his refuge in France. Witnessing the destruction of European Jewry and Europe itself, he did not so much question the narrative of progress as highlight the destruction it left in its wake. Months before his suicide in 1940, he compiled his "Theses on the Philosophy of History." The ninth was a reflection on the 1920 painting by Paul Klee titled *Angelus Novus* (see accompanying image). Benjamin bought it in 1921, seeing in it "the angel of history." When he wrote about it in 1940, it would have been unknown to his readers. But his description has now been cited so often in so many contexts that it is at once iconic and cliché. Indeed, we have stripped the picture of the very "aura" that Benjamin attributed to art, that numinous quality lost in the process of mechanical reproduction. I nevertheless invoke Benjamin's thoughts on Klee's painting to restore them to their context of a broader philosophical interrogation, prompted by the world wars, of the idea that history must be a narrative of progress. The angel looks "as though he is about to move away from something he is fixedly contemplating. His eyes are staring, his mouth is open, his wings are spread. . . . His face is turned toward the past." This was not an angel that intervened, as a divine actor, in the unfolding of human history. History was too swift for him to perform the healing magic he might, and he is reduced to a helpless witness: "Where we perceive a chain of events, he sees one single catastrophe which keeps piling wreckage upon wreckage and hurls it in front of his feet. The angel would like to stay, awaken the dead, and make whole what has been smashed. But a storm is blowing from Paradise; it has got caught in his wings with such violence that the angel can no longer close them. The storm irresistibly propels him into the future to which his back is turned, while the pile of debris before him grows skyward. This storm is what we call progress."[38] Benjamin killed himself while fleeing

Nazi forces. His possessions were passed on to his fellow Frankfurt School philosopher Theodor Adorno, who likewise questioned the narrative of progress in the face of the Holocaust. The French historian of ideas Michel Foucault questioned it based on its serial exclusion of the mad, the deviant, the homosexual, and so on, as "abnormal."[39] To Foucault, discourses are what constitute and empower the subjects that make history; they are thus the proper objects of historical study. Indeed, this book is in many ways a study of how the discourse of history shaped empire. Yet Foucault remained committed to the Hegelian understanding of philosophy as a critical reflection on our present in which we employ conceptual tools inherited from the past.

Writing in New Zealand, the exiled Austrian philosopher Karl Popper also developed a critique of historicism, arguing that the idea that history must evolve inexorably according to some knowable general laws had produced the totalitarian movements of his time. His 1957 book *The Poverty of Historicism* argued that the unpredictable development of human knowledge, which had an important causal role in history, prohibited predictable functioning of any such laws.[40] In addition to fascism, he was disturbed by the way that Marxist doctrine enabled violence by convincing believers that more would die through class struggle than through a swift revolution to end it. He recognized, in other words, how certain historical scripts informed ethical decisions in the present. He argued instead that human history as a whole is a single unique event, made up of contingencies; study of the past may reveal trends but not laws with predictive power. These ideas also appear in his 1945 book on the "open society," which remains a popular defense of Western liberal values.[41] Popper's readings of thinkers like Hegel and Marx have been much criticized; more importantly, he did not recognize that the liberal values he valorized as an alternative to fascism and communism *also* originated in a view of history guided by natural laws and had furnished the intellectual breeding ground of colonialism, in which fascism was rooted. Popper's conclusions were at once radical and conservative, locating the source of "our greatest troubles" in "our impatience to better the lot of our fellows." He rightly lauded democracy and warned of the dangers of those presuming the role of "great men" but continued to place faith in technocracy and the goal of individual freedom. Though something of an iconoclast, neither social democrat nor libertarian, he mistook liberal ideals for historical reality in holding up Western liberal democracies as societies that had peacefully

Paul Klee, *Angelus Novus*, 1920. (Photo © The Israel Museum, Jerusalem, by Elie Posner)

improved over time—as if the United States, the United Kingdom, and France had not constitutively depended on imperialism. E. P. Thompson's depiction of the simultaneously libertarian and communitarian values of the English working class alluded exasperatedly to Popper's indictment of the "persecuted . . . as forerunners of oppression." He reclaimed the "open society" as the patrimony of the Radical Left, beginning with Paine, asserting that "democracy," putting the people at the center, means setting in motion forces that can be neither controlled nor foreseen.[42]

For Thompson, like Benjamin, history-writing might perform a more poetic redemptive function in the face of unremitting loss. Another of Benjamin's theses affirmed that major and minor events both had a place in the record of the past: "Nothing that has ever happened should be regarded as lost for history." But the "fullness of its past" was available only to a "redeemed mankind."[43] The recovery of history, then, is a measure of our species' accountability to conscience; Benjamin writes, "Each moment it [redeemed mankind] has lived becomes a *citation à l'ordre du jour*—and that day is Judgment Day." In the very completing of the secular record of history lies proof of the moral reckoning of mankind and the end of time itself. The problem with the narrative of progress was precisely its presumption of "homogeneous, empty time," when in fact "history is the subject of a structure whose site is not homogeneous, empty time, but time filled by the presence of the now."[44]

E. P. was also a poet, and this was an important part of his sense of agency as a thinker and activist, perhaps because of his childhood exposure to "poets and political agitators." He assembled his history of the English working class with an eye on the Romantic poets of their time. To E. P., explains the historian Joan Scott, poetry stood for "deeply inspired action. . . . The poet was crucial to revolutionary politics, for he could articulate the longings that, along with practical programs, inspired men to act." Blake, especially, "embodied the possibility of poetry and politics, romantic yearning and rational resistance in a single movement."[45] The Thompsons' intergenerational attempts to revolutionize the discipline involved an effort to infuse it with an ethical outlook derived from poetry rather than the judgment of time that had long been its end. This was notably also when Aimé Césaire published his *Discourse on Colonialism* (1950) in poetic prose to achieve a kind of transcendent "clairvoyance."[46]

And yet, the year before, Adorno famously pronounced, "To write [lyric] poetry after Auschwitz is barbaric."[47] Lyric poetry can perhaps be

said to have come into its own with Shakespeare, with *Hamlet* exemplifying the preoccupation with individual moral agency that so tragically
failed the millions who died in the Holocaust. Adorno meant one cannot
use the art form of the total society that produced Auschwitz to memorialize that event. Art holds a mirror to society, but a total and thoroughly
sinister society left no moral space or form through which to offer a reflection on it. Culture and criticism were complicit in each other: "In the open-
air prison which the world is becoming, it is no longer so important to know
what depends on what, such is the extent to which everything is one." He
later modified his stance to acknowledge the need and right to express suffering: "It may have been wrong to say that after Auschwitz you could no
longer write poems. But it is not wrong to raise the less cultural question
whether after Auschwitz you can go on living." Any life after it must be a
nightmare of memory and self-doubt. To Marx's idea that philosophy must
not only interpret but change the world, he answered in 1966 that philosophy
"lives on because the moment to realize it was missed."[48] The time for revolutionary action was over. His work on identity, however, contributed a central
idea to the massive protest movements of 1968, that self-making was itself an
exercise of political agency—the personal as political.[49] Indeed, the modern
historical profession's very preoccupation with "agency," the idea of autonomous selves with the power to make history, is rooted in this moment.

Adorno saw "negative identity" as prior to the liberating identity of
modern selfhood. But in other spaces and traditions of thought, dissolution of the self was evidence not of weakness, uncertainty, and alienation
leading inevitably to fascism but of resilience and openness. Those other
moral spaces survived the traumas of the mid-twentieth century—that
thread of antihistorical thought that evolved from the colonial period
through the present and that has depended on the form of poetry as
much as on ethical content pulled from alternative sources. The Holocaust opened up a chasm in history; on this side of it, the limits of art,
perception, philosophy, reason, all stood exposed. And yet, the present is
seeded with thoughts and ways of being from outside its unspeakable
reality. Adorno may not have perceived these, but E. P. Thompson's turn
to poetry as a way forward just then suggests that his exposure to Blake,
eighteenth-century working-class song, and anticolonial "poets and political agitators" in his own time gave him a glimpse into those ways of
being. Indeed, those poets were attempting just then to write lyric poetry
about the unspeakable trauma of Partition, albeit often obliquely.[50]

Benjamin's prophetic recovery of lost time—his perception of fragments that might be redeemed from the power of the totality—and Thompson's effort to recover lost causes evoke Faiz's contemplation of the moon
from behind prison bars. Thompson found new ethical inspiration in the
creative—poetic—radical traditions of eighteenth-century workers, regardless of their effectualness in their own time. For him they provided a
stark contrast to the rigid, "scientific" materialism embraced by the Communist Party of Great Britain in *his* time. In recovering the imaginative
play of the ideas animating earlier activists, he sought to offer a new guide
to agency in his own time, an alternative to the uninspired conformism
demanded of the strict historical vision of the party. (As Dipesh Chakrabarty observes, in European Romanticism, "imagination" has deep connections to Christian conceptions of the divine, which later secular forms
never fully overcame.[51]) He searched for a new historical script for exercising agency in his own time, judging its ethical merit not from its ultimate effectualness but from its aesthetic and social qualities. The role of
poetry, he felt (in Scott's luminous phrasing), was to "leaven politics with
imagination," to suggest a "middle ground between . . . disenchantment
with perfectionist illusions and complete apostasy"—"the demanding, yet
creative space of continuing aspiration."[52] This is a resonant echo of what
Urdu poets processing Partition attempted to do in their work—to find a
middle ground between apostasy and disenchantment. Indeed, his father's
relationship with anticolonial poet-activists from India helped produce
the historical discipline's revised ethical commitments in the late twentieth century. His father's generation had turned to poetry to cope with the
incomprehensible scale of death and disaster wrought by the First World
War; so, too, did the Partition generation. The scale of mass violence and
loss that marked these two events made them resonate at a visceral level as
moral narratives, moral tragedies, events in which all the folly of human
history was flagrantly on display. History proved inadequate to the moral
tragedy they posed, and survivors turned instead to poetry for their bearings, however inadequate it, too, was to their experiences. The historian
Thomas Laqueur writes of the World War I poets: "Theirs was a poetry
that longed for redemption while knowing full well that it was impossible
and that even the hope of redemption threatened to betray the reality of
suffering. The anger, bitterness, irony, as well as the lyricism—and also the
Biblical and mythical references—of so much war poetry come from the
poet's knowledge that experience, like the past, is a fleeting thing, impos-

sible and yet desperately important to convey."[53] They wrote poems, but it was clear that no one not present then "could claim to know, or have the moral authority to understand or speak about, what mass death and destruction meant." That pain drove figures like the elder Thompson to use their lingering belief in their potential for heroic action to question the historical imagination that had given them that belief. They invented a new kind of history, infused with poetry, going forward.

To be sure, E. P. Thompson's radical approach to history was itself limited in effect because of his intensely domestic focus on England, unwittingly echoing the "Little England" vision of nineteenth-century thinkers (burnished by historians in the 1920s–1940s). In 1953, partly exercised by the possibility that Indian independence in 1947 might merely represent a transition to more informal imperial control, the historians John Gallagher and Ronald Robinson showed, in what is reputedly among the most cited historical articles ever published, how incongruous the idea of mid-Victorian "anti-imperialism" was with the reality of imperial expansion in that period.[54] But over the course of the 1950s, understandings of decolonization shifted, with continual news of the Kenyan "Emergency" and other conflicts and, more decisively, the humiliating British defeat that was the Suez Crisis of 1956: an abortive invasion of Egypt brought home the lesson that Britain could no longer flex its military muscle without American say-so, bringing down the government of Anthony Eden. The narrative of decolonization as a story of imperial fulfillment and continuity within the Commonwealth was now challenged by the "decline thesis" of British history, a sense of history's betrayal of Britain. Rather than doing justice to Britain's past, history seemed to be mocking it: What future might they possess now? Old narratives of the rise and fall of empires were trotted out to explain Britain's postwar fortunes. The generation of would-be colonial administrators who emerged from public schools and Oxbridge encountered a new political reality and responded with anger and, more productively, derision, launching a rich satire trend ridiculing well-worn ideas about duty and service to nation and empire and the civilizing mission. As the Tory journalist Peregrine Worsthorne wrote in 1959, "Everything about the British class system begins to look foolish and tacky when related to a second-class power on the decline."[55] The perception of decline was somewhat at odds with the historical reality of the time—an era of British affluence and a triumphant welfare state. In due course, it would fuel the imperial nostalgia that led to the Thatcher era and the current

Brexit movement. But at the time, apart from satire and anger, some took an ostrich position vis-à-vis the empire. E. P. Thompson's work was in this vein.[56]

Despite his cosmopolitan experiences as an ex-soldier and his up-bringing and family history, Thompson's historical work strove to redis-cover England, avoiding empire altogether as it began to fall apart and refugees and immigrants arrived in thousands. This focus was partly dic-tated by embarrassment and partly by a desire to rethink and remake British identity in a time of decolonization in terms of the communitarian values of the working class rather than the long vaunted paternalistic values of the (imperial) ruling class. Between the wars, George Orwell had immersed himself in the troubles of the British working classes in search of redemption from his service in the Indian Imperial Police. Thompson similarly turned to the working class for redemption and escape from em-pire. He came from a family that conceived of radical struggle "Byroni-cally," as a bond between a penitent Englishman and an enslaved people. Significantly, his wife, the historian Dorothy Thompson, had long been re-searching the life and work of Chartism's Byronic leader Ernest Jones. The mood of postwar imperial nostalgia was just then resurrecting the char-acter of the "gentleman" that Jones had claimed—a type invested with chivalry, daring, and altruism.[57] The gentlemanly radical was back. From the eighteenth century, news of rebellion abroad had had an impact on British radicalism. If anticolonial rebellion was more effectual in the post–World War II period, the rupture it produced in historical thinking was proportionately pivotal.

E. P. wrote his history while attempting to make history himself as a teacher, by inculcating a sense of working-class agency among his adult students at the Workers' Educational Association and by taking a lead role in the popular Campaign for Nuclear Disarmament, which in its own way was a nostalgic bid for Britain to take a great, redemptive, role in leading the world. This mode of action, and Thompson's explorations of earlier socialist thought and practice, emerged from his perception that the Marxist historical imagination had been hijacked in service of authori-tarian exercise of agency. In 1956, as the Suez Crisis unfolded, the Soviet Union crushed the Hungarian uprising, confirming his and other Marxists' fears about the "party" line against the right of ordinary people to make their own history. E. P. was a key figure in the establishment of the New Left that broke with the Soviet line in hopes of recovering more democratic forms of revolutionary agency. In 1960, he cofounded the *New Left Review* with the Jamaican-born cultural theorist Stuart Hall, later departing in high dudgeon as devotees of "theory" gained sway among its editors. Like Madani, he, too, objected to the notion that history must conform to theory, hence his suspicion of the very idea of progress.

The story of the elder and younger Edward Thompson allows us to trace the changing purpose of historical understanding and history-writing as faith in the progress narrative fractured in the first half of the twentieth century. Whatever E. P. Thompson's own limitations, with the launch of "history from below," we began to write and rewrite the past to produce ever more just and inclusive narratives. Certainly, there were other, crucial sources for this methodological turn, including, especially, the influence of French historians like Georges Lefebvre and Marc Bloch and the Annales school, but that story lies somewhat beyond the scope of this history of how historical thinking made the empire and was in turn remade in the era of decolonization. And, arguably, however influential French developments were, in terms of methods and theory, the *ethos* of British "history from below" was shaped significantly by the anticolonial and postimperial imperatives traced here. After E. P.'s sense of history's compact with poetry, history was claimed for a different kind of progressive and poetically redemptive discourse. Joan Scott noted E. P.'s exclusion of women's stories; the histories of forgotten peoples and regions has been slowly rediscovered, by degrees, in fits and starts.[58] We show where even the weak and the voiceless exercised agency and left their mark on the world. From the era of the Enlightenment through the Suez Crisis, the powerful had claimed the discipline of history for themselves. Historians were not hobbyists on the sidelines, but the very makers of history. From the eighteenth century and the Hastings era, when towering Orientalist scholars like Sir William Jones served as Supreme Court justice in Calcutta, through to the Mills and Macaulay, and the very end of empire under Churchill's disapproving gaze, historians were key architects of empire. They shaped their present based on their understanding of the past, which they narrated to wide audiences. The elder Thompson, an ex-missionary, drew on the religious vocabulary of "atonement" to alter this trend. However secular, a prominent strand of British history-writing after him promised to fulfill morally and politically redemptive purposes. This kind of history is society's atonement, but also the discipline's own enactment of penance for its central role in the unfolding of the morally questionable events in the modern past. The very act of communing with dead subalterns through our research, writing, and reading is supposed to be redemptive—we rescue history's losers from "the enormous condescension of posterity," in E. P.'s much quoted phrase.[59] This is a common view of the discipline today; it is recent, shaped by intellectual and political activism in the era of *decolonization.*[60]

And it is not the only view. Many historians remain in the grip of the imperialist approach to history, which also remains something of a cultural default in popular understandings of history and "development." Indeed, the discipline's new redemptive ethos, like the early nineteenth-century Romantic search for redemption, can be shoehorned into those understandings. In the second half of the twentieth century, certainly, eschatological visions of progress, both socialist and liberal, continued to guide history's unfolding. E. P. Thompson's mistrust of theory was redoubled when he visited India for six weeks during Indira Gandhi's Emergency of 1975–1977. He was warmly welcomed in acknowledgment of his father's close friendship with Indira Gandhi's father, Jawaharlal Nehru. But he was horrified at the abandonment of democracy, meeting with persecuted students and academics in secret. The Moscow-directed Indian Communist Party supported the government's repressive measures, to his utter horror, as did the British Left. The role of Indian Communist Party intellectuals in coining theoretical abstractions to justify the Emergency's abuses intensified his suspicion of theory, fueling the vehemence of his critique in his 1978 essay "The Poverty of Theory."[61] The Indian nationalist leader J. B. Kripalani, then in his eighties, was jailed in the Emergency for opposing Indira Gandhi's growing authoritarianism. Still, E. P. looked to him to guide India back to its democratic path. Forty years earlier, when Kripalani was general secretary of the All-India Congress Committee, Thompson's father had described him: "With his black hair and clear-cut features and spare athletic body he looks like the hero of one of Byron's wilder romances, as if he had just arrived leading a horde of Tartar bandits."[62]

The visit left E. P. profoundly disturbed by the convergence of Western modernizing theory—the latest iteration of the liberal narrative of history—with orthodox Moscow-directed socialist theory: Both envisioned a modern urban intellectual elite with know-how imposing modernity and progress upon the nation. Both prioritized top-down, capital-intensive technologically driven development depending on a disciplined workforce for national economic takeoff. Marxism's economic determinism echoed utilitarian notions of historical progress.[63] Both, to him, were vulgar in their unpoetic political vision. They shared a similar vision of history and historical agency, as their respective parent theories— Marxism and liberalism—had. Unmoored from its Romantic origins, Marxism had become lifeless and authoritarian. Mahatma Gandhi had embraced the vision of village India partly out of a certainty that the alternative of mass industrialization would entail exploitation of villagers. Yet his and other creative visions yielded to the Congress Party's investment in a modernist, industrial vision of India's future—a willing embrace of developmental progress as the objective of India's history, without perceiving that the mirage of development was what had justified colonial rule and India's resulting poverty.[64]

Indeed, after empire, while the discipline of history was being remade, India fell under the spell of a new, postcolonial notion of time that was insistently forward-looking and called for a rapid shedding of the past, not least because of the traumatic crucible of Partition in which it was forged. If the British looked at the *form* of independence (dominion status, Commonwealth membership) for a verdict on empire, Indians and Pakistanis felt an urgent need to prove the validity of their assertions that they would be better off without colonial rule. Turn-of-the-century intellectuals like Dadabhai Naoroji had challenged the liberal historical narrative with its own methods: using statistics gathered by the British Indian government, they showed that Britain had actually drained wealth from the subcontinent. They argued on intellectual and ethical grounds laid by the British. And so in 1947, with the shackles off, the burden was to show, swiftly, Indians' true potential. Five-year plans and big dams were centerpieces of this effort, which entailed a sharp discounting of the long-term effects of imperialism, including deadly episodes of famine and Partition. Britain's indebtedness to India is roughly $45 trillion, according to recent estimates.[65] And yet, the expectation remains that the historic damage represented by this figure does not have an impact on the region's postindependence potential, that India can simply "move on" and "develop" and "catch up" once and for all. Moreover, the proof of "development" will depend on favorable comparison of GDP and demographic data with other places in the world—in line with the notion of comparability integral to late-Victorian evolutionary historical thought, when experts began to identify and classify differences as reflective of levels of development.

To be sure, the Indian economist and Nobel laureate Amartya Sen later helped redefine "development" in terms of "capabilities" that enable people to expand "substantive freedoms" to lead the lives they desire.[66] It is no surprise that this flexible, non-teleological understanding of development was shaped by the anticolonial, antihistorical intellectual tradition described in Chapter 5: Tagore gave Amartya Sen his name, and Amartya was a student at Santiniketan in the 1940s. Dependency and world-systems theorists also chipped away at the normative postcolonial view of development. But despite such interventions, mainstream notions of "development" remain in the old mode of competitive national modernization. The postcolonial hangover is evident in ex-colonies' continued membership in the Commonwealth (except, notably, Ireland): Though it allows them to perform their "equality" in cricket and other athletic contests, its perks include technical assistance to support economic growth. The end of the Cold War, especially, sealed the procrustean rule of the old Victorian narrative in the guise of neoliberalism, which hailed it as the "end of history"[67]—despite the absence of evidence that global free-market capitalism could ever be more than an exploitative, extractive, environmentally devastating producer of gross inequality and widespread poverty, especially given the poor terms on which countries emerging from the imperial framework that had inaugurated this global system were expected to participate in it. As in the eighteenth century, a state of continual war, underwritten by orientalist cultural tropes and humanitarian cant, drives the economic "progress" of the most powerful participants in the system.

If many scholarly historians today no longer take progress as their guiding assumption, the development goal is a legacy of liberal empire so deeply embedded in political and institutional structures and practices that it is difficult for postcolonial societies to shake off; indeed, it is what makes postcolonial societies *postcolonial*. They struggle to "move on" from, even forget, the colonial past to "catch up" and arrive at a long-deferred future marked by freedom and prosperity.[68] But to move only forward in time, to lose the *fullness* of time, the way the past lives in the present and shapes the future, is itself an inhuman and impossible expectation, given how intimately such societies have been shaped by the colonial past—including the historical imagination envisioning progress towards some developmental end. Meanwhile, Western carping about the enduring "failure" of formerly colonized societies to "catch up" woefully underesti-mates "the immense distortion" empire introduced into the lives of gen-erations of people well into the postcolonial period, as Edward Said put it. Those who would dwell on the depredations of empire are accused of en-gaging in self-indulgent victimology and evading responsibility for the failures of the postcolonial present.[69]

Disappointment with India is inescapably built into Western historicism—including E. P. Thompson's postwar cultural-Marxist ap-proach. The historic intellectual entanglement of colonialism, nationalism, and historicism dooms any assessment of postcolonial India to an endless loop of lament without hope of practical recovery. After all, the industrial revolution that enabled the making of the first English working class si-multaneously ruined the Indian handloom textile industry whose prod-ucts it sought to imitate. Yet, absurdly, taking that working class as an ideal, we search for its analogues in the very place upon whose ruin its formation depended. And we are disappointed by the Indian subjectivities we find. But those subjectivities were shaped in different directions by the very historical processes that produced our English "norm." This is why there can be no national "models" of history; all national histories have been shaped by transnational historical forces. As Stuart Hall argued, the national frames of old historical narratives cannot serve us; colonial his-tory has made it impossible to conceive of specific communities and tradi-tions with settled and fixed boundaries and identities.[70] E. P. Thompson's framing of British social history in the era of Indian nationalism, as a kind of escape from decolonization, depended on denial of precisely those transnational bonds. Today, others persist in pinning India's failures to the fact that "castes are not classes," in the words of Thompson's theory-loving nemesis Perry Anderson, author of a popular recent book on India's post-colonial failures.[71]

Notwithstanding history's reformed ethos with the rise of "history from below," Dipesh Chakrabarty's *Provincializing Europe* still had to ex-plain in the year 2000 that Western historical models, in all their whig-gish, Marxist, or post-Marxist variants, cannot but see the history of most of the world in terms of "lack"—the lack of the right social classes to fulfill the right political roles to make the appropriate historical transitions to lead to the correct telos.[72] After all, habits of historical thought were shaped by the history of empire; history came of age in the hands of Macaulay and Mill, defining "progress" through the rhetorical exclusion of Africans and

Indians from that narrative. This is why, Chakrabarty argues, it is difficult to think with historicism, which is based on Enlightenment concepts of universal human experience and secular modernity, to understand change in non-European parts of the world. Its assumptions about the path to modernity inevitably lead us to a conclusion that capitalist transition in other parts of the world has been incomplete or lacking. Chakrabarty's solution is to renew European thought from the margins—to "provincialize Europe." This is a necessary and important intervention; at the same time, it is important to highlight that historicism did not get the European story right either, insofar as it imagined European progress as isolated from the narrative of empire that it *also* underwrote.

Chakrabarty's attitude towards our common European intellectual patrimony is one of "anticolonial . . . gratitude." Neither social scientists nor ordinary people can do without it, he argues, especially since our institutions for administering justice require us to speak and think through the secular language and logic of history. Moreover, we cannot simply insert ourselves into alternative regional intellectual lineages that have become "matters of historical research for most" scholars, traditions that are treated as "truly dead, as history."[73]

Here, Chakrabarty himself falls prey to a sense of helplessness before history. Have we in fact arrived at a settled state of intellectual affairs? Might we not resurrect "lost causes" or learn again from practices and thoughts long consigned to the dustbin of history? As Chakrabarty urges, to provincialize Europe is to see "the modern as . . . contested," to "write over . . . privileged narratives . . . other narratives of human connections" based on "dreamed-up pasts and futures where collectivities are defined neither by the rituals of citizenship nor by the nightmare of 'tradition' that 'modernity' creates."[74] Dare we imagine that recovery of other ways of being and intellectual traditions—the dreams that "the modern represses in order to be"—might still have practical and institutional purchase, especially as we confront the planetary crisis produced by dominance of the European tradition? The competing interwar dreams of a liberal versus Soviet-style international order may have failed, but, as we have seen in Chapter 5, these were not the only intellectual traditions reaching beyond the imaginative horizon of the nation-state.

Anthropologists and literary scholars have reckoned with their disciplines' complicity in modern empire in ways that have forced reconsideration of methods and theory—critical work stimulated by anticolonialism via figures like the Palestinian literary scholar Edward Said (whom Faiz met in Beirut) and the anthropologist Talal Asad (son of Muhammad Asad). Though historians have tried to dismantle the narratives that underpinned empire, their efforts to decolonize the discipline have primarily taken the form of making it more inclusive—and that, too, with limited success. British publishers have co-opted even anticolonial thought into the neo-imperial project of extending British cultural influence.[75] (The UK publishers of this book refused to relinquish Indian rights to it.) Even despite the changes following the work of E. P. Thompson, Foucault, and others, historians have not fully confronted the ways in which the historical craft and some of its most authoritative practitioners have been implicated in the making of empire. Nor is it clear that Chakrabarty asks us to.

Religion's persistently awkward fit in historical work exemplifies the problem. Historicism evolved in the age of empire when orientalism identified religiosity as the mark of backwardness. "Progress" thus meant secularization (or at least abandonment of Indian and "other" religions). Christianity was as intolerable in more radical accounts; the spiritually ecumenical Byron satirized Christianity (and Islam) for using the threat of punishment and promise of rewards in the afterlife to promote violent competition between armies.[76] The recovering Christian Edward John Thompson wrote to Nehru in 1939 that religion was the "greatest pest in the world,"[77] a view E. P. shared: For all his empathy towards the working classes, even he could not redeem from the enormous condescension of posterity the historical force represented by Methodism, the creed his father had preached (and in which he had been schooled). He attacked it with an emotional fervor of, frankly, Methodist intensity, charging it with having sapped the revolutionary energies of the English working classes by distracting them with concern for the afterlife and elevating emotion over intellect.[78] In short, it disrupted their proper exercise of agency and took history down the "wrong" path. Methodism ruined the heroic tale Thompson would otherwise have been able to tell about eighteenth-century Britain. Hinduism and Islam are, of course, typically alleged to have derailed democracy in South Asia and the Middle East through precisely the same mechanisms—emotionalism, the distraction of the afterlife.

But the history of religious belief is immanent in the history of colonialism and nationalism.[79] Anticolonialism did not just answer colonialism on its own ethical grounds; it also challenged those grounds, recognizing the kind of suspension of ethics entailed by its historicist commitments.

To do so, it did not go "back" to religious ethics; it used them as a resource for conceiving a new ethical vision for a postcolonial and perhaps even postnational world. Among British anticolonial thinkers, too, it was figures like Wilfrid Blunt and the Theosophist Annie Besant, for whom religion provided a powerful means of identifying with colonial subjects, who were most able to think outside the progressive catechism of the historical idiom.[80] Religion is everywhere in the diverse modernities of the globe, not as an atavism but as a constitutive element of those modernities.[81] Even the West's "secular" model of society is imbued with religious vestiges, as we have seen from the start of this book. An ascetic Christianity suffuses Western political economy from Adam Smith through Marxism. Edward John Thompson's Byronism was founded on the remnants of Methodist belief in the value of redemptive suffering and sacrifice. Byronism itself depended on Old Testament mythology, on the idea of a chosen people with a common stock of memories and hopes coming into its own—national messianism.[82] Recognizing the paradoxical nature of what we call secularism might enable us to think and write with less condescension about religion and the religiously minded in the modern period. We might have to come to terms with the irrational quotient of human nature or even expand our sense of the rational to include the spiritual explorations that are at the core of what it means to be human and social. We might see that they are not what gets in the way of the unfolding of history; they lie at the heart of the story of human self-discovery that history might take as its proper subject. Chakrabarty does go this far: "I take gods and spirits to be existentially coeval with the human, and think from the assumption that the question of being human involves the question of being with gods and spirits."[83] Many anticolonial movements tried hard to assemble alternative systems of public ethics rather than adopt wholesale the eschatologically structured ethics of the nation-state that was part of the cultural and political inheritance of colonialism. The audacity of the Indian anticolonial vision—the demand for self-rule now, for Indians as they were, however illiterate, religious, and so on—captured the imagination of the elder Thompson. But the historical imagination through which he refracted that vision and through which his son endeavored to understand Methodist workers could never fully accommodate that audacity. Anticolonial thinkers who adapted Marxist history to their own ends, when Lenin and Mao enabled imagination of new kinds of historical scripts, likewise could not. The Constitution of Medina, Gandhi's village utopia—despite these various attempts to parry historicism, postcolonial societies remained captive to colonial narratives of history. This is partly because their categories are so deeply embedded in the discipline, as Chakrabarty explains. Even methodological innovations spawned by the Subaltern Studies collective have not shaken the hold of those narratives. That is why India's stubborn "anti-modernity" haunts those who would rummage through the regions of the earth in search of the right kind of progress. Despite a series of anticolonial educational experiments that sought to shake the hold of the disciplines and modes of thought that enabled colonialism, their institutional stickiness continues to drive a seemingly incurable global postcolonial hangover.[84]

What then is the historian's place in history today? The inclusion of scholars of diverse backgrounds has transformed our knowledge of race, gender, and culture, undermining the narratives that underpinned empire and other forms of racial inequality. Let's leave aside the sheer slowness of the process, exacerbated by periodic backlash. As I observed at the outset of this book, academic historians' policy-relevant research is often willfully ignored by policymakers precisely because it tends to cast a critical light on the current political order. Historians actively participated in the debate about the catastrophic Iraq War, a vocal majority cautioning against it.[85] Distinguished historians submitted an amicus brief cautioning against an overly expansive interpretation of the Second Amendment in the 2008 Supreme Court *Heller* decision.[86] But such voices are systematically drowned out, to the point that American political culture has become the site of a crisis around the very concept of truth. Not only historians but the voices of masses of citizens are ignored in these matters: Citizens increasingly confront the reality that the modern state in Western polities is not amenable to democratic check. Corporations and lobbies have hijacked that role. Galton discerned the beginnings of this military-industrial nexus in his time, which the radical William Cobbett soon after named the "Thing." It morphed through the history recounted here into the Cold War secret state, a "new, and entirely predatory complex" of private industry, especially military contracts, and the state, that E. P. Thompson called a "new Thing."[87] This is not a set of political institutions open to being unmasked. The elder Thompson saw history-writing as truth-telling against the state, and, indeed, today, the critical historian's role is often that of one who tells the truth but is powerless to exert real influence on public opinion or policy. An influential minority of historians nostalgic for the days when the discipline abetted power offers supportive endorsement to policy echoes of that time, while historians in the updated, anticolonial mold have become critics of this complex. That is their redemptive power. The idea of "history from below" is that great-man history wrongly gave credit to singular heroic actors. It came, ironically, from the Thompsons' sense of their own great-man capacity to change history. But it entailed an ethical transformation for history consumers and writers since then. But if most professional historians no longer credit the making of history to great men, those who dream of exercising great-man agency continue to find scripts in popular history and in the vaunting of expertise—of a certain kind.

The paradoxical outcome has been that while historians have adopted a critical posture towards power, new kinds of "experts," especially economists and political scientists, have happily seized the helm of power itself, as the new makers of history: "as human expertise overcoming nature, as the progress of reason and modernity, or as the expansion and development of capitalism."[88] From the mid-twentieth century, a new cultural dogma increasingly came to equate expertise with quantitative analysis, and ethical action with the objectivity claimed by these disciplines.[89] These disciplines foster an intrinsically antihistorical, universalist approach to understanding political change. But they are not antihistorical in the manner of the creative anticolonial thinkers described in this book. They are antihistorical in the way the historian Thomas Macaulay was, in their envisioning of change based on abstract principles rather than a working through and with existing circumstances. Historians like Macaulay were the first "technocrats," policymakers claiming the legitimacy of applying apolitical rationality in shaping societies. They launched the idea of "development" as an apolitical "technical" problem, which strengthened the hold of faith in history as a story of *universal* progress, of progress without loss. This is the unacknowledged historical imagination of the social sciences implicit in their blindness to the past. Chapter 4 traced the early incumbency of the idea of the expert as someone possessed of abstruse knowledge in close, even closeted, dialogue with the powerful. In this sense, social scientists are history's own monster. Timothy Mitchell has shown us how the discourse of development constituted itself as a form of knowledge standing apart from its objects—poor colonies like India—despite the central fact of the British Empire's powerful role in shaping that poverty.[90] History was essential to the formation of that discourse before it became the province of economics and before history itself became the province of mutiny.

Certainly, revisionist historians must assert their expertise on policy matters against the monopolistic claims of social scientists—and proponents of great-man history. Doing history also has its own ethical valence; it is its own kind of activism since the revisionism of the 1960s. Indeed, historians might even reprise the Smithian project of arriving at (new) judgments of value through history. Insofar as this book offers historical examples of anticolonial, antihistorical thought, it, too, invites us to derive new values *from history*. We might draw on those alternative ethical visions to find a fruitful way forward for the historical discipline itself: Throwing out all our tainted historical scripts may not be as liberating as it seems. We might instead draw from the scripts with the most liberatory potential, without foreclosing possibilities of what "liberation" might look like. E. P. Thompson tried to steer clear of a deterministic view of historical agency, and his vaunting of lost causes did much to transform the discipline's sense of purpose. Still, he saw value in "utopias that permit critical assessment of the present in terms of some deep moral commitment and unleash imaginative longing for a particular kind of future." Such utopias were necessary for practical politics.[91] Hence his enormous appreciation for William Morris, as a poetic *and* utopian thinker.[92] That said, when that utopia takes the form of a possible future, as opposed to a way of being *now*, when it presumes the linear flow of time, it cramps the space for ethical maneuver.

This, in a sense, was what happened when Leftist British historians tried to contest the Right's appeal to nationalist sentiments in the 1980s. Under Margaret Thatcher, a Britain burdened by the decline thesis turned towards the Victorian past, or, more aptly, a mythical vision of that past, including unapologetic imperialism and militarism. The 1982 war over the Falkland Islands depended on and profoundly appealed to historically minded nationalist sentiment that had been frustrated since the Suez Crisis, as E. P. Thompson, Eric Hobsbawm, Stuart Hall, and other Leftist intellectuals perceived, having spilled much ink critically analyzing the "heritage" industry that had tried to compensate for the apparent poverty of the present with a nostalgic vision of the past. Raphael Samuel, another proponent of "history from below," who founded the History Workshop movement at Ruskin College in Oxford, felt the Left needed to do more than criticize; it had to offer a compelling alternative narrative of patriotism.

But rather than a coherent alternative, the resulting History Workshop conference and book collection emphasized the contested and ad hoc ways in which people make sense of and use the past. The work was criticized for its eclecticism and ambiguity, and for rehearsing the same opposition between the "jingoistic," manufactured patriotism of the state (diagnosed by Hobson) and the democratic patriotism of the people long celebrated by Orwell and E. P. Thompson in the time of fascist and Stalinist totalitarianism.[93] By failing to "separate the study of patriotism in the past from their own attitudes towards patriotism in the present," socialist historians had landed in a historiographical "cul de sac," pronounced Miles Taylor. Samuel's willingness to consider history a necessarily "national question" (akin to Thompson's "Little Englander" vision) constrained the liberatory potential of this effort to reappropriate patriotism for the Left.[94] Nor did he question history's conventional moral function. As the Thatcher government proceeded to create a national, and nationalistic, history curriculum (the source of today's imperial amnesia), Samuel conceded that heroes were a "necessary fantasy" in history, since "we all seek out people to believe in, patterns to follow, examples to take up."[95]

We might instead go further along the lines of poet-thinkers who infused liberal and socialist narratives of historical progress with a metaphysical appeal, an imaginative promise of acting in a manner that enabled transcendence of worldly time itself—the Romantics, the Mughal rebels, the Progressive Writers. Instead of looking to technology or blind confidence in a liberatory future to save us, despite the unending disasters that pile up before the angel of history, it is time to reinvent the possibility and promise of poetic action that might enable a truer reckoning with the legacies of empire. While Britain's Left continued to struggle in the face of pressing questions of race and national identity (as imminent Brexit makes irrevocably clear), Samuel's *Theatres of Memory* (1994), on the way memory dynamically and actively shapes the past, offered another way forward: It urged history's value as a form of knowledge distinct from memory in facilitating critical inquiry and, importantly, called on professional academic historians to engage with the wider culture of popular history-making.[96]

The very word "history" comes from the Greek *istoreo,* meaning "to inquire." More than truth-telling or a search for models, we might reclaim it as an open-ended search for truth, in the manner of poetry. It is, after all, a verb, not a noun: to find out for yourself. Current conversations about history, including this book, are multiplying spaces and opportunities for poetic historical understanding that layers past, present, and future together in productive, nonlinear ways. History still offers an ethical vision, as Enlightenment philosophers hoped, but in a different, less future-oriented way. As historians have backed down from their old positions at the helm of state power and adopted a critical posture, their work has become pivotal in countless conversations and legal actions around reparations, restitution, apologies, and, most importantly, memorialization, which all attempt to make new history. Once again, historians have become central to the making of history, but in a new way: by engaging with the wider culture, in which a vast industry of popular history remains captive to the old great-man mode of narrating the past and inspiring action in the present.

Byron died for Greece partly to atone for Britain's plundering of the Parthenon: From 1801 to 1805, Lord Elgin took from there sculptures, inscriptions, and architectural features. The British Museum today defiantly asserts in placards around the exhibit of "Elgin's marbles" that it is "certain" that Elgin's actions spared the sculptures "further damage by vandalism, weathering and pollution" and that thanks to Elgin, generations had been able to see them "at eye level rather than high up on the building." This rather lame advantage is accompanied by the assurance that Elgin had received an Ottoman firman, or letter of permission, allowing him to remove the sculptures.[97] Greece has demanded return of these artifacts for at least a century. The British refuse, partly out of concern for the precedent such an act would establish. But Brexit, for all its pretense of restoring Britain's freedom and global power, may force capitulation, as Greece has inserted a clause addressing permanent return of the sculptures in Britain's draft free trade deal with the European Union.[98] Meanwhile, the governor of Easter Island is begging the British Museum for the return of one of its famous statues: the Hoa Hakananai'a, one of the most spiritually important monoliths of the Chilean island. The Indian government dithers about demanding the return of the Kohinoor diamond, the 106-carat gem that became part of the Crown jewels after the conquest of Punjab. The British seized the diamond, which had passed from ruler to ruler of the region, insinuating themselves into the line of political inheritance symbolized by its history. Given this political symbolism, it makes little sense for them to continue to hold it now that they have ceded control of the region itself. In 2015, the Indian diplomat Shashi Tharoor called for the return of treasures but also at least symbolic payment of reparations for the economic looting of the subcontinent. Such calls for restitution of stolen objects are not about undoing history but making new history.

Tharoor also suggests formal apology as a gesture of atonement and active effort to teach British schoolchildren what their country owes to the colonies Britain held, in a manner similar to the way German children are taught about concentration camps.[99] This is all the more urgent given Indians' fading sense of the enduring legacies of British colonialism. The Amritsar Massacre of 1919 has become central to debates about apologies. That event, in the wider context of the "Punjab Disturbances" of the time, was, in fact, historically pivotal to notions of colonial legal culpability: In the early 1920s, Indians successfully demanded financial compensation for Indian victims from a government that until then had only compensated European victims of violence (by levying indemnities on Indians).[100] The British prime minister David Cameron visited the site in 2013 but did not make an apology. The mayor of London, Sadiq Khan, urged such a gesture when he visited Amritsar in 2017. On the centenary of the event last year, Jeremy Corbyn, the Labour Party leader, called for an unequivocal apology, but Prime Minister Theresa May only went so far as to express "regret."[101]

In South Africa, meanwhile, the "Rhodes Must Fall" movement succeeded in securing the removal of the statue of Cecil Rhodes from the University of Cape Town, inspiring likeminded movements elsewhere and echoing movements to remove Confederate statues and symbols in American universities. These are efforts to change popular views of colonialism but also to decolonize educational institutions created in the time of empire.[102] And such conversations are gaining some traction.[103] Last year, the French government called on French museums to return thousands of African artworks taken without consent.[104] The United Kingdom's National Army Museum agreed to repatriate two locks of hair taken from the Ethiopian emperor to Ethiopia.[105] Australian Aboriginals won the right to sue for colonial land loss.[106] Belgium apologized for kidnapping children from its African colonies.[107] There is an active international conversation about returning the stolen Benin Bronzes to Nigeria.[108] Kenyan survivors of British concentration camps in the 1950s have also successfully sued for reparations, thanks largely to the work of the historian Caroline Elkins. Catherine Hall (who was married to Stuart Hall until his death in 2014) meanwhile leads a group of historians producing the database Legacies of British Slave-ownership.[109]

The Brexit movement, however, is a sort of memorial in the antithetical direction, the very opposite of coming to terms with the imperial past in favor of instead glorifying its memory—without bad conscience, making penance both impossible and even more urgently necessary. Brexit hails the desperate return to power of an expiring "history boys" culture in almost caricature form, with Jacob Rees-Mogg, author of a nostalgic collection of biographies, *The Victorians: Twelve Titans Who Forged Britain* (2019), serving as leader of the House of Commons and Boris Johnson, a Churchill biographer who takes Churchill and Disraeli as his models of a politician-writer, as prime minister. In this climate, the *Times,* panicking at British universities' evident willingness to return looted objects to "pressure groups," declared such acts of atonement "neither morally required nor conducive to learning about the past." The editors neither imagine the possibility of the objects' use in historical inquiry in the places to which they are being returned, nor value the possibility of making new history through their return. Duly acknowledging the justice of returning artworks looted by the Nazis, they baldly assert that "it is less clear that historical artefacts from the colonial era meet the same criteria."[110] This continued lack of bad conscience has been the biggest obstacle to the idea of moral reparation for historical wrong in the area of colonialism when it has proven successful in other cases. Restitution of objects taken by the Nazis depended on an irrevocable consensus about the illegitimacy of property transfers under Nazi rule.[111] Likewise, efforts to seek reparations and official apologies for victims of American slavery are founded on a clear sense of the moral depravity of the slave system. The effort to achieve restitution of colonial seizure of cultural objects has been comparatively tepid because of continued ambivalence around the moral case against empire. The German precedent makes clear the productive potential of such actions, explains Catherine Gallagher. In the 1950s, West Germany signed a restitution agreement with Israel to help compensate victims of the Holocaust, setting several important precedents: that a successor government can inherit and make good on the culpability of a prior regime, that compensation can productively be made to a designated descendant group of the original victims; that reparations need not depend on exact calculations of damages; and that acceptance of reparation does not imply an erasure or undoing of past injustices.[112] Reparations for slavery, for instance, is not about compensation for past injustices, explains the journalist Ta-Nehisi Coates, but "a national reckoning that would lead to spiritual renewal[,] ... a revolution of the American consciousness."[113]

Such a reckoning is urgent with respect to empire, too, as new works continue to defend even the most scandalous moments of its record, including the Amritsar Massacre.[114] Indeed, without that wider reckoning, an apology for an isolated incident like the massacre, if it ever happens, risks strengthening the myth of liberal empire. As the historian Kim Wagner has warned, persistent myths surrounding the event make it unlikely that an apology will lead to an honest reckoning with the event, especially given the current British political climate in which, far from regretting the imperial past, a revived nostalgia and xenophobia have fueled the Brexit demand.[115] In short, an apology specifically for the Amritsar Massacre risks repeating the ethical duplicity of the Hastings trial, when the narrow focus on a few bad men or moments of excess blinded Britons to the illegitimacy of the entire imperial enterprise.

By the same token, the effort to hold individual men accountable for international crimes and financial recessions, rather than accept such events as the inevitable fallout of economic and political "progress," encounters pushback on the grounds that prosecuting a few individuals reinforces the impunity of more powerful actors, given the structural nature of inequality.[116] In short, more trials of more Hastingses are not going to deliver justice; they risk performing the same kind of moral cleansing work that the Hastings trial did for British rule in India—or the Galton disownment did for war-invested Quakers. More collective accountability, on the other hand, can wind up giving personal immunity to those who do not merit it. Helpful as German reparations to Israel were, Gallagher argues, they also served the politically expedient purpose of freeing particular Nazis from responsibility. Instead of facing criminal prosecution, they were reintegrated into German life. The rash of individual prosecutions for crimes against humanity from the 1990s sought to end that impunity, to enact retributive *and* reparative historical justice. But the state itself remains immune from criminal responsibility, as if it had no agency of its own.[117] Perhaps the answer is a combination of strategies that hold individuals, collectives, and state institutions accountable. More importantly, it is *the continuing struggle for justice* that matters. With empire, that struggle remains feeble and abortive as long as the wider public remains either ignorant or committed to the historical narratives of great men and progress that enabled it. Amnesia is one problem. But added to that is the continued deflection of the "scandal of empire" by the old habit of weighing its pros and cons. Indeed, the moral case *for* imperialism is still actively defended,[118] even though, as Mike Davis puts it, "imperial policies towards starving 'subjects' were often the exact moral equivalents of bombs dropped from 18,000 feet."[119]

The problem with weighing pros and cons is that it presumes there is a point at which the story is over, the accounts are closed, and we can actually tot up the balance. It also depends on the premise that empire was a legitimate political and economic form. This premise subverts the laborious and sacrificial work of generations who fought to end empire on the grounds that it was illegitimate—the imposition of an autocratic, racist, violent, and extractive form of rule. Historical evaluation of racist despotisms in Europe—for instance, fascist regimes—are never written about as legitimate, and yet many write about empire as though it *can* be evaluated neutrally.[120] No historian in her right mind would say, yes, Hitler was horrible to the Jews, but, on the other hand, he built the autobahn! The question is not when and where did the imperial state err or fail or prove incompetent, but why we presume an illegitimate form of government could but err and fail and prove incompetent.

Secondly, the very act of totting up pros and cons rests on the fallacy of counterfactual history, the idea that, absent the British presence, there would be no railroads or dams or any sort of "progress" in India.[121] This sort of thinking merely reproduces the legitimizing narratives of liberal empire—the idea that India would have no history without the British presence, that it would have stood still in time. We already know that pre-colonial trends in management of food security and water were better suited to the region.[122] Moreover, the British worked hard from the beginning to stifle indigenous manufacturing.[123] Those still skeptical of the possibility of Indian industrial takeoff might at least be persuaded that there is no evidence that Indians would not have been as good at imitating British industry as the Japanese and Germans proved to be. The British ensured that they did not have an opportunity to do so, for they needed India to supply raw materials.[124]

Finally, it is not clear the alleged "pros" were in fact "pros."[125] British-built railroads in India, for instance, served British economic and political needs rather than the needs of Indians. The East India Company guaranteed a 4–5 percent profit plus free land and other facilities to British investors in their construction. Indian taxpayers thus massively subsidized these corporate profits. The railroads also drew on British industrialism in a manner that prevented them from stimulating Indian industry. In 1853, Marx believed railroad construction would fuel industrialism in India; he did not realize that most of the capital raised for their construction was spent in Britain, that workers came from Britain and were paid twice the home rate plus passage and other allowances. Rails, locomotives—everything came from abroad, despite the capacity to make locomotives in India. India became more dependent on British industry, settling into the role of raw material supplier for world markets. In the 1870s, it was clear to those who cared to know that the British-made railroads exacerbated rather than alleviated the effects of famine.[126] They served British rather than Indian security, as did irrigation projects. All alleged "public works" projects in the subcontinent were designed to enable the imperial bureaucracy to preserve its power as cheaply as possible.[127] In the 1840s and 1850s, they were supported only when they promised to either mitigate revenue loss caused by famine or strengthen the British military position in war. After the rebellion of 1857, they were part of a new assertion of British authority over the land and space of the subcontinent. John Stuart Mill's official defense of the East India Company in 1858 propagandized such "improvements."[128] Although it did not save the company from extinction, it set a trend for annual post-mutiny government reports titled "Moral and Material Progress" in India, assembled without consulting Indians.[129] Thus, too, was the colony the initial site of the "territorial framing of an economy," as Mitchell tells us.[130] It is important to recognize the political function of such narratives—and the gap between the real and the recorded.[131] These were the claims that figures like Naoroji disputed. And yet they continue to unduly color our own assessments of the purpose and effects of British rule in India.

The ideas and actions of anticolonial thinkers changed the world. But the ever-shifting forces of colonialism remained at large, as we have seen in Chapter 5. They are what encourage some scholars to continue to stubbornly resist characterization of it as "violent usurpation and enslavement . . . *by definition,* devoid of redeeming features."[132] And so anticolonial historians have had to continually affirm both that empire mattered and that it was and is a morally and politically illegitimate form of rule.[133] Recognizing empire's intrinsic illegitimacy and dependence on violence and slavery does not imply a belief in British malignancy, any more than recognizing the violence of Nazism implies a belief in Germans as existentially evil;

rather it has driven a great deal of scholarship aimed at understanding how Britons reconciled their claims of good intentions with the violence they continually unleashed.[134] Indeed, the contradictions between the liberatory claims and repressive tendencies of "liberal empire" are a staple of this scholarship. This book has forwarded that effort by arguing that certain historical narratives were critical in enabling imperialism. Karuna Mantena rightly calls the ever-shifting rationalizations of empire "a rhetoric of evasion." But no one needed to think they were being evasive because theories of history evolved to buffer that realization. Mantena answers those who protest the wholly negative characterization of empire well, explaining that once we realize that violence and racism were constitutive of empire, we can no longer judge empire on the basis of the purity of moral intentions or the universalism of liberal ideals.[135] Understanding those intentions and their articulation remains important for understanding how empire becomes thinkable, but those stated intentions do not change the nature of the enterprise. They have the odor of protesting too much about a system that depended on violence, looting, and destruction.

We know that empire, including slavery, definitely made many contributions to *British* economic and institutional development and to British intellectual, social, and cultural development.[136] Still, the idea that it opened the floodgates of modernity and prosperity *for all,* despite some understandable growing pains and a few scandals here and there, remains seductive. And that is because without this idea, we would lose our sense of history itself. The stakes for remaining invested in some positive notion of empire are high. But they are dangerous in that they help perpetuate inequalities dating from the imperial era and fuel political movements like Brexit that draw from the same racist well. The disastrous Iraq War that the United States launched in 2003 was grounded in Victorian arguments about benevolent empire, boosted by the British prime minister Tony Blair—the spread of democracy, humanitarian goals, and so on. In the shadow of that mission's failure, the moral argument shifted to the duty to provide security to a people incapable of providing it for themselves, as though the American intervention was not the very source of that insecurity in the first place.[137] There is a fundamental contradiction in Britain's celebration of its role in defeating the Nazis while also celebrating its empire rooted in violence and racism—the imperialism to which thinkers from Césaire to Arendt traced Nazism's origins. British neo-Nazis were among the most stridently anti-immigration groups from the 1970s. Anti-immigration sentiment remains politically potent. How then has Nazism been fully defeated? The very reason to hold collectives as well as individuals accountable for the crimes of empire is so that we remain alive to the continued danger of such crimes. This was why Arendt emphasized the banality of Adolf Eichmann's evil in her 1963 book. He was at fault, but simply eradicating an individual like him would not remove the possibility of continued evil; the collective in which he was situated provided him with the anonymity, impunity, and passivity that enabled his crimes.[138]

Memorialization, by bridging professional and public history, is one strategy that may compel fresh moral reckoning with the imperial past and make new history possible for the present and future. In the United States, the Equal Justice Initiative (EJI), a nonprofit law firm in Montgomery, Alabama, hopes that putting up memorials to the African American victims in the counties where they were lynched will force a healing confrontation with the past—if they can overcome local resistance to such memorialization. As racial equality remains elusive, such efforts to memorialize the painful and resilient history of African Americans can address amnesia *and* shift the American conscience in a manner that can affect things today. After all, the endurance of inequality is rooted partly in the way late-nineteenth-century memorialization of the Confederacy, with statues of Robert E. Lee and Stonewall Jackson, shaped public memory about slavery. (Taking them down thus is not about erasing history but undoing *their* erasure of history.) The EJI's Montgomery museum on lynching compels visitors to confront the reign of terror endured by African Americans, for which no one was ever held accountable. Thomas Laqueur explains, "All this narrative work has been carried out in the hope that the recognition of past wrongs and moral blindness will make those in the present not only recognise our complicity in this history but also the continuity of past and present."[139] EJI's strategy is to change cultural narratives in order to change hearts and minds, which Laqueur likens to "a sort of Christian piercing of the heart[,] . . . something like the conversions of old." Laqueur concludes pessimistically, however: "One would like to believe that remembering a difficult history can change hearts, but this does not seem like a hopeful moment in the United States for mastering a past of racial injustice." This pessimism is understandable given the current political climate in the United States. But it also emerges from an expectation that the Christian piercing of the heart must lead somewhere, that we must arrive at a new historical destination, but if we dispense with this historical ambition, we might see the experience of the piercing—and the ethically transformative work it does—as an end in itself. Intriguingly, in this regard, in the 1950s, the transformation of the distinguished British historian of Africa, the Oxford don Margery Perham, from a liberal imperialist into a profound skeptic of empire was accompanied by a return to Christian faith.[140]

If apologies help heal old wounds, expressions of gratitude for past kindnesses also raise the possibility for making new kinds of anticolonial history. In 2018, a sculpture commemorating the Choctaw Nation's bond with the Irish was unveiled in Cork, Ireland. The bond was forged when the Choctaw sent donations for famine relief to the Irish in the 1840s. At the unveiling, Chief Batton said, "Your story is our story."[141] Members of his nation had scraped their pockets for the donations, having just endured their own tragic Trail of Tears. The Irish prime minister's visit to the Choctaw Nation in 2019 affirmed gratitude for the "sacred memory" and "sacred bond." "Our nations have shared a similar history of tragedy, perseverance and strength," said Chief Batton, "a kindred spirit." This invocation of the past is explicitly about making new history now. The news report of the visit opens, "History was made for the Choctaw nation . . ." The Irish prime minister Leo Varadkar announced a new scholarship program for Choctaws to study in Ireland. Varadkar, the son of an Indian father and Irish mother, is conscious of the power of shared anticolonial pasts.

The parts of the world that clamor for apologies and reparations, decades after the end of empire, do so out of the knowledge that "only that which does not cease to hurt remains in memory." Laqueur borrows this line from Nietzsche to explain that mourning demands "that the past is somehow kept present," to insure against the inevitable fading of the pain of immediate loss, even though we know "just how utterly past the past is, how historical it is, how even the worst horrors lose their sting."[142] They seek apology and reparations not to indulge in victimology, but because the necessary moral, cultural, and spiritual reckoning has yet to transpire, as evidenced by persistent empire, amnesia about empire, and defenses of empire. Those with power drink from the river Lethe, whose waters offer complete forgetfulness. In Greek myth, the shades of the dead drank from this river in the underworld of Hades to forget their earthly lives; Virgil told us that this was so that they might be reincarnated anew. But this is a form of reincarnation that does not permit the working of karma. Forgetting frees one from accountability to conscience, from the obligation of atonement. And the forgotten and silenced truth is supplanted with myths perpetuated beyond the academy.

Memorialization can thus do important cultural and justice work vis-à-vis the British Empire. Memorials to the Indian national movement exist, but not to the crimes that fueled it, with the occasional exception such as the much-visited memorial to the Amritsar Massacre of 1919. Where are the memorials to famine victims, forced laborers, rebels blown from cannons, the displaced, the victims of everyday racism? There is, incredibly, not a single museum dedicated to empire.[143] Quite apart from the moral work such sites can do, they are necessary today to counter nostalgic romanticization and glamorization of the imperial past, which remains alluring enough to feed the frenzy for Brexit in hopes that Britain might revive a more glorious relationship to the rest of the world. Without those memorials, the violent reality of empire, precisely because it is so monstrous, will begin to appear increasingly implausible and yield to the romance narrative.[144] This romanticization is as noxious as nostalgia for the Confederacy in the American South and the revival of Nazi sentiment in the United States and Europe. We revile Holocaust deniers but continue to argue points with empire nostalgics as if their position falls within the pale of reason and ethical respectability.[145] Memorialization can help make the atrocities of empire common knowledge, for the sake of avoiding future repetitions and to ensure that Britons are aware of what their country owes the world, as such awareness can critically shape relationships among its citizens and between Britain and the world.[146] We live in a postcolonial world in which the division between haves and have-nots extends divisions created in the era of European colonialism. Without a clear-eyed understanding of that colonial past, people around the world will continue to turn to myths of liberal empire and racial and cultural prejudices to understand their inequality. We remain prisoners of those myths because the history of empire has not ended. "Who controls the past controls the future," wrote Orwell. "*Who controls the present controls the past.*"[147] This line appears in his novel *1984* (1949) envisioning a totalitarian Britain. At the Ministry of Truth, Winston Smith alters the historical record to accord with the party's official version. By silencing the past, the regime normalizes the present as the only possible present.

The reality is that professional historians do not control the present or the past. Their production of history flows into a vast lake of historical production to which politicians, "popular historians," museums, novels, films,

TV dramas, activists, and countless members of the public contribute. The narratives of empire that the public consumes are not those produced by academic historians but nostalgic TV series, great-man histories, and other pageants of empire. Even fresh defenses of Hastings continue to appear.[148] The very fact of continued debate about empire, its unending debatability, is evidence of empire's continuing presence. Its relevance in our lives today does not proceed directly from its original impact. As Trouillot explains, we routinely underestimate the size, relevance, and complexity of the overlapping sites where history is produced. Indeed, "we are all amateur historians with varying degrees of awareness about our production."[149] And so, while Britain continues to celebrate the empire's role in defeating Nazism, formerly fringe neo-Nazi views of nonwhite immigration to Britain have fueled the xenophobic Brexit movement. This was only possible because of the silencing of the imperial past, the record of British violence abroad in the very same period in which the Nazis came to power in Germany. Without this historical consciousness, Britons today cannot be conscious of the meaning of their present actions. Nor can Indians and citizens of other postcolonial places.

Memorialization and other kinds of public history are crucial also because the historical discipline's efforts to redeem itself from complicity in empire are severely limited by the discipline's declining strength since it renounced its pact with power. Undergraduate majors in history have plummeted in the United States, faster than any other major in recent years.[150] The UK history curriculum erases and whitewashes the history of empire. Alan Bennett's play *The History Boys* captured a culture that was already passing when it premiered in 2004, as social-scientific regimes of expertise displaced the old faith, since the days of Macaulay at least, that the study of history was the ideal preparation for a young man with political ambitions, understood as great-man aspirations. There, too, the number reading history at university has declined by about a tenth in the last decade, reports *The Economist*, lamenting the discipline's displacement from its "central position in national life," where it had long served as "a ticket into the elite . . . , as Alan Bennett documented." The storied liberal publication places blame squarely on the shoulders of the historical profession for going too far in its preoccupation with "the marginal rather than the powerful, the poor rather than the rich"—another instance of backlash.[151] Decrying the apparent absence of an "intellectual movement focused on understanding the dynamics of progress," journalists farcically call for creation of a new discipline of "Progress Studies"—at once proving growing collective ignorance of what the discipline of history has been and what postwar thinkers recognized it ought to be.[152] In this dismal state of affairs, greater engagement with public history offers historians the possibility of reorienting the discipline towards informing utopian ways of being now, rather than guiding us towards some presumed horizon of progress. Embracing this new value may burnish the discipline's standing in universities, but engaging for the sake of that possible institutional payoff would defeat its poetic purpose.

In engaging in this new kind of history-making, we might take inspiration from the educational experiments of anticolonialists who recognized history's complicity in empire and sought to recover different notions of time. This critique is implicit in an awareness of history's compact with power. As Trouillot puts it, "The past does not exist independently from the present." It exists only in relation to the present; the present makes something be the past: "In that sense, the past has no content." We cannot identify the past *as past*. The terms through which we, as subjects, summon the past belong to the present. We are constituted as subjects through our continuous creation of the past. We do not succeed the past but are its contemporaries.[153] Apart from the realm of apologies and reparations, what would a sense of history based on an awareness of the simultaneity of past and present, the fullness of time, look like? The celebrated Indian poet Javed Akhtar is the son of the Progressive poet Jan Nisar Akhtar, himself descended from a poet-leader of the 1857 rebellion. His poem "*Waqt*" (Time) offers an intriguing vision of this possibility. It opens with the poet's contemplation of the meaning of time:

Ye waqt kya hai	What is this thing time
Ye kya hai akhir ki jo musalsal	What is this after all that
guzar raha hai	continually passes
Ye jab na guzra tha	When this had not passed
Tab kahan tha	Then where was it
Kahin to hoga	It must have been somewhere
Guzar gaya hai	[If] it has passed
To ab kahan hai	Then where is it now
Kahin to hoga	It must be somewhere.

After reflecting on the perspective from a moving car, which makes stationary objects look as though they are moving away, he wonders:

To kya ye mumkin hai	So then is it possible
Saari sadiyan	That all the centuries
Qatar-andar-qatar apni jagah	Are standing in place,
khardi hon	line upon line
Ye waqt sakit ho	That this time is static
Aur hum hi guzar rahe hon	And it is we who are passing
Is ek lamhe mein	That in this one moment
Saare lamhe	All moments
Tamam sadiyan chhupi hui hon	All centuries are hidden
Na koi ainda	Not any future
Na guzishta	Nor past
Jo ho chuka hai	What has happened
Jo ho raha hai	What is happening
Jo hone vaala hai	What will happen
Ho raha hai	Is happening

The poem goes on to imagine a place in the universe where time has not yet come and the existential awareness compelled by such contemplation of the "whereness" of time.[154] It playfully asks the reader to let go of the comfortable, automatic assumption of linear time to recover a sense of its fullness, of the contemporaneity of past, present, and future. After all, at a basic level, what we perceive as time's passage *forward* is in fact the cyclical movement of our planet in a loop, repeated revolutions in space that entail continual return to the same *place*.

To be sure, Western orientalists have long been fascinated by such "oriental" understandings of time. In the nineteenth century, Thomas Carlyle affirmed that "all deep souls . . . the Hindoo Mythologist, the German Philosopher" recognize that "this world is after all but a show,—a phenomenon or appearance, no real thing," that we are, as Shakespeare knew, "such stuff as Dreams are made of!" He meditated explicitly on the "great mystery of TIME . . . rolling, rushing on, swift, silent . . . on which we and all the Universe swim like exhalations, like apparitions which are, and then are *not*." The ineffable universe was a "Force which is *not* we . . . Force, Force, everywhere Force; we ourselves a mysterious Force in the centre of that." Through writing, man miraculously related "the Past and Distant with the Present in time and place; all times and all places with this our actual Here and Now."[155] This magic changed everything. Carlyle recognized here the power of history-writing to transform lives in the present. Though there are common threads in his and Akhtar's meditations on time, Akhtar takes us to a very different end. He does not ask us to harness the power to imagine the past in the present for any particular purpose. Rather, he asks us to simply imagine it and to consider that imagining as part of our humanity, to recognize that we are passing through a forever time. In William Blake's poem "London" (1794), the poet wandering the city detects in the cries of pain around him the sound of "the mind-forg'd manacles."[156] It is a lament on the straitjacket of reason that produced the ugly modernity before him; the instrumentalizing of a linear conception of time towards that end was the essence of those manacles, a relentless curbing of the imagination to enforce a sense of helplessness before circumstance, theory, history. These mind-forg'd manacles produced the hubris that led us to think that great men must act in time, must *make* our time. Perhaps Tagore had the phrase in mind when he bewailed Western nationalism's production of "neatly compressed bales of humanity" bound in "iron hoops."[157] We might regain our ethical bearings with an awareness that it is we who pass through time, that time—all past, present, future—makes us, forges bonds between disparate individuals and their environment, and that this forging is itself the recurring end of history. Kate Bowler, a historian of Christianity coping with cancer, writes that Christianity's eschatological structure—which informed Enlightenment ideas of time as "the arena of progress"—orients its followers to the future in a manner that, for her, "poisoned the sacred work of living in the present." She explores as a counter the notions of cyclical time embraced by the Stoics, who believed in living fully in the present. In thinking through these ideas and contemplating her past, Bowler describes a kind of temporal transcendence, "the past and the future experienced together in moments where I can see a flicker of eternity." She adopts an attitude towards the future that rests on memorializing the past and present: "the way forward dotting the path behind me."[158]

Akhtar's epiphanic reversal of our position vis-à-vis time, envisioning us flowing through it, fits neatly with the dawning realization that our preoccupation with human history has long blinded us to its essentially ephemeral nature. We very much are flowing through time. The multiple sets of fathers and sons in this modern story—the Galtons, Macaulays, Mills, Stephens, Gladstones, Thompsons, Akhtars, Asads, and so on—are testimony to the past's contemporaneity with the present and to the way an inherited sense of historic destiny, even entitlement, extends the life of great-man agency even as professional historians have increasingly abandoned that mode of narrating history. The stories recounted here are about elites whose sense of historic destiny shaped their actions, how the discourse of history shaped the unfolding of imperial history—how a certain set of men acted to become "such stuff as dreams are made on."

Apart from these generational bonds, the past is also fully contained within the present insofar as the current climate represents "the totality of human actions over time"; it expresses "the entirety of our being over time."[159] Though history is the study of settled human life, covering a few millennia at most, it blends beyond into the history of man as a species, into biology, which in turn merges eventually with geology, the history of the planet, which at some point flows into the history of the cosmos—astronomy. (This inter-temporal perception of disciplinary connections is distinct from those imagined by eighteenth- and nineteenth-century philosophers presuming their common governance by universal laws.) Historians have lately acknowledged this realm of "deep history," particularly in the context of highlighting the human impact on the history of the planet. They have imported the geological term "Anthropocene" into the historical discipline.[160] To be sure, the species approach towards studying the Anthropocene obscures the differing moral responsibilities of different groups for the apocalyptic moment in which we find ourselves. For instance, European killing of Native Americans altered the global climate, producing the Little Ice Age.[161] It is not "man" or "human nature"— something biologically inevitable—that led to our present discontents. They are the result of particular actions by particular classes and cultures: the Fausts constructing dams and dikes, building castles on reclaimed land; the mine owners and mill owners confident in their entitlement to make history; not the miners or cotton growers, whose evolution and articulation of historical subjectivity and agency were themselves mutinous. Some argue that we might more accurately call this epoch the "Capitalocene." Those committed to the idea of modern history as a story of progress must reconcile that conviction with the reality of the destruction of not only lives—which we have always known—but the planet itself. Consumption of geologically ancient *fossil* fuels—driven by particular classes—has altered the planet, and that environmental impact is in turn shaping the evolution of human history. Beyond the realm of geology, scientific explorations of the modern age have introduced new elements into space—man-made satellites and probes with unknown micro effects on celestial forces that may play out in millennia to come. What will be the butterfly effect of Neil Armstrong's moon landing? If the universe shapes human action, human action now shapes the universe, too, and the fate of the planet and innumerable other species.

The Anthropocene, the industrial era, is a mere moment on the timescale of existence or the geological timescale. But if human action now has interplanetary effects and "deep history" connects the scale of human time with geological and astronomical timelines, we have left the realm of earthly time altogether. What would it mean to experience the "fullness" of time on such a scale, an experience of time in which past and present commingle to produce the future? The notion of the Anthropocene insists that we acknowledge our (destructive) impact on the planet, and yet by calling our attention to the way history shades into biology, geology, and astronomy, it at once reminds us of the relative insignificance of our existence *and* of the change we have wrought in a universe with its own timeless dynamism and dialectic of creative destruction. Is the study of human history legitimate against this scale? Are the dynamics of change that we uncover—the contexts, factors, contingencies—*real,* given the ephemeral nature of human existence, its belatedness and imminent vanishing? Dinosaurs were here for 179 million years, vanishing 66 million years ago. Hominids appeared less than 2 million years ago; humans like us only 200,000 years ago. Is it hubris to call our time "Anthropocene," given the insignificance of our presence in astronomical time? Or is it humility, insofar as it entails recognition of our reckless use of our hoary planet? Might we even more humbly and soberly recognize that we are merely the most extreme among creatures transforming Earth, including animals, trees, photosynthetic organisms, the Amazon?[162]

The fatal flaw in having allowed our historical sensibility to shape our consciences in the modern period may be its fundamentally human-centric nature; we are only now, belatedly, perceiving history's ties to biology, geology, and astronomy (in a manner different from the way eugenicists conceived of the continuities between biology and history). Until now, modern history and modern literature, however progressive, put man at their center, in a position of power over nature and other species. The very measure of "progress" has been the extrication of culture from nature. (Protecting Indians from "man-eating" "wild" animals was also important to marketing empire, most famously the heroic feats of the tiger hunter Jim Corbett.) Even the most revisionist of historians have focused on human redemption, giving voice to heretofore voiceless people, without considering the countless voiceless creatures implicated by our dreams of progress. Some of the antihistorical strains of thought we've glimpsed were also antihumanist in refusing to put man at the center of the universe. The basic thrust of humanism is that the purpose of the universe is man and that the universe is man's responsibility. Even environmentalists calling on us to resist climate change are invested in this notion. None would entertain the notion of "man's essential ephemerality in this unfathomable universe," to borrow a phrase from Mahmood Farooqui.[163] This would, indeed, be antihistory; it would mean man cannot save the universe, or that the universe does not need saving—an undoing of the Enlightenment, which reassigned that role from God to man.

As animals lose their habitats, and humans, too, we might stand a chance of looking at both as the center of the universe and recognize our conjoined fates. As Amitav Ghosh puts it, the uncanniness of the freakish effects of climate change lies in "the fact that in these encounters we recognize something we had turned away from[,] . . . the presence and proximity of nonhuman interlocutors." Many are belatedly confronting the reality that nonhuman forces can intervene and have always intervened in human thought,[164] though many others have long recognized the mutual shaping of the human and nonhuman. Certainly one might read this as an expansion of our arena of ethical responsibility, from a preoccupation with humans to include animals and the planet, in whiggish terms, a further extension of the liberal narrative of history as progress. After all, many abolitionists turned their attentions next to the animal rights and antivivisection movements. But as Ghosh recognizes, what is required is not so much progress as recovery from the imaginary of progress. In fact, that activism depended on the mingling of liberalism with an older awareness of the shared nature of human and other animal experience. The first use of the term "crime against humanity" was in a printed sermon against cruelty towards "any living creature of life" in the context of badger baiting.[165] This is a different sense of the word "humanity" than what we usually assume with the phrase; it refers not to the object of the crime—other humans—but to the way that we lose our own humanity when we are cruel to others, whatever the species, and *for whatever end.*

The climate crisis preying on many a conscience today demands re-covery of such modes of thought. Kant compared the stability of the natural laws guiding human progress to that of the laws governing the seemingly "unstable weather, which we likewise cannot determine in ad-vance, but which, in the large, maintain the growth of plants[,] the flow of rivers, and other natural events in an unbroken uniform course."[166] And yet, in the very moment in which he wrote, humans were beginning to disrupt the laws governing weather. At the same time, we know of that disruption only because colonialism stimulated the emergence of climate science as an effort to understand the planetary weather system for the sake of managing far-off colonies. It was the gift of British officials strug-gling to make sense of monsoons and drought.[167] Our appreciation of Earth's cosmic timescale and our impact on it likewise owes something to the search for the experience of a cosmic timescale that drew Britons to the deserts of the Middle East between the wars, where they, too, reinvented notions of human agency. Indeed, our entire concept of nature, as a realm of which humans are not a part, was forged through our continual disrup-tion of it.[168] The cultural theorist Raymond Williams noted, "The idea of nature contains, though often unnoticed, an extraordinary amount of human history."[169] This is why the story of Sakuntala so appealed to Eu-ropean Romantics: it was about history-making man's denial of the es-sence and fount of existence, his compact, even union, with the earth.[170] Now, writing ourselves into the history of the planet reinserts us into "na-ture," subverting that stark, illusory opposition since the Enlightenment between man and nature. We have not mastered nature, and, increasingly, we know we cannot.

Liberal theorists like Francis Fukuyama prematurely declared the end of history and the triumph of liberalism with the end of the Cold War, blissfully unaware of the catastrophic toll the past was wreaking on the world. But some historians have long been aware of the complex interplay of environment and human history. Foucault's contemporary Fernand Braudel precociously imagined history to unfold in ways beyond the reach of conscious actors, especially would-be revolutionaries with an exagger-ated sense of their historical agency. Culture and environment constrain our actions, and change transpires over such a long *durée* that it transcends the consciousness of those who make it. Striving to move beyond the un-derstanding of history as a record of human events, he traced instead the gradual unfolding of human history within the slow, cyclical unfolding of environmental time.[171]

Reckoning with man's ephemerality might force us to reconsider history as cyclical, if not aimless. The Abrahamic religions have left their linear millenarian imprint on liberal and Marxist visions of liberation, as well as on linear scientific theories of the origin and expansion of the universe.[172] What would a cyclical outlook look like? I don't mean the narratives of decline-and-fall associated with Gibbon or later historians like Toynbee, anxious over the security of Britain's empire—or the apocalyptic "decline of the West" texts that have emerged since his time expressing a kind of siege mentality licensing preemptive strengthening (e.g., Oswald Spengler's "Caesarism") or aggression against would-be usurpers elsewhere in the world. I mean rather a view of time that is not linear—like Akhtar's or the idea of yugas. The minute we accommodate as historical actors humans who believe in rebirth, we are forced to accommodate a worldview in which humans can morph into other forms: a monkey this life, human in the next; a human in this life, a snake in the next. This worldview is no longer human-centric; it is one in which the story of man cannot but blur into the story of other species, where all life is truly interrelated.[173] What would be the implications for conscience, then? How should our chastened acknowledgment that we have wittingly or unwittingly authored an "Anthropocene" era weigh on our collective conscience? Reflecting on Partition, the Pakistani writer Intizar Husain invoked the fatalistic wisdom of Ved Vyas that what is bound to happen happens: "Our understanding calls it a historical act."[174] This is an idea of man as both ephemeral and deeply flawed and of history as a narrative form that creates sense and structure where there is often not. That man suffers from bad conscience is itself the result of historical contingency. If we had remained God's property, as we were before the Enlightenment, the earth would not be on our conscience. Epic remembrance, like that offered by the *Mahabharata*, is a reminder that the past is infinite—as are lives and existence.

Try as we might to keep our eyes fixed steadily on the future and progress, we do live in the fullness of time: medieval patterns—and Victorian revivals of them—decorate our textiles; we live among redwood trees as old as those patterns; we live alongside ruins; we dream of jinn who knew the Prophet Muhammad; we anticipate the end of times; we imbibe lessons from previous yugas, reconstruct the Mesozoic era and the origins of the cosmos, and commune with the dead, as we have even by reading this book. Some of this is testimony to the power of human scientific investigation, but all of it is testimony to the imagination that spurs both curiosity and the ability to contend with realities beyond the scale of our own. That imaginative power is what enables us to grasp, even fleetingly, the illusory or ephemeral or subjective nature of worldly reality, that enables us to imagine earthly human life as a world at the end of a rabbit hole on the space-time continuum—the sense of the world as *maya* or cosmic *leela* (play) in Hindu tradition. Perhaps we write human history to redeem *it* from the enormous condescension of the scale of geological time. Like the traversable wormholes of quantum theory, history allows time travel; it allows us to ask, What if we had been there, *would we have done the same?* Britons today have taken refuge in pretty myths rather than the lived reality of the empire; it is time to wake from that long night of stories, from that dreamworld down the rabbit hole, and find new connection with the family of the living. Escape from human-centered history, from history framed as conquest and progress, is its own atonement.

There is much, then, that we can salvage from the historical discipline. We might provincialize Europe, certainly. Indeed, Kant had almost called for that with his 1784 essay "Idea for a Universal History," which remains an elusive disciplinary goal, a kind of Borgesian map of human development that we strain ever harder to create. Kant's idea of universal history (though positing a typically orientalist hierarchy with European societies at the top) foresaw the end of history as a federation characterized by a cosmopolitan moral culture.[175] But, at the same time, Kant acknowledged the impossibility of ever completely solving the problem of governance, for any administrator of the law, being human, would himself require governance from above: This is the problem of crooked timber. In this, he exhibited an affinity with later antihistorical thinkers with their nonchalance towards ends in preference to renewal of ethical means. Rather than make his peace with this unattainability and find meaning in the connections that someone like Faiz later found in the struggle towards it, Kant advocated belief in a happy end of history as the only antidote to the despairing conclusion that we might find meaning only in another world. He knew that in peddling history-as-progress he was peddling a lie. Successive German philosophes unmasked it—from Goethe to Benjamin. We know history is emplotted, a literary narrative. But it was anticolonial thinkers who ultimately found a way out of the cul-de-sac that worried Kant by seeking meaning not in the possibility of progress towards a perfect federation but in the possibility of connection *now*. There was a sense, implicit in the Sufi idiom, that worldly experiences were merely instrumental in the real game, which was connection—with the divine and the living, serially or simultaneously. This was a historical sensibility in which worldly affairs are a jumble of events transpiring off the main stage, conducing towards an end that is transcendental or otherworldly. The ideas of figures like Blake or Gandhi or Maulana Madani are not passé, the stuff of naive atavism; as Barbara Metcalf observes, Madani drew skillfully on a rich Islamic scholarship tradition in political debates in a manner that both showed and renewed its relevance.[176] The transregional nature of such conversations ensured that they left a deep imprint on European thought, too.[177] Accessing them may require breaking free from an exclusive commitment to the textual sources that have been the basis of historical inquiry since it took shape in the era of colonialism, delving into memory, myth, and oral traditions where we find survivals of otherwise marginalized intellectual traditions.[178]

At the moment, climate change negotiations remain captive to the legacy of empire, as postcolonial nation-states demand the right to prove their capacity to catch up, while their former colonizers paternalistically ask them to renounce that dream in the name of climate conservation. But the crisis is a collective one; it will require recovery of the idea of the collective, long exiled from many arenas of modernity. Lost causes—including Gandhi's utopia of village republics—may provide fresh inspiration as we contend with the reality that the vision of modernity for which so many sacrificed so much can in fact be practiced only by a small minority; it is unsustainable as a way of life for the world. In 1928, Gandhi already knew this: "God forbid that India should ever take to industrialism after the manner of the West," he warned. "If an entire nation of 300 millions took to similar economic exploitation, it would strip the world bare like locusts."[179]

Our very sense of selfhood is implicated in a shift from an ethical outlook grounded in progress to one grounded in connection. It may be true that the current crisis is unintended and thus no one's fault in particular, or the fault of our collective flawed humanity, but it also remains true that it is the result of certain cultural propensities prioritizing individuals, material progress, a deferring of ethical judgment, that we granted excessive status. The idea of coherent selfhood underlay deep investment in the power of human agency that at once rendered nature docile: The Victorians bequeathed us a sense of geological change as predictable and gradual, likening belief in freakish events to delusional belief in supernatural agents guiding human life.[180] As the idea of human historical agency gained sway, the domain of acts of God shrank; the disenchanting of the world entailed a view of nature as tame. Now that the myth of gradual geological change has been punctured, and we can see earthquakes and floods as the prodigies that they are, we might also acknowledge the myths of history and human agency on which it depended. Three centuries of investment in the historical sensibility that led, via capitalism and imperialism, to the current climate crisis depended on the idea of coherent, rational selfhood (however illusory it was and however vexed the idea remained); altering that sensibility will entail adapting that sense of self into something more tolerant of incoherence, incompleteness, a layering of ways of being, a capacity to shift shape—perhaps an excavation of repressed cultural memory of shapeshifters like those who became wolves according to the revelation of the moon. This is a self that is not only multitudinous (in the manner of Walt Whitman's "I contain multitudes") but porous, aware of its social and inter-temporal character. Pope Francis's encyclical of 2015 openly criticized "the idea of infinite or unlimited growth" so dear to economists and technology experts, the "irrational confidence in progress and human abilities" that has marked our time—in short, the confidence in great-man historical power that this book has sought to dissect. The encyclical instead insists on the connection between concern for nature, inner peace, and social justice.[181] Many other religious leaders and organizations have echoed these concerns, and, as Ghosh notes, such organizations, partly because of their transnational quality and transcendent view of time, may prove the most effectual in mobilizing people for climate change. He, too, ends with a call for an ethics of connection: The hope that future generations will be able to "transcend the isolation in which humanity was entrapped in the time of its derangement; that they will rediscover their kinship with other beings."[182]

Some worry that throwing out the idea of directional history is neither possible nor desirable given the way that idea has already structured so much of our world and the way we live.[183] But apart from the way this protest itself propagates the notion of helplessness before history, we now know that world to be unsustainable. Certainly, the idea of modernization has been dogged by criticism since the Romantics. We have tended to read that criticism as "dissent." But it was not merely a gasket for expressing frustration and disappointment with the secular vision of progress; Blake, Gandhi, the Martiniquan revolutionary philosopher Frantz Fanon, and others put practicable alternative ways of being on the table, programmatically. Interwar anticolonial activists denied liberation was a singularly European humanistic preoccupation, demonstrating partly on the basis of the very history of rebellion "that impulses towards freedom and equality can be seen to arise across multiple contexts and cultures . . . and as such would be impulses towards reclamation *from* rather than bestowal by Western benevolence," as summarized by the literary scholar Priyamvada Gopal.[184] In his lectures during World War I, Tagore cautioned against "modernizing" as "nothing but mimicry."[185] Gandhi's notion of *swaraj* depended on a moral transformation at the level of the self, a freeing from the "mind-forg'd manacles" of colonialism; it is literally "self" rule in the sense of freedom from all government control: "It is Swaraj when we learn to rule ourselves."[186] Independence comes from the bottom up. It was the straining after this goal that mattered: "Let India live for the true picture, though never realisable in its completeness."[187] After World War II, Fanon, too, categorically deplored "nauseating mimicry" of Europe and becoming "obsessed by the desire to catch up with Europe," which was headed to an abyss; doing so had turned the United States into a "monster."[188] E. P. Thompson sympathized with Fanon's text, whose context made it "not only comprehensible but inevitable." But he defensively (and rightly) protested against the conclusion that the "West" had "nothing to offer"; the insularity of his work was partly in a spirit of defiant redemption. "For us," he wrote to the editorial board of the *New Left Review* in his resignation letter (prompted by his long argument with Perry Anderson about theory), "the 'European game' can never be finished": "If 'our' tradition has failed . . . then it is for us to put it in repair" rather than hastily conclude that "the humanist values discovered in the West are corrupted beyond recall."[189] It was 1963, the year that saw publication of *The Making of the English Working Class,* his attempt at recovering England's radical humanistic values.

In short, it is not true that we are stuck only with the intellectual patrimony of what we might call the canonical traditions of the European Enlightenment. More than a particular set of ideas, the Enlightenment's legacy is the spirit of critical inquiry. Blake is as much a part of this heritage as Mill. Even Kant's historical commitments were more transcendental than we have grasped. *And* the humanistic values of such "Western" thinkers were shaped through engagement with other traditions, and vice versa (as Thompson's own intellectual formation shows). Alternative ideas of history and the purpose of historical agency remain with us, if we choose to shake off our mind-forg'd manacles and grasp them. Just as Frankenstein's monster turns out to be more human than monster, so history turns out to have richer ethical force than has typically been allowed. Decolonizing the discipline—its redemption—will involve not only provincializing Europe but also thinking, like interwar South Asians, outside the box of the historicist imagination of the nation. Historians of the modern period might fruitfully think like medievalists, who approach their subjects with a sense of common humanity without presuming a common cultural and ethical outlook; they are certainly not thrown by invocations of divine agency. We allow medieval people to tell us their stories on their own terms, without faulting them for the absence of some evolutionarily determined trait; so should we allow moderns, too, with their complex, layered identities shaped by the history of empire. As Chakrabarty reminds us, the Santal rebel of 1855, and humans from any other period and region, "are always in some sense our contemporaries: that would have to be the condition under which we can even begin to treat them as intelligible to us. Thus the writing of history must implicitly assume a plurality of times existing together, a disjuncture of the present with itself. Making visible this disjuncture is what subaltern pasts allow us to do." It is because we have access to the fullness of time, because we live among the fragments of worlds that have passed, that we are able to historicize at all. Chakrabarty writes, "It is because we live in time-knots that we can undertake the exercise of straightening out, as it were, some part of the knot (which is how we might think of chronology)."[190]

The "cure" for "social evils" imagined by E. P. Thompson is not an event that will announce the "end of social evolution." Rather, it is the way of being that comes about when we search together for a "cure" *knowing* that we will not find it, that the "cure" is in our very search for it together. It is the moon outside the prison bars. Urdu Progressive poets often used the metaphor of "dawn" for freedom, implying that the time of suffering is like a long night, but, like every night, it must end in dawn. As Faiz wrote: "*Lambi hai gham ki shaam magar shaam hi to hai*" (Long is the night of sorrow, but it is still just a night).[191] This is a future-oriented optimistic ethos. But, crucially, everyone knows that just as dawn reliably follows night, so night reliably follows dawn. We are not going to reach the end of social evolution; time is cyclical. Liberation is not a condition we achieve at the end of linear time but something we experience in fits and starts in the very pursuit of liberation. It lies in the gap between Ghalib's *"Shama har rang mein jalti hai seher hote tak"* (The candle burns in every color till morning happens) and Khamosh Ghazipuri's *"Har shab-e-gham ki seher ho ye zaruri to nahin"* (That every night of sorrow should end in morning is not necessary).[192]

As this book goes to press, Indians are thronging sites of historic public belonging to protest new citizenship laws that abrogate the secular mission of the Indian constitution; their language of protest draws heavily on this political and poetic legacy. Urdu poetry has always been a social and collective endeavor; the performance of the poem in a *mushaira* incorporates the audience. Even in silent reading, the reader identifies with the genderless first-person voice of the poet. The poet's place in history becomes the reader's, too. Whatever such movements achieve, their anticolonial antihistorical ethos is intrinsically liberatory.

As Thompson reminds us, this is not an exclusively South Asian or non-European idea. For, as Stuart Hall admonished, modern history makes it impossible to conceive of specific traditions within fixed boundaries. In the time of the French Revolution, Thompson's narrative tells us, the English radical and poet John Thelwall deduced, "Whatever presses men together . . . is . . . ultimately promotive of human liberty."[193] Recently the historian Timothy Snyder invoked the importance of "corporeal politics" in response to the global rise of populist authoritarianism: "Power wants your body softening in your chair and your emotions dissipating on a screen. Get outside. Put your body in unfamiliar places with unfamiliar people." That experience of connection *is* the subversion of power, the end in itself. A journalist writing on the massive, optimistic people's march against Brexit in March 2019 recalled this line from Snyder's book, noting that though the marchers' time and effort would inevitably be judged fruitless, it mattered the way mass marches always do: "as a reminder . . . that democracy is not a settled state, but a shifting expression of collective will."[194] Poetry remains important to such movements all over.[195]

Kant and Intizar Hussain were right about the flawed nature of humanity. And yet, so many in the modern period believed that conquest and nation-building might be exercises in virtue—perhaps the biggest proof of that flawed nature. Billions of us now are working out our destinies in the shadow of states and political relationships that are the wreckage of that folly. History has been a great enabler of that undeservedly easy conscience, and it is time that the producers and consumers of history together concede that there is no narrative of progress that might justify a moral wrong. If we remove that cloak of narrative deception, we will find that our other inherited modes of ethical accountability remain with us, intact, available. We may draw on them to assess our place on the scale of Time, our obligations to one another and to the planet and the cosmos. We will need history to understand how we got here—the tension between a historical and antihistorical outlook will be permanent in our souls. We might tell new, more encompassing, perhaps more chaotic stories that will return us to the fullness of time. In their telling, we may make new history, too. That history can have no end; the struggle to renew humanity is an end in itself.

NOTES

INTRODUCTION

1   Alan Bennett, *The History Boys* (London: Faber and Faber, 2004).

2   J. R. Seeley, *Lectures and Essays* (London: Macmillan, 1870), 296.

3   See, for instance, Eric Alterman, "The Decline of Historical Thinking," *New Yorker,* February 4, 2019. On overspecialization as a cause of the apparent decline of historians' influence, see, for instance, David Armitage and Jo Guldi, *The History Manifesto* (Cambridge: Cambridge University, 2014). In fact, academic historians are like other scholarly agents, including economists, who produce work that may or may not be amenable to popular readership—something that depends on shifts in public education and culture as well as on the work itself. At a deeper level, humanistic endeavors are intrinsically valuable and require no practical justification. Moreover, concern about "overspecialization" too often offers cover to concern with the way greater diversity and attention to diversity have changed the profession. *The Economist,* thus, lately blamed historians' declining influence on their preoccupation with "the marginal rather than the powerful, the poor rather than the rich." "Bagehot," "The End of History," *The Economist,* July 20, 2019, 49. See also note 19. Whatever their scholarly proclivities, historians, like other scholars, engage in public-facing work as teachers, public interlocutors, institutional figures, activists, and authors of specialized monographs as well as popular books, essays, and so on. This public role—through which they fulfill their cultural function—is what I am interested in.

4   On liberalism and empire, see, especially, Uday Mehta, *Liberalism and Empire: A Study in Nineteenth-Century British Liberal Thought* (Chicago: University of Chicago Press, 1999); Jennifer Pitts, *A Turn to Empire: The Rise of Imperial Liberalism in Britain and France* (Princeton, NJ: Princeton University Press, 2005). One might tell related stories about the French *mission civilisatrice* and the American notion of "manifest destiny."

5   Immanuel Kant, "Idea for a Universal History with a Cosmopolitan Point of View," 1784, trans. Lewis White Beck, from Kant, *On History* (Indianapolis: Bobbs-Merrill, 1963), Thesis 6, transcribed by Rob Lucas, Marxist Internet Archive, https://www.marxists.org/reference/subject/ethics/kant/universal-history .htm. Note that I have used this translation elsewhere in the text, but in the particular line cited above from the Sixth Thesis, I have opted for the translation popular-

ized by Isaiah Berlin. Beck translates the line thus: "from such crooked wood as man is made of, nothing perfectly straight can be built."

6   See, paradigmatically, James Scott, *Seeing Like a State: How Certain Schemes to Improve the Human Condition Have Failed* (New Haven, CT: Yale University Press, 1999).

7   Dipesh Chakrabarty, *Provincializing Europe: Postcolonial Thought and Historical Difference* (Princeton, NJ: Princeton University Press, 2000), 7.

8   Notably, Mehta groups many of the thinkers covered here as "political theorists." *Liberalism and Empire,* 6. This book shows that the historical imagination that structured their political thought did important ethical work in enabling empire.

9   Mohandas K. Gandhi, quoted in Nirmal Kumar Bose, ed., *Selections from Gandhi* (Ahmedabad: Navajivan, 1948), 203.

10   Will Dahlgreen, "Rhodes Must Not Fall," YouGov, January 18, 2016, http://yougov.co.uk/topics/politics/articles-reports/2016/01/18/rhodes-must-not-fall; Jon Stone, "British People Are Proud of Colonialism and the British Empire, Poll Finds," *The Independent,* January 19, 2016; Robert Booth, "UK More Nostalgic for Empire Than Other Ex-Colonial Powers," *Guardian,* March 11, 2020.

11   Paul Cornish, Nigel Biggar, Robert Johnson, and Gareth Stansfield, "Interests, Ethics and Rules: Renewing UK Intervention Policy," January 11, 2020 (Beckington, Nr Frome: Cityforum, 2020), 19.

12   Clement Atlee, *Empire into Commonwealth: The Chichele Lectures Delivered at Oxford in May 1960 on Changes in the Conception and Structure of the British Empire during the Last Half Century* (New York: Oxford University Press, 1961). Though even in Atlee's time, some historians, such as Margery Perham, recognized that colonial subjects fought and won their freedom in the teeth of British recalcitrance, the myth has echoed down to our present in the work of historians such as David Cannadine and John Darwin. See Priyamvada Gopal, *Insurgent Empire: Anticolonial Resistance and British Dissent* (London: Verso, 2019), 3, 12, 432–433.

13   See also Afua Hirsch, "Britain's Colonial Crimes Deserve a Lasting Memorial," *Guardian,* November 27, 2017.

14   On this, see also Priya Satia, *Spies in Arabia: The Great War and the Cultural Foundations of Britain's Covert Empire in the Middle East* (New York: Oxford University Press, 2008), introduction.

15   On representations and empire, see, generally, Edward Said, *Orientalism* (orig. 1978; repr., New York: Vintage, 2003).

16   Samuel Galton, "To the Friends of the Monthly Meeting at Birmingham," 1795, Birmingham City Archives: MS3101/B/16/2.

17   Priya Satia, "Byron, Gandhi and the Thompsons: The Making of British Social History and the Unmaking of Indian History," *History Workshop Journal* 81 (2016): 135–170; Satia, "Poets of Partition: The Recovery of Lost Causes," in Arie Dubnov and Laura Robson, eds., *Partitions: A Transnational History of Twentieth-Century Territorial Separatism* (Stanford, CA: Stanford University Press, 2019), 224–256.

18   See, for instance, Martin Malia, *The Soviet Tragedy: A History of Socialism in Russia, 1917–1991* (New York: Free Press, 1994); Martin Amis, *Koba the Dread: Laughter and the Twenty Million* (New York: Vintage, 2002). A vast literature points out the comparable features of Nazism and Stalinism.

19   This conference of over thirty white men (but for one woman who chaired a panel) in March 2018 created a scandal in a profession made up of growing numbers of nonwhite and female scholars. See Maya Salam, "Stanford History Event Was 'Too White and Too Male,' Organizer Admits," *New York Times,* March 17, 2018, 21; Emma Kerr, "'Multiple Steves and Pauls': A History Panel Sets Off a Diversity Firestorm," *Chronicle of Higher Education,* March 15, 2018, http://www .chronicle.com/article/Multiple-Steves-and/242841; Allyson Hobbs and Priya Satia, "An Academic Conference Featured 30 White Men and One White Woman. How Should the University Respond?" *Washington Post,* March 26, 2018. The conference's demographic makeup was not incidental to its purpose, which was to address the supposed fact that the "majority of academic historians have tended to shy away from questions of contemporary interest, especially to policy makers." "Previous generations were less shy of such questions," claimed the conference website. "Applied History," seminar program, available at axsonjohnsonfoundation.org/wp-content/uploads/2018/03/Applied-History.pdf. The conference's primary organizer, Niall Ferguson, had already expressed dismay at the "significant price" of growing attention to diversity to the historical discipline. See Ferguson, "The Decline and Fall of History," speech, October 2016, Folger Shakespeare Library, Washington, DC, http://www.youtube.com/watch ?v=7WXNF6Vyo7A. I defended the contributions today's historians make to policymaking and public debate. See Priya Satia, "The Whitesplaining of History Is Over," *Chronicle of Higher Education,* March 28, 2018, http://www .chronicle.com/article/The-Whitesplaining-of-History/242952.

20   This is why writing longer-term narratives, as David Armitage and Jo Guldi urge in *The History Manifesto,* is no necessary fix: longer-term narratives do not secure us from the kind of counterproductive policymaking that arises from deferring judgment to the future. That requires a reimagining of the ethical logic of history (leaving aside the scope for effectively applying such knowledge in existing state structures) (Chapter 6). Moreover, in exhorting historians to influence policymakers as they once did, Armitage does not distinguish between influence exercised from within and without state institutions. See Armitage, "Why Politicians Need Historians," *Guardian,* October 7, 2014. But a work of history that engages a wide readership influences policymakers differently from "in-house" historians advising civil servants and policymakers from within state offices. These are distinct modes of public "relevance." Here, I recount history's rise as the disciplinary outlook of empire-builders and the subsequent anticolonial reclamation of it as the province of critics speaking *outside* the imperial state. This is the disciplinary history from which historians today must envision their role in public debate.

21   On the last, see also Dane Kennedy, *Imperial History Wars: Debating the British Empire* (London: Bloomsbury, 2018), chap. 7.

22   Those looking for philosophical works on conscience or the intellectual history of the concept of conscience might instead consult Martin van Creveld, *Conscience: A Biography* (London: Reaktion, 2015); Richard Sorabji, *Moral Conscience through the Ages: Fifth Century BCE to the Present* (Oxford: Oxford University Press, 2014); Martha Nussbaum, *Political Emotions: Why Love Matters for Justice* (Cambridge, MA: Belknap Press of Harvard University Press, 2013); Kenan Malik, *The Quest for a Moral Compass: A Global History of Ethics* (London: Atlantic, 2014); Paul Strohm, *Conscience: A Very Short Introduction* (Oxford: Oxford University Press, 2011).

1. THE PROGRESS OF WAR

Epigraph: Lin-Manuel Miranda, "Hamilton: An American Musical," in *Hamilton: The Revolution,* ed. Jeremy McCarter (New York: Grand Central Publishing, 2016), 120.

1 For interesting play with this idea, see Michelle Alexander, "What If We're All Coming Back?" *New York Times,* October 29, 2018.

2 On the early importance of John Locke's work in this shift, see Paul Strohm, *Conscience: A Very Short Introduction* (Oxford: Oxford University Press, 2011), 41–42.

3 Henry St. John Bolingbroke, *The Works of Lord Bolingbroke. With a Life, Prepared Expressly for This Edition, Containing Additional Information Relative to His Personal and Public Character, Selected from the Best Authorities. In Four Volumes* (orig. 1752; repr., London: Henry G. Bohn, 1844), 2:193. The letters were printed privately before his death.

4 Emma Rothschild, "*The Theory of Moral Sentiments* and the Inner Life," in *The Philosophy of Adam Smith: The Adam Smith Review,* vol. 5, *Essays Commemorating the 250th Anniversary of "The Theory of Moral Sentiments,"* ed. Vivienne Brown and Samuel Fleischacker (London: Routledge, 2010), 28, 29, 30, 33.

5 Strohm, *Conscience,* 48.

6 Immanuel Kant, "Idea for a Universal History with a Cosmopolitan Point of View," 1784, trans. Lewis White Beck, from Kant, *On History* (Indianapolis: Bobbs-Merrill, 1963), Eighth and Ninth Theses, transcribed by Rob Lucas, Marxist Internet Archive, https://www.marxists.org/reference/subject/ethics/kant/universal-history.htm. To be sure, elsewhere Kant affirmed more transcendental moral values, exhorting us to "act that you use humanity, whether in your own person or in the person of any other, always at the same time as an end, never merely as a mean." *Groundwork for the Metaphysic of Morals,* chap. 2, quoted in Manfred Kuehn, "Reason as a Species Characteristic," in Amélie Rorty and James Schmidt, eds., *Kant's "Idea for a Universal History with a Cosmopolitan Aim": A Critical Guide* (Cambridge: Cambridge University Press, 2009), 86.

7 Rüdiger Bittner, "Philosophy Helps History," in Rorty and Schmidt, *Kant's "Idea for a Universal History,"* 235.

8 Eckart Förster, "The Hidden Plan of Nature," in Rorty and Schmidt, *Kant's "Idea for a Universal History,"* 189.

9 David Bell, *The Cult of the Nation in France: Inventing Nationalism, 1680–1800* (Cambridge, MA: Harvard University Press, 2001), 15.

10 David Hume to William Strahan, August 1770, in *The Letters of David Hume,* vol. 2, ed. J. Y. T. Greig (orig. 1932; repr., Oxford: Oxford University Press, 2011), 230.

11 Benedict Anderson, *Imagined Communities: Reflections on the Origin and Spread of Nationalism* (London: Verso, 1983).

12 Herodotus, *The Histories,* trans. Tom Holland (orig. 5th cent. BCE; repr., New York: Penguin, 2015).

13 Thucydides, *History of the Peloponnesian War,* ed. M. I. Finley, trans. Rex Warner (orig. 5th cent. BCE; trans. 1954; repr., New York: Penguin, 1972).

14 See, for instance, Matthew Gabriele, "Islamophobes Want to Recreate the Crusades. But They Don't Understand Them at All," *Washington Post,* June 6, 2017.

15 Euan Cameron, "The Protestant Reformers and World History: How Cosmic Time Became Theological Time," lecture, Humanities Center, Stanford University, November 8, 2019.

16   David Como, "In Due Time: Apostasy, Apocalypse, and the English Revolution," talk, Humanities Center, Stanford University, November 8, 2019.

17   Nicholas Dirks, *The Scandal of Empire: India and the Creation of Imperial Britain* (Cambridge, MA: Harvard University Press, 2008), 256–257.

18   For an overview of scholarship on the place of God and Christianity in the Enlightenment, see Charly Coleman, "Resacralizing the World: The Fate of Secularization in Enlightenment Historiography," *Journal of Modern History* 82:2 (2010): 368–395.

19   Catherine Gallagher, *Telling It Like It Wasn't: The Counterfactual Imagination in History and Fiction* (Chicago: University of Chicago Press, 2018), 17.

20   Gallagher, *Telling It Like It Wasn't*, 18.

21   Talal Asad, *Formations of the Secular: Christianity, Islam, Modernity* (Stanford, CA: Stanford University Press, 2003), 27.

22   Kant, "Idea for a Universal History with a Cosmopolitan Point of View," Eighth Thesis.

23   Genevieve Lloyd, "Providence as Progress," in Rorty and Schmidt, *Kant's "Idea for a Universal History,"* 202.

24   Bittner, "Philosophy Helps History," 245–249.

25   See Kuehn, "Reason as a Species Characteristic," 72.

26   Henry Allison, "Teleology and History in Kant: The Critical Foundations of Kant's Philosophy of History," in Rorty and Schmidt, *Kant's "Idea for a Universal History,"* 27.

27   Kuehn, "Reason as a Species Characteristic," 83.

28   Kant, "Idea for a Universal History with a Cosmopolitan Point of View," Introduction.

29   Kant, "Idea for a Universal History with a Cosmopolitan Point of View," Ninth and Fourth Theses.

30   Joseph Priestley, *Lectures on History and General Policy, to Which Is Prefixed, An Essay on a Course of Liberal Education for Civil and Active Life,* 2 vols. (orig. 1788; repr., London: J. Johnson, 1793), 1:48, 64–65, 83.

31   Gallagher, *Telling It Like It Wasn't*, 21–22.

32   Priestley, *Lectures on History*, 2:467–468; 1:80; 2:441. Italics on closing phrase are mine.

33   Charles Davenant, *An Essay Upon the Probable Methods of Making a People Gainers in the Ballance of Trade* (orig. London: Printed for James Knapton . . . , 1699; repr., Ann Arbor: Text Creation Partnership, 2011), 154–155, https://quod.lib.umich.edu/cgi/t/text/text-idx?c=eebo;idno=A69897.0001.001. I thank Jon Cooper for this reference. On luxury in this period, see Maxine Berg and E. Eger, eds., *Luxury in the Eighteenth Century: Debates, Desires and Delectable Goods* (London: Palgrave, 2003). By association with commerce and desire, other behaviors invited moral questioning in a new way. See, for instance, Thomas Laqueur, *Solitary Sex: A Cultural History of Masturbation* (New York: Zone, 2003).

34   I thank Max Ashton for this observation.

35   Thucydides, *History of the Peloponnesian War,* 82, 242.

36   Priestley, *Lectures on History*, 2:451, 453, 454, 467. Italics in original.

37   See Priya Satia, *Empire of Guns: The Violent Making of the Industrial Revolution* (New York: Penguin, 2018).

38   Samuel Galton, "To the Friends of the Monthly Meeting at Birmingham," 1795, Birmingham City Archives: MS3101 / B / 16 / 2. Italics in original.

39   Joseph Freame to Mary Freame, June 16, 1762, Friends House Library: Temp MSS: 403/1/1/1/6.

40   Emma Rothschild, *The Inner Life of Empires: An Eighteenth-Century History* (Princeton, NJ: Princeton University Press, 2011), 123–124. See also 132–133 and 150–153.

41   Quoted in Peter Brock, *Pacificism in Europe to 1914* (Princeton, NJ: Princeton University Press, 1972), 308.

42   See, generally, Satia, *Empire of Guns.*

43   Trevor Jackson, "Markets of Exception: An Economic History of Impunity in Britain and France, 1720–1830" (PhD diss., University of California, Berkeley, 2017).

44   T. Asad, *Formations of the Secular,* 25.

45   Amitav Ghosh, *The Great Derangement: Climate Change and the Unthinkable* (Chicago: University of Chicago Press, 2016), 123.

46   "Notoriously historical work": Rothschild, "*The Theory of Moral Sentiments* and the Inner Life," 26; Smith quotations: Adam Smith, *An Enquiry into the Nature and Causes of the Wealth of Nations,* ed. Edwin Cannan (orig. 1776; repr., New York: Modern Library, 1994), 765.

47   Priestley, *Lectures on History,* 2:355–358.

48   See Priya Satia, "Are 100 Years Enough?" *The New Republic,* November 9, 2018, http://newrepublic.com/Article/152153/100-years-enough.

49   Galton, "To the Friends of the Monthly Meeting at Birmingham."

50   Strohm, *Conscience,* 14–15.

51   Roy Porter, *English Society in the Eighteenth Century* (New York: Penguin, 1982), 323.

52   Ghosh, *Great Derangement,* 127–128.

53   Charles Taylor, *A Secular Age* (Cambridge, MA: Belknap Press of Harvard University Press, 2007).

54   See Thomas W. Laqueur, "Bodies, Details, and the Humanitarian Narrative," in *The New Cultural History,* ed. Lynn Hunt (Berkeley: University of California Press, 1989), 176–204; Lynn Hunt, *Inventing Human Rights: A History* (New York: Norton, 2007), chap. 1.

55   Miles Taylor, *Ernest Jones, Chartism, and the Romance of Politics, 1819–1869* (Oxford: Oxford University Press, 2003), 256.

56   Coleman, "Resacralizing the World," 395.

57   Stefan Collini, *Public Moralists: Political Thought and Intellectual Life in Britain, 1850–1930* (Oxford: Clarendon, 1991). As Collini shows, "intellectuals" is a dynamic category of the period. I will not have space to explore the shifting domains that shaped them and their work in this book.

58   Dror Wahrman, *The Making of the Modern Self: Identity and Culture in Eighteenth-Century England* (New Haven, CT: Yale University Press, 2004), xi.

59   Ian Baucom, *Specters of the Atlantic: Finance Capital, Slavery, and the Philosophy of History* (Durham, NC: Duke University Press, 2005), 239, 245.

60   Adam Smith, *The Theory of Moral Sentiments,* ed. D. D. Raphael and A. L. Mafied (orig. 1759–61; repr., Indianapolis: Liberty Fund, 1982), pt. 3, chap. 3.

61   Karl Marx, "A Contribution to the Critique of Hegel's Philosophy of Right," Introduction, in *Deutsch-Französische Jahrbucher,* February 1844, "Works of Karl Marx 1843," Marxists Internet Archive, https://www.marxists.org/archive/marx/works/1843/critique-hpr/intro.htm.

62   David Hume, *An Enquiry concerning Human Understanding* (orig. 1748; London: A. Millar, 1777), 98, Hume Texts Online, https://davidhume.org/texts/e/.

63   See Dana Rabin, *Identity, Crime, and Legal Responsibility in Eighteenth-Century England* (London: Palgrave, 2004), 169.

64   Thomas Paine, "To the Representatives of the Religious Society of the People called Quakers . . . ," in appendix to *Common Sense*, 3rd ed., 1776, reprinted in *The Writings of Thomas Paine*, vol. 1, *1774–1779*, ed. Moncure Daniel Conway (New York: Putnam's, 1894), 124.

65   *Epistle from the Yearly Meeting in London to the Quarterly Meetings*, May 4, 1779, Birmingham City Archives: MS695 / 26 / 6.

66   See Satia, *Empire of Guns*, 127–130.

67   Wahrman, *Making of the Modern Self.*

68   Satia, *Empire of Guns*, chap. 6.

69   On the history of knowledge of this communal landholding, see Karuna Mantena, *Alibis of Empire: Henry Maine and the Ends of Liberal Imperialism* (Princeton, NJ: Princeton University Press, 2010), 130–131.

70   Satia, *Empire of Guns*, chaps. 6, 7.

71   Such concerns were assuaged by the logic that abstaining from such sales would only send these customers into the arms of rival suppliers or encourage indigenous arms-making. The British would thereby forfeit profit, prestige, and diplomatic influence. Satia, *Empire of Guns*, chap. 7; Satia, "Guns and the British Empire," Aeon, February 14, 2018, aeon.co/essays/is-the-gun-the-basis-of-modern-anglo-civilisation.

72   Smith, *Theory of Moral Sentiments*, 92–93, 100. Philosophical preoccupation with "intention" continues to enable passivity in the face of political and moral crisis. See, for instance, S. Matthew Liao, "Do You Have a Moral Duty to Leave Facebook?" *New York Times*, November 25, 2018, 3.

73   See Satia, *Empire of Guns*, 245–247.

74   Walter Benjamin, "The Work of Art in the Age of Mechanical Reproduction," in *Illuminations: Walter Benjamin: Essays and Reflections*, ed. Hannah Arendt (orig. 1937; repr., New York: Schoken, 1968), 217–251.

75   Satia, *Empire of Guns*, 247–255.

76   Christopher Leslie Brown, *Moral Capital: Foundations of British Abolitionism* (Chapel Hill, NC: University of North Carolina Press, 2006), 52–53.

77   On the company's earlier history, see Philip Stern, *The Company-State: Corporate Sovereignty and the Early Modern Foundations of the British Empire in India* (New York: Oxford University Press, 2011).

78   Jackson, "Markets of Exception." As Jackson notes, after the South Sea Bubble of 1720, some attacked Robert Walpole's administration as corrupt, but he defended himself sufficiently to remain in power for two decades after.

79   Jackson, "Markets of Exception," 106.

80   Paine, *Common Sense*, 1776, in *The Writings of Thomas Paine*, 96.

81   Paine, "Reflections on the Life and Death of Lord Clive," *Pennsylvania Magazine*, March 1775, reprinted in *The Writings of Thomas Paine*, 29–35.

82   William Dalrymple, *The Anarchy: The Relentless Rise of the East India Company* (New York: Bloomsbury, 2019), 235.

83   Paine, "A Serious Thought," *Pennsylvania Journal*, October 18, 1775, reprinted in *The Writings of Thomas Paine*, 65–66.

84   Paine, "The Crisis," no. VII, "To the People of England," November 21, 1778, in *The Writings of Thomas Paine*, 274.

85   Smith, *Wealth of Nations*, 693, 666.

86   Smith, *Wealth of Nations*, 675–676.

87   Edward Gibbon, *The History of the Decline and Fall of the Roman Empire*, vol. 1 (London: Strahan and Cadell, 1776).

88   See Dirks, *Scandal of Empire*, 10, 13, 18, 21, 39, 43, 80–81.

89   Burke, speech in Parliament, Fourth Day of the Impeachment Trial of Warren Hastings, February 16, 1788, in *Writings and Speeches of Edmund Burke*, vol. 6, *India: The Launching of the Hastings Impeachment, 1786-1788*, ed. Paul Langford and P. J. Marshall (Oxford: Oxford University Press, 1991), 346.

90   Uday Mehta, *Liberalism and Empire: A Study in Nineteenth-Century British Liberal Thought* (Chicago: University of Chicago Press, 1999), 175.

91   Edmund Burke, *Reflections on the Revolution in France, and on the Proceedings in Certain Societies in London . . .* (London: J. Dodsley, 1790), 8–9.

92   Thomas Paine, *Rights of Man: Being an Answer to Mr. Burke's Attack on the French Revolution*, ed. Hypatia Bradlaught Bonner (orig. 1791; repr., London: Watts, 1937).

93   Keith Baker, "Revolution 1.0," *Journal of Modern European History* 11:2 (2013): 194–195. See also, generally, Steve Pincus, *1688: The First Modern Revolution* (New Haven, CT: Yale University Press, 2009).

94   Baker, "Revolution 1.0," 200–201, 210.

95   Priestley, *Lectures on History*, 1:iv.

96   Edmund Burke to French Laurence, July 28, 1796, quoted in Dirks, *Scandal of Empire*, 128.

97   Soldiers like Cortés succeeded against powerful empires in the New World largely thanks to contingent factors, but legends about them—rooted in Cortés's own vanity—furnished a model for modern imperial heroes.

98   Quoted in Dalrymple, *The Anarchy*, 234.

99   Dalrymple, *The Anarchy*, 240, 287.

100   As E. P. Thompson discerned with respect to the Burke-Paine dispute, "Neither writer was systematic enough to rank as a major political theorist. Both were publicists of genius, both are less remarkable for what they say than for the *tone* in which it is said." *The Making of the English Working Class* (orig. 1963; repr., New York: Vintage, 1966), 90.

101   Dirks, *Scandal of Empire*, 92.

102   Thomas Metcalf, *Ideologies of the Raj* (orig. 1995; repr., New York: Cambridge University Press, 1997), 19.

103   It is a measure of the historically complex play of moral relativism and universalism in British liberal thought that Burke found Thomas Paine's defense of the *Rights of Man* equally objectionable.

104   Dirks, *Scandal of Empire*.

105   See Brown, *Moral Capital*.

106   Brown, *Moral Capital*, 3, 10–11.

107   Brown, *Moral Capital*, 28, 352, 388, 418, 424.

108   Brown, *Moral Capital*, 437.

109   John Ashworth, "The Relationship between Capitalism and Humanitarianism," in Thomas Bender, ed., *The Antislavery Debate: Capitalism and Abolitionism as a Problem in Historical Interpretation* (Berkeley: University of California Press, 1992), 186–187.

110   David Brion Davis, "Reflections on Abolitionism and Ideological Hegemony," in T. Bender, *The Antislavery Debate*, 177–178.

111   Kant rejected slavery in principle but, by contrast, seems to have tolerated it as another evil that would ultimately drive civilizational advance. Thomas McCarthy,

Race, Empire, and the Idea of Human Development (Cambridge: Cambridge University Press, 2009), 64. See also Pauline Kleingeld, "Kant's Changing Cosmopolitanism," in Rorty and Schmidt, *Kant's "Idea for a Universal History,"* 184.

112 Brown, *Moral Capital*, 153, 231.

113 Thomas Haskell, "Capitalism and the Origins of the Humanitarian Sensibility, Part I," in T. Bender, *The Antislavery Debate*, 110–111; Haskell, "Capitalism and the Origins of the Humanitarian Sensibility, Part 2," in T. Bender, *The Antislavery Debate*, 140.

114 See Satia, *Empire of Guns*, 329.

115 Joseph Priestley, *A Sermon on the Subject of the Slave Trade; Delivered to a Society of Protestant Dissenters at the New Meeting, in Birmingham; and Published at Their Request* (Birmingham: Pearson and Rollason, 1788), 5; Priestley, *Lectures on History*, 2:207.

116 On "war capitalism," see Sven Beckert, *Empire of Cotton: A New History of Global Capitalism* (New York: Knopf, 2014).

117 David Bell describes this as the rise of political charisma. *Men on Horseback: The Power of Charisma in the Age of Revolution* (New York: Farrar, Straus and Giroux, 2020).

118 Bell, *Men on Horseback*, 29; 53–89; Personal communication with David Bell, March 27, 2020.

119 Samuel Galton to John Howard Galton, December 11, 1815, Birmingham City Archives: MS3101/C/D/10/9/53.

120 Brown, *Moral Capital*, 437, 439, 441, 444. See Thomas Clarkson, *The History of the Rise, Progress and Accomplishment of the Abolition of the Slave-Trade by the British Parliament* (Philadelphia: James P. Parke, 1808).

121 Brown, *Moral Capital*, 5.

122 On the consolidation of caste, see Nicholas Dirks, *Castes of Mind: Colonialism and the Making of Modern India* (Princeton, NJ: Princeton University Press, 2001).

123 See, for instance, Yuri Slezkine, *The House of Government: A Saga of the Russian Revolution* (Princeton, NJ: Princeton University Press, 2017), 37, on student "conversion" of workers to socialism in the time of the Russian Revolution.

124 Karl Marx, *The Eighteenth Brumaire of Louis Bonaparte*, trans. Saul Padover from the 1869 German edition (orig. 1852), chap. 1, 2nd para, "Works of Marx & Engels 1852," Marxist Internet Archive, www.marxists.org/archive/marx/works/1852/18th-brumaire/.

125 Slezkine, *House of Government*, 36–41.

126 Baker, "Revolution 1.0," 189–190, 201.

127 Baker, "Revolution 1.0," 212–213.

128 G. W. F. Hegel, *Lectures on the Philosophy of History*, trans. J. Sibree (orig. 1837; trans. 1857; repr., London: G. Bell, 1914), 22.

129 G. W. F. Hegel, *The Philosophy of Right*, trans. Alan White (orig. [1820]; Indianapolis: Hackett, 2002), 10.

130 Karl Marx, *Theses on Feuerbach* (orig. 1845; trans. from 1888 German edition), in Frederick Engels, *Ludwig Feuerbach and the End of Classical German Philosophy* (Peking: Foreign Languages Press, 1976), Eleventh Thesis, 65.

131 T. Asad, *Formations of the Secular*, 192–193.

132 V. I. Lenin, *What Is to Be Done? Burning Questions of Our Movement*, in Lenin, *Collected Works*, vol. 5, trans. Joe Fineberg and George Hanna (orig. 1902; Moscow: Foreign Languages Publishing House, 1961), 347–530. See Slezkine,

House of Government, chaps. 2 and 3, on the historical scripts that animated Russian revolutionaries.

133 For one subtle study of the complex avenues of ancient Roman influence on British colonialism, see Ananya Kabir, "Consecrated Groves: British India and the Forests of Germania," in *Germania Remembered, 1500–2009: Commemorating and Inventing a Germanic Past,* ed. Christina Lee and Nicola McClelland (Tempe, AZ: ACMRS, 2012), 155–171.

134 Dipesh Chakrabarty, *Provincializing Europe: Postcolonial Thought and Historical Difference* (Princeton, NJ: Princeton University Press, 2000), 108. See also, generally, chaps. 3, 4. See also Ranajit Guha, "The Prose of Counter-Insurgency," in *Selected Subaltern Studies,* ed. Ranajit Guha and Gayatri Spivak (orig. 1983; repr., Oxford: Oxford University Press, 1988), 45–84.

135 E. P. Thompson, "The Moral Economy of the Crowd," *Past & Present* 50 (1971): 76–136.

136 E. P. Thompson, *Making of the English Working Class,* 68–74.

137 E. P. Thompson, *Making of the English Working Class.*

138 John Steinbeck, *The Grapes of Wrath* (orig. 1939; repr., New York: Penguin, 2002), 349.

139 Primo Levi, *Survival in Auschwitz: The Nazi Assault on Humanity,* trans. Stuart Woolf (orig. 1947; trans. 1959; repr., New York: Touchstone, 1996), 73.

140 Clausewitz, *On War,* c. 1820s, quoted in Gallagher, *Telling It Like It Wasn't,* 43.

141 Catherine Hall nicely summarizes Hayden White's arguments on this: "Historical narratives are manifestly 'verbal fictions', . . . 'the contents of which are as much invented as found and the forms of which have more in common with their counterparts in literature than they have with those in the sciences.'" Quoting White, "The Historical Text as Literary Artifact," in *Tropics of Discourse* (London, 1973), 42. White explains that we create coherence by tailoring the facts, leaving things out. Emplotting events is ultimately a literary operation. Hall, *Macaulay and Son: Architects of Imperial Britain* (New Haven, CT: Yale University Press, 2012), 291.

142 Annette Richards, "C. P. E. Bach, the Musical Portrait and the Making of Music History," talk at Humanities Center, Stanford University, October 16, 2018.

143 Winston Churchill, interview with Gustavus Ohlinger, "WSC: A Midnight Interview, 1902," *Michigan Quarterly Review,* February 1966, reprinted in *Finest Hour* 159 (Summer 2013), winstonchurchill.org/publications/finest-hour/finest-hour-159/wsc-a-midnight-interview-1902/.

144 Chris Otter, *The Victorian Eye: A Political History of Light and Vision in Britain, 1800–1910* (Chicago: University of Chicago Press, 2008); Patrick Joyce, *The Rule of Freedom: Liberalism and the Modern City* (London: Verso, 2003).

145 See also Slezkine, *House of Government,* 74–75.

146 See also Thomas Laqueur, *The Work of the Dead: A Cultural History of Mortal Remains* (Princeton, NJ: Princeton University Press, 2015).

147 Ghosh, *Great Derangement,* 138.

148 Kant, quoted in Mehta, *Liberalism and Empire,* 210.

2. PROGRESS AS PENANCE

Epigraph: William Bentinck to James Mill, 1827, quoted in Uday Mehta, *Liberalism and Empire: A Study in Nineteenth-Century British Liberal Thought* (Chicago: University of Chicago Press, 1999), 13.

1   *Yes Minister,* episode 20, "The Whisky Priest," Dec. 16, 1982.

2   Thomas Paine, *Common Sense,* 3rd ed., 1776, reprinted in *The Writings of Thomas Paine,* vol. 1, *1774–1779,* ed. Moncure Daniel Conway (New York: Putnam's, 1894), 69.

3   Stefan Collini, *Public Moralists: Political Thought and Intellectual Life in Britain, 1850–1930* (Oxford: Clarendon, 1991), 67, 113.

4   Samuel Coleridge, *Ode on the Departing Year* (Bristol: N. Biggs, 1796), 5, 12, 15; Morton Paley, *Apocalypse and Millennium in English Romantic Poetry* (Oxford: Clarendon, 1999), 128.

5   Samuel Coleridge, "The Rime of the Ancient Mariner," 1798, in *The Norton Anthology of Poetry,* ed. Alexander Allison et al., 3rd ed. (New York: Norton, 1983), 581.

6   Samuel Coleridge, *Biographia Literaria, or Biographical Sketches of My Literary Life and Opinions,* 2 vols. (orig. 1817; repr., London: William Pickering, 1847), 2:2.

7   See also Talal Asad, *Formations of the Secular: Christianity, Islam, Modernity* (Stanford, CA: Stanford University Press, 2003), 13, 41, 194.

8   Johann Wolfgang von Goethe, *Faustus* (1808, 1832), available as *Faust: Part One,* trans. David Luke (trans. 1987; repr., Oxford: Oxford University Press, 2008); Goethe, *Faust: Part Two,* trans. David Luke (trans. 1994; repr., Oxford: Oxford University Press, 2008).

9   Oxford University Press published Coleridge's 1821 translation in 2007, inciting some controversy. *Faustus, from the German of Goethe,* trans. Samuel Taylor Coleridge, ed. Frederick Burwick and James C. McKusick (Oxford: Oxford University Press, 2007).

10 Mary Shelley, *Frankenstein, or The Modern Prometheus* (orig. 1816, introduction 1831; repr., New York: Signet, 1965), 200.

11 M. Shelley, *Frankenstein,* author's introduction, xi.

12 On the similarities between Goethe's and Kant's visions of the role of evil in human striving towards good, see also Allen Wood, "Kant's Fourth Proposition: The Unsociable Sociability of Human Nature," in Amélie Rorty and James Schmidt, eds., *Kant's "Idea for a Universal History with a Cosmopolitan Aim": A Critical Guide* (Cambridge: Cambridge University Press, 2009), 128.

13 William Blake, *America: A Prophecy,* 1793, available at The William Blake Archive, http://www.blakearchive.org/work/america.

14 William Blake, *A Vision of the Last Judgment,* c. 1810, in Alexander Gilchrist, *Life of William Blake, with Selections from his Poems and Other Writings,* vol. 2 (London: Macmillan, 1880), 198.

15 Lord George Gordon Byron, *Don Juan, in Sixteen Cantos, with Notes* (orig. 1819–1824; repr., Halifax: Milner and Sowerby, 1837).

16 Caroline Franklin, "'Some Samples of the Finest Orientalism': Byronic Philhellenism and Proto-Zionism at the Time of the Congress of Vienna," in *Romanticism and Colonialism: Writing and Empire, 1780–1830,* ed. Tim Fulford and Peter Kitson (New York: Cambridge University Press, 1998), 231.

17 Lord George Gordon Byron, *The Siege of Corinth: A Poem* (London: John Murray, 1816).

18 Franklin, "'Some Samples of the Finest,'" 225–226.

19 Malcolm Kelsall, "'Once Did She Hold the Gorgeous East in Fee . . .': Byron's Venice and Oriental Empire," in Fulford and Kitson, *Romanticism and Colonialism,* 258.

20   Thomas Paine, *Rights of Man: Being an Answer to Mr. Burke's Attack on the French Revolution,* ed. Hypatia Bradlaught Bonner (orig. 1791; repr., London: Watts, 1937), 206.

21   See Priya Satia, "Byron, Gandhi and the Thompsons: The Making of British Social History and the Unmaking of Indian History," *History Workshop Journal* 81 (2016): 135–170. For a record of resistance around the world to British rule in this period, see Richard Gott, *Britain's Empire: Resistance, Repression and Revolt* (London: Verso, 2011).

22   Thomas, Earl of Dundonald, *Narrative of Services in the Liberation of Chili, Peru, and Brazil, from Spanish and Portuguese Domination,* vol. 1 (London: James Ridgway, 1859), xi.

23   Quoted in Thomas, Eleventh Earl of Dundonald, and H. R. Fox Bourne, *The Life of Thomas, Lord Cochrane, Tenth Earl of Dundonald,* vol. 1 (London: Richard Bentley, 1869), 159. Cochrane wrote condescendingly of the local populations, highlighting the "redeeming feature" that most of the officers were "English and North American" (Dundonald, *Narrative of Services,* 23). He likened Chileans to "Orientals" in their "exaggerated" recourse to "flowery rhetorical phrases" (21).

24   Dundonald, *Narrative of Services,* 58, 125–126.

25   Linda Colley, *Britons: Forging the Nation, 1707–1837* (New Haven, CT: Yale University Press, 1994).

26   See, for instance, Percy Shelley, *Alastor, or The Spirit of Solitude: And Other Poems* (orig. 1816; repr., London: Reeves and Turner, 1885). See also Lord George Gordon Byron, *Childe Harold's Pilgrimage* (orig. 1812–1818; repr., Oxford: Clarendon, 1920).

27   Siraj Ahmed, *Archaeology of Babel: The Colonial Foundation of the Humanities* (Stanford, CA: Stanford University Press, 2017), introduction.

28   William Jones, trans., *Sacontalá or The Fatal Ring: An Indian Drama by Cálidás* (Calcutta: J. Cooper, 1789).

29   G. W. F. Hegel, *Lectures on the Philosophy of History,* trans. J. Sibree (orig. 1837; trans. 1857; repr., London: G. Bell, 1914), 109.

30   See Aakash Singh Rathore and Rimina Mohapatra, *Hegel's India: A Reinterpretation, with Texts* (Oxford: Oxford University Press, 2017).

31   Edward Said, *Orientalism* (orig. 1978; repr., New York: Vintage, 2003). See also Thomas Metcalf, *Ideologies of the Raj* (orig. 1995; repr., New York: Cambridge University Press, 1997), 7.

32   Charles Grant, *Observations on the State of Society among the Asiatic Subjects of Great-Britain, Particularly with Respect to Morals; and on the Means of Improving It* (written in 1792, presented to the East India Company in 1797), 15, 38, 178.

33   See, for instance, Nicholas Dirks, *The Scandal of Empire: India and the Creation of Imperial Britain* (Cambridge, MA: Harvard University Press, 2008), 32, 34, 298

34   See Dirks, *Scandal of Empire,* and T. Metcalf, *Ideologies of the Raj,* 24.

35   Quoted in T. Metcalf, *Ideologies of the Raj,* 24.

36   On the British writing of Indian history in the eighteenth and nineteenth centuries, see Dirks, *Scandal of Empire,* and T. Metcalf, *Ideologies of the Raj.*

37   See Javed Majeed, *Ungoverned Imaginings: James Mill's "The History of British India" and Orientalism* (Oxford: Clarendon, 1992), 127–128, 134–135.

38   J. S. Mill, quoted in Majeed, *Ungoverned Imaginings,* 135.

39   James Mill, *The History of British India,* vol. 1 (London: Baldwin, Cradock and Joy, 1817), x, xv, 429. Emphasis in original. See also Karuna Mantena, *Alibis of Empire: Henry Maine and the Ends of Liberal Imperialism* (Princeton, NJ: Princeton University Press, 2010), 26–27; Majeed, *Ungoverned Imaginings,* 135.

40   On Mill's break with previous modes of British historical discourse on India, see Theodore Koditschek, *Liberalism, Imperialism, and the Historical Imagination: Nineteenth-Century Visions of a Greater Britain* (Cambridge: Cambridge University Press, 2011), chap. 2.

41   James Mill, *History of British India,* abridged and with an introduction by William Thomas (Chicago, 1975), xxxiii, quoted in Catherine Hall, *Macaulay and Son: Architects of Imperial Britain* (New Haven, CT: Yale University Press, 2012), 208.

42   Mantena, *Alibis of Empire,* 29.

43   Majeed, *Ungoverned Imaginings,* 128.

44   See also T. Metcalf, *Ideologies of the Raj,* 30–31.

45   Jon Wilson, *The Chaos of Empire: The British Raj and the Conquest of India* (New York: Public Affairs, 2016), 205.

46   Koditschek, *Liberalism, Imperialism, and the Historical Imagination,* 87.

47   See also T. Metcalf, *Ideologies of the Raj,* 94.

48   Thomas Babington Macaulay, "Minute of 2nd February 1835 on Indian Education," in *Macaulay, Prose and Poetry,* selected by G. M. Young (Cambridge, MA: Harvard University Press, 1957), 721–724, 729, in Internet Modern History Sourcebook, Fordham University, https://sourcebooks.fordham.edu/mod/1833 macaulay-india.asp.

49   Koditschek, *Liberalism, Imperialism, and the Historical Imagination,* 113.

50   Majeed, *Ungoverned Imaginings,* 192.

51   Jon Wilson, *Chaos of Empire,* 214.

52   Hall, *Macaulay and Son,* 321–322, 331–332.

53   For an excellent description of the work, see Hall, *Macaulay and Son,* 276–278.

54   Koditschek, *Liberalism, Imperialism, and the Historical Imagination,* 134–138. On Macaulay's formation, see Hall, *Macaulay and Son.*

55   Dirks, *Scandal of Empire,* 323, 325.

56   Macaulay, "Warren Hastings," October 1841, quoted in Hall, *Macaulay and Son,* 248.

57   Thomas Babington Macaulay, *The History of England from the Accession of James the Second,* vol. 4 (Leipzig: Bernhard Tauchnitz, 1855), 239.

58   See also Catherine Hall's discussion of Hayden White here in *Macaulay and Son,* 289.

59   Hall, *Macaulay and Son,* 290.

60   As Catherine Hall notes, few women dared to write within the formal model of history. *Macaulay and Son,* 269, 298. One recalls the unfortunate reviews of the fictional Lady Carbury's *Criminal Queens* in Anthony Trollope's *The Way We Live Now* (orig. 1875; repr., London: Oxford University Press, 1941).

61   Thomas Carlyle, *The French Revolution: A History,* 3 vols. (London: James Fraser, 1837).

62   Thomas Carlyle, *On Heroes, Hero-Worship, and the Heroic in History,* ed. George Wherry (orig. 1841; repr., Cambridge: Cambridge University Press, 1911), 1, 2, 14, 79, 147, 158.

63   Thomas Carlyle, "Occasional Discourse on the Negro Question," *Fraser's Magazine for Town and Country* 15 (1849): 670–679.

64   J. S. Mill, *Considerations on Representative Government* (orig. 1861; repr., London: Longmans, Green, 1919), 141.

65   J. S. Mill, *On Liberty* (orig. 1959; repr., New York: Henry Holt, 1879), 116–120.

66   See also Collini, *Public Moralists*, 110, 133–134.

67   J. S. Mill, *On Liberty*, 24–25. See Koditschek, *Liberalism, Imperialism, and the Historical Imagination*, 61–63. T. Metcalf, *Ideologies of the Raj*, 31–32.

68   J. S. Mill, "Civilization," in *Dissertations and Discussions* (orig. 1836; repr., London: Routledge, 1910), 134; Mantena, *Alibis of Empire*, 33.

69   On British profits from India, see Chapter 6. See also Dirks, *Scandal of Empire*, chap. 4; Sven Beckert, *Empire of Cotton: A New History of Global Capitalism* (New York: Knopf, 2014).

70   Gregory Claeys, *Imperial Sceptics: British Critics of Empire, 1850–1920* (Cambridge: Cambridge University Press, 2010), 49–52.

71   See Meredith Martin, "'Imperfectly Civilized': Ballads, Nations, and Histories of Form," *Arcade*, May 18, 2018, https://arcade.stanford.edu/content/imperfectly -civilized-ballads-nations-and-histories-form-1.

72   See Claeys, *Imperial Sceptics*, 28–36.

73   On Whig historiography's fit in its cultural context, see John Burrow, *A Liberal Descent: Victorian Historians and the English Past* (Cambridge: Cambridge University Press, 1981).

74   Quoted in Mehta, *Liberalism and Empire*, 13.

75   Mehta, *Liberalism and Empire*, 45.

76   M. Shelley, *Frankenstein*, 210.

77   Charlotte Brontë [Currer Bell, pseud.], *Jane Eyre* (London: Smith, Elder, 1847).

78   Jon Wilson, *Chaos of Empire*, 174.

79   Priya Satia, "Guns and the British Empire," Aeon, February 14, 2018, aeon.co /essays/is-the-gun-the-basis-of-modern-anglo-civilisation.

80   Lauren Benton and Lisa Ford, *Rage for Order: The British Empire and the Origins of International Law, 1800–1850* (Cambridge, MA: Harvard University Press, 2016), 14. See also, for instance, James Epstein, *Scandal of Colonial Rule: Power and Subversion in the British Atlantic during the Age of Revolution* (Cambridge: Cambridge University Press, 2012).

81   E. P. Thompson, *The Making of the English Working Class* (orig. 1963; repr., New York: Vintage, 1966), 710.

82   Antoinette Burton, *The Trouble with Empire: Challenges to Modern British Imperialism* (New York: Oxford University Press, 2015), 63; Gott, *Britain's Empire*.

83   Mark Doyle, *Communal Violence in the British Empire: Disturbing the Pax* (London: Bloomsbury, 2016), 2.

84   See the forthcoming work of Matthew Wormer on how the opium trade fit into the liberal myth of empire.

85   Caitlyn Lundberg, "From Defeat to Glory: The First Anglo-Afghan War and the Construction of the Victorian Military Machine, 1837–1851" (PhD diss., Stanford University, 2016), chap. 2.

86   John William Kaye, *History of the War in Afghanistan*, 2 vols. (London: Richard Bentley, 1851).

87   Lundberg, "From Defeat to Glory," 229, quoting Kaye, *History of the War in Afghanistan*, 1:195n.

88   Lundberg, "From Defeat to Glory," 234.

89   Review of *History of the War in Afghanistan*, in *The Calcutta Review* 30 (June 1, 1851), 424, quoted in Lundberg, "From Defeat to Glory," 235.

90   See G. J. Alder, "The 'Garbled' Blue Books of 1839: Myth or Reality?" *Historical Journal* 15:2 (1972): 229–259.

91   Frederick Gibbon, *The Lawrences of the Punjab* (London: J. M. Dent, 1908), 68–69. In 1909, the *Globe* also wrote of Auckland's "unfortunate mistake." See Lundberg, "From Defeat to Glory," 214.

92   Lundberg, "From Defeat to Glory," chap. 3.

93   Christopher Herbert, *War of No Pity: The Indian Mutiny and Victorian Trauma* (Princeton, NJ: Princeton University Press, 2008), 101, 106, 110–112.

94   Jon Wilson, *Chaos of Empire*, 5.

95   See also Crispin Bates, ed., *Mutiny at the Margins: New Perspectives on the Indian Uprising of 1857,* vol. 1, *Anticipations and Experiences in the Locality* (London: Sage, 2013).

96   William Pinch, "Micro-history, Macro-history, and 1857," lecture, Stanford University, April 4, 2016.

97   Faisal Devji, *Muslim Zion: Pakistan as a Political Idea* (London: Hurst, 2013), 132–133.

98   Mahmood Farooqui, *Besieged: Voices from Delhi 1857* (orig. 2010; repr., Gurgaon: Penguin, 2012), 255, 283, 285, 430–431.

99   Farooqui, *Besieged*, 95.

100 Maulvi Mohammed Baqar, *Delhi Urdu Akhbar*, June 14, 1857, in Farooqui, *Besieged*, 358–62, 366.

101 Farooqui, *Besieged*, 400–401.

102 Quoted in William Dalrymple, *The Last Mughal: The Fall of a Dynasty: Delhi, 1857* (orig. 2006; repr., New York: Vintage, 2008), 69.

103 Rakhshanda Jalil, *Liking Progress, Loving Change: A Literary History of the Progressive Writers' Movement in Urdu* (Delhi: Oxford University Press, 2014), 21–23.

104 On precolonial historical thought in South India, for instance, see Velcheru Narayana Rao, David Shulman, and Sanjay Subrahmanyam, *Textures of Time: Writing History in South India, 1600–1800* (Delhi: Permanent Black, 2001). See also Manan Ahmed Asif's forthcoming book *The Loss of Hindustan: Tarikh-i-Firishta and the Work of History* (Cambridge, MA: Harvard University Press, 2020).

105 See, for instance, William Dalrymple, *The Anarchy: The Relentless Rise of the East India Company* (New York: Bloomsbury, 2019). Eighteenth-century British Orientalist-historians relied on works such as Muhammad Casim Ferishta's *Tarikh-e-Ferishti* (translated by Alexander Dow in 1768 under the title *History of Hindostan*), which was written in Persian in the late sixteenth century.

106 Dalrymple, *The Anarchy,* 397.

107 S. Rahman, "'Delhi Renaissance': Intellectuals and the 1857 Uprising," *People's Democracy* 31:26 (July 2007), https://archives.peoplesdemocracy.in/2007/0701 /07012007_1857.htm. See also Gail Minault, "Master Ramchandra of Delhi College: Teacher, Journalist, and Cultural Intermediary," *Annual of Urdu Studies* 18 (2003): 95–104.

108 Baqar, *Delhi Urdu Akhbar,* June 21, 1857, in Farooqui, *Besieged,* 373; *Delhi Urdu Akhbar,* July 5, 1857, in *Besieged,* 383.

109 Farooqui, *Besieged*, 5.

110 Baqar, *Delhi Urdu Akhbar,* June 21, 1857, in Farooqui, *Besieged,* 370.

111 Baqar, *Delhi Urdu Akhbar,* June 21, 1857, in Farooqui, *Besieged,* 368.

112 Farooqui, *Besieged*, 401.

113 Farooqui, *Besieged*, 427.

114 Baqar, *Delhi Urdu Akhbar,* July 5, 1857, in Farooqui, *Besieged,* 377.

115 Baqar, *Delhi Urdu Akhbar,* July 5, 1857, in Farooqui, *Besieged,* 380.

116 Farooqui, *Besieged,* 7, 404.

117 Baqar, *Delhi Urdu Akhbar,* July 5, 1857, in Farooqui, *Besieged,* 377.

118 Said, quoted in Ned Curthoys and Debjani Ganguly, *Edward Said: The Legacy of a Public Intellectual* (Melbourne: Melbourne University Publishing, 2007), 199n34. This exercise in understanding Persian poetry and Islam fed Goethe's ideas about *Weltliteratur,* "the study of all the literatures of the world as a symphonic whole which could be apprehended theoretically as having preserved the individuality of each work without losing sight of the whole." Edward Said, "A Window on the World," *Guardian,* August 1, 2003. As Ahmed (*Archaeology of Babel,* chap. 1) notes, Said's (and Goethe's) privileging of the court poet Hafez is a thoroughly imperial legacy, entailing marginalization of other, non- or extra-textual poetic discourses.

119 Mir Taqi Mir, "*Faqirana aae sada kar chale,*" available at Rekhta, https://rekhta .org/ghazals/faqiiraana-aae-sadaa-kar-chale-meer-taqi-meer-ghazals; Momin Khan Momin, "*Asar us ko zara nahin hota,*" available at Rekhta, https://rekhta .org/ghazals/asar-us-ko-zaraa-nahiin-hotaa-momin-khan-momin-ghazals.

120 Faisal Devji, *The Impossible Indian: Gandhi and the Temptation of Violence* (Cambridge, MA: Harvard University Press, 2012), 20–21.

121 See, for instance, Francis Joseph Steingass, *A Comprehensive Persian-English Dictionary, Including the Arabic Words and Phrases to Be Met with in Persian Literature* (London: Routledge and K. Paul, 1892). Indian loyalists to the British also used the word in that way, for example, Zahir Dehlvi's *Dastan-e-Ghadar* (1897).

122 Farooqui, *Besieged,* 10, 394, 428–430.

123 Karl Marx, "The Indian Bill," *New-York Daily Tribune,* July 24, 1858, in Karl Marx and Friedrich Engels, articles in the *New-York Daily Tribune,* Marxists Internet Archive, https://www.marxists.org/archive/marx/works/subject/newspapers /new-york-tribune.htm.

124 Quoted in Jon Wilson, *Chaos of Empire,* 258.

125 Macaulay, journal entry, October 1857, quoted in Hall, *Macaulay and Son,* 326–327.

126 See also Burton, *Trouble with Empire,* 58–68.

127 Herbert, *War of No Pity,* 40–41, 53, 203.

128 Lundberg, "From Defeat to Glory," 250.

129 Friedrich Engels, *The Condition of the Working Class in England* (orig. German 1845; trans. New York, 1887).

130 Karl Marx and Friedrich Engels, *The Communist Manifesto* (orig. 1848; trans. 1888; repr., New York: Bantam, 1992), 24. See also Marshall Berman, *All That Is Solid Melts into Air: The Experience of Modernity* (London: Verso, 1983), and Berman, "Tearing Away the Veils: The *Communist Manifesto,*" *Dissent,* May 6, 2011, https://www.dissentmagazine.org/online_articles/tearing-away-the-veils -the-communist-manifesto.

131 See Burrow, *Liberal Descent.*

132 See also John Gallagher and Ronald Robinson, "The Imperialism of Free Trade," *The Economic History Review* 6:1 (1953): 1–15; Mike Davis, *Late Victorian Holocausts: El Niño Famines and the Making of the Third World* (London: Verso, 2001), 295.

133 Karl Marx, "The Future Results of British Rule in India," *New-York Daily Tribune,* August 8, 1853. My italics. See also Said, *Orientalism,* 153–156.

134 Karl Marx, "The British Rule in India," *New-York Daily Tribune*, June 25, 1853.

135 See, for instance, Karl Marx, "Indian News," *New-York Daily Tribune*, Aug. 14, 1857; Karl Marx, "The Indian Revolt," *New-York Herald Tribune*, Sept. 16, 1857. The orientalist motifs on the whole seem more evident in Engels's columns than in Marx's.

136 Karl Marx, "The Revolt in the Indian Army," *New-York Daily Tribune*, July 15, 1857.

137 Karl Marx, "Investigation of Tortures in India" *New-York Daily Tribune*, Sept. 17, 1857.

138 Marx, "The Indian Revolt," *New-York Daily Tribune*, Sept. 16, 1857.

139 Karl Marx, "British Incomes in India," *New-York Daily Tribune*, Sept. 21, 1857.

140 Friedrich Engels, "The Capture of Delhi," *New-York Daily Tribune*, Dec. 5, 1857.

141 Friedrich Engels, "Details of the Attack on Lucknow," *New-York Daily Tribune*, May 25, 1858.

142 Congreve, 1859, quoted in Claeys, *Imperial Sceptics*, 61. Notably, Congreve's discipline, philosophy, offered access to other, nonhistorical modes of ethical thought.

143 Karl Marx, "The Annexation of Oude," *New-York Daily Tribune*, May 28, 1858.

144 Miles Taylor, *Ernest Jones, Chartism, and the Romance of Politics, 1819–1869* (Oxford: Oxford University Press, 2003), especially 34, 79, 99, 102, 254.

145 The poem was initially titled "The New World" and may have been written just when Jones was released from prison in 1850. It was first published in 1851 and then republished in August 1857, just as British suppression of the rebellion got under way. Taylor, *Ernest Jones*, 142–144, 183–184. For other dissenting British interpretations of the revolt, see Priyamvada Gopal, *Insurgent Empire: Anticolonial Resistance and British Dissent* (London: Verso, 2019), chap. 1.

146 See Gopal, *Insurgent Empire*, 60–66. As Gopal notes, the republication of "The New World" under a title referring to India just then was somewhat opportunistic (63). On Marx's and Jones's mutual influence, see 69–71.

147 See Hall, *Macaulay and Son*, 289–290, 326–327.

148 Marx, "The Indian Bill," *New-York Daily Tribune*, July 24, 1858.

149 J. S. Mill, "A Few Words on Non-Intervention," *Fraser's Magazine*, December 1859, reprinted in *Dissertations and Discussions*, vol. 3 (London: Longman's, Green, Reader, and Dyer, 1867), 173.

150 J. S. Mill, *Considerations on Representative Government*, 26.

151 John William Kaye, *A History of the Sepoy War in India*, vol. 1 (orig. 1864; repr., London: W. H. Allen, 1870), xii.

152 Kaye, *History of the Sepoy War*, 1:170, 177; Herbert, *War of No Pity*, 195–196. On the ambivalence of mutiny literature, see generally Herbert, *War of No Pity*.

153 John William Kaye, *A History of the Sepoy War*, vol. 3 (orig. 1880; repr., London: Longmans, Green, 1896), 427.

154 John William Kaye, *A History of the Sepoy War*, vol. 2 (London: W. H. Allen, 1870), 217.

155 Lundberg, "From Defeat to Glory," 247.

156 See also Lundberg, "From Defeat to Glory," 256–257.

157 Samuel Smiles, *Self-Help; with Illustrations of Character and Conduct* (London: John Murray, 1859), chap. 8.

158 See, for instance, Seema Alavi, *Muslim Cosmopolitanism in the Age of Empire* (Cambridge, MA: Harvard University Press, 2015).

159 Timothy Mitchell, *Rule of Experts: Egypt, Techno-Politics, Modernity* (Berkeley: University of California Press, 2002), 63–64.

160 Hall, *Macaulay and Son*, 334–335.

3. PROGRESS OF ELIMINATION

Epigraph: George Bernard Shaw, *The Man of Destiny: A Trifle* (orig. 1897; repr., London: Constable and Constable, 1914), 201.

1 Caitlyn Lundberg, "From Defeat to Glory: The First Anglo-Afghan War and the Construction of the Victorian Military Machine, 1837–1851" (PhD diss., Stanford University, 2016), 248–249.

2 This and the defeat in 1857 were key moments in the consolidation of martial race theory—the idea that men of the northwestern region of South Asia were natively martial (though martial did not necessarily imply honorable). See also Heather Streets, *Martial Races: The Military, Race and Masculinity in British Imperial Culture, 1857–1914* (Manchester: Manchester University Press, 2004), and Lundberg, "From Defeat to Glory," 249.

3 To be sure, the American rebels were also denigrated with racial language. See Dror Wahrman, *The Making of the Modern Self: Identity and Culture in Eighteenth-Century England* (New Haven, CT: Yale University Press, 2004), chap. 6.

4 Christopher Herbert, *War of No Pity: The Indian Mutiny and Victorian Trauma* (Princeton, NJ: Princeton University Press, 2008), 34.

5 John William Kaye, *A History of the Sepoy War*, vol. 3 (orig. 1880; repr., London: Longmans, Green, 1896), 649. My emphasis.

6 Quoted in Thomas Metcalf, *Ideologies of the Raj* (orig. 1995; repr., New York: Cambridge University Press, 1997), 45.

7 *Pace* Karuna Mantena, *Alibis of Empire: Henry Maine and the Ends of Liberal Imperialism* (Princeton, NJ: Princeton University Press, 2010), 11, 17, 22.

8 Mantena, *Alibis of Empire*, 12, 22.

9 Mantena, *Alibis of Empire*, 110, 154.

10 Stefan Collini, *Public Moralists: Political Thought and Intellectual Life in Britain, 1850–1930* (Oxford: Clarendon, 1991), 277.

11 Morley and Maine, quoted in Collini, *Public Moralists*, 279.

12 Henry Maine, "Prinsep's Punjab Theories," October 26, 1866, in *Minutes by Sir H. S. Maine, 1862–69* (Calcutta: Superintendent of Government Printing, 1892), 106. Emphasis in original.

13 Mantena, *Alibis of Empire*, 112.

14 Mantena, *Alibis of Empire*, 15.

15 Mantena, *Alibis of Empire*, 137.

16 Maine, "The Effects of Observation of India upon European Thought," the Rede Lecture of 1875, in *Village-Communities in the East and West* (London, 1876), 236–237, quoted in Mantena, *Alibis of Empire*, 148.

17 Maine, quoted in Mantena, *Alibis of Empire*, 138.

18 Mantena, *Alibis of Empire*, 138–139.

19 Maine, *Village-Communities in the East and West*, quoted in Mantena, *Alibis of Empire*, 144.

20 Mantena, *Alibis of Empire*, 149, 163, 165.

21 Mantena, *Alibis of Empire*, 146.

22 Priyamvada Gopal, *Insurgent Empire: Anticolonial Resistance and British Dissent* (London: Verso, 2019), 106.

23 Which Gordon insistently denied. Antoinette Burton, *The Trouble with Empire: Challenges to Modern British Imperialism* (New York: Oxford University Press, 2015), 155–156. I am less prepared to comment on Jamaican notions of agency

than Indian ones—though the pitfalls of emic observation are not necessarily fewer than those of etic knowledge—even despite the fact that English-speaking Jamaican voices were more accessible even to Britons then than those of Indians in 1857 (Gopal, *Insurgent Empire*, 87). As with all peasant insurgencies, motivations would have been mixed and articulate in varying degrees.

24   See also Jill Bender, *The 1857 Indian Uprising and the British Empire* (Cambridge: Cambridge University Press, 2016).

25   Eyre to Cardwell, October 20, 1865, *Parliamentary Papers: Papers Relating to the Disturbances in Jamaica*, Part I, Despatches from Governor Eyre (London: Harrison, 1866), 3, 7.

26   J. Bender, *The 1857 Indian Uprising*, chap. 5.

27   Quoted in Burton, *Trouble with Empire*, 154.

28   Catherine Hall, *Civilising Subjects: Metropole and Colony in the English Imagination, 1830–1867* (Oxford: Polity, 2002), 406; Burton, *Trouble with Empire*, 155–156.

29   *Birmingham Daily Post*, November 21, 1865, quoted in Hall, *Civilising Subjects*, 407.

30   J. S. Mill, "The Disturbances in Jamaica (2)," July 31, 1866, item 33 in *The Collected Works of John Stuart Mill*, vol. 28, *Public and Parliamentary Speeches Part I November 1850–November 1868*, ed. Bruce Kinzer and John Robson (Toronto: University of Toronto Press, 1988), https://oll.libertyfund.org/titles/mill-the-collected-works-of-john-stuart-mill-volume-xxviii-public-and-parliamentary-speeches-part-i?q.

31   Quoted in Peter Daniel, "The Governor Eyre Controversy," *New Blackfriars* 50:591 (August 1969): 576.

32   Quoted in J. Bender, *The 1857 Indian Uprising*, 157.

33   T. Metcalf, *Ideologies of the Raj*, 53.

34   Quoted in Theodore Koditschek, *Liberalism, Imperialism, and the Historical Imagination: Nineteenth-Century Visions of a Greater Britain* (Cambridge: Cambridge University Press, 2011), 166.

35   Herbert, *War of No Pity*, 234.

36   On these legal intricacies, see Peter Handford, "Edward John Eyre and the Conflict of Laws," *Melbourne University Law Review* 32 (2008): 822–860.

37   Jon Connolly, "'A Melancholy Example of Declension and Decay': Interpreting the Morant Bay Uprising," unpublished paper, 2011.

38   Diana Paton, "State Formation in Victorian Jamaica," in *Victorian Jamaica*, ed. Timothy Barringer and Wayne Modest (Durham, NC: Duke University Press, 2018), 131.

39   Some working-class activists did express solidarity with the Jamaican rebels. See Gopal, *Insurgent Empire*, 88.

40   John Ruskin, "The Jamaica Insurrection," *The Daily Telegraph*, Dec. 20, 1865, in *The Complete Works of John Ruskin*, vol. 18, *Arrows of the Chase* (Philadelphia: Reuwee, Wattley & Walsh, 1891), 226–227. Emphasis added.

41   Amitav Ghosh and Dipesh Chakrabarty, "A Correspondence on *Provincializing Europe*," *Radical History Review* 83 (2002): 148, 152.

42   On global reactions to the rebellion, see Crispin Bates and Marina Carter, eds., *Mutiny at the Margins: New Perspectives on the Indian Uprising of 1857*, vol. 3, *Global Perspectives* (London: Sage, 2013).

43   J. S. Mill to Dr. William Ireland, June 22, 1867, in *The Collected Works of John Stuart Mill*, vol. 16, *The Later Letters of John Stuart Mill, 1849–1873, Part III*, ed.

Francis Mineka and Dwight Lindley (Toronto: University of Toronto Press, 1972), 1282. See also generally Jimmy Klausen, "Violence and Epistemology: J. S. Mill's Indians after the 'Mutiny,'" *Political Research Quarterly* 69:1 (2016): 96–107.

44   J. S. Mill, "Petition concerning the Fenians," June 14, 1867, item 62, in *The Collected Works,* vol. 28.

45   William Gladstone, March 30, 1838, in M. R. D. Foot, ed., *The Gladstone Diaries,* vol. 2 (Oxford: Clarendon, 1968), 358. See also Gladstone, "Speech Delivered in the House of Commons on the Motion of Sir George Strickland," March 30, 1838 (London: J. Hatchard, 1838). I thank Emma Rothschild for these citations. See, generally, Roland Quinault, "Gladstone and Slavery," *The Historical Journal* 52:3 (2009): 363–383.

46   C. W. de Kiewiet, 1929, quoted in John Gallagher and Ronald Robinson, "The Imperialism of Free Trade," *The Economic History Review* 6:1 (1953): 3. For an interesting effort in 1930 to assemble all these facts into a consistent image of Gladstone as a "Christian statesman," see William Harbutt Dawson, "Gladstone as a Christian Statesman," *Contemporary Review* 137 (1930): 317–326.

47   See Gregory Claeys, *Imperial Sceptics: British Critics of Empire, 1850–1920* (Cambridge: Cambridge University Press, 2010), 35, on Bright's logic here.

48   Collini, *Public Moralists,* 217, 226.

49   J. R. Seeley, *The Expansion of England: Two Courses of Lectures* (London: Macmillan, 1883), 193, 208, 214, 251. See also Mantena, *Alibis of Empire,* 46–8. Mantena sees Seeley as severing empire from distinct moral aim. I disagree.

50   Seeley, *Expansion of England,* 8, 214, 255, 304–306.

51   In an interesting twist of fate, my first outing with the ideas in this book was a piece in the science magazine *Nature,* founded in 1869 with a name inspired by a line from Wordsworth and whose early publications included works by Spencer and other supporters of Darwinian theory. See Priya Satia, "What Guns Meant in Eighteenth-Century Britain," *Nature,* Palgrave Communications, September 10, 2019, www.nature.com/articles/s41599-019-0312-z.

52   Herbert Spencer, *The Principles of Biology,* vol. 1 (London: Williams and Norgate, 1864), 453.

53   Thomas McCarthy, *Race, Empire, and the Idea of Human Development* (Cambridge: Cambridge University Press, 2009), 78.

54   Priya Satia, *Empire of Guns: The Violent Making of the Industrial Revolution* (New York: Penguin, 2018), 380–381.

55   Koditschek, *Liberalism, Imperialism, and the Historical Imagination,* 14. Emphasis in original.

56   W. D. Hay, *Three Hundred Years Hence; or, A Voice from Posterity* (London: Newman, 1881), 249–250, in *British Future Fiction,* vol. 2, *New Worlds,* ed. I. F. Clarke (London: Pickering & Chatto, 2001).

57   T. Metcalf, *Ideologies of the Raj,* 200.

58   Seeley, *Expansion of England,* 50–51.

59   Cited in *Anti-Slavery Reporter,* Nov. 1, 1858, quoted in Hall, *Civilising Subjects,* 361.

60   Stephen, letter to the *Times* March 1, 1883, quoted in Uday Mehta, *Liberalism and Empire: A Study in Nineteenth-Century British Liberal Thought* (Chicago: University of Chicago Press, 1999), 196–197.

61   Mantena, *Alibis of Empire,* 42.

62   Stephen, quoted in Collini, *Public Moralists*, 284.

63   Jon Wilson, *The Chaos of Empire: The British Raj and the Conquest of India* (New York: Public Affairs, 2016), 310. See also Elizabeth Kolsky, *Colonial Justice in British India* (Cambridge: Cambridge University Press, 2010).

64   See Nasser Hussain, *The Jurisprudence of Emergency: Colonialism and the Rule of Law* (Ann Arbor: University of Michigan Press, 2003).

65   James Fitzjames Stephen, *The Story of Nuncomar and the Impeachment of Sir Elijah Impey*, 2 vols. (London: Macmillan, 1885).

66   See also T. Metcalf, *Ideologies of the Raj*, 210; Mantena, *Alibis of Empire*, 39–41, 45.

67   On the controversy, see Partha Chatterjee, *The Black Hole of Empire: History of a Global Practice of Power* (Princeton, NJ: Princeton University Press, 2012). The Nawab of Bengal, after militarily pushing back against the East India Company's refusal to cease construction of fortifications, held the remaining British and Indian company soldiers captive in the brig at Fort William, where the majority perished overnight in sweltering heat.

68   R. E. Holmes, *History of the Indian Mutiny* (1883), quoted in Herbert, *War of No Pity*, 204.

69   James Fitzjames Stephen, *Liberty, Equality, Fraternity* (orig. 1872; repr., New York: Holt and Williams, 1873), 331.

70   See Paul Strohm, *Conscience: A Very Short Introduction* (Oxford: Oxford University Press, 2011), 64–67.

71   Friedrich Nietzsche, "On the Use and Abuse of History for Life," trans. Ian Johnston, originally published in *Untimely Meditations* (1874; repr. 2010), http://johnstoi.web.viu.ca//nietzsche/history.htm.

72   John Morley, *On Compromise* (orig. 1874; repr., London: Macmillan, 1888), 28.

73   Baron Acton to Mandell Creighton, April 1887, in *Appendix of "Historical Essays and Studies by . . . First Baron Acton,"* ed. J. N. Figgis and R. V. Laurence (London: Macmillan, 1907), 504–505.

74   John Acton, *The Rambler*, March 1862, in *The History of Freedom and Other Essays by . . . First Baron Acton*, ed. J. N. Figgis and R. V. Laurence (London: Macmillan, 1907), 240, 242.

75   Quoted in Mike Davis, *Late Victorian Holocausts: El Niño Famines and the Making of the Third World* (London: Verso, 2001), 32.

76   Jon Wilson, *Chaos of Empire*, 318.

77   Davis, *Late Victorian Holocausts*, 6–9, 12. See also Sunil Amrith, *Unruly Waters: How Rains, Rivers, Coasts, and Seas Have Shaped Asia's History* (New York: Basic, 2018).

78   Davis, *Late Victorian Holocausts*, 32, 58.

79   See Satia, *Empire of Guns*; Satia, "Guns and the British Empire," Aeon, February 14, 2018, aeon.co/essays/is-the-gun-the-basis-of-modern-anglo-civilisation.

80   Aidan Forth, *Barbed-Wire Imperialism: Britain's Empire of Camps* (Oakland: University of California Press, 2017).

81   Nicholas Dirks, *The Scandal of Empire: India and the Creation of Imperial Britain* (Cambridge, MA: Harvard University Press, 2008), 308.

82   T. Metcalf, *Ideologies of the Raj*, 123–125.

83   See also John Ellis, *The Social History of the Machine Gun* (orig. 1975; repr., Baltimore: Johns Hopkins University Press, 1986).

84   Robert Routledge, *Discoveries and Inventions of the Nineteenth Century* (orig. 1876; repr., London: Routledge, 1903), 170.

85   Clive Ponting, *Churchill* (London: Sinclair-Stevenson, 1994), 100–105.

86   Winston Churchill, interview with Gustavus Ohlinger, "WSC: A Midnight Interview, 1902," *Michigan Quarterly Review,* February 1966, reprinted in *Finest Hour* 159 (Summer 2013), winstonchurchill.org/publications/finest-hour/finest-hour-159/wsc-a-midnight-interview-1902/.

87   Churchill, addressing the Peel Commission in 1937, quoted in Samar Attar, *Debunking the Myths of Colonization: The Arabs and Europe* (Lanham, MD: University Press of America, 2010), 9.

88   As recorded by Leo Amery, quoted in Madhusree Mukerjee, *Churchill's Secret War: The British Empire and the Ravaging of India during World War II* (orig. 2010; repr., New York: Basic, 2011), 205.

89   James Vernon, *Hunger: A Modern History* (Cambridge, MA: Harvard University Press, 2007).

90   Quoted in Davis, *Late Victorian Holocausts,* 58.

91   Quoted in Davis, *Late Victorian Holocausts,* 58.

92   Quoted in Davis, *Late Victorian Holocausts,* 8.

93   Alfred Russel Wallace, *The Wonderful Century: Its Successes and Its Failures* (New York: Dodd, Mead, 1898), 338–340. See also Wilfrid Blunt's grim appraisal, "The Shame of the Nineteenth Century," quoted in Gopal, *Insurgent Empire,* 164, 341, 342.

94   A critical exception is Davis, *Late Victorian Holocausts.*

95   On British socialist and anti-imperialist thought in this period, see, for instance, Claeys, *Imperial Sceptics;* A. P. Thornton, *The Imperial Idea and Its Enemies: A Study in British Power* (orig. 1959; repr., New York: Anchor, 1968); Gopal, *Insurgent Empire.*

96   Quoted in Claeys, *Imperial Sceptics,* 238; see also, generally, 249–253.

97   Collini, *Public Moralists,* 276.

98   Davis, *Late Victorian Holocausts,* 59.

99   Shaw, *Man of Destiny,* 201.

100   See Forth, *Barbed-Wire Imperialism.* The camp embodied the tension between the imperial promise of freedom and uplift and the imperial impulse to discipline and control movement.

101   See Derek Sayer, "British Reaction to the Amritsar Massacre 1919–1920," *Past & Present* 131:1 (1991): 130–164; Kim Wagner, *Amritsar 1919: An Empire of Fear and the Making of a Massacre* (New Haven, CT: Yale University Press, 2019); Wagner, "'Calculated to Strike Terror': The Amritsar Massacre and the Spectacle of Colonial Violence," *Past & Present* 233:1 (2016): 185–225.

102   Churchill [speech in the Commons, July 8, 1920], quoted in Sayer, "British Reaction to the Amritsar Massacre," 131.

103   Quoted in Ferdinand Mount, "They Would Have Laughed," *London Review of Books* 41:7 (April 4, 2019): 9–12.

104   Jeffrey Auerbach, *Imperial Boredom: Monotony and the British Empire* (New York: Oxford University Press, 2018), introduction and chap. 3.

105   See also, generally, Graham Dawson, *Soldier Heroes: British Adventure, Empire, and the Imagining of Masculinity* (London: Routledge, 1994).

106   Max Weber, *The Protestant Ethic and the Spirit of Capitalism,* trans. Talcott Parsons (orig. 1904; trans. 1930; repr., London: Unwin University Books, 1965), 181.

107   Max Weber, "Science as a Vocation," 1917, in H. H. Gerth and C. Wright Mills, eds. and trans., *From Max Weber: Essays in Sociology* (orig. 1946; repr., New York: Oxford University Press, 1958), 155.

108 Sung Ho Kim, "Max Weber," in *The Stanford Encyclopedia of Philosophy*, winter 2017 ed., ed. Edward Zalta, section 4.3, "Modernity *contra* Modernization," https://plato.stanford.edu/archives/win2017/entries/weber/.

109 Max Weber, "Parliament and Government in Germany under a New Political Order," 1918, in *Weber: Political Writings*, trans. and ed. Peter Lassman and Ronald Speirs (Cambridge: Cambridge University Press, 1994), 159.

110 Elleke Boehmer, quoted in Helen Carr, "Imagism and Empire," in *Modernism and Empire*, ed. Howard J. Booth and Nigel Rigby (Manchester: Manchester University Press, 2000), 80.

111 Stephen Kern, *The Culture of Time and Space, 1880–1918* (Cambridge, MA: Harvard University Press, 1983), 38.

112 For the story of the standardization of time, see Vanessa Ogle, *The Global Transformation of Time: 1870–1950* (Cambridge, MA: Harvard University Press, 2015).

113 Benedict Anderson, *Imagined Communities: Reflections on the Origin and Spread of Nationalism* (London: Verso, 1983)—borrowing Benjamin's concept of "homogenous empty time."

114 William Morris, *News from Nowhere, or An Epoch of Rest, Being Some Chapters from a Utopian Romance* (orig. 1890; repr., London: Longmans, Green, 1905).

115 On Blatchford, see Claeys, *Imperial Sceptics*, 172–180.

116 Quoted in Claeys, *Imperial Sceptics*, 174.

117 On the contested sovereignty of these states, see the forthcoming dissertation of Madihah Akhter.

118 See also T. Metcalf, *Ideologies of the Raj*, 63, 75, 91.

119 Fredrick Lugard, *The Dual Mandate in British Tropical Africa* (London: William Blackwood, 1922).

120 Claeys, *Imperial Sceptics*, 201.

121 *Pace* Mantena, *Alibis of Empire*, 55.

122 Mantena, *Alibis of Empire*, 74–75, 150, 156. See, generally, Nicholas Dirks, *Castes of Mind: Colonialism and the Making of Modern India* (Princeton, NJ: Princeton University Press, 2001).

123 Joseph Conrad, *The Heart of Darkness* (orig. serial 1899; orig. book 1902; repr., New York: Dover, 1990), 22, 45–46, 68.

124 Edward Said, *Culture and Imperialism* (orig. 1993; repr., New York: Vintage, 1994), 25.

4. THE REDEMPTION OF PROGRESS

Epigraph: T. E. Lawrence, *The Seven Pillars of Wisdom: A Triumph* (orig. 1926; repr., New York: Anchor, 1991), 24.

1 Samuel Lloyd, *The Lloyds of Birmingham*, 2nd ed. (Birmingham: Cornish Brothers, 1907), 120–129. On views of war in this time, see I. F. Clarke, *Voices Prophesying War: Future Wars 1763–3749* (orig. 1966; repr., Oxford: Oxford University Press, 1992).

2 "The Will to Believe" was the title of an 1896 lecture by the American philosopher William James.

3 Alex Owen, *The Place of Enchantment: British Occultism and the Culture of the Modern* (Chicago: University of Chicago Press, 2004), 22.

4 Thomas Laqueur, "The Past's Past," *London Review of Books* 18:18 (September 19, 1996): 3–7. On the relationship between spiritualism and traditional Christianity in this period, see the forthcoming dissertation of Murphy Temple.

5   See Judith Walkowitz, *City of Dreadful Delight: Narratives of Sexual Danger in Late-Victorian London* (Chicago: University of Chicago Press, 1992).

6   Lytton Strachey, *Eminent Victorians* (New York: Garden City, 1918).

7   See also Eitan Bar-Yosef, "The Last Crusade? British Propaganda and the Palestine Campaign, 1917–18," *Journal of Contemporary History* 36 (2001): 87–109.

8   Lawrence, *Seven Pillars of Wisdom*, 23.

9   Priya Satia, *Spies in Arabia: The Great War and the Cultural Foundations of Britain's Covert Empire in the Middle East* (New York: Oxford University Press, 2008), chaps. 4, 5.

10   See Joanna Bourke, *An Intimate History of Killing: Face-to-Face Killing in Twentieth-Century Warfare* (London: Granta, 1999).

11   Lawrence, *Seven Pillars of Wisdom*, 31, 181–182, 633.

12   See literature cited throughout Satia, *Spies in Arabia*.

13   Lawrence, *Seven Pillars of Wisdom*, 25.

14   Vernon, CID to S/S CO, 25 June 1925, The National Archives: CO 727/11. See also Satia, *Spies in Arabia*, 319–321.

15   See Benedict Anderson, *Under Three Flags: Anarchism and the Anti-colonial Imagination* (London: Verso, 2006); Ilham Khuri-Makdisi, *The Eastern Mediterranean and the Making of Global Radicalism, 1860–1914* (Berkeley: University of California Press, 2010).

16   I am also working on a book-length exploration of the network of the "global Left" across time and space.

17   Johan Mathew, *Margins of the Market: Trafficking and Capitalism across the Arabian Sea* (Oakland: University of California Press, 2016), 83, 93, 96. On this arms trade, see also Seema Alavi, *Muslim Cosmopolitanism in the Age of Empire* (Cambridge, MA: Harvard University Press, 2015), 74–84.

18   Winston Churchill, *The Story of the Malakand Field Force, an Episode of Frontier War* (New York: Longmans, 1898), 5.

19   J. G. Lorimer, *Gazetteer of the Persian Gulf, Oman, and Central Arabia*, vol. 1, *Historical*, pt. 2 (orig. 1915; repr., Calcutta: Superintendent Government Printing, 1970), 2586–2587.

20   Mathew, *Margins of the Market*, 91, 96, 110.

21   Satia, *Spies in Arabia*, chap. 1, 34–36.

22   Mead, *Fragments of a Faith Forgotten* (1912), quoted in Demetres Tryphonopoulos, "History of the Occult Movement," in *Literary Modernism and the Occult Tradition*, ed. Leon Surette and Demetres Tryphonopoulos (Orono: The National Poetry Foundation, University of Maine, 1996), 23.

23   Douglas Carruthers, *Arabian Adventure: To the Great Nafud in Quest of the Oryx* (London: H. F. & G. Witherby, 1935), 68. See Satia, *Spies in Arabia*, chaps. 2, 3.

24   David Hogarth, review of *Amurath to Amurath*, by Gertrude Bell, *Geographical Journal* 37 (1911): 435.

25   G. Wyman Bury [Abdulla Mansur, pseud.], *The Land of Uz* (London: Macmillan, 1911), xxi.

26   Gertrude Bell, *Amurath to Amurath* (New York: Dutton, 1911).

27   Mark Sykes, *The Caliph's Last Heritage: A Short History of the Turkish Empire* (London: Macmillan, 1915), 5, 118.

28   On Blunt's anticolonialism, see Priyamvada Gopal, *Insurgent Empire: Anticolonial Resistance and British Dissent* (London: Verso, 2019), chap. 3.

29   David Hogarth, "Problems in Exploration I. Western Asia," *Geographical Journal* 32 (1908): 549–550.

30 Satia, *Spies in Arabia,* chap. 2.

31 Ferdinand Tuohy, *The Secret Corps: A Tale of "Intelligence" on All Fronts* (London: John Murray, 1920), 172.

32 Meredith Townsend, *Asia and Europe: Studies Presenting the Conclusions Formed by the Author in a Long Life Devoted to the Subject . . .* (orig. 1901; repr., New York: G. P. Putnam's, 1904), 305–307. On the influence of this book's "prophetic pages," see John Strachey, *The Adventure of Living: A Subjective Autobiography* (New York: G. P. Putnam's, 1922), 231.

33 Mark Sykes, *Dar-ul-Islam; A Record of a Journey through Ten of the Asiatic Provinces of Turkey* (London: Bickers & Son, 1904), 12, 12n.

34 Sykes, *Caliph's Last Heritage,* 303.

35 Sykes, *Dar-ul-Islam,* 219.

36 Louisa Jebb, *By Desert Ways to Baghdad* (Boston: Dana, Estes, 1909), 264–265.

37 Satia, *Spies in Arabia,* chap. 3.

38 Sykes, *Caliph's Last Heritage,* 57.

39 Townsend, *Asia and Europe,* 305–306.

40 David Hogarth, *A Wandering Scholar in the Levant,* 2nd ed. (London: J. Murray, 1896), 1–2.

41 Satia, *Spies in Arabia,* 130–131, 134.

42 Townsend, *Asia and Europe,* 167.

43 Jebb, *By Desert Ways,* 16–17.

44 Bell to Valentine Chirol, April 5, 1914, quoted in Elizabeth Burgoyne, *Gertrude Bell: From Her Personal Papers,* 2 vols. (London: E. Benn, 1958–1961), 1:304.

45 Frederic Lees, introduction to Philip Baldensperger, *The Immovable East: Studies of the People and Customs of Palestine* (Boston: Small, Maynard, 1913), vii. The actual Arab intellectual and scientific traditions of this period are, alas, beyond the scope of this book.

46 N. N. E. Bray, *Shifting Sands* (London: Unicorn, 1934), 14.

47 Lord George Gordon Byron, *The Corsair: A Tale* (London: John Murray, 1914); Byron, *The Siege of Corinth: A Poem* (London: John Murray, 1816).

48 N. N. E. Bray, *A Paladin of Arabia: The Biography of Brevet Lieut.-Colonel G. E. Leachman . . .* (London: Unicorn, 1936), 190.

49 Satia, *Spies in Arabia,* chap. 4.

50 Mead, "The Rising Psychic Tide," *Quest* 3 (1911–12), 420, quoted in Tryphonopoulos, "History of the Occult Movement," 22.

51 "A fellow officer," obituary for Leachman, *Daily Telegraph,* August 21, 1920.

52 Satia, *Spies in Arabia,* chap. 4.

53 Reginald Savory, quoted in Satia, *Spies in Arabia,* 168.

54 Eleanor Franklin Egan, *The War in the Cradle of the World: Mesopotamia* (New York: Harper, 1918), 74.

55 Satia, *Spies in Arabia,* 80, 144–145.

56 A. F. Wavell, *Allenby: Soldier and Statesman* (London: George G. Harrap, 1944), 162.

57 T. E. Lawrence, "Military Notes," *Arab Bulletin* 32 (Nov. 1916), 480, Princeton University: Firestone Library: Arab Bureau Papers: FO 882. See also T. E. Lawrence, "Twenty-Seven Articles," *Arab Bulletin* 60 (Aug. 1917), article 22.

58 T. E. Lawrence, "Evolution of a Revolt," *Army Quarterly,* Oct. 1920, reprinted in *Oriental Assembly,* ed. A. W. Lawrence (London: Williams & Norgate, 1939), 112–115.

59 T. E. Lawrence to Vyvyan Richards, July 15, 1918, in *The Letters of T. E. Lawrence,* ed. David Garnett (London: Jonathan Cape, 1938), 244.

60   Lawrence, "Twenty-Seven Articles," articles 20 and 22; Harold Dickson, 1916, quoted in Satia, *Spies in Arabia*, 140.

61   Harold Dickson and Edmund Dane, quoted in Satia, *Spies in Arabia*, 146. See, generally, *Spies in Arabia*, 145–149.

62   Lawrence, Report on Intelligence of IEF "D," May 1916, in Jeremy Wilson, *Lawrence of Arabia: The Authorised Biography of T. E. Lawrence*, appendix 3 (London: Heinemann, 1989), 949–952.

63   Ferdinand Tuohy, *The Crater of Mars* (London: William Heinemann, 1929), 173.

64   Harold Dickson, 1916, quoted in Satia, *Spies in Arabia*, 141.

65   Lawrence, "Evolution of a Revolt," 128–129.

66   Harold Dickson, letter, Feb. 7, 1915, quoted in Satia, *Spies in Arabia*, 158.

67   Air Staff, "On the Power of the Air Force and the Application of that Power to Hold and Police Mesopotamia," March 1920, The National Archives: AIR 1/426/15/260/3. For more on British airpower in the Middle East, see Satia, *Spies in Arabia*, chaps. 4, 7.

68   Satia, *Spies in Arabia*, 159–160.

69   Geoffrey Salmond to General, n.d. (36 hours after the battle), The National Archives: AIR 1/725/115/1.

70   Lionel Evelyn Charlton, *Deeds That Held the Empire, by Air* (London: J. Murray, 1940), 82–88.

71   Group Captain Amyas Borton, "The Use of Aircraft in Small Wars," February 25, 1920, *Journal of the Royal United Services Institute* 65 (1920): 310–319; Leith-Ross, "The Tactical Side of I(a)," n.d., 8–9, National Army Museum: ARC 1983-12-69-10 ; J. E. Tennant, *In the Clouds above Baghdad, Being the Records of an Air Commander* (London: Cecil Palmer, 1920), 163.

72   H. Birch Reynardson, *Mesopotamia, 1914–15: Extracts from a Regimental Officer's Diary* (London: Andrew Melrose, 1919), 272; A. J. Barker, *The Bastard War: The Mesopotamian Campaign of 1914–1918* (New York: Dial, 1967), 42.

73   See the forthcoming dissertation of Murphy Temple.

74   Major quoted in Martin Swayne, *In Mesopotamia* (London: Hodder & Stoughton, 1917), 166.

75   Review of *By Tigris and Euphrates*, by E. S. Stevens, *Times*, December 14, 1923, 8.

76   Edwyn Bevan, *The Land of Two Rivers* (London: E. Arnold, 1918), 112.

77   Conrad Cato, *The Navy in Mesopotamia* (London: Constable, 1917), 117.

78   A. G. Wauchope, "The Battle That Won Samarrah," chap. 8 in *With a Highland Regiment in Mesopotamia: 1916–1917*, by One of Its Officers (Bombay: Times Press, 1918), 85.

79   Sykes, 1917, quoted in Satia, *Spies in Arabia*, 176.

80   Richard Coke, *The Arab's Place in the Sun* (London: Thornton Butterworth, 1929), 13, 305–307.

81   Mann to his mother, January 25, 1920, in [Mann, James Saumarez], *An Administrator in the Making: James Saumarez Mann, 1893–1920*, edited by his father [James Saumarez Mann Sr] (London: Longmans, Green, 1921), 206. See also Satia, *Spies in Arabia*, 178–179.

82   Satia, *Spies in Arabia*, chaps. 5, 9.

83   Herbert Baker, in A. W. Lawrence, ed., *Lawrence by His Friends* (orig. 1937; abridged ed., London: Jonathan Cape, 1954), 205.

84   Basil Henry Liddell Hart, *"T. E. Lawrence": In Arabia and After* (London: Jonathan Cape, 1934), 447 (last page).

85   Quoted in Satia, *Spies in Arabia*, 196.

86   Robert Graves, *Lawrence and the Arabs* (London: J. Cape, 1927), 57.

87   Sykes, 1917, quoted in Simon Ball, "Britain and the Decline of the International Control of Small Arms in the Twentieth Century," *Journal of Contemporary History* 47:4 (2012): 820–821.

88   Quoted in Ball, "Britain and the Decline of the International Control of Small Arms," 821.

89   Quoted in David Stone, "Imperialism and Sovereignty: The League of Nations' Drive to Control the Global Arms Trade," *Journal of Contemporary History* 35 (2000): 218. See also, generally, Priya Satia, *Empire of Guns: The Violent Making of the Industrial Revolution* (New York: Penguin, 2018), chap. 10.

90   Lawrence, quoted in Satia, *Spies in Arabia*, 301–302.

91   "The Risings in Mesopotamia," *Times*, August 7, 1920, 11.

92   Vita Sackville-West, *Passenger to Tehran* (London: Hogarth Press, 1926), 57–61.

93   See Satia, *Spies in Arabia*, chap. 7.

94   Lawrence to Liddell Hart, 1933, in *Letters of T. E. Lawrence*, 323.

95   Jeremy Wilson, *Lawrence of Arabia*, 1153.

96   Satia, *Spies in Arabia*, chap. 7.

97   Timothy Mitchell, *Rule of Experts: Egypt, Techno-Politics, Modernity* (Berkeley: University of California Press, 2002), 102–103, 108.

98   Quoted in Satia, *Spies in Arabia*, 245.

99   Air Staff, "On the Power of the Air Force and the Application of that Power to Hold and Police Mesopotamia," March 1920. It differed crucially from Bentham's panopticon in that there was no provision for public surveillance of the aerial inspectors.

100   Philby, 1919, quoted in Satia, *Spies in Arabia*, 245.

101   *Illustrated London News*, February 1, 1919, 149. The quotation alludes to Stephen Phillips's poem "Marpessa," first published in 1897. See also Priya Satia, "Developing Iraq: Britain, India and the Redemption of Empire and Technology in the First World War," *Past & Present* 197 (2007): 211–255.

102   Hubert Young, *The Independent Arab* (London: J. Murray, 1933), 338.

103   R. H. Peck, "Aircraft in Small Wars," *Journal of the Royal United Services Institute* 73:491 (1928): 541.

104   Captain R. J. Wilkinson, "The Geographical Importance of Iraq," *Journal of the Royal United Services Institute* 61:468 (1922): 665.

105   Quoted in Satia, *Spies in Arabia*, 253. The draft of the Air Staff's "Notes on the Method of Employment of the Air Arm in Iraq," presented to Parliament in August 1924, carried this sentence almost verbatim. Later drafts omitted it and stressed air control's humaneness.

106   Worthington-Evans, quoted in Satia, *Spies in Arabia*, 237.

107   Chairman [Lord Peel?] of the Central Asian Society, quoted in Satia, *Spies in Arabia*, 247.

108   Quoted in Satia, *Spies in Arabia*, 248.

109   John Glubb, *Story of the Arab Legion* (London: Hodder & Stoughton, 1948), 149; Glubb, *Arabian Adventures: Ten Years of Joyful Service* (London: Cassell, 1978), 148.

110   Glubb, *Story of the Arab Legion*, 161.

111   General Staff, "Notes on Modern Arab Warfare Based in the Fighting round Rumaithah and Diwaniyah, July–August 1920," appendix 9, in Aylmer Haldane, *The Insurrection in Mesopotamia, 1920* (Edinburgh: W. Blackwood, 1922), 333.

112 Wilson to the Chief of the General Staff, Mesopotamia, March 4, 1920, in Air Staff, Memo on effects likely to be produced by intensive aerial bombing of semi-civilised people, n.d., The National Archives: CO 730/18: 58212.

113 Trenchard, 1930, quoted in Satia, *Spies in Arabia,* 248.

114 Glubb, 1926, quoted in Satia, *Spies in Arabia,* 196.

115 Aylmer Haldane to Churchill, 1921, quoted in Satia, *Spies in Arabia,* 249; Lawrence, 1930, quoted in Satia, *Spies in Arabia,* 249.

116 J. M. Spaight, *Air Power and War Rights* (London: Longmans, Green, 1924), 23–24, 102–103.

117 Bell to her parents, March 16, 1922, quoted in Burgoyne, *Gertrude Bell,* 2:266.

118 F. H. Humphreys to Sir John Simon, December 15, 1932, The National Archives: AIR 8/94.

119 [Lawrence, June 1930], quoted in Basil Henry Liddell Hart, *The British Way in Warfare* (New York: Macmillan, 1933), 159.

120 Humphreys to Simon, December 15, 1932.

121 Spencer, quoted in Daniel Pick, *War Machine: The Rationalisation of Slaughter in the Modern Age* (New Haven, CT: Yale University Press, 1993), 77.

122 "The Royal Air Force," *Times,* July 2, 1927, 13.

123 Satia, *Spies in Arabia,* chap. 10.

124 Sir John Slessor, *The Central Blue: The Autobiography of Sir John Slessor* (New York: Praeger, 1957), 57.

125 John Glubb, *The Changing Scenes of Life: An Autobiography* (London: Quartet, 1983), 105; Philip Anthony Towle, *Pilots and Rebels: The Use of Aircraft in Unconventional Warfare 1918–1988* (London: Brassey's Defence Publishers, 1989), 54.

126 Satia, *Spies in Arabia,* 257.

127 Hubert Young to Shuckburgh, October 23, 1921, The National Archives: CO 730/16.

128 Robert Brooke-Popham, lecture, 1921, quoted in Satia, *Spies in Arabia,* 257; C. H. Keith, April 30, 1929, "Mosul," in *Flying Years* (Aviation Book Club ed., London: J. Hamilton, 1937), 240–241; Prudence Hill, *To Know the Sky: The Life of Air Chief Marshal Sir Roderic Hill* (London: W. Kimber, 1962), 96–97.

129 Bell, November 4, 1920, quoted in Burgoyne, *Gertrude Bell,* 2:181.

130 Percy Cox to Cabinet Committee on Iraq, February 1923, The National Archives: AIR 8/57.

131 Edwin Montagu, note on the causes of the outbreak in Mesopotamia, [c. August 25, 1920], The National Archives: FO 371/5229: 2719.

132 Churchill, 1920, quoted in Satia, *Spies in Arabia,* 225.

133 Valentine Chirol, "The Reawakening of the Orient," in *The Reawakening of the Orient and Other Addresses by Valentine Chirol, Yusuke Tsurumi, Sir James Arthur Salter* (New Haven, CT: Yale University Press, 1925), 6.

134 Satia, *Spies in Arabia,* chap. 6.

135 Lawrence, note, [September 20, 1919], The National Archives: FO 371/4236: 129405.

136 Toynbee, India Office memorandum, 1918, quoted in Satia, *Spies in Arabia,* 210.

137 Quoted in Arie Dubnov, "The Architect of Two Partitions or a Federalist Daydreamer? The Curious Case of Reginald Coupland," in *Partitions: A Transnational History of Twentieth-Century Territorial Separatism,* ed. Arie Dubnov and Laura Robson (Stanford, CA: Stanford University Press, 2019), 70.

138 See Satia, *Spies in Arabia*, 310–311.

139 Thomas Lyell, *Ins and Outs of Mesopotamia* (London: A. M. Philpot, 1923), 214.

140 "National Defence in the Air," *Times*, March 15, 1923, 13.

141 "Musings without Method," *Blackwood's* (September 1919), 434–437.

142 S/S to HC Mesopotamia, October 23, 1920, The National Archives: WO 106/200. See, generally, Satia, *Spies in Arabia*, 221–222.

143 Bell to her mother, November 16, 1920, quoted in Burgoyne, *Gertrude Bell*, 2:183.

144 See Satia, *Spies in Arabia*, 133, 290, 323 and chaps. 2, 5.

145 Anti-Semitic conspiracy theories like the infamous *Protocols of the Elders of Zion* were part of this culture. See Satia, *Spies in Arabia*, 312–313.

146 Arnold Toynbee, *A Study of History* [vol. 1] (London: Oxford University Press, 1934).

147 H. G. Wells, *The Open Conspiracy: Blue Prints for a World Revolution* (Garden City, NY: Doubleday, Doran, 1928), 198.

148 Hannah Arendt, *Imperialism: Part Two of "The Origins of Totalitarianism"* (orig. 1951; repr., New York: Houghton Mifflin, 1968), 100.

149 See, for instance, Gopal, *Insurgent Empire*, chap. 6.

150 See Satia, *Spies in Arabia*, chaps. 7, 10.

151 Commons debate, 1924, quoted in Satia, *Spies in Arabia*, 303.

152 See Satia, *Spies in Arabia*, 294.

153 George Orwell, "Politics and the English Language," 1945, in *George Orwell: Essays, Selected and Introduced by John Carey*, ed. Peter Davison (New York: Knopf, 2002), 963.

154 See Satia, *Spies in Arabia*, 299–304 passim.

155 Satia, *Spies in Arabia*, 296–298.

156 *Round Table*, December 1919, quoted in A. P. Thornton, *The Imperial Idea and Its Enemies: A Study in British Power* (orig. 1959; repr., New York: Anchor, 1968), 206.

157 "The Position in Mesopotamia," *Times*, September 6, 1920, 11.

158 George Orwell, *Burmese Days* (orig. 1934; repr., New York: Harcourt, 1962), 68–72. Flory's estranged love interest, Elizabeth, also shares a name with the love from whom the monster divides his double, Victor Frankenstein. On Orwell's thinking about empire, see also Orwell, "Shooting an Elephant," 1936, in Peter Davison, *George Orwell*, 42–49.

159 Satia, *Spies in Arabia*, 300.

160 Quoted in Union of Democratic Control, *The Secret International: Armament Firms at Work* (London: The Union of Democratic Control, 1932), 7n1.

161 Quoted in Union of Democratic Control, *Secret International*, 43–45.

162 *Report of the Royal Commission on the Private Manufacture of and Trading in Arms*, 1936, 29–31, 33, 65, *Parliamentary Papers*: Cmd. 5292.

163 Satia, *Spies in Arabia*, 324.

164 Churchill and James Masterton-Smith, quoted in Satia, *Spies in Arabia*, 230.

165 Quoted in Satia, *Spies in Arabia*, 231.

166 H. St. John B. Philby, preface, 1945, Riyadh, in *Arabian Days: An Autobiography* (London: R. Hale, 1948), xvi. Interestingly, two of the infamous Cambridge Five, the Soviet moles in British intelligence during the Cold War, were connected to this generation of contrarian spies in Arabia: Kim Philby was the son of St. John Philby, and Anthony Blunt was a cousin of Wilfrid Blunt's. Satia, *Spies in Arabia*, 334.

167 Graves, *Lawrence and the Arabs,* 54.

168 Jeremy Wilson, *Lawrence of Arabia,* 858.

169 Shaw to Lawrence, December 1, 1922, in *Letters to T. E. Lawrence,* ed. A. W. Lawrence (London: J. Cape, 1962), 161–163.

170 Quoted in Satia, *Spies in Arabia,* 321.

171 Quoted in Satia, *Spies in Arabia,* 320.

172 Major C. S. Jarvis, *Arab Command: The Biography of Lieutenant-Colonel F. G. Peake Pasha* (orig. 1942; repr., London: Hutchinson, 1946), 129.

173 See Satia, *Spies in Arabia,* 318–321.

174 Air Staff, Note on the Status of the RAF in Iraq when that country becomes a member of the League of Nations, September 7, 1929, The National Archives: AIR 2/830.

175 Air Policy with Regard to Iraq, n.d. [October–November 1929], The National Archives: AIR 2/830. On the limits on the league's ability to fulfill its idealistic ambitions of oversight, see Priya Satia, "Guarding *The Guardians:* Payoffs and Perils," *Humanity* 7:3 (Winter 2016): 481–498.

176 Satia, *Spies in Arabia,* 275–277.

177 Quoted in Satia, *Spies in Arabia,* 277, 278.

178 Peck, "Aircraft in Small Wars," 545.

179 This was explicitly stated in Air Marshal Sir J. M. Salmond, Report on Command from 1 Oct. 1922 to 7 Apr. 1924, n.d. [c. April 1924], The National Archives: AIR 23/542.

180 Churchill, quoted in W. G. Sebald, *On the Natural History of Destruction,* trans. Anthea Bell (orig. 1999; trans., New York: Modern Library, 2003), 19–24. For more on how interwar experience in Iraq shaped the RAF's activities in World War II, see Satia, *Spies in Arabia,* 253–254.

181 The closest he came to uttering these words was in a Commons speech of January 23, 1948, in which he said, "For my part, I consider that it will be found much better by all Parties to leave the past to history, especially as I propose to write that history myself."

182 On techno-science and experts, see Mitchell, *Rule of Experts,* 15; on Arabist experts' influence on wartime development of Iraq, see Satia, "Developing Iraq."

183 Mitchell, *Rule of Experts,* 82–83; see also 4–6.

184 Arendt, *Imperialism,* 101.

185 Edward Carson, quoted in Jon Wilson, *The Chaos of Empire: The British Raj and the Conquest of India* (New York: Public Affairs, 2016), 397.

186 David Edgerton, *England and the Aeroplane: An Essay on a Militant and Technological Nation* (Basingstoke, UK: Macmillan in association with the Centre for the History of Science, Technology and Medicine, University of Manchester, 1991), 107; Jon Lawrence, "Forging a Peaceable Kingdom: War, Violence, and Fear of Brutalization in Post–First World War Britain," *Journal of Modern History* 75 (2003): 557–589.

187 Satia, *Spies in Arabia,* 334–337; Priya Satia, "Drones: A History from the British Middle East," *Humanity* 5:1 (2014): 1–31.

188 Dexter Filkins, "Tough New Tactics by U.S. Tighten Grip on Iraq Towns," *New York Times,* December 7, 2003, 13.

189 Colonel David Kilcullen, cited in "U. S. Considers Halting Drone Attacks on Pakistan," *Daily Telegraph,* May 5, 2009.

5. THE DIVISION OF PROGRESS

Epigraph: Benedict Anderson, *A Life beyond Boundaries: A Memoir* (London: Verso, 2016), x.

1 Churchill speech, quoted in Thomas Metcalf, *Ideologies of the Raj* (orig. 1995; repr., New York: Cambridge University Press, 1997), 232.

2 George Orwell, *The Road to Wigan Pier* (orig. 1937; repr., San Diego, 1958), 147–148.

3 George Orwell, "The Lion and the Unicorn: Socialism and the English Genius," 1941, in *George Orwell: Essays, Selected and Introduced by John Carey,* ed. Peter Davison (New York: Knopf, 2002), 337–339.

4 George Orwell, War-Time Diary, August 10, 1942, in *George Orwell: The Collected Essays, Journalism & Letters,* vol. 2, *My Country Right or Left, 1940–1943,* ed. Sonia Orwell and Ian Angus (orig. 1968; repr., Boston: Nonpareil, 2019), 443.

5 A. Dirk Moses, "Epilogue: Partitions, Hostages, Transfer: Retributive Violence and National Security," in *Partitions: A Transnational History of Twentieth-Century Territorial Separatism,* ed. Arie Dubnov and Laura Robson (Stanford, CA: Stanford University Press, 2019), 277.

6 See Yasmin Khan, *The Great Partition: The Making of India and Pakistan* (New Haven, CT: Yale University Press, 2007).

7 Mark Doyle, *Communal Violence in the British Empire: Disturbing the Pax* (London: Bloomsbury, 2016), 4, 41–42, 82–83.

8 Strachey, *India,* quoted in Doyle, *Communal Violence in the British Empire,* 2.

9 T. Metcalf, *Ideologies of the Raj,* 13.

10 Nicholas Dirks, "Castes of Mind," *Representations* 37 (Winter 1992): 59.

11 Quoted in Jon Wilson, *The Chaos of Empire: The British Raj and the Conquest of India* (New York: Public Affairs, 2016), 373.

12 Witnessing these events informed the anticolonial thought of British radicals like Hyndman. See Priyamvada Gopal, *Insurgent Empire: Anticolonial Resistance and British Dissent* (London: Verso, 2019), chap. 4.

13 Quoted in T. Metcalf, *Ideologies of the Raj,* 224.

14 Barbara Metcalf, *Husain Ahmad Madani: The Jihad for Islam and India's Freedom* (Oxford: Oneworld, 2009), 83–84.

15 Doyle, *Communal Violence in the British Empire,* 177, 201.

16 B. Metcalf, *Husain Ahmad Madani,* 104.

17 Both these stories of partition also involve enormously complex histories beyond the scope of this book. For fuller consideration of the transnational connections between these cases, see Dubnov and Robson, *Partitions.*

18 Arie Dubnov, "The Architect of Two Partitions or a Federalist Daydreamer? The Curious Case of Reginald Coupland," in *Partitions: A Transnational History of Twentieth-Century Territorial Separatism,* ed. Arie Dubnov and Laura Robson (Stanford, CA: Stanford University Press, 2019), 59–61.

19 Quoted in Dubnov, "The Architect of Two Partitions or a Federalist Daydreamer?" 78.

20 Dubnov, "The Architect of Two Partitions or a Federalist Daydreamer?" 78–79.

21 Quoted in Dubnov, "The Architect of Two Partitions or a Federalist Daydreamer?" 83.

22 Christopher Leslie Brown, *Moral Capital: Foundations of British Abolitionism* (Chapel Hill, NC: University of North Carolina Press, 2006), 9.

23   W. H. Auden, "Partition" (1966), in *City without Walls and Other Poems* (New York: Random House, 1969), 86.

24   Arie Dubnov and Laura Robson, "Introduction: Drawing the Line, Writing beyond It: Toward a Transnational History of Partitions," in *Partitions: A Transnational History of Twentieth-Century Territorial Separatism*, ed. Arie Dubnov and Laura Robson (Stanford, CA: Stanford University Press, 2019), 4.

25   Dubnov, "The Architect of Two Partitions or a Federalist Daydreamer?" 84.

26   Quoted in Catherine Gallagher, *Telling It Like It Wasn't: The Counterfactual Imagination in History and Fiction* (Chicago: University of Chicago Press, 2018), 257.

27   Dubnov and Robson, "Introduction," 2–3, 27.

28   Dubnov, "The Architect of Two Partitions or a Federalist Daydreamer?" 84. India was a dominion until it became a republic on January 26, 1950. Commonwealth rules were changed to allow India to remain a member, setting a new precedent for allowing republics within the body. Pakistan ceased to be a dominion in 1956 on the creation of the Islamic Republic of Pakistan.

29   Faisal Devji, *The Impossible Indian: Gandhi and the Temptation of Violence* (Cambridge, MA: Harvard University Press, 2012), 160.

30   Dubnov "The Architect of Two Partitions or a Federalist Daydreamer?" 81.

31   Katherine Watt, "Thomas Walker Arnold and the Re-evaluation of Islam, 1864–1930," *Modern Asian Studies* 36:1 (2002): 69.

32   Faisal Devji, "From Minority to Nation," in Dubnov and Robson, *Partitions*, 33.

33   Priya Satia, *Spies in Arabia: The Great War and the Cultural Foundations of Britain's Covert Empire in the Middle East* (New York: Oxford University Press, 2008), 130–131, 134.

34   On anticolonial pushback against universalist notions of time, see also Vanessa Ogle, *The Global Transformation of Time: 1870–1950* (Cambridge, MA: Harvard University Press, 2015).

35   Devji, "From Minority to Nation," 35–36.

36   Quoted in Devji "From Minority to Nation," 36.

37   Devji, "From Minority to Nation," 44.

38   Muhammad Iqbal, "*Jawab-e-Shikwa*" (1913), available at Rekhta, https://www.rekhta.org/nazms/javaab-e-shikva-dil-se-jo-baat-nikaltii-hai-asar-rakhtii-hai-allama-iqbal-nazms.

39   From Iqbal's *nazm*, "*Tulu-e-Islam*," available at Rekhta, https://rekhta.org/nazms/tuluu-e-islaam-daliil-e-subh-e-raushan-hai-sitaaron-kii-tunuk-taabii-allama-iqbal-nazms.

40   Muhammad Iqbal, "*Shama aur Shayar*," (1912), in *Baang-e-Dara* (orig. 1924; repr., Delhi: Kutub Khana Hameediya, 1990), 144.

41   Muhammad Iqbal, *The Reconstruction of Religious Thought in Islam* (orig. 1930; repr., London: Oxford University Press, 1934), 178.

42   Muhammad Iqbal, *Zarb-e-Kaleem, Yaani Elan-e-Jung Daur-e-Hazir Ke Khilaaf* (orig. 1936; repr., n.d.), 99, available at Rekhta, https://www.rekhta.org/ebooks/zarb-e-kaleem-elan-e-jang-daur-e-haazir-ke-khilaf-allama-iqbal-ebooks/.

43   Muhammad Iqbal, "McTaggart's Philosophy," in *Speeches, Writings and Statements of Iqbal*, ed. Latif Ahmad Sherwani (orig. 1944, 1977; repr., Lahore: Iqbal Academy Pakistan, 1995), 187.

44   Devji, "From Minority to Nation," 45–47.

45   Devji, "From Minority to Nation," 52, 54–55.

46   Muhammad Asad, *The Road to Mecca* (New York: Simon and Schuster, 1954), 11, 44, 76, 193.

47   Muhammad Asad and Pola Hamida Asad, *Home-coming of the Heart [The Road to Mecca, Part 2]* (Lahore: The Truth Society, 2012), 29, 34–35.

48   M. Asad, *Road to Mecca*, 54.

49   M. Asad, *Road to Mecca*, 4.

50   Iqbal to Thompson, March 4, 1934, transcribed in S. Ahmad, *Iqbal: His Political Ideas at Crossroads: A Commentary on Unpublished Letters to Professor Thompson, with Photographic Reproductions of the Original Letters* (Aligarh: Printwell, 1979), 80. Original printed on 94.

51   Faisal Devji, *Muslim Zion: Pakistan as a Political Idea* (London: Hurst, 2013), 22.

52   M. Asad and P. Asad, *Home-coming of the Heart*, 97.

53   Muhammad Asad, "Uniqueness of Pakistan Movement in the Muslim World: Its Ideological Basis," *Arafat*, Lahore, May 1947, in "A Matter of Love: Muhammad Asad and Islam," ed. Ismail Ibrahim Nawwab, *Islamic Studies* 39:2 (Summer 2000): 210–11. Emphasis in original. Back in Europe, Asad's father, sister, and stepmother perished in the Holocaust. Asad himself was interned as an enemy alien in India during the war (notwithstanding his Jewish heritage).

54   M. Asad, "Dangers Facing Pakistan," *Arafat*, Lahore, May 1947, in "A Matter of Love," 212.

55   M. Asad, "Enthusiasm of Indian Muslims for Pakistan," *Arafat*, Lahore, May 1947, in "A Matter of Love," 209.

56   M. Asad and P. Asad, *Home-coming of the Heart*, 116.

57   M. Asad and P. Asad, *Home-coming of the Heart*, 117–118.

58   Venkat Dhulipala, *Creating a New Medina: State Power, Islam, and the Quest for Pakistan in Late Colonial North India* (Delhi: Cambridge University Press, 2015), 4. See also Faisal Devji, "Young Fogeys: The Anachronism of New Scholarship on Pakistan," review of Venkat Dhulipala's *A New Medina*, The Wire.in, October 4, 2015, https://thewire.in/books/young-fogeys-the-anachronism-of-new-scholarship-on-pakistan; Barbara Metcalf, "Review of *Creating a New Medina: State, Power, Islam and the Quest for Pakistan in Late Colonial India*, by Venkat Dhulipala," *The Book Review* 39:6 (2015).

59   Watt, "Thomas Walker Arnold," 81.

60   There is not space to go into this matter deeply here. For the particularities of parts of the United Provinces, for instance, see Dhulipala, *Creating a New Medina*.

61   M. Asad, "Enthusiasm of Indian Muslims for Pakistan," 209.

62   On this, see Devji, *Muslim Zion*, e.g., 3.

63   Devji, *Muslim Zion*, chap. 1, 99, 138.

64   Khan, *Great Partition*, 49, 83.

65   Khan, *Great Partition*, 129.

66   Quoted in Khan, *Great Partition*, 78.

67   Certainly, some thinkers had raised the idea of population transfer, such as B. R. Ambedkar in *Pakistan, or The Partition of India* (orig. *Thoughts on Pakistan*, 1940) (Bombay: Thackers, 1945). Jinnah did not like the idea. See also Faisal Devji, "National Identity Is a Political Project. Turning That into a Religious Endeavour Does Not Work," *Naya Daur*, February 15, 2019, nayadaur.tv/2019/02/national-identity-is-a-political-project-turning-that-into-a-religious-endeavour-does-not-work/.

68   Jon Wilson, *Chaos of Empire,* 451. Wilson writes that between 1,060 and 2,500 protestors were killed and 60,000 to 90,000 imprisoned in appalling conditions.

69   Quoted in Jon Wilson, *Chaos of Empire,* 451.

70   Khan, *Great Partition,* 50–51.

71   Khan, *Great Partition,* 49–50, 55.

72   Jinnah, speech at Muslim League meeting, July 19, 1946, quoted in Tarun Vijay, "Jinnah. He Had a Pistol. He Used It," *Times of India,* August 19, 2009, https://timesofindia.indiatimes.com/blogs/indus-calling/jinnah-he-had-a-pistol/.

73   Hamlet's "To Be Or Not To Be" speech, Shakespeare's *Hamlet,* Act 3, Scene 1, available at Poetry Foundation, https://www.poetryfoundation.org/poems/56965/speech-to-be-or-not-to-be-that-is-the-question.

74   Ranabir Samaddar, "Policing a Riot-Torn City: Kolkata, 16–18 August 1946," *Journal of Genocide Research* 19:1 (2017): 39–60.

75   Khan, *Great Partition,* 64–65.

76   Khan, *Great Partition,* 112. See also Dhulipala, *Creating a New Medina,* 468–469, on the United Provinces.

77   Khan, *Great Partition,* 106. Guneeta Singh Bhalla, founder of the oral-history collection The Partition Archive, has also concluded from thousands of interviews that the violence was not caused by neighbors turning against one another overnight, as British theories of Hindu-Muslim enmity would have it, but by gangs licensed by local political leaders. Bhalla, "What Really Caused the Violence of Partition?" *The Diplomat,* August 28, 2019, https://thediplomat.com/2019/08/what-really-caused-the-violence-of-partition/.

78   Khan, *Great Partition,* 102, 128.

79   Khan, *Great Partition,* 127.

80   The Partition Archive, www.1947partitionarchive.org.

81   See also Khan, *Great Partition,* 138–140.

82   On the colonized mind, see Frantz Fanon, *The Wretched of the Earth,* trans. Constance Farrington (orig. 1961; trans., New York: Grove Weidenfeld, 1963); Ashis Nandy, *The Intimate Enemy: Loss and Recovery of the Self under Colonialism* (Delhi: Oxford University Press, 1983). See also the critical work of Homi Bhabha on mimicry, and Antonio Gramsci on the concept of cultural hegemony in *Selections from The Prison Notebooks,* ed. and trans. Quintin Hoare and Geoffrey Nowell Smith (orig. 1929–1935; New York: International, 1971).

83   Dipesh Chakrabarty, *Provincializing Europe: Postcolonial Thought and Historical Difference* (Princeton, NJ: Princeton University Press, 2000), 8–9.

84   See also Devji, *Muslim Zion,* chap. 2; Ali Raza, Franziska Roy, and Benjamin Zachariah, eds., *The Internationalist Moment: South Asia, Worlds, and World Views, 1917–1939* (Los Angeles: Sage, 2015); Manu Goswami, "Imaginary Futures and Colonial Internationalisms," *American Historical Review* 117 (Dec. 2012): 1461–1485. Goswami notes, "The neglect of colonial internationalisms has impoverished our understanding of the global making of twentieth-century political modernism" (1485).

85   Gopal, *Insurgent Empire,* 141–143, 148–150. See also Seema Alavi, *Muslim Cosmopolitanism in the Age of Empire* (Cambridge, MA: Harvard University Press, 2015).

86   See Michael Martel, "'The Island Councils Too': Late-Victorian Epic Romance and Caribbean Multiracial Self-Governance," PCCBS paper, UC Merced, March 2019; Christopher Taylor, *An Empire of Neglect: The West Indies in the Wake of British Liberalism* (Durham, NC: Duke University Press, 2018). See

also, generally, Paul Gilroy, *The Black Atlantic: Modernity and Double Consciousness* (London: Verso, 1993).

87 Frederick Cooper, *Africa in the World: Capitalism, Empire, Nation-State* (Cambridge, MA: Harvard University Press, 2014), 64–70, 95. See also Cooper, *Citizenship between Empire and Nation: Remaking France and French Africa, 1945–1960* (Princeton, NJ: Princeton University Press, 2014). On the continued play of such notions in Guadeloupe, see Yarimar Bonilla, *Non-sovereign Futures: French Caribbean Politics in the Wake of Disenchantment* (Chicago: University of Chicago Press, 2015).

88 Mrinalini Sinha, *Specters of Mother India: The Global Restructuring of an Empire* (Durham, NC: Duke University Press, 2006), 154.

89 Rabindranath Tagore, "Where the Mind Is without Fear," song 35, in *Gitanjali*, in *Collected Poems and Plays of Rabindranath Tagore* (London: Macmillan, 1920), 16. The original Bengali version was published in 1910. Tagore's own English translation of the poem appeared in 1913.

90 Tagore, quoted in Goswami, "Imaginary Futures and Colonial Internationalisms," 1474.

91 Rabindranath Tagore, *The Religion of Man, Being the Hibbert Lectures for 1930* (New York: Macmillan, 1931), appendix 1; Tagore, *Creative Unity* (New York: Macmillan, 1922), 73.

92 Devji, *Impossible Indian*, 44.

93 William Morris, *News from Nowhere, or an Epoch of Rest, Being Some Chapters from a Utopian Romance* (orig. 1890; repr., London: Longmans, Green, 1905), 32, 79, 152.

94 Mohandas K. Gandhi, *Hind Swaraj, or Indian Home Rule* (orig. 1909; repr., Ahmedabad: Navajivan, 1946), 56–57. See also Devji, *Muslim Zion*, 108–9.

95 Iqbal, quoted in Devji, *Impossible Indian*, 95–96.

96 Gandhi, *Hind Swaraj*, 65.

97 See also Priya Satia, "In Trying to Defy Colonialism, Draft NEP Walks the Path of the Colonisers," The Wire.in, July 20, 2019, https://thewire.in/education/in-trying-to-defy-colonialism-draft-nep-walks-the-path-of-the-colonisers.

98 Mohandas K. Gandhi, *Gita the Mother*, ed. Jag Parvesh Chander (Lahore: Indian Printing Works, 1946), 31.

99 Quoted in Devji, *Impossible Indian*, 105.

100 Devji, *Impossible Indian*, 115.

101 Prathama Bannerjee, "*Bhagavad Gita* Wasn't Always India's Defining Book," The Print.In, December 15, 2019, https://theprint.in/opinion/bhagavad-gita-not-indias-defining-book-another-text-was-more-popular/334904/.

102 Ashis Nandy, "From Outside the Imperium: Gandhi's Cultural Critique of the 'West,'" *Alternatives: Global, Local, Political* 7:2 (1981): 172, 183. See also Nandy, "The Psychology of Colonialism: Sex, Age, and Ideology in British India," *Psychiatry* 45:3 (1982): 214–217.

103 Devji, *Impossible Indian*, 93. This idea echoed the thought of Bal Gangadhar Tilak, a leader of the swadeshi movement of 1905–1911, who defined freedom *as* an act of agency. See Gopal, *Insurgent Empire*, 184–185.

104 Uday Mehta, *Liberalism and Empire: A Study in Nineteenth-Century British Liberal Thought* (Chicago: University of Chicago Press, 1999), 97, 113.

105 Mohammad Ali Jauhar, 1923, reproduced in Rachel Fell McDermott et al., eds., *Sources of Indian Tradition: Modern India, Pakistan, and Bangladesh*, vol. 2 (New York: Columbia University Press, 2013), 409.

106 On the complex motivations of Indians who fought in that war, see Santanu Das, *India, Empire, and First World War Culture: Writings, Images, and Songs* (Cambridge: Cambridge University Press, 2018).

107 See Alavi, *Muslim Cosmopolitanism*.

108 Norman Bray, note, March 25, 1917 (and synopsis thereof), The National Archives: FO 371/3057: 103481.

109 B. Metcalf, *Husain Ahmad Madani*, 11, 46, 72.

110 Satia, *Spies in Arabia*, 218

111 Yasmin Saikia, "*Hijrat* and *Azadi* in Indian Muslim Imagination and Practice: Connecting Nationalism, Internationalism, and Cosmopolitanism," *Comparative Studies of South Asia, Africa and the Middle East* 37:2 (2017): 202, 207. See also, generally, Gajendra Singh, "India and the Great War: Colonial Fantasies, Anxieties and Discontent," *Studies in Ethnicity and Nationalism* 14:2 (2014): 343–361.

112 Saikia, "*Hijrat* and *Azadi* in Indian Muslim Imagination and Practice," 202–203

113 Saikia, "*Hijrat* and *Azadi* in Indian Muslim Imagination and Practice," 206–207.

114 Quoted in Kama Maclean, *A Revolutionary History of Interwar India: Violence, Image, Voice and Text* (New York: Oxford University Press, 2015), 15; Maclean, *Revolutionary History of Interwar India*, 31.

115 On the intersections, see Maclean, *Revolutionary History of Interwar India*.

116 Maclean, *Revolutionary History of Interwar India*, 140–141.

117 Rajendra Prasad, *India Divided* (Bombay: Hind Kitabs, 1946), 26.

118 Khan, *Great Partition*, 21.

119 Dirks is helpful in identifying this problem. See Nicholas Dirks, *Castes of Mind: Colonialism and the Making of Modern India* (Princeton, NJ: Princeton University Press, 2001), coda, "The Burden of the Past: On Colonialism and the Writing of History."

120 Muhammad Iqbal, "*Tarana-i-Hindi*," 1904, available at Rekhta, https://www.rekhta.org/nazms/taraana-e-hindii-saare-jahaan-se-achchhaa-hindostaan-hamaaraa-allama-iqbal-nazms.

121 Amrita Pritam, "*Ajj Aakhaan Waris Shah Nu*," written c. 1948, available at YouTube, https://www.youtube.com/watch?v=aFkKOro8-jw.

122 See also Amir Mufti, *Enlightenment in the Colony: The Jewish Question and the Crisis of Postcolonial Culture* (Princeton, NJ: Princeton University Press, 2007), 211–212, 216, 221–224, 239, 243.

123 Saadat Hasan Manto, "*Toba Tek Singh*," in *Phundne* (Lahore: Maktabah-e-Jadid, 1955).

124 Quoted in Khan, *Great Partition*, 194.

125 Sahir Ludhianvi, "*Chakle*," in *Talkhiyaan* (orig. 1945; repr., Delhi: Hali, 1949), 74–77.

126 Faiz Ahmad Faiz, "*Subh-e-Azadi*," 1951, in *Dast-e-Saba* (Delhi: Shafiq, 1952), 22–24.

127 Ali Sardar Jafri, "*Fareb*," available at Rekhta, https://www.rekhta.org/nazms/fareb-ali-sardar-jafri-nazms. Other Urdu poets who criticized the "dawn" included Sahir Ludhianvi, Nadeem Qasimi, Jan Nisar Akhtar, Kaifi Azmi, Majrooh Sultanpuri, Naresh Kumar Shad, Jigar Moradabadi, and Qateel Shifai. More hopeful were Majaz Lucknavi and Jagan Nath Azad. For much of this poetry, see Rekhta, www.rekhta.org.

128 Faiz Ahmad Faiz, "*Aaye kuchh abr kuchh sharab aaye*," available at Rekhta, https://rekhta.org/ghazals/aae-kuchh-abr-kuchh-sharaab-aae-faiz-ahmad-faiz-ghazals.

129 Worldly experiences of exile and refuge gave *hijr* and *birha* a range of new secular connotations, Mufti notes. *Enlightenment in the Colony,* 211–212, 216, 221–224, 239, 243.

130 Faiz Ahmad Faiz, *"Zindaan Ki Ek Shaam,"* available at Rekhta, https://www .rekhta.org/nazms/zindaan-kii-ek-shaam-shaam-ke-pech-o-kham-sitaaron-se -faiz-ahmad-faiz-nazms.

131 Mufti, *Enlightenment in the Colony,* 165.

132 B. Metcalf, *Husain Ahmad Madani,*118.

133 Mufti, *Enlightenment in the Colony,* 179.

134 B. Metcalf, *Husain Ahmad Madani,* 149.

135 Quoted in B. Metcalf, *Husain Ahmad Madani,* 151. On some of the differences between Madani's and Azad's thought, see 116–119.

136 B. Metcalf, *Husain Ahmad Madani,* 133–136.

137 Jagan Nath Azad, *"Na Puchho Jab Bahar Aayi,"* in *Intikhab-e-Kalam* (Aligarh: Anjuman Taraqqi, 1957), 7–8. Munir Niazi also expressed this sense of never being quite at home and yet being always at home. *Ajnabi shehr* ("strange city") is a common trope in Urdu poetry for a reason.

138 Faiz Ahmad Faiz, *"Marsia"* ("Elegy"), in *Sar-e-Vaadi-e-Seena* (Lucknow: Kitabi Duniya, 1962), 90; Mufti, *Enlightenment in the Colony,* 220–221.

139 Jagan Nath Azad, *"Ashaar, Lahore Mein Keh Gaye,"* in *Watan Mein Ajnabi* (orig. 1951; repr., Delhi: Maktaba Jamia, 1964), 70.

140 A few examples: The Leftist Pakistani poet Ibn-e-Insha (born in Jalandar in 1927) composed *"Tu Kahan Chali Gayi Thi"* ("Where Had You Gone") in the 1950s, gesturing with equal ease towards Karachi and Delhi. Nazir Qaiser's poetry is as ecumenical in its geography. Shiv Kumar Batalvi (often referred to as Punjab's Byron) drew on the ancient epic about Puran Bhagat of Sialkot for his epic verse play *Loona* in 1965. Jagan Nath Azad came to India, but his poetry dwelled on memories of his homeland, his lost *chaman* (garden).

141 See also Mufti, *Enlightenment in the Colony,* 223–224.

142 Bollywood has often dramatized the split self as literally split with the "double-role" genre. Themes of cataclysmic displacement are common in movies, like the earthquake that scatters the family in Yash Chopra's *Waqt (Time)* (1965) or the many tales of brothers separated at birth or orphans. *"Deewar"* (wall) is also a frequent motif in poems, films, and plays. See Priya Satia, "Poets of Partition: The Recovery of Lost Causes," in Arie Dubnov and Laura Robson, eds., *Partitions: A Transnational History of Twentieth-Century Territorial Separatism* (Stanford, CA: Stanford University Press, 2019), 230n11.

143 See Vazira Zamindar, *The Long Partition and the Making of Modern South Asia: Refugees, Boundaries, Histories* (New York: Columbia University Press, 2007).

144 Anam Zakaria, *The Footprints of Partition: Narratives of Four Generations of Pakistanis and Indians* (New Delhi: Harper Collins, 2015), 84. My emphasis.

145 I thank Hamida Chopra for sharing this story.

146 Lawrence to Charlotte Shaw, October 14, 1931, in *T. E. Lawrence: The Selected Letters,* ed. Malcolm Brown (New York: Paragon, 1992), 459.

147 Lawrence to Robin Buxton, March 4, 1927, in *The Selected Letters,* 319. See also Lawrence to Ezra Pound, December 7, 1934, in *The Selected Letters,* 507. Though positioned at the center of the maelstrom of interwar politics and culture, both also created spaces of hermetic withdrawal where they created new kinds of society (Gandhi's ashram, Lawrence's cottage). Both leapt to the head of liberation movements abroad in Byronic style (Gandhi arriving in India from South

Africa), "going native" in the process. Notably, Churchill admired Lawrence in his Arab robes as "one of Nature's great princes" (Winston Churchill, *Great Contemporaries* [orig. 1937; repr., London: Odhams, 1949], 131) but despised Gandhi's transformation into a "half naked fakir"—the phrase emanated from his speech of February 23, 1931, in which he described the humiliating spectacle of "a seditious Middle Temple lawyer, now posing as a fakir of a type well-known in the East, striding half-naked up the steps of the Vice-regal palace . . . to parley on equal terms with the representative of the King-Emperor." Quoted in Richard Toye, *Churchill's Empire: The World That Made Him and the World He Made* (New York: Henry Holt, 2010), 176.

148   See the work, especially, of the Berkeley-based Partition Archive at www
      .1947partitionarchive.org.

149   Devji, *Muslim Zion*, 248.

150   Dubnov and Robson, "Introduction," 1.

151   Tom Nairn, *The Break-Up of Britain: Crisis and Neonationalism* (London: NLB,
      1977).

152   Anderson, *A Life beyond Boundaries*, 124.

153   Fintan O'Toole, "Are the English Ready for Self-Government?" *The Irish Times*,
      March 19, 2019, https://www.irishtimes.com/opinion/fintan-o-toole-are-the
      -english-ready-for-self-government-1.3830474?mode=amp.

6. THE PAST AND FUTURE OF HISTORY

Epigraph: Toni Morrison, Nobel Lecture, December 7, 1993, https://www
.nobelprize.org/prizes/literature/1993/morrison/lecture/.

1   See Caroline Elkins, *Imperial Reckoning: The Untold Story of Britain's Gulag in
    Kenya* (New York: Henry Holt, 2005).

2   Quoted in Elkins, *Imperial Reckoning*, 352.

3   Jon Wilson, *The Chaos of Empire: The British Raj and the Conquest of India*
    (New York: Public Affairs, 2016), 496–497.

4   In this speech of April 20, 1968, Powell alluded to a line from Virgil's *Aeneid*:
    "As I look ahead, I am filled with foreboding. Like the Roman, I seem to see 'the
    River Tiber foaming with much blood.'"

5   V. D. Savarkar, *The Indian War of Independence, 1857* (London: n.p., 1909).

6   Kama Maclean, *A Revolutionary History of Interwar India: Violence, Image,
    Voice and Text* (New York: Oxford University Press, 2015), 91. On the history of
    Indian history-writing on the "mutiny," see Crispin Bates, ed., *Mutiny at the
    Margins: New Perspectives on the Indian Uprising of 1857*, vol. 6, *Perception,
    Narration and Reinvention: The Pedagogy and Historiography of the Indian Up-
    rising* (London: Sage, 2014).

7   Syed Ahmed Khan, *Asbab-e-Baghawat-e-Hind* (orig. 1859; repr., Aligarh: Uni-
    versity Publishers, 1958).

8   E. P. Thompson, *Alien Homage: Edward Thompson and Rabindranath Tagore*
    (Delhi: Oxford University Press, 1993), 72–73.

9   E. J. Thompson, *Mesopotamian Verses* (London: Epworth, 1919); Thompson,
    Atonement: A Play of Modern India, in Four Acts (London: Ernest Benn, 1924).

10 E. J. Thompson, *The Other Side of the Medal* (orig. 1925; repr., London: Hogarth
    Press, 1930), 27–28.

11 E. P. Thompson, *Alien Homage*, 89.

12   Priti Joshi, review of *War of No Pity: The Indian Mutiny and Victorian Trauma,* by Christopher Herbert, *Romanticism and Victorianism on the Net* 53 (Feb. 2009), https://www.erudit.org/fr/revues/ravon/2009-n53-ravon2916/029909ar/.

13   Quoted in Mary Lago, *India's Prisoner: A Biography of Edward John Thompson, 1886–1946* (Columbia: University of Missouri Press, 2001), 212.

14   Priya Satia, "Byron, Gandhi and the Thompsons: The Making of British Social History and the Unmaking of Indian History," *History Workshop Journal* 81 (2016): 138, 145.

15   E. J. Thompson to Frank Thompson, 1936, quoted in Peter Conradi, *A Very English Hero: The Making of Frank Thompson* (London: Bloomsbury, 2012), 79.

16   E. J. Thompson, *The Making of the Indian Princes* (London: Oxford University Press, 1943), 269.

17   E. J. Thompson and Geoffrey Garratt, *The Rise and Fulfillment of British Rule in India* (London: Macmillan, 1934).

18   See Gregory Claeys, *Imperial Sceptics: British Critics of Empire, 1850–1920* (Cambridge: Cambridge University Press, 2010), 5–6, 33 passim. For this literature, see, for instance, R. L. Schuyler, *The Fall of the Old Colonial System: A Study in British Free Trade, 1770–1870* (orig. 1945; repr., Hamden, CT: Archon, 1966), and Schuyler, "The Climax of Anti-Imperialism in England," *Political Science Quarterly* 36 (1921): 537–560.

19   J. A. Hobson, "Social Thinkers in Nineteenth-Century England," *Contemporary Review* 137 (1930): 457.

20   See, for instance, Priyamvada Gopal, *Insurgent Empire: Anticolonial Resistance and British Dissent* (London: Verso, 2019), part 2; Marc Matera, *Black London: The Imperial Metropolis and Decolonization in the Twentieth Century* (Oakland: University of California Press, 2015). That anti-imperialism did not become a mainstream feature of British leftist thought testifies to the limits of historicist radical thought. It took a rejection of historicism to repudiate empire.

21   C. L. R. James, *The Black Jacobins* (London: Secker & Warburg, 1938).

22   Christopher Leslie Brown, *Moral Capital: Foundations of British Abolitionism* (Chapel Hill, NC: University of North Carolina Press, 2006), 12. See Eric Williams, *Capitalism and Slavery* (orig. 1944; repr., Chapel Hill: University of North Carolina Press, 1994).

23   Michel-Rolph Trouillot, *Silencing the Past: Power and the Production of History* (orig. 1995; repr., Boston: Beacon, 2015), 13.

24   E. J. Thompson, *Making of the Indian Princes,* vi.

25   E. P. Thompson, "The Nehru Tradition," in *Writing by Candlelight* (London: Merlin, 1980), 138.

26   See Satia, "Byron, Gandhi and the Thompsons," 146–152.

27   E. P. Thompson, *Beyond the Frontier: The Politics of a Failed Mission, Bulgaria 1944* (Stanford, CA: Stanford University Press, 1997), 14, 33–34.

28   Quoted in Dennis Dworkin, *Cultural Marxism in Postwar Britain: History, the New Left, and the Origins of Cultural Studies* (Durham, NC: Duke University Press, 1997), 17.

29   Milovan Djilas, quoted in Philip Knightley, *The Second Oldest Profession: The Spy as Bureaucrat, Patriot, Fantasist and Whore* (London: Andre Deutsch, 1986), 121.

30   E. P. Thompson, *Alien Homage,* viii, 73–74, 93.

31 E. P. Thompson, "The Peculiarities of the English," 1965, in *The Poverty of Theory & Other Essays* (New York: Monthly Review Press, 1978), 266; E. P. Thompson, "The Secret State," *Race & Class* 20:30 (1979): 219–242; E. P. Thompson, "An Alternative to Doomsday," *New Statesman,* December 21, 1979, in *Britain and the Bomb: The "New Statesman" Papers on Destruction and Disarmament* (Manchester: Manchester Free Press, 1981), 9–18. See also David Edgerton, *Warfare State: Britain, 1920–1970* (Cambridge: Cambridge University Press, 2006).

32 Dworkin, *Cultural Marxism in Postwar Britain,* 114.

33 See, especially, E. P. Thompson, *Witness Against the Beast: William Blake and the Moral Law* (Cambridge: Cambridge University Press, 1993).

34 To be sure, there was some delay, given Thompson's early preoccupation with the "nation," partly out of embarrassment about empire. On this, see Satia, "Byron, Gandhi and the Thompsons," 154. The framing of British social history in the era of Indian anticolonialism, as, indeed, an escape from decolonization, depended on denial of transnational bonds.

35 E. P. Thompson, *The Making of the English Working Class* (orig. 1963; repr., New York: Vintage, 1966), 13, 551.

36 Quoted in Catherine Gallagher, *Telling It Like It Wasn't: The Counterfactual Imagination in History and Fiction* (Chicago: University of Chicago Press, 2018), 25.

37 E. P. Thompson, "Time, Work-Discipline and Industrial Capitalism," *Past & Present* 38 (1967): 93.

38 Walter Benjamin, "Theses on the Philosophy of History," 1940, in *Illuminations: Walter Benjamin: Essays and Reflections,* ed. Hannah Arendt (New York: Schoken, 1968), thesis 9, 257–258.

39 See, for instance, Michel Foucault, *The History of Sexuality,* 3 vols. (orig. 1976–84; trans., London: Allen Lane / Penguin, 1978–1984).

40 Karl Popper, *The Poverty of Historicism* (London: Routledge, 1957).

41 Karl Popper, *The Open Society and Its Enemies* (London: Routledge, 1945).

42 E. P. Thompson, *Making of the English Working Class,* 101.

43 Benjamin, "Theses on the Philosophy of History," thesis 3, 254.

44 Benjamin, "Theses on the Philosophy of History," theses 13 and 14, 260–261.

45 Joan W. Scott, "Women in *The Making of the English Working Class,*" in *Gender and the Politics of History* (orig. 1988; repr., New York: Columbia University Press, 1999), 80–81, citing Henry Abelove.

46 Robin D. G. Kelley, "A Poetics of Anticolonialism," introduction to Aimé Césaire, *Discourse on Colonialism,* 1955, trans. Joan Pinkham (orig. 1955; trans., 1972; repr., New York: Monthly Review, 2000), 17.

47 Theodor Adorno, "Cultural Criticism and Society," 1949, in *Prisms,* trans. Samuel Weber and Shierry Weber (orig. 1967; trans., 1981; Cambridge, MA: The MIT Press, 1983), 34.

48 Theodor Adorno, *Negative Dialectics,* trans. E. B. Ashton (orig. 1966; trans., 1973; repr., London: Taylor & Francis, 2004), 3, 362–363.

49 Eric Oberle, *Theodor Adorno and the Century of Negative Identity* (Stanford, CA: Stanford University Press, 2018), 3.

50 See, generally, Priya Satia, "Poets of Partition: The Recovery of Lost Causes," in Arie Dubnov and Laura Robson, eds., *Partitions: A Transnational History of Twentieth-Century Territorial Separatism* (Stanford, CA: Stanford University Press, 2019), 224-256. Nevertheless, a new anthology of poetry on Partition claims there was not much poetic response to the event—prompting a reviewer

to invoke Adorno's line about the impossibility of poetry after Auschwitz. Ameer Imam, "Filling the Lacuna: First Anthology of Poetry on the Partition of India in 1947," *The Levant News,* June 4, 2019, the-levant.com/filling-lacuna -first-anthology-poetry-partition-india-1947/.

51 Dipesh Chakrabarty, *Provincializing Europe: Postcolonial Thought and His-torical Difference* (Princeton, NJ: Princeton University Press, 2000), 174.

52 Scott, "Women in *The Making of the English Working Class,*" 81–82. The adage "pessimism of the intellect, optimism of the will," attributed to the communist thinker Antonio Gramsci, coined while he was imprisoned in Fascist Italy, also strained after this middle ground. One recalls also Toni Morrison's words: "There is no time for despair, no place for self-pity, no need for silence, no room for fear. We speak, we write, we do language. That is how civilizations heal." Toni Mor-rison, "No Place for Self-Pity, No Room for Fear," *The Nation,* March 23, 2015.

53 Thomas Laqueur, "The Past's Past," *London Review of Books* 18:18 (September 19, 1996): 3–7.

54 John Gallagher and Ronald Robinson, "The Imperialism of Free Trade," *The Economic History Review* 6:1 (1953): 1–15.

55 Peregrine Worsthorne, "Class and Conflict in British Foreign Policy," *Foreign Affairs* 37:3 (April 1959): 431.

56 E. H. Carr traced the sense of despair and skepticism of this time to the intel-lectual elite. His *What Is History?,* ed. R. W. Davies (orig. 1961; repr., London: Penguin, 1990), explained how history-writing and historians were shaped by their own time and place but also reasserted the importance of understanding history as progress.

57 Miles Taylor, *Ernest Jones, Chartism, and the Romance of Politics, 1819–1869* (Oxford: Oxford University Press, 2003), 16, 254.

58 Scott, "Women in *The Making of the English Working Class.*"

59 E. P. Thompson, *Making of the English Working Class,* 12.

60 See also Priya Satia, "The Whitesplaining of History Is Over," *Chronicle of Higher Education,* March 28, 2018, http://www.chronicle.com/article/The-Whitesplaining -of-History/242952; Satia, "Byron, Gandhi and the Thompsons."

61 Satia, "Byron, Gandhi and the Thompsons," 155–156.

62 Quoted in E. P. Thompson, "Indira: the Light That Failed," *Guardian,* No-vember 16, 1978, 7. On the distinctly postcolonial imperatives that led to the Emergency, see Gyan Prakash, *The Emergency Chronicles: Indira Gandhi and Democracy's Turning Point* (Princeton, NJ: Princeton University Press, 2019).

63 Scott Hamilton, *The Crisis of Theory: E. P. Thompson, the New Left, and Postwar British Politics* (Manchester: Manchester University Press, 2011), 159–162; Ham-ilton, "'An Appetite for the Archives': New Light on E. P. Thompson," lecture at History Department, University of Auckland, in *Reading the Maps* (blog), March 29, 2007, readingthemaps.blogspot.co.nz/2007/03/appetite-for-archives -new-light-on-ep.html. See also Tim Rogan, *The Moral Economists: R. H. Tawney, Karl Polyani, E. P. Thompson, and the Critique of Capitalism* (Princeton, NJ: Princeton University Press, 2017).

64 See also Majid Rahnema and Victoria Bawtree, eds., *The Post-Development Reader* (London: Zed Books, 1997).

65 "How Much Money Did Britain Take Away from India?" in *Business Today,* November 19, 2018, https://www.businesstoday.in/current/economy-politics /this-economist-says-britain-took-away-usd-45-trillion-from-india-in-173 -years/story/292352.html; Jason Hickel, "How Britain Stole $45 Trillion from

India," *Al Jazeera*, December 19, 2018, https://www.aljazeera.com/indepth /opinion/britain-stole-45-trillion-india-181206124830851.html.

66   Amartya Sen, *Commodities and Capabilities* (orig. 1985; repr., New York: Oxford University Press, 1999).

67   See, paradigmatically, Francis Fukuyama, *The End of History and the Last Man* (New York: Free Press, 1992).

68   See also Anand Taneja, *Jinnealogy: Time, Islam, and Ecological Thought in the Medieval Ruins of Delhi* (Stanford, CA: Stanford University Press, 2018), 51, 57.

69   Edward Said, *Orientalism* (orig. 1978; repr., New York: Vintage, 2003), preface (2003), xxii.

70   See James Vernon, "When Stuart Hall Was White," *Public Books*, January 23, 2017, www.publicbooks.org/when-stuart-hall-was-white/.

71   Perry Anderson, *The Indian Ideology* (London: Verso, 2013), 154. He is the brother of the theorist of nationalism Benedict Anderson.

72   Chakrabarty, *Provincializing Europe*, 8–9.

73   Chakrabarty, *Provincializing Europe*, 5–6, 86, 107, 255.

74   Chakrabarty, *Provincializing Europe*, 46.

75   See the forthcoming book, Caroline Ritter, *Imperial Encore: The Cultural Project of the Late British Empire* (Berkeley: University of California Press, 2021).

76   Caroline Franklin, "'Some Samples of the Finest Orientalism': Byronic Philhellenism and Proto-Zionism at the Time of the Congress of Vienna," in *Romanticism and Colonialism: Writing and Empire, 1780–1830*, ed. Tim Fulford and Peter Kitson (New York: Cambridge University Press, 1998), 233–234.

77   Quoted in Conradi, *Very English Hero*, 128.

78   See E. P. Thompson, *Making of the English Working Class*, chap. 11.

79   See also Talal Asad, *Formations of the Secular: Christianity, Islam, Modernity* (Stanford, CA: Stanford University Press, 2003), 200.

80   As noted also by Claeys, *Imperial Sceptics*, 9.

81   Chakrabarty writes: "Although the God of monotheism may have taken a few knocks . . . in the nineteenth-century European story of 'the disenchantment of the world', the gods and other agents inhabiting practices of so-called 'superstition' have never died anywhere." *Provincializing Europe*, 16.

82   Franklin, "'Some Samples of the Finest,'" 242, citing Hans Kohn.

83   Chakrabarty, *Provincializing Europe*, 16.

84   Priya Satia, "In Trying to Defy Colonialism, Draft NEP Walks the Path of the Colonisers," The Wire.in, July 20, 2019, https://thewire.in/education/in-trying -to-defy-colonialism-draft-nep-walks-the-path-of-the-colonisers.

85   The January 2003 American Historical Association meeting saw the formation of the group Historians against the War. Some 2,200 historians signed its initial petition against the war. See https://historiansagainstwar.org. The historian Juan Cole launched an influential blog, *Informed Comment* (www.juancole.com), providing factual critique of the war and of the official story about the Middle East. British historians were also roundly critical. See, for instance, Matt Seaton, "Blast from the Past," *Guardian*, February 23, 2003.

86   See Brief of Amici Curiae, Jack N. Rakove, Saul Cornell, et al., in *DC v. Heller* (2008), https://www.scotusblog.com/wp-content/uploads/2008/01/07-290_amicus _historians.pdf.

87   E. P. Thompson, "The Peculiarities of the English," 266.

88   Timothy Mitchell, *Rule of Experts: Egypt, Techno-Politics, Modernity* (Berkeley: University of California Press, 2002), 53.

89   There is not space to do justice to the rise of this dogma here.

90   Mitchell, *Rule of Experts,* 210–211, 223.

91   Scott, "Women in *The Making of the English Working Class,*" 80.

92   See E. P. Thompson, *William Morris: Romantic to Revolutionary* (London: Lawrence & Wishart, 1955).

93   Miles Taylor, "Patriotism, History and the British Left in Twentieth-Century Britain," *The Historical Journal* 33:4 (1990): 987.

94   Raphael Samuel, "The Case for National History," paper, quoted in Sophie Scott-Brown, *The Histories of Raphael Samuel,* chap. 6 (Acton: Australian National University Press, 2017), https://press-files.anu.edu.au/downloads/press/n2443 /html/cho6.xhtml?referer=&page=11#. On Samuel's engagement with nationalism in these years, see, generally, Scott-Brown, *Histories of Raphael Samuel,* chap. 6. Paul Gilroy's *The Black Atlantic: Modernity and Double Consciousness* (London: Verso, 1993) also called out the absence of attention to race and transnational experience in British working-class movements of the 1970s and 1980s.

95   Raphael Samuel, "The People with Stars in Their Eyes," *Guardian,* September 23, 1995, quoted in Scott-Brown, *Histories of Raphael Samuel,* chap. 6.

96   Scott-Brown, *Histories of Raphael Samuel,* chap. 6.

97   Placards titled "London and Athens" and "Lord Elgin and the Parthenon," British Museum, as seen by the author on July 18, 2017.

98   Bruno Waterfield, "Greece Demands Elgin Marbles for EU Trade Deal," *Times,* February 19, 2020.

99   See Shashi Tharoor, "Britain Does Owe Reparations," speech hosted by Oxford Union, May 28, 2015, https://www.youtube.com/watch?v=f7CW7S0zxv4; Tharoor, *An Era of Darkness: The British Empire in India* (New Delhi: Aleph, 2016).

100   Hardeep Dhillon, "Redress and Compensation in Matters of Colonial State Violence: Valuing Colonial Lives of the 'Punjab Disturbances,'" paper presented at Princeton University, April 19, 2019.

101   Manika Parasher, "After 100 Years, Britain 'Regrets' Jallianwala Bagh Massacre That Killed Hundreds of Indians," Indiatimes.com, April 10, 2019, https://www .indiatimes.com/trending/after-100-years-britain-regrets-jallianwala-bagh -massacre-that-killed-hundreds-of-indians-365215.html.

102   See also Richard Drayton, "Rhodes Must Not Fall? Status, Postcolonial 'Heritage' and Temporality," *Third Text* 33 (2019): 651–666.

103   Colonial reparations were the subject of the blockbuster movie of the winter of 2019, *Frozen II.* See Priya Satia, "*Frozen II* Isn't Just a Cartoon: It's a Brilliant Critique of Colonialism," *Washington Post,* December 5, 2019.

104   Ruth Maclean, "France Urged to Change Heritage Law and Return Looted Art to Africa," *Guardian,* November 21, 2018.

105   Mark Brown, "UK Museum Agrees to Return Ethiopian Emperor's Hair," *Guardian,* March 4, 2019.

106   Bill Code, "Australia Aboriginals Win Right to Sue for Colonial Land Loss," *Al Jazeera,* March 14, 2019, https://www.aljazeera.com/news/2019/03/australia-ab originals-win-sue-colonial-land-loss-190315062311052.html.

107   Milan Schreuer, "Belgium Apologizes for Kidnapping Children from African Colonies," *New York Times,* April 4, 2019.

108   See Alex Marshall, "Will These Treasures Ever Go Home?" *New York Times,* January 26, 2020, 23–24.

109   See Legacies of British Slave-ownership, UCL, https://www.ucl.ac.uk/lbs/; Catherine Hall, Nicholas Draper, Keith McClelland, Katie Donnington, and

Rachel Long, *Legacies of British Slave-ownership: Colonial Slavery and the Formation of Victorian Britain* (Cambridge: Cambridge University Press, 2014).

110   "The Times View on Returning Artefacts: Spoils of History," *Times,* February 10, 2020.

111   See Prashant Reddy Thikkabarapu, "A Rock and a Hard Place," *Caravan,* September 1, 2016, https://www.caravanmagazine.in/perspectives/myopic-approach-artefacts-kohinoor. See also Priya Satia, "Why Political Contest over Kohinoor Is a Must," *Tribune,* May 12, 2016, https://www.tribuneindia.com/news/comment/why-political-contest-over-kohinoor-is-a-must/235216.html.

112   Gallagher, *Telling it Like It Wasn't,* 180.

113   Ta-Nehisi Coates, "The Case for Reparations," *The Atlantic,* June 2014, www.theatlantic.com/magazine/archive/2014/06/the-case-for-reparations/361631/.

114   See, for instance, Kim Wagner, "Review of Nick Lloyd, *The Amritsar Massacre: The Untold Story of One Fateful Day* (I. B. Tauris, 2011)," *Reviews in History* 1224 (March 15, 2012), https://reviews.history.ac.uk/review/1224.

115   Kim Wagner, "Viewpoint: Should Britain Apologise for Amritsar Massacre?" BBC.com, February 19, 2019, https://www.bbc.com/news/world-asia-india-47070534.

116   Trevor Jackson, "Markets of Exception: An Economic History of Impunity in Britain and France, 1720–1830" (PhD diss., University of California, Berkeley, 2017), 277.

117   Gallagher, *Telling It Like It Wasn't,* 305, 307, 308.

118   See, for instance, Niall Ferguson, *Empire: The Rise and Demise of the British Empire* (London: Allen Lane, 2002); Jeremy Black, *Imperial Legacies: The British Empire around the World* (New York: Encounter, 2019); Nigel Biggar's "Ethics and Empire" project at Oxford University's McDonald Centre, which hosted a private conference in 2018, reported in Camilla Turner, "Oxford Professor's Colonialism Conference Held in Private for Fear of Disruption from Activists," *The Telegraph,* December 19, 2018 https://www.telegraph.co.uk/education/2018/12/19/oxford-professor-had-hold-academic-conference-inprivate-fear/. Academics around the world question the intellectual basis of the "Ethics and Empire" project. See Richard Adams, "Oxford University Accused of Backing Apologists of British Colonialism," *Guardian,* December 22, 2017.

119   Mike Davis, *Late Victorian Holocausts: El Niño Famines and the Making of the Third World* (London: Verso, 2001), 22.

120   See also Nicholas Dirks, *The Scandal of Empire: India and the Creation of Imperial Britain* (Cambridge, MA: Harvard University Press, 2008), 329.

121   As Césaire put it, "Colonialist Europe is dishonest in trying to justify its colonizing activity *a posteriori* by the obvious material progress that has been achieved in certain fields under the colonial regime—since *sudden change* is always possible, in history as elsewhere; since no one knows at what stage of material development these same countries would have been if Europe had not intervened; since the technical outfitting of Africa and Asia, their administrative reorganization, in a word, their 'Europeanization', was (as is proved by the example of Japan) in no way tied to the European *occupation;* since the Europeanization of the non-European continents could have been accomplished otherwise than under the heel of Europe; since this movement of Europeanization *was in progress;* since it was even slowed down; since in any case it was distorted by the European takeover." *Discourse on Colonialism,* 45–46.

122   Davis, *Late Victorian Holocausts,* 286–287.

123 See, for instance, Priya Satia, "Guns and the British Empire," Aeon, February 14, 2018, aeon.co/essays/is-the-gun-the-basis-of-modern-anglo-civilisation; Amitav Ghosh, *The Great Derangement: Climate Change and the Unthinkable* (Chicago: University of Chicago Press, 2016), 106–107; Tharoor, *An Era of Darkness,* especially chap. 1.

124 See Ghosh, *Great Derangement,* 107. On the West's dependence on oil extraction in the Middle East in the twentieth century, see Timothy Mitchell, *Carbon Democracy: Political Power in the Age of Oil* (London: Verso, 2011).

125 See also Tharoor, *An Era of Darkness.*

126 Davis, *Late Victorian Holocausts,* 111.

127 Jon Wilson, *Chaos of Empire,* 269.

128 J. S. Mill, *Memorandum of the Improvements of the Administration of India during the Last Thirty Years, and the Petition of the East-India Company to Parliament* (London: Wm. H. Allen, 1858).

129 Jon Wilson, *Chaos of Empire,* 288.

130 Mitchell, *Rule of Experts,* 6. See also Manu Goswami, *Producing India: From Colonial Economy to National Space* (Chicago: University of Chicago Press, 2004).

131 On this gap, see also Bhavani Raman, *Document Raj: Writing and Scribes in Early Colonial South India* (Chicago: University of Chicago Press, 2012).

132 Christopher Herbert, *War of No Pity: The Indian Mutiny and Victorian Trauma* (Princeton, NJ: Princeton University Press, 2008), 5.

133 The stickiness of the notion of "absentminded" imperialists fuels the effort to prove it mattered (though Seeley himself pressed the empire's importance even while whitewashing its origins). See, for instance, Bernard Porter, *Absent-Minded Imperialists: Empire, Society, and Culture in Britain* (New York: Oxford University Press, 2006). Works like Philippa Levine, *The British Empire: Sunrise to Sunset* (New York: Pearson Longman, 2007), and Catherine Hall, *Civilising Subjects: Metropole and Colony in the English Imagination, 1830–1867* (Oxford: Polity, 2002), push back against this narrative. Narratives of imperial benevolence have inspired pushback from Dirks, *Scandal of Empire;* Davis, *Late Victorian Holocausts;* Tharoor, *An Era of Darkness;* and Elkins, *Imperial Reckoning.* Most recently, Gopal's *Insurgent Empire* creatively makes the case against empire by tracing a lineage of British anticolonial thought that was informed by thinkers from and in the colonies. Jon Wilson's recent *The Chaos of Empire* falls somewhere in between the effort to prove empire mattered and that it was illegitimate: Arguing that the pros of empire have been greatly exaggerated, Wilson implies that it might have been somewhat redeemed if the British had done more for "development." The book persists in evaluating the empire in terms of its "achievements." In his zealous effort to prove the lack of order in the empire, Wilson winds up echoing Seeley at times, writing, for instance, that "beyond Curzon's band of supporters, imperialism had few allies" (389) and that the British exercised power only "sporadically" (481). He even concludes that British India had been "disconnected . . . from the main currents of British life" (491). Having gone to such lengths to prove the empire's true, violent nature, he absolves Britons themselves of accountability for it. William Dalrymple's *The Anarchy: The Relentless Rise of the East India Company* (New York: Bloomsbury, 2019) likewise acknowledges the violence of British imperialism in India but pins blame narrowly on the company, while also excusing the incursion somewhat as the product of Mughal anarchy. One reviewer was happily reassured that "eighteenth-century India was just a tough place to live." Ian Morris, "When a Private British Corporation Ruled India," *New York Times*

Review of Books, September 12, 2019. On *The Anarchy,* see also Priya Satia, "An Epic Struggle for Mastery of a Subcontinent," *Los Angeles Review of Books,* March 3, 2020, https://lareviewofbooks.org/article/an-epic-struggle-for-mastery -of-a-subcontinent/.

134   Césaire said this long ago: "Do not seek to know whether personally these gentlemen are in good or bad faith, whether personally they have good or bad intentions. Whether personally—that is, in the private conscience of Peter or Paul—they are or are not colonialists, because the essential thing is that their highly problematical subjective good faith is entirely irrelevant to the objective social implications of the evil work they perform as watchdogs of colonialism." *Discourse on Colonialism,* 55.

135   Karuna Mantena, *Alibis of Empire: Henry Maine and the Ends of Liberal Imperialism* (Princeton, NJ: Princeton University Press, 2010), 187–188.

136   See, for instance, Dirks, *Scandal of Empire; Legacies of British Slave-ownership;* Myriam Francois, "It's Not Just Cambridge University—All of Britain Benefited from Slavery," *Guardian,* May 7, 2019.

137   See also Mantena, *Alibis of Empire,* 179–180.

138   Gallagher, *Telling It Like It Wasn't,* 280. See Hannah Arendt, *Eichmann in Jerusalem: A Report on the Banality of Evil* (New York: Viking, 1963).

139   Thomas Laqueur, "Lynched for Drinking from a White Man's Well," *London Review of Books* 40:19 (October 11, 2018): 11–15.

140   Gopal, *Insurgent Empire,* 426.

141   "Irish Prime Minister Visits Choctaw Nation to Thank Them for Famine Donation Made 172 Years Ago," *Native News Online,* March 17, 2019, https://native newsonline.net/currents/irish-prime-minister-visits-choctaw-nation-thank -famine-donation-made-172-years-ago/.

142   Laqueur, "The Past's Past."

143   See also Afua Hirsch, "Britain's Colonial Crimes Deserve a Lasting Memorial," *Guardian,* November 27, 2017.

144   As with Holocaust denial; see Gallagher, *Telling It Like It Wasn't,* 301.

145   Not that controversies around the Holocaust and slavery have been put to bed: Recall the 1970s controversy over Robert Fogel and Stanley Engerman, *Time on the Cross: The Economics of American Negro Slavery* (New York: Norton, 1974), and the *Historikerstreit* debates in Germany in the 1980s.

146   See also Maya Goodfellow, "But, Do You Think Empire Was Really All That Bad?" *Media Diversified,* January 29, 2016, mediadiversified.org/2016/01/29/but -do-you-think-empire-was-really-all-that-bad/.

147   George Orwell, *1984* (orig. 1949; repr., New York: Signet, 1983), 32. My italics.

148   See Dalrymple, *The Anarchy,* esp. 237–240.

149   Trouillot, *Silencing the Past,* 19–20.

150   Marc Wortman, "History Majors Are Becoming a Thing of the Past, Except in the Ivy League," *The Daily Beast,* January 4, 2019, https://www.thedailybeast.com /history-majors-are-becoming-a-thing-of-the-past-except-in-the-ivy-league.

151   "Bagehot," "The End of History," *The Economist,* July 20, 2019, 49.

152   Patrick Collison and Tyler Cowen, "We Need a New Science of Progress," *The Atlantic,* July 30, 2019.

153   Trouillot, *Silencing the Past,* 15–16.

154   Javed Akhtar, "*Waqt,*" in *Tarkash* (orig. 1995; repr., Delhi: Star, 2004), 117-124.

155   Thomas Carlyle, *On Heroes, Hero-Worship, and the Heroic in History,* ed. George Wherry (orig. 1841; repr., Cambridge: Cambridge University Press, 1911), 8–9, 37–38, 164.

156   William Blake, "London" (1794), in *The Norton Anthology of Poetry*, ed. Alexander Allison et al., 3rd ed. (New York: Norton, 1983), 506.

157   Rabindranath Tagore, *Nationalism* (London: Macmillan, 1917), 6.

158   Kate Bowler, "How Cancer Changes Hope," *New York Times*, December 30, 2018, 1, 4.

159   Ghosh, *Great Derangement*, 115.

160   See, especially, Dipesh Chakrabarty, "The Climate of History: Four Theses," *Critical Inquiry* 35:2 (2009): 197–222.

161   Lauren Kent, "European Colonizers Killed So Many Native Americans That It Changed the Global Climate, Researchers Say," CNN.com, February 2, 2019, https://www.cnn.com/2019/02/01/world/european-colonization-climate-change-trnd/index.html.

162   See Ferris Jabr, "Our Planet Is Just as Alive as We Are," *New York Times*, April 21, 2019, Sunday Review, 4. Anticipating Earth's eventual inability to support life, Charles Darwin recognized that "to those who fully admit the immortality of the human soul, the destruction of our world will not appear so dreadful." *The Autobiography of Charles Darwin*, ed. Nora Barlow (orig. 1887; repr., London: Collins, 1958), 92.

163   Mahmood Farooqui, *A Requiem for Pakistan: The World of Intizar Husain* (New Delhi: Yoda, 2016), 217–218.

164   Ghosh, *Great Derangement*, 30–31, 80. See also Mitchell, *Rule of Experts*, chap. 1.

165   Rev. John Trusler (1735–1820), quoted in Thomas Laqueur, lecture (unpublished paper), North American Conference on British Studies, 2017.

166   Immanuel Kant, "Idea for a Universal History with a Cosmopolitan Point of View," 1784, trans. Lewis White Beck, from Kant, *On History* (Indianapolis: Bobbs-Merrill, 1963), Introduction, transcribed by Rob Lucas, Marxist Internet Archive, https://www.marxists.org/reference/subject/ethics/kant/universal-history.htm.

167   See Davis, *Late Victorian Holocausts*; Sunil Amrith, *Unruly Waters: How Rains, Rivers, Coasts, and Seas Have Shaped Asia's History* (New York: Basic, 2018).

168   See also Mitchell, *Rule of Experts*, 35–36.

169   Raymond Williams, "Ideas of Nature," in *Problems of Materialism and Culture: Selected Essays* (London: Verso, 1980), 67.

170   See Siraj Ahmed, *Archaeology of Babel: The Colonial Foundation of the Humanities* (Stanford, CA: Stanford University Press, 2017), chap. 4.

171   See Fernand Braudel, *The Mediterranean and the Mediterranean World in the Age of Philip II*, 2 vols. (orig. 1949; trans. and repr., Berkeley: University of California Press, 1996).

172   Evident in the long-presumed unitary narrative of the universe with a clear, singular beginning (the Big Bang). A new model emerging from the work of Egyptian physicist Ahmed Farag and Canada-based Indian physicist Saurya Das suggests the universe in fact has no beginning or end—a theory that would align more with non-Abrahamic religious cosmologies. See Lisa Zyga, "No Big Bang? Quantum Equation Predicts Universe Has No Beginning," Phys.org, February 9, 2015, https://phys.org/news/2015-02-big-quantum-equation-universe.html.

173   For Intizar Husain's intriguing thoughts along these lines, see Farooqui, *A Requiem for Pakistan*, 221–231.

174   Translated and quoted by Farooqui, *A Requiem for Pakistan*, 259.

175   On Kant's changing views of race in this period, see Pauline Kleingeld, "Kant's Changing Cosmopolitanism," in *Kant's "Idea for a Universal History with a Cosmopolitan Aim": A Critical Guide*, ed. Amélie Rorty and James Schmidt (Cambridge: Cambridge University Press, 2009), 184–186.

176   Barbara Metcalf, *Husain Ahmad Madani: The Jihad for Islam and India's Freedom* (Oxford: Oneworld, 2009), 7.

177   I have focused here on E. P. Thompson. But one might think of many, many others, for example, the French philosopher Simone Weil or Maude Royden (on whom, see the forthcoming dissertation of Meade Klingensmith). The wider networks at play here, entwining the anticolonial and Byronic modes, will be the subject of a later book. See also Gopal, *Insurgent Empire.*

178   See also S. D. Ahmed, *Archaeology of Babel,* introduction. As an example of such a work, see Haroon Khalid, *Walking with Nanak: Travels in His Footsteps* (New Delhi: Tranquebar, 2016).

179   Quoted in Ghosh, *Great Derangement,* 111.

180   Ghosh, *Great Derangement,* 20–21.

181   Quoted in Ghosh, *Great Derangement,* 159. See also 154, 157.

182   Ghosh, *Great Derangement,* 160, 162.

183   Thomas McCarthy, *Race, Empire, and the Idea of Human Development* (Cambridge: Cambridge University Press, 2009), 222.

184   Gopal, *Insurgent Empire,* 348.

185   Tagore, *Nationalism,* 75.

186   Mohandas K. Gandhi, *Hind Swaraj, or Indian Home Rule* (orig. 1909; repr., Ahmedabad: Navajivan, 1946), 47.

187   Mohandas K. Gandhi, "Gandhi's Political Vision: The Pyramid vs. the Oceanic Circle (1946)," in Gandhi, *Hind Swaraj, and Other Writings,* ed. Anthony J. Parel (Cambridge: Cambridge University Press, 1997), 189.

188   Frantz Fanon, *The Wretched of the Earth,* trans. Constance Farrington (orig. 1961; trans., New York: Grove Weidenfeld, 1963), 310–313.

189   E. P. Thompson, "Where Are We Now?" (unpublished memo, 1963), in *E. P. Thompson and the Making of the New Left: Essays & Polemics,* ed. Cal Winslow (New York: Monthly Review, 2014), 239, 242–243. See also Rogan, *Moral Economists,* 169.

190   Chakrabarty, *Provincializing Europe,* 109, 112.

191   Faiz Ahmed Faiz, *"Ham par tumhari chaah ka ilzam hi to hai,"* available at Rekhta, https://www.rekhta.org/ghazals/ham-par-tumhaarii-chaah-kaa-ilzaam -hii-to-hai-faiz-ahmad-faiz-ghazals.

192   Mirza Ghalib, *"Aah ko chahiye ik umr asar hote tak,"* available at Rekhta, https://www.rekhta.org/ghazals/aah-ko-chaahiye-ik-umr-asar-hote-tak-mirza -ghalib-ghazals; Khamosh Ghazipuri, *"Umr jalvon mein basar ho ye zaruri to nahin,"* available at Rekhta, https://www.rekhta.org/ghazals/umr-jalvon-men -basar-ho-ye-zaruurii-to-nahiin-khamosh-ghazipuri-ghazals.

193   Thelwall, 1796, quoted in E. P. Thompson, *Making of the English Working Class,* 185.

194   Tim Adams, "Put It to the People March," *Guardian,* March 23, 2019. It remains to be seen how the coronavirus pandemic may alter our capacity for such expression.

195   See, especially, global attraction to hip-hop as a means of political empowerment. See Hasan Minhaj, "Hip Hop and Streaming," episode of "Patriot Act," March 10, 2019, https://www.youtube.com/watch?v=MEZV6EE8JMA. See also Rowan Williams, "Why Poetry Matters," *New Statesman America,* October 23, 2019, https://www.newstatesman.com/culture/books/2019/10/why-poetry-matters.

ACKNOWLEDGMENTS

I wrote the first draft of this book in a white heat from the fall of 2018 to the spring of 2019. I owe the staff and administration at the Stanford Humanities Center a huge debt for the freedom to write so consumingly and for the exceptional interlocutors the center provided in the form of my fellow Fellows that year. The mark of conversations with them—and even particular presentations of their projects—is all over this book. I want especially to thank Omnia El Shakry, Elizabeth Marcus, Jennifer Scappettone, J'Nese Williams, Caroline Winterer, and Adrian Zakar. I must also thank Yasmin Samrai, my intrepid research assistant at the center, who helped me get the sources I needed, offered stimulating insights, and gamely immersed herself in the life and thoughts of Muhammad Asad and Shashi Tharoor for the duration. It was thanks to my department at Stanford and the School of Humanities and Sciences that I was able to take this year of sabbatical leave, and I am grateful for the opportunity.

I had intended to write a book on global networks of anticolonial thought from the time of Thomas Paine to Edward Said. But I soon realized that I had over many years nurtured a book on the role of historical thinking in empire that was the necessary precursor to that book on the "global Left," and, indeed, that implicit in much of that anticolonial thought was antihistorical thought, too. And so, I wrote this book.

I owe that realization partly to the opportunity to visit Case Western Reserve University as the Strauss Lecturer in the Humanities in September 2018, for which I must thank John Broich and Peter Knox. It was in the course of preparing my lectures for the visit that I began to articulate the central place of questions of conscience in all my work as a historian—though the realization of the key role the historical discipline played in managing imperial conscience required another leap. A conversation about writing with John Broich on a staircase in Cleveland also stayed with me as I wrote this book. At home, Shaili Jain's contagious fearlessness about writing also spurred me on.

I wrote it feverishly, reminding myself of Dr. Frankenstein at work on his demonic creation, dead to the rest of the world. A few dear friends insisted that I stay in it. I have not always thanked friends by name in earlier books, but I must do so in this book about the ethics of connection. In finding you, I find myself: Guneeta Singh Bhalla, Anshu Nagpal Chatterjee, Melanie Gurunathan, Allyson Hobbs, Purvi Kapadia, Abhimanyu Katyal, Rebecca Manley, Ana Minian, Divya Patnam, Nimmi Paulraj, Sonia Sandhu, and Ashima Yadav. Beyond friendship, Rebecca and Ana ("My Favorite") also gave me helpful feedback, and my cousin-sister Anshu helped me with Weber.

It was Abhi Katyal's turn as astrologer that jolted me awake, enabling me to think through how different narrative traditions shape our sense of agency. As Abhi wisely observes about human beings: "We can justify *anything*." In listening to him describe the planetary transits that shape our perceptions and agency, I became conscious of the diverse cultural influences that have until now shaped my own sense of agency, which in turn helped me home in on the role of history in shaping my historical actors' sense of agency. How do I think through what I do, insofar as those actions aren't the unthinking or automatic product of my geographical, gender, racial, caste, and social position? I realized that I draw on some ineffable cultural amalgam of dharmic, Gandhian, and Sufi thought absorbed from family, religious teaching, movies, myth, and so on; Punjabi notions of community; anticolonial lineage; compulsions derived from the family trauma of Partition; notions of civic duty and rights, but also of cultural and racial marginality, absorbed through American schooling; gender-based ideas of helplessness; an awareness, emerging from my study of history, of my obligation as a woman of color to acknowledge and exercise agency when I see the opportunity to; and much else.

I have had, at once, too much sense of an obligation to act, however ineffectually, and too much sense of an obligation *not* to act, to quietly accept, surrender. I wrote this book in a time in which I have felt powerless in areas of my own life. That may be *why* I wrote it—my moon through prison bars. The book emerged partly from an effort to understand why and when we think we can act, why and when we do not, why and when in different versions of the story Sakuntala and Raja Dusyanta do and don't do what they do. Certainly, the answers may lie significantly in the terrain of psychology and temperament—or perhaps, Abhi might add, astrology. But the way we *articulate* our duty or inability to act matters. Galton's alibi was Providence. And I discovered that that particular form of self-consolation echoed through the history of empire. It is a record of history itself underwriting endless mayhem in a manner with which we have not contended.

My graduate students have been an important influence on this book: Aidan Forth, Caitlyn Lundberg, Jonathan Connolly, Madihah Akhter, Murphy Temple, Meade Klingensmith, Matthew Wormer, Jon Cooper, and Jeffery Chen. Many of my thoughts on the way history has informed empire have been shaped in the course of working with them, as my notes testify. I also want to acknowledge deeply helpful exchanges with David Bell, Hardeep

Dhillon, Trevor Jackson, Abhishek Kaicker, and Mircea Raianu. Thank you also to Ghazala Ansari and Shaheer Khan. My comrade in British history at Stanford, David Como, provided essential insight on early modern historical thought. My wonderful colleagues Joel Cabrita, Paula Findlen, Jessica Riskin, and Richard Roberts answered impromptu queries. I am also grateful to Keith Baker for helping me understand and think through why things happen and, most intriguingly and infuriatingly, why they don't. In the nick of time, Alex Woloch generously indulged my theories about Orwell. With characteristic care, my dear mentor and colleague James Vernon pointed me in the right direction at a helpful time. I shared my first stab at the first chapter with my beloved teacher Thomas Laqueur, who indulged me with feedback over lunch that blew the bolts of the book open for me—not least his counsel that I immediately revisit the Melian Dialogue. He also generously showed me where the joints still leaked in the draft manuscript. I cannot aspire to Tom's sensitivity and wisdom, but I am infinitely grateful to be on the receiving end of it. When I needed to know the context in which "crime against humanity" was first used—badgers, he told me—he shared with me a paper on the history of humanitarianism that he gave one year at the North American Conference on British Studies. In considering the fate of the antivivisection movement, the paper ends on a ledge: "The claim for a universalist morality is impossible. That said, the limits on such claims are not terribly attractive either." The valiant ability to inhabit this agonistic space of uncertainty, in the gap of this unresolved ending, is what this book seeks to affirm. The inimitable Mrinalini Sinha also very generously read the complete manuscript, and her encouragement was worth every ounce of the effort that went into writing it. Finally, I must thank, with wholly inadequate words, Emma Rothschild, both for her warm support of the book and for her wise and perceptive reading, at such short notice, which allowed me to address essential gaps and flaws. Remaining errors in the text are of course entirely my own.

I was fortunate to present some of the material in this book at the Stanford Humanities Center, the Pacific Coast Conference of British Studies in 2019, Syracuse University, and the 2019 conference of the North American Victorian Studies Association, and I thank the audiences there for their stimulating feedback. Entire paragraphs emerged from my reflection on those thoughtful questions. The incisive, indeed prophetic, insight of my agent Jin Auh helped me turn my initial draft into the book I actually wanted to write and helped the book find the right publishing homes. Thank you also to Emma Smith and Alexandra Christie for their help in that process. Sharmila Sen, my visionary editor at Harvard University Press, provided essential feedback and shepherded the book through speedy publication, with the help of her indefatigable assistant Heather Hughes and the press's brilliant design and editorial team. I also want to thank Casiana Ionita and her team at Penguin UK for their support of the book.

Lastly, I want to acknowledge the support and care of my parents and my family, in the United States and in India. My dear nieces and nephews, Sukanya, Uday, Surya, Saavan, Janav, Noor, and Armaan, provide the sweetest inspiration. My beloved Aprajit Mahajan, you have been by my side through every labor of my life—mental, physical, emotional (heroically plowing through this manuscript twice!). There is no thank-you adequate to that. As always, my children, Amann and Kabir, fill my mind and heart as I write. Everything is for you, my darlings: the possibility of finding meaning in connection and in grasping the fullness of time, which you both make more real for me. This time you share the dedication page with your dadi and my mother-in-law, C. P. Sujaya, whose inspiration marks this book. Illness takes Mummy from us each day, and I dedicate this to her in loving tribute to her fearless and sensitive mind and soul, and the remarkable life she has lived. It was she who first introduced me to the art of "managing contradiction" in explaining why she likes green chilies and sweets on her plate at once and through the example of the way she has lived her life of love, activism, and scholarship. I feel so fortunate to have her blessing and to have seen in her eyes that she sees in me something of herself.